The *The* Home Office *and* Small Business Answer Book

Solutions to the

most frequently asked

questions about

starting and running

home offices and

small businesses

Janet Attard

A Henry Holt Reference Book
Henry Holt and Company   New York

A Henry Holt Reference Book
Henry Holt and Company, Inc.
Publishers since 1866
115 West 18th Street
New York, New York 10011

Henry Holt® is a registered
trademark of Henry Holt and Company, Inc.

Published in Canada by Fitzhenry & Whiteside Ltd.,
91 Granton Drive, Richmond Hill, Ontario L4B 2N5.

Library of Congress Cataloging-in-Publication Data
Attard, Janet.
The home office and small business answer book: solutions to the
most frequently asked questions about starting and running home
offices and small businesses/Janet Attard.—1st ed.
 p.   cm.—(A Henry Holt reference book)
Includes bibliographical references and index.
1. Home-based businesses.   2. Small business.   I. Title   II. Series.
HD2333.A75   1992   92–35504
658′.041—dc20   CIP

ISBN 0-8050-2078-0
ISBN 0-8050-2565-0 (An Owl Book: pbk.)

First Edition—1993

Designed by Claire N. Vaccaro

Printed in the United States of America
All first editions are printed on acid-free paper. ⊗
1 3 5 7 9 10 8 6 4 2

For Jay, Steve, and Vicki

Contents

Contents

Contents

Acknowledgments

Writing this book and simultaneously keeping the online information areas my company manages running smoothly would have been impossible without the help of a number of very special people. My heartfelt thanks go out to Jeff Chasalow, Joan Kumpitsch, Jim Peabody, Kent Seitzinger, and Jack Slick, who are assistant sysops in the Home Office/Small Business RoundTable (HOSB) on GEnie; Gerry Elman, Hal Zoller, Paul Mayer, and Robert Schenot, who help out in the HOSB; John Lichtenberger and Jim Smith, who are assistants for the Business Resource Directory on GEnie; and Ben Mandell, who helps manage the message board area in the Microsoft Small Business Center on America Online. All of these people are experts in their own fields and provided useful insights and comments as well as encouragement while I was writing the book.

I am deeply indebted, too, to my agent, Sam Mitnick, and to Ken Wright and Paula Kakalecik at Henry Holt for their efforts in making this book happen. No author could have a more understanding or helpful team behind her. My daughter, Vicki, deserves a hand, too, for her editorial assistance with parts of the book.

Finally, I would like to acknowledge the role online computer information services have played in making this book possible. Many of the businesspeople and professionals I interviewed for the book were found through the information areas I run on GEnie and America Online. Many of the interviews I did for the book were conducted partially or completely through electronic mail, eliminating phone tag and avoiding many of the problems inherent with communicating with people who live and work in different time zones. Additionally, I was able to save a tremendous amount of time on research—and do research at hours libraries are normally closed—by using the Dow Jones News Retrieval service and the database services available on GEnie.

The Home Office *and*
Small Business
Answer Book

Introduction

I was just about to leave for lunch when the switchboard operator told me I had a phone call.

Puzzled, since I was new on the job and was not expecting any calls, I walked back to my desk and picked up the phone. It was my 10-year-old son.

"Hi, Mom, it's me."

"Stephen? . . . *Stephen?*"

"Yeah, it's me."

"Why did you call? Is anything the matter?"

"I'm at Mike's house."

"You're supposed to be in school. Why are you at Mike's house?"

"The school caught on fire and they sent everyone home . . ."

"What do you mean the school caught on fire . . . ?"

"So I got on Mike's bus and went to his house."

". . . If the school caught on fire and you're at Mike's house, *where's Vicki?*"

"I put her on our bus and told her to go to Nina's."

"Did Nina say it was OK?"

"I don't know, I'm at Mike's house."

As it turned out, 7-year-old Vicki was indeed at Nina's, but that phone call made me start to reconsider whether taking the job as a staff writer on a business trade magazine had been the right thing to do. Although the job was exactly the

1

type of work I had wanted, and it allowed me to schedule my hours around the children's school schedule, I just didn't feel comfortable about working away from home.

It wasn't long before I started to resent the hour and fifteen minutes I had to spend traveling to and from work each day. I also realized that the costs of going to work (for new clothes, gasoline, tires, lunch from the deli on days I didn't have time to make my lunch or forgot to take it with me) were all eating into the extra income I thought I'd gain by working at a "real" job instead of free-lancing from home as I had been doing for the ten years prior.

So a few months later, when my husband took a new job and we had to move to another part of the state, I decided to give self-employment another go-round— at least until the children were a few years older.

That was more than 10 years ago. These days the children, like others their age, show up mostly to eat, sleep, and borrow gas money. But I'm still self-employed and still work out of a home office.

Over the years the focus of my work has changed somewhat, and the amount of work that gets handled from my office has grown significantly. But more importantly, technologic advances have reduced both the cost and the physical size of powerful business machines. Millions of people now find it practical and affordable to equip a room at home or a small away-from-home business with many of the same high-powered tools used by the biggest corporations.

As a result, in a phenomenon that might best be called the "American Home Office and Small Business Revolution," millions of people have already traded in their glassed-in, climate-controlled, ulcer-producing corporate jobs for the convenience, personal satisfaction, challenge, and potentially easier-going life-style that comes with self-employment. Millions more wish to follow in their footsteps.

Not everyone finds the going easy, however. For instance:

▶ The highly skilled engineer who wants to kiss his 9-to-5 job good-bye may be at a loss to know how to find customers for the consulting service he wants to start or what kind of health insurance policy to buy when he is no longer covered by the company plan.

▶ The programmer who has developed what could be the hottest new program of the decade may not know how to market her work or how to protect it with copyrights, trademarks, or patents.

▶ The secretary who has started a word processing business so she can stay home with her children may not know how to price her services or whether to believe the salesperson who says if she'll pay a fee of several hundred dollars he may be able to make it possible for her to accept credit cards from her customers.

In the past, finding practical answers to questions like these has not been easy. Although plenty has been written about the benefits of being self-employed and what one *ought* to do to start a business, textbook rules often don't work in real-life home offices and very small businesses.

The *Home Office and Small Business Answer Book* provides those real-life answers. The questions in the book are based on real questions received from business owners and would-be business owners throughout the United States and Canada since 1988 when my company, Attard Communications, began providing home office and small business information first to General Electric Company's GEnie computer information network, and later to the Microsoft Small Business Center on America Online. The answers are based on information I've gathered during my own twenty years of self-employment and on real-life experiences of business owners and professionals in many different trades and industries.

The book was written with another practical consideration in mind, too: the time crunch every business owner faces. Although it would be useful to learn how to start and run a business one step at a time, few people have the time to do it that way. Instead, they forge ahead, looking for answers and information as they need it at various stages of their business.

This book has therefore been organized to help you find answers as you need them. The first part of the book deals with common questions and concerns about choosing, equipping, and starting small and home businesses. Following that is nuts-and-bolts information about getting customers, running the "business side" of the business, and dealing with problems that may arise along the way. Finally, you'll find information about growing your business and lists of useful resources.

In short, the *Home Office and Small Business Answer Book* should help you gather the information you need quickly and easily so you can focus your efforts on running your business and achieving success.

I.

Taking
the Tiger
by the Tail

1.

Can You Really Make
Money at Home?

This week more than 39 million people in the United States are likely to spend some time tapping away at home computer keyboards, tinkering with gadgets in slightly musty basements, loading boxes or barrels or tools into vans or garages, or pursuing any number of other activities, all in pursuit of one common goal—making money at home. *

Who are these people? How successful are they at making money at home? More importantly, should *you* work at home and will *you* be successful? Here are some insights and information to guide you in your decision.

Q **Who works at home?**

Almost everyone works at home, or so it often seems! There's that guy up the street who has a little wallpapering business on the side, the woman around the corner who translates scientific papers into German, your sister in Chicago who works as a free-lance direct mail copywriter, and your brother-in-law in California who leads corporate training seminars.

* This figure is based on findings of the eighth annual National Work-at-Home Survey released in July 1992 by LINK Resources Corporation, a New York–based technology research and consulting firm. The figure represents a 9.4 percent growth in home workers over the previous year. Of the 39 million workers, 30.4 million worked on their own from home or worked as telecommuters, while 8.6 million brought work home from the office to do after hours. The data was based on a random sampling of 2,500 households.

Then, too, there's the auto mechanic who makes house calls, the homebased word processor your company hires occasionally, the woman who does your taxes every year, the computer consultant who just installed a new inventory system in your company's warehouse, and the young man in a suburban New York community who grew his "little" newspaper delivery route into an enterprise so profitable that it let him put aside enough money to pay for his college education *and* make a down payment on a condominium he purchased for rental income—*before he turned 18*. (Because of his age, the young man's parents had to cosign the contract. Not surprisingly, this individual went on to become an accountant.)

And, let's not forget your old school pal Jim Douglas. Jim is that guy you haven't seen in 15 years who called last week just to say hello—and to share information with you about a wonderful business opportunity he's discovered that could help you save for a financially secure retirement.

Q **How much money do people who work at home make?**

Some people earn as much as $250,000 a year working from home. Others work sporadically from home and make just a few hundred to a few thousand dollars annually. Still others grow their businesses so big they have to move them out of their homes to nearby business or industrial space. Results of a June 1992 study conducted by the Home Office/Small Business RoundTable on the GEnie computer information service suggest most full-time self-employed people gross $30,000 or more each year; 10 percent of them gross more than $100,000 per year. (More than 900 business people who use computers and modems responded to the survey.)

Q **How many self-employed people work for themselves full-time?**

Based on the 1992 LINK Resources study and on the survey conducted by the Home Office/Small Business RoundTable, 31 to 32 percent (a little more than 12 million) self-employed individuals derive their primary income from self-employment.

Q **What kinds of businesses can be started at home?**

Almost any kind! Profitable newsletters, chemical distributorships, electroplating businesses, and mail order companies have all been started at home. So have candy distributorships, used-car sales operations, precision tool-and-die companies, word processing and desktop publishing businesses, catering firms, landscaping services, and transcription services. In fact, the number of business that can be started from home is almost unlimited.

Q **Is there anything I can't do at home?**

There are certain products that it is illegal to produce in the home. Fireworks and other explosives and medical supplies and drugs are prohibited in most states. The manufacture of food and clothing at home is highly regulated or prohibited in some localities. (If you are allowed to produce food for resale at home, you will have to comply with strict health regulations.) Generally, if what you do can affect the health and safety of others, it will be regulated and could be prohibited as a home business. In addition, some communities have outdated zoning laws forbidding any type of business to be conducted in the home. Often such laws are blatantly ignored; sometimes they are enforced. Check your local laws if you have any doubts. (See chapter 10 for information on zoning and other laws that may affect you.)

Q **Do people ever lose money trying to start a home business?**

Yes, they do. Thousands of people each year throw good money away chasing get-rich schemes and scams. Thousands more see their investments turn sour because what they sell just doesn't attract the demand they expected it would, or because they stumble into some unforeseen pitfall along the way. This book will help you avoid many of these obstacles to success.

Q **What are the benefits of working for myself?**

I asked a crusty old industrial plant owner that question years ago, and he wagged his finger at me and said, "Young lady, there is only one reason to be in business: to make money, make more money, and make still more money."

Although this kind of obsession with money is a motivator for some business owners, 40 percent of the people who took the Home Office/Small Business survey cited a desire to improve the quality of their life as a reason for being self-employed or wanting to start a home business.

Broadcast consultant Ron Tindiglia explains it this way: "For me, this is a time in my life when the *how* I make money is more important than the dollar amount. The funny thing is, when I concentrate on the *how*, the money seems to take care of itself." Tindiglia was vice president of news for CBS-owned television stations prior to 1986 when he started his production and consulting company. Today, he still runs Ron Tindiglia Enterprises, Inc., from an office in his home in Westchester County, New York. His staff doubled in 1991, he says, when his wife, Misti, joined him in the business to help with marketing and client services.

Q **Can people who don't have a lot of contacts or a lot of corporate management experience build satisfying and successful businesses from home?**

Yes! They may not be able to build a profitable business overnight, but if they are patient and build the business slowly but steadily, they can build successful and very satisfying businesses.

Jerry Lunsford, a former backcountry ranger, is one good example. Lunsford was seeking a better way of life when he started his business, Camelid Capers, in 1985. At the time, he was searching for something to do that would keep him outdoors. Camelid Capers, which takes tourists on guided day hikes in the Point Reyes National Seashore, was born when Lunsford attended a llama auction in Grants Pass, Oregon, and, as he puts it, "I couldn't sit on my hands." Lunsford manages the business on an entry-level Macintosh computer, and although it hasn't made him rich, it keeps him outdoors doing things he loves to do. Says Lunsford, "The llamas carry the gear, the customers lead the llamas. The favorite scenario seems to be lunch on the beach with llamas." If the business continues to grow as it has been, he hopes it will soon allow him to give up his winter job doing technical support for a computer company.

Q **What are the benefits of starting a business from home?**

The obvious advantage is a reduction in overhead costs. Putting your office in a corner of your home eliminates monthly office rental and utility expenses. In addition, having your business at home may also:

- provide substantial tax deductions
- reduce transportation costs
- eliminate commuting time
- reduce expenditures for work clothes and lunches out
- reduce child-care worries and expense
- reduce interruptions and increase your productivity
- allow you to work when it is most convenient for you to work
- minimize involvement with office politics
- provide better customer service
- let you take control of your own destiny

Q **Are there any drawbacks?**

Yes, there can be some drawbacks. Chief among them is the need to wear all the hats in the business. Instead of being able to delegate marketing, billing, filing, bookkeeping, routine correspondence, and other office functions to a staff, most people who work at home have to handle all of these functions themselves. Other potential problems include:

- finding or attracting customers may be more difficult
- making important business contacts may be harder
- getting merchant status can be difficult and/or costly
- financing and suppliers credit may be hard to come by
- family interruptions may be disruptive
- family members may not be supportive of your business
- family privacy may be disturbed if you have customers come to your home
- start-up expenses may be higher than you expected

Q **What does it take to build a successful home business?**

Business school professors, venture capitalists, and bankers will say it takes a combination of these factors to build a successful business:

- a good product or service at the right price
- a sizable market (a substantial number of customers)

- a clear-cut plan for reaching that market in a reasonable amount of time
- sufficient financing
- an experienced management team
- the technical competence to produce and deliver the product
- the means to market the product or service
- an emphasis on customer satisfaction
- the ability to collect from customers
- an accurate method of keeping records
- an awareness of tax and other laws affecting the business
- a watchful eye on the competition and market trends
- the flexibility to change direction when change is needed
- an owner who is at once optimistic, persistent, realistic, and enthusiastic about the product

Q **Are there any special character traits I'll need?**

People who have bootstrapped their way to success in homebased or other small businesses point over and over again to the importance of the business owner's enthusiasm and dedication.

"Textbook businesses always seem to have investors, be highly capitalized, and have sophisticated business plans," says Duane Long, owner of Long Transportation Services, Inc., a trucking and transportation brokerage in Raleigh, North Carolina. But, while those things are important, says Long, "the textbook scenario is far different than the way the majority of small businesses start."

Long speaks from experience. An entrepreneur himself, he launched his transportation brokerage from his kitchen table in 1984 with only $500. The company, which is no longer homebased, now grosses close to $20 million annually.

As Long sees it, the two traits needed for success in business are knowledge and commitment. "You have to know the product, know what the business is all about, and then put your blood, sweat, and tears into it. You have to become almost obsessed. If you don't, it will fail."

Q **Is it still possible to start a business from the kitchen table?**

Yes. Businesses often get started with little more than a manila envelope, a notebook, an index-card file box, and the family telephone. Some run that way forever, but most people add a separate business phone line when they start getting a lot of phone calls. As the businesses grow, they add a file cabinet and/or desk and move out of the kitchen into a spare room or basement, if the space is available.

Q Besides the willingness to work hard, what other personal character traits do I need?

Enthusiasm and belief in your product or service are critical to building a successful business. Your ability to convince customers to buy from you, suppliers to sell to you on credit or at a discount, and family and/or friends to loan money to you all depend on your ability to sell others on the value of your offerings. If you dislike the business or what you have to do to make money in the business, your ability to make the needed sales, contacts, and loans will be crippled.

In addition, most successful business owners generally possess the following characteristics:

▸ They are self-starters. They don't sit around waiting for someone else to tell them what to do or when to do it.
▸ They get along with most other people.
▸ They believe in listening to and learning from others.
▸ They set long-term goals as well as short-term goals.
▸ They look to the future and live for the future, not the past.
▸ They are both optimistic and realistic.
▸ They like to take charge and make decisions.
▸ They don't complain about life; they make life happen.
▸ They are flexible but not wishy-washy.
▸ They are honest and considerate in their dealings with other people.
▸ They believe in themselves.

Q I have little children at home. How many hours will I have to work a week to make money?

There is no minimum number of hours you have to work each week to make money. One of the wonderful things about building your own business is you can build it to suit you and your needs. Your earnings won't be sky-high if you can only work a few hours a week, but you can still make money. Furthermore, if you plan for the long run, the business you start on a small scale now could grow into a substantial source of income as the time you have to devote to it increases in later years.

For example, if you have the skills and equipment, you might want to start a small word processing business from home, doing a limited number of jobs when the children are asleep. As they grow, you might take on more work, take courses in commercial art and layout (if you have the interest), and expand into desktop publishing. Later you might add other services or even move the business out of the house. The same kind of gradual growth and expansion of time and income can be maneuvered in many other fields.

Q **Is there an easy way to make money in my own business?**

Working for yourself can be highly enjoyable, highly rewarding, and highly profitable, but there is no easy road to riches.

Q **Is there any good way to make money in a hurry?**

Although there are some businesses that can be started faster than others, you can't count on making money in a hurry in any business. Even if you find customers immediately, you may have to wait for payment, or you may need the profits to buy inventory, supplies, equipment, or improve your cash position.

Q **What home and small businesses make the most money?**

The businesses that make the most money are almost always those that allow you to hire other people, make commissions on work other people do, or sell products to many people. Income from businesses requiring your individual attention is always going to be limited by the number of hours you can personally devote to client work. If it takes you 50 hours to write a computer program you sell to one company for $1,000, you have made $20 an hour. If you can turn around and sell that same program unchanged to ten other companies, even allowing for marketing time your earnings per hour on that program have multiplied tremendously.

Similarly, if you do word processing and do all the work yourself, the money you make will be limited by the time you devote to marketing the service and performing it. However, if instead of doing the work yourself you become a temporary employment agency and match workers to available jobs, you could greatly increase your income.

 Do many home businesses fail?

There are no accurate statistics on failure rates for home businesses. Although statistics for all businesses show 80 to 90 percent of all new businesses fail in the first year and 95 percent fail within five years, such statistics don't really apply to home businesses.

The reason is that many home businesses are run from a corner of the family checkbook as well as a corner of the family den. Having relatively low start-up costs, no business rent to pay each month, and no payroll to meet each week, few home businesses ever really fail. The majority can stay in business even if customers are few and far between. This is particularly true when a business is a moonlight operation, provides a second income for a family, and/or is supplemented with income from part-time or temporary employment.

In addition, owners of home businesses are usually far more flexible than traditional away-from-home businesses. If one business idea doesn't work out, often the owner of a home business will simply redirect his or her focus to some other income-producing activity. Thus, the individual selling decorative wreaths may switch to selling jewelry or collectibles, a seamstress may go into the image consulting business, or a computer consultant might start a software publishing company.

Finally, when a home business doesn't work out, equipment and supplies purchased for the business can often be used for other purposes. The computer that was bought to run a business may wind up being used by one or more members of a household to prepare homework or to acquire word processing, spreadsheet, or other computer skills needed to get a job. Supplies, samples, or inventory may also get used up by family, given away as gifts, or packed up to await sale at the next neighborhood garage sale or a local flea market.

Thus, while some home businesses do fail, the overall risks are minimal compared to starting businesses outside of the home.

 Are there any common traits among unsuccessful home businesses?

Some home businesses fall prey to the problems that traditionally cause small businesses to fail: undercapitalization and poor management. However, even when cash runs out, the underlying reason for the disintegration of a home business can often be attributed to one or more of these factors:

- lack of owner enthusiasm and dedication
- lack of knowledge of the business or industry
- failure to get to know the customer and/or make contacts
- lack of self-confidence
- no market for the products or services
- the product or service isn't profitable to produce and sell
- the product or service is grossly overpriced compared to comparable products and services
- poor-quality goods or services
- owner's focus is on making money with little or no regard for the customer or what is being sold
- no real product or service is being offered
- lack of professionalism in dealing with and corresponding with customers
- no clear-cut plans
- need for cash
- inability to compete against bigger or more established companies

Q **I have a good idea, but I'm afraid I'll lose money if it doesn't work. Is there any way to avoid the risk?**

No. If you want to be in business for yourself you are going to have to take some risks. But, be sure they are calculated risks. In other words, do all your homework, find out as much as you can about the industry, the customers, the competition, and what it takes to make—or break—the business you want to start. Then decide if you can live with the risk. If you can't, you may have to settle for a different type of business or for working as someone's employee until the time comes when you can afford to take the risk.

Q **Can I work for myself a few hours a week without starting a business?**

There are people who call their businesses a hobby for years. However, there are several problems with doing that:

- If you aren't reporting the income, you are operating illegally and could find yourself sued for tax evasion or fraud sometime down the road by both the federal and state government.
- If you are reporting your income, you may be missing out on important tax deductions and leaving yourself open to penalties (for not paying self-employment tax on business income) if you are ever audited and found to be running a business instead of pursuing a hobby.
- Should you need a business loan to expand your "hobby," you won't have the financial information bankers or other investors are going to want to see before loaning you money.

Q **I'm not sure I want to start my own business. Are there any jobs that would let me work at home?**

More and more companies are experimenting with hiring people to work at home or allowing existing employees to do part or all of their work at home. These employees are often called "telecommuters" because they communicate with the main office over the telephone and often deliver work (via computer or fax) over the telephone lines as well. The LINK Resources study showed that there were 6.6 million telecommuters in the U.S. in 1992, an increase of 20 percent from the preceding year.

These jobs aren't easy to find, but if you bang on enough doors, you may be able to turn up something to your liking, particularly if you have computer skills and a computer available to you. If you are employed in an occupation that doesn't require your presence in the office, consider whether your present employer might allow you to work at home part or all of the time. If you can show the employer the advantages of fewer interruptions, increased productivity, and better-quality work—he or she may agree to the arrangement, or at least to test the concept.

2.

The Million Dollar
Question:
What Kind of Business
Can I Start?

You don't have to read many success stories before you start wishing you could work for yourself. The opportunity to be your own boss and the potential for high income are strong enticements. But what can you do? What kind of business would be suitable for you to start? This chapter may help you discover some answers.

 I want to start a business, but don't know what to start. How do I decide what would be a good business to pursue?

The most successful home and small businesses are generally those that:

▶ are based on the owner's skills, interests, and knowledge
▶ involve doing something the owner likes to do and does well
▶ sell products or services that many people need and are willing to buy or must buy

One way to close in on the most promising businesses for you, personally, is to get out a sheet of paper and divide it into four vertical columns. In the first column, list everything you like to do, and in the second column, list the things you are expert at doing or about which you have some or a great deal of knowledge. In the third column, list businesses that might make use of the interests and skills you have listed in the first two columns. In the last column, make notations about how many customers there might be for each type of business you have listed (see Table 2.1 on page 20).

Use the notes you've made as a paper "think tank." They should let you immediately spot which of your interests (things you like to do) match up with businesses that have a potentially large base of customers. If you also have the skills required by the business(es), you now have one or more specific targets to investigate as a possible business.

Here's an example: Suppose you work or have worked as a secretary in a large corporation. Your "Do Well" list might include a variety of job-related tasks such as word processing, scheduling, filing and organizing, taking messages, and answering phones. It is also likely that you've included non-job-related tasks like planning parties, cleaning, organizing school fund-raisers, and cooking.

If your "Like to Do" list includes organizational things like arranging meeting details, running the school fair, or rearranging closets or cabinets for efficiency, businesses that would fit in with what you like to do and know how to do might be a word processing or general secretarial service, a meeting planning service, or a personal organization service—just for starters. For a secretarial service, the "Potential Customer" column might include local businesses, students, and job hunters. You may not know offhand who would buy meeting or planning services, but you can research these if they are of interest and fill them in later.

Have a supportive spouse or friend suggest businesses that match your skills and interests. They may see business possibilities you don't. If your spouse or friends tend not to be supportive, don't discuss your ideas with them. Try to find someone who is, or keep your ideas to yourself.

Q   **Where do I get business ideas?**

The list of business ideas on page 455, the Yellow Pages of your phone book, and the articles and ads in popular magazines and trade publications are good sources to jog your thinking. However, don't get taken in by the get-rich-quick ads or the "Make thousands of dollars in your own business" ads. Make a list of the types of businesses that pique your interest, then investigate the most promising ones to see if any would make a suitable business for you.

Table 2.1: Business Selection Worksheet

Instructions: Fill in appropriate information under the headings "Like to Do" and "Do Well." Then, under "Business Possibilities," list, in the order they occur to you, any ideas for possible businesses based on your skills and interests. Finally, next to each business idea, put some rough "guestimate" of how many people would buy from the business and who those people might be. Your notations should help you spot potentially good businesses for you to consider.

Like to Do (interests, hobbies, etc.)	Do Well (skills, expertise, experience)	Business Possibilities	Potential Customers and Income

Table 2.2: Sample Worksheet

Like to Do (interests, hobbies, etc.)	Do Well (skills, expertise, experience)	Business Possibilities	Potential Customers and Income
Experiment with new recipes	Word processing	Meeting planner	Large corporations; potentially substantial fee for each meeting organized
Organize school fundraisers	Scheduling		
	Filing	Word processing service	Students, small businesses, bigger businesses with work overloads; relatively small profit per job but can do many separate jobs
Play the piano	Organizing meetings		
Plan parties	Taking messages		
Travel	Writing letters		
Read	Coordinating multiple tasks		
Rearrange closets		Image consulting and personal organization services	Upper income customers; executive women who don't have time to organize their closets; relatively few customers but fun work
		Wedding or party planning service	Anyone who schedules parties in halls or other major events
		Formal clothing rental service	Party-goers—male and female; likely to be repeat customers
		Complete office and resume service center	Mostly business customers or individuals needing resumes written and typeset; many customers; small profit likely for each sale

Q **What else makes a business successful?**

The businesses with the best track record for success are those for which the owner:

- knows the business, the industry, and the customer
- can produce a top-quality product or service for which there is a need
- can produce the product or service better, less expensively, or more quickly (or sometimes all three) than competitors
- knows how to reach the customer
- knows how long it will take to get the business going and plans accordingly
- starts off with one or more customers, often former employers

Q **Which businesses are the simplest to start?**

A service business in an industry you know well or a service that involves doing tasks others don't like to do or don't have time to do will usually be the easiest to launch. Often such businesses can be started by getting on the phone, calling potential customers, and asking for their business.

Q **Is there anything I should avoid?**

Steer clear of ads or "friends" promising that you can start earning a big income right away, particularly if they ask you to send money for information. For the most part such ads and telemarketing scripts have been carefully written to push your "hot buttons" (greed, desire for status, need to provide for your family) and pry you and your money apart.

Q **How long will it take before the business is successful?**

Don't expect overnight miracles. Like growing flowers, growing a business takes time. If you know who your customers will be before you start your business, you may be fortunate enough to start making sales right away. But it still may take months to build a stream of customers steady enough to make the business successful.

I want to start a business but don't have any skills. Is there anything I can do?

Everyone has some kind of skills. You probably just haven't discovered yours or may need more training to turn one of your skills into a business. Vocational schools, high schools, and colleges in your area may offer adult education courses that you could take to develop or improve skills. Additionally, you might be able to get a part-time job working for a company where you could gather industry knowledge or on-the-job training.

 I'd like to start a business in a totally different field than the one I'm in now. How do I know what kinds of things I'd be best at doing?

Think about the things you like to do and are good at doing. Do you like to help people? Do you spend a lot of time at a hobby? Do you like to build or make things? Table 2.1 on page 20 should help you explore your interests and skills.

Consider, too, whether there is something you've always wanted to do that makes money but which you were discouraged from doing. For instance, when I was in junior high school I wanted to be a writer. Well-meaning parents, teachers, and guidance counselors all suggested I would be better off pursuing some other career since writers tend not to make much money and because I was "so good in math and science." What they said seemed logical, so I started college as a chemistry major.

No one, including me, ever considered whether I really *liked* math or science. And, despite top grades in the subject, I really didn't like math. In fact, by the end of my first year in college I *loathed* math and changed my major to English. Shortly after graduating college I started working on—and writing for—a daily newspaper.

Is there a writer buried inside you? A photographer? An artist? A dancer? An actor? Or is there some other field you always wanted to pursue but never did? Do you have, or could you acquire, sufficient skills to turn your avocations into a part-time or even a full-time business?

 There are a lot of businesses that sound interesting to me. How do I decide which business is the right one?

Look for the business that comes closest to your interests and capabilities and that fits in with your long- and short-range financial goals. For each business you think you might want to start, ask yourself the questions below. Write your answers down on a piece of paper so you can more easily compare the relative benefits and drawbacks of one business over another.

▶ Do I really know much about this business?
▶ Do I have all the skills needed to start and run this business?
▶ Would I really enjoy doing whatever is necessary to sell this product or service?
▶ How much money do I need to make each week?
▶ How much money could this business make each week?
▶ How long would it take (realistically!) to start generating that much money?
▶ How much will it cost to start this business and run it until it starts producing income on a steady basis?
▶ Can I afford to put that much into the business?
▶ What money will I use to live on until the business starts making money?
▶ How fast do I need to generate money?
▶ Are there really enough people who want to buy this product or service? (See chapter 7, "Planning: Your Personal Road Map to Success")
▶ Do I know how to find them?
▶ How many hours a week can I work now?
▶ How many hours a week will it take to do all the work (finding customers, producing or getting the product or service to them, billing them, doing the bookkeeping)?
▶ How big could the business grow?
▶ How big do I want it to grow?

Q **Do I need to know about a business before starting it if I'm going to buy a franchise? Won't the franchisor teach me all I need to know?**

People who buy a franchise or a home "business" without knowing anything about the business and without learning about the business in advance are taking

24

a big risk. Without some idea of what the business is all about, you have no way of determining if you will like the business, if there is a market for its products and services in your area, or if you have what it takes to bring in a steady stream of customers. Additionally, while a true franchise provides training, less expensive turnkey businesses and opportunity ventures often provide only a manual and perhaps a little phone support to help you get started.

 Where do I get the money to start a business?

Most people dig into their own pockets to start their businesses. They pull extra income from weekly paychecks, suck it out of savings accounts, take out personal loans or second mortgages, use charge cards to buy equipment, use inheritances or, occasionally, pension funds, borrow from relatives, barter, make deals, and so on.

 How much time should I spend investigating an idea?

As much time as you need to get the facts, but no more. Remember, no matter how good your idea is, you can't turn it into a business until you act on the idea. Do take the time to gather all the details you need to determine your chances for success, but don't get so tied up looking into the business that you never get your own business going. If you are procrastinating because you're worrying about failure, try starting the business on a very limited scale to allow you to judge your interest and chances for success if you were to go after the business in a bigger way.

 How much money will I need to start a business?

People have started profitable businesses with not much more than the sweat of their brow, but realistically you should count on having to spend a minimum of a few hundred dollars, even if the business you want to start can be run without purchasing equipment or inventory. The reason: you will need money for business cards, stationery, phone calls, office supplies, postage, and perhaps for ads or brochures. (See chapter 7 for planning information.)

 Can I start a newsletter with $200?

Realistically, no. Even if you were to do all the writing, editing, and layouts yourself, you would still have the printing, marketing, and mailing costs to cover. To find out how much money you will need, determine how many pages the newsletter will be; what fees you may have to pay for writing, editing, or layouts; what it will cost to print and mail it; and how much you will need to spend for direct mail solicitations. Newsletters are usually supported entirely by subscription fees, which may take time to collect, so allow yourself enough money to market the newsletter effectively and to get out several issues.

Whether you are creating a newsletter or any other type of business, working out the cost figures is essential. If you see that the costs are higher than you can afford, rethink your idea. Determine if the skills needed for the original idea could be used to start a business that takes less cash. For instance, if you have the skills to write, edit, and produce a newsletter but not the money to print, market, and mail it, consider doing sales and marketing literature for other businesses. You probably *could* get that type of business started with $200 if you had another source of income to pay your bills until the service developed steady customers and income.

Q   **I have a lot of expensive computer equipment. What would be the best computer business to start?**

The only real computer businesses are those that involve the sale, programming, or repair of computers. In almost all other businesses a computer is nothing more than a tool to accomplish a specific task. If you used a typewriter instead of a computer to write letters, type spreadsheets, write legal contracts or books, you wouldn't consider yourself in the typewriter business. Using a computer is no different. You start with the skill or business and use the computer to help produce the work of that business faster or more efficiently.

Q   **I'm disabled. What kind of business could I start?**

The answer will depend on your abilities and interests. Holly Phillips, a woman in Pennsylvania who is confined to a wheelchair due to a form of muscular dystrophy, has enough strength in her arms and hands to use a computer and scanner and does typing and optical character recognition (OCR) scanning from her home. After Robert Martin, who lives in Nashville, Tennessee, lost the use of both of his legs in an accident, he started a homebased locksmith business that evolved into a computer security business; it not only supported himself and his family but also provided employment for several other handicapped workers. For information about adaptive devices to help you work at home, contact your state office of rehabilitation. You can also get information by calling the IBM Special Needs Information Referral Center in Atlanta at (800) 426–3333 or the Apple Worldwide Disability Solutions Group at (800) 732–3131.

Q **Should I start several businesses at once to see which makes money?**

I wouldn't recommend doing that. It takes a lot of time and effort to start one business. If you try to start several at the same time, you won't be able to devote sufficient time and attention to any one of them.

If you are seriously interested in two or more different businesses because you like the products and services of each, try this strategy: start one business, get it on its feet and running smoothly, and then start the second venture. If your second venture is in any way related to the first, your start-up will be easier, and you may eventually find that each business can feed customers to the other. If you start a lawn-care service, for instance, and later a pool maintenance service, your lawn-care company should be able to tell the pool service what homes in a neighborhood to target for pool openings, closings, cleaning, and repair. If you are a technical writer and are good at writing manuals, you might start a sideline business doing computer training. Training sessions at corporations may bring you technical or other writing assignments, or your writing may lead to training opportunities.

Be sure, however, to allow yourself time to establish customers and expertise in one business before attempting to start the next.

Q **I'd like to start a little business my spouse could run while I'm at work. What would be good?**

The only good business for your spouse to run while you are at work is one that he or she *wants* to start. Remember, it takes commitment, dedication, and time to start and run a business. If your spouse doesn't have the time or interest to research a business, he or she is unlikely to be very happy or successful running one you start. (The same is true for starting businesses for your children to take over.) If the business is something you'll do as a joint venture, talk it out together.

See what he or she likes to do or might like to do and how that matches up with what you could do after work or on weekends. One team-up situation that works well for some couples is for the at-home spouse to be the marketing and customer service end of the business (drumming up business, taking service calls or orders during the day) while the work-away-from-home spouse becomes the one responsible for doing the work or making the product that was ordered.

 An acquaintance has asked me to come to her home this weekend to learn how I could make money in my spare time, but she wouldn't tell me any more than that. Should I go?

That tactic is commonly used to get people to go to meetings to recruit distributors for "network marketing" or multilevel marketing (MLM) organizations. What you will probably hear is that you can make money by being a distributor for the company. As a distributor, one of your main tasks will be to build a "downline," which is to bring more distributors into the organization under you. Your distributors will be encouraged to bring in still more distributors, and so on.

If you attend the meeting be aware that while some people make money in these ventures, many spend far more on sample kits, motivational tapes, and leaflets than they ever make in profits. Furthermore, certain MLM operations are prohibited in some states. Others that pop up from time to time are outright scams. If you decide to get involved, move cautiously and learn as much as you can about the organization. If you have any doubts about a group's legitimacy, check them out with the state or county district attorney's office and/or with the Better Business Bureau. Computer modem users can also get information about MLM organizations they are considering in the Home Office/Small Business RoundTable on the GEnie service. One category in the RoundTable is devoted entirely to MLM businesses. (See chapter 4 for further discussion of MLM.)

 How can I tell the difference between a real business opportunity and a scam?

Memorize this phrase: **If it sounds too good to be true, it probably is.** There is no quick and easy way to make money, no way to make megabucks for stuffing or opening envelopes, and no secret method to go from near bankruptcy to Mercedes ownership overnight. Neither is it very likely that you will make $4,000 a month part-time using your computer while you still retain your full-time job, as one company claims. There are people who do make more than that with a part-time business, but usually they reach this income because they have become experts at something or because they have gradually accumulated a list of repeat customers.

Remember, the only true opportunity is one that will let you make a profit selling a product or service at a reasonable price that people want to buy. If you will have to wheedle, cajole, use high-pressure sales tactics, or stretch or hide the truth to win customers, your business will be short-lived and your profits non-existent.

Q What should I do first?

Once you've chosen a business, there are a number of organizational and legal tasks to perform before you get started. Among them:

- prepare a business plan (explained in chapter 7)
- choose and register a business name
- check zoning laws
- determine what special permits or licenses might be needed and apply for them
- apply for an employer identification number
- apply for a sales tax number (resale number) if needed
- open a business checking account

Some specific steps will vary according to your local laws and the type of business you run. The start-up checklist on pages 35–39 lists some common start-up tasks and includes some suggestions for who to call about various requirements.

Q How long will it take me to get started?

It could take a month or more to complete all the tasks that need to be done. If your local laws require you to place a public notice in a newspaper stating your intent to do business under a fictitious name (or even your own name), you may have to run the notice for several weeks before you can start the business officially. An employer identification number and sales tax number, if you need them, may also take a little time to be assigned. Other tasks usually can be accomplished fairly quickly unless you have to take and pass any tests, as you might need to do in order to get a license or get special insurance.

Q **Will I have to collect sales taxes? And if I do, will I have to incorporate?**

You will have to find out what products and services have a sales tax in your state and collect taxes if you sell any of those products or services. Your state tax department should be able to give you information about taxable items. Don't be surprised if the regulations seem confusing and arbitrary or if they change from county to county and city to city within your state. You may have several different tax rates if you sell in more than one area of the state. Each sale is subject to the tax rates and regulations that apply to the customer's location.

Q **Do I have to collect sales tax on out-of-state sales?**

The Supreme Court looked at this issue in 1992 in the case of *Quill* v. *North Dakota* and decided that states may force out-of-state vendors to collect sale tax *if* Congress allows them to. At the time of writing, Congress had yet to pass such a resolution.

Because of the undue hardship that tracking all the tax rates and regulations in all the counties and cities in all the states throughout the United States would place on small businesses, it is hoped that Congress will not pass a law forcing businesses to collect out-of-state taxes.

Q **Where can I get help if I need it?**

The legal requirements for starting a business vary from state to state, and even from county to county or city to city within any one state. They also vary according to the type of business you are starting. Unfortunately there is little consistency in the way the offices responsible for administering the regulations are named. In one locality you might need to contact an office of permits; in another, the county clerk's office. In some cases you will need to comply with regulations issued by several different state or local offices.

The first place you should turn for help, therefore, is the blue government listings in your county or regional telephone directory. For information about registering your business name and getting a business certificate, look for a county or city clerk's office or an office of business permits and licenses. Call and ask if that office is the right place to register your business name, and if there are other local or state regulations that the type of business you are thinking about starting must comply with.

Don't be surprised or get discouraged if the first office you call doesn't have the information you need and doesn't know where to refer you. Clerks in any one government office often know little about what goes on in other government offices. A man in Chicago called and wrote letters to several Illinois state offices; then, when he got no response after two weeks, decided "it was time to trek on down to the State of Illinois Building."

There, he says, he asked four different people if there was "any central office to find out all the licenses and permits that might be required of a business or for a contractor doing a particular job." Three out of the four people he asked were of no help at all. "One of them, upon my saying the word 'job,' said that anyone looking for a job should go see personnel and pointed me in that direction.

"A fourth came through, but not with a one-stop answer. She said that various agencies and departments handled various areas. Incorporation, for instance, would be handled via the secretary of state. Licensing, on the other hand, would be the department of revenue."

If you can't quickly find out what permits and licenses you may need and where to apply for them, a nearby office of the Small Business Administration (SBA) or the Service Corps of Retired Executives (SCORE) should be able to help. Other government-funded agencies that may be able to help you find your way through the maze of red tape are Small Business Development Centers (SBDCs), Economic Development Agencies, Minority Business Development Centers (MBDCs), and Offices of Women's Business Ownership. (See pages 473–499 for phone numbers of SBA, SCORE, SBDC, MBDC, and Women's Business Ownership offices throughout the country.) You also can get the phone number of a local SBA by calling the SBA answer desk in Washington, D.C. That phone number is (800) 827-5722. When you dial that number you get a prerecorded message giving you a menu of options from which to choose. One of the options tells you how to contact local branch offices of the SBA.

Local business groups such as the chamber of commerce, regional industrial associations, and Lion's Clubs can be helpful. Colleges and universities that offer business classes may also offer some help.

In addition to securing any necessary licenses and permits, you may also need to apply for a state sales tax number. The place to get that information as well as information about state income taxes is often called the state tax department or state revenue service. (See the list of state tax department addresses and phone numbers in appendix 4.) If you will be hiring employees, contact your state department of labor to find out about any state labor laws with which you must comply.

Information on federal income taxes for businesses and on payroll deductions you are required to make if you hire employees is available from the U.S. Internal Revenue Service (IRS). If you aren't sure what forms or information you need, call the IRS help line at (800) 829–1040.

Q   Should I quit my job to start my business?

The answer really depends on your financial status. If you need your income to pay for food, clothing, shelter, and bills, try to develop some customers and have at least 6 months' to a year's worth of living expenses put aside in the bank before quitting your job. Here's why:

Suppose you are a graphic artist. You quit your job, start your home business, and, after two weeks, meet someone from a medium-sized ad agency who says he has a job for you but is waiting for the client to give the go-ahead. Two weeks later, the agency contact calls you and sets up a meeting for the following week with you and a copywriter with whom you'll be working.

After the meeting, you do a rough layout but have to wait for the writer to send you the copy before you can continue. That takes another week. You finally finish the job and send it to the agency, they send it to the client, and a few days later the client requests a minor change. You make it, and at long last you can bill for the job.

At this point, a month or more has elapsed since you first heard about the job. *It is likely to be another 30 to 45 days or perhaps longer from the time you submit your bill until you get paid.* That makes the total elapsed time from the day you heard about the assignment until you actually get a check in your hands close to 75 days. If the check is big and drawn on an out-of-town company you may have to wait 5 days more for the check to clear your bank and the money to become available. If the check was drawn on an out-of-state bank, it could take 2 weeks.

While quitting your job may be tempting, a better path to follow, if possible, would be to work at the business part-time until the following factors are in place:

- You have a cash reserve that will last you 6 months to 1 year.
- You have run the business long enough to see there is a lasting demand for the product or service.
- You know how long it takes to collect payment from customers.
- You have a steady stream of customers.
- Profits allow you to pay yourself a salary and replace medical insurance or other benefits you'll lose when you quit your job.
- The business has grown enough that it requires your attention full-time.

Q   If I use my own name as the business name do I have to register with anyone?

That depends on where you live. In some states you are required to register your business even if it operates under your own name. In other states, you don't have to register the business unless it operates under a different name.

Q   Must I have fancy business cards and stationery made up?

If you are serious about being in business, you should have business cards and business stationery made up. If your business is one where appearances and creativity are important, you will need well-designed business cards, letterhead, and envelopes all printed on a good stock (*stock* is a term used in the printing industry to describe kinds of papers). If your business is something like a car repair service, you can probably get by with a plain white business card and inexpensive stationery. You may also need things like sales slips, shipping labels, and invoice forms.

Q   Do I need a computer?

Owning and knowing how to use a computer is almost essential in some businesses. In others, it's optional.

For instance, any business where you have to communicate or exchange information with another business or where there is repetitive typing or number crunching to do practically requires the use of a computer these days. Computer use is the norm in advertising, publicity, translation services, and writing, as well as in law offices, management consulting, personnel recruiting, and other office services. In fields such as these you simply will not project a professional appearance without a computer and, as a result, won't get the customers and clients you should.

Many other businesses don't require a computer to bring in business but could benefit from using a computer to stay in touch with customers, track parts and inventory, or do accounting and taxes.

Don't make the mistake of assuming a computer is the magic ingredient that will put you into business, however. If you don't already have a computer available at home, wait to buy one until you know how to use one and know what you will use it for. Most local schools and colleges offer adult education computer courses. (Unless you want to start a new career as a programmer, though, don't bother with programming courses. Look for courses that teach you what you can do with a microcomputer and/or how to use frequently used computer applications such as word processing, databases, and spreadsheets. See chapter 12 for information on buying a computer.)

Q   **Do I need any special training to start a business?**

If you have no previous experience running a business, you will need to acquire some basic knowledge of business practices and procedures. Most of that basic knowledge can be acquired inexpensively through reading, networking with other businesspeople, and attending inexpensive business conferences in your area.

Q   **I never finished high school. Will I be able to run my own business?**

Yes. One of the nice things about being the boss is there's no one to tell you that you can't be hired because you don't have a high school or college degree.

Q   **Do I need an attorney or accountant to start a business?**

It would be wise to consult an attorney or accountant since you will need to know what civil and tax laws affect you and how to keep at least simple financial records. However, many home business owners don't feel they can afford professional help and gather the information they need from books, friends, the library, seminars, or other sources. If you choose to go that route, be aware that there are some situations in which you would be foolish *not* to consult professional help. Among them:

- if you have to sign or offer contracts
- if you deal in large sums of money or hold money or property for customers
- if you plan to invest a substantial amount of money in your business
- if you plan to buy a business or franchise
- if you have no knowledge of taxes
- if what you sell might potentially cause injury or loss of any kind to someone else
- if you will be working with another person in a formal or informal partnership
- if you are going to incorporate
- when you develop a product, design, or name that you wish to protect from future use by unauthorized parties
- whenever you encounter unfamiliar or puzzling legal or financial matters

Table 2.3: Business Start-up Checklist

The list below is meant to remind you of the tasks you may have to perform to start your business. It includes some contact information and notes that may be of use to many business; blank spaces would be filled in on your own list with names and numbers you collect as you proceed with your plans.

Task	Contact	Notes	Date Done
Assess your skills and interests			
Research the business idea		Investigate the business (will it make money? how much? what do you need to start it?)	
Write a business plan and market plan		You may not need an elaborate business plan with high-powered spreadsheets for a small home business. You should at least create an informal plan, however, both to help you decide if the business will make	

(continued)

Table 2.3—*Continued*

Task	Contact	Notes	Date Done
		money, and to give your activities focus and direction. If you need financing, you will need a formal business plan.	
Choose a business name and verify right to use the name	Yellow Pages; county clerk's office records	Normally, you can't register a business name if another business is using a similar name. Therefore you should check the Yellow Pages for similar names before going to register yours. It's also advisable to have several alternate choices ready. Some businesses that have registered names may not be in the phone book.	
Register or reserve corporate name		Only if you plan to incorporate.	
Register or reserve state or federal trademark	U.S. Patent and Trademark Office	Advisable if you will be selling nationally and want to protect symbol and names from use by others.	
Register copyrights	U.S. Copyright Office	Registration isn't required to protect your copyright, but registering a copyright gives you more recourse against infringers. It is also inexpensive and relatively easy to do.	
Apply for patent if you will be marketing an invention	U.S. Patent and Trademark Office	Assistance from a patent attorney is advisable.	
Check zoning laws	County, city, or town zoning board		

Table 2.3—*Continued*

Task	Contact	Notes	Date Done
Choose a location for the business or make space in the house for it			
Register business name and get a business certificate	Usually handled by the county or city clerk's office	A business certificate may be called a DBA (doing business as) or a fictitious name certificate. You may also need a business permit from your town or city to operate your business, as well as other licenses or permits. Determine what you will need by asking local authorities or other local business people.	
File partnership or corporate papers		It is highly advisable to have an attorney help you prepare the papers if you plan to operate as a partnership or corporation. See chapter 11 for additional information.	
Get any required business licenses or permits	City or county licensing or clerk's office		
Order any required notices of your intent to do business in the community		Some states require you to run a public notice in a newspaper indicating your intent to operate a business. You should be able to find out how to place such notices and how long it must run when you register your business name.	
Have business phone or extra phone lines installed	Local phone company		

(*continued*)

Table 2.3—*Continued*

Task	Contact	Notes	Date Done
Check into business insurance needs		Equipment and auto/vehicle insurance or fire, theft, and liability insurance may be needed. Your personal vehicle and house insurance may not cover your business needs. (See chapter 22 for additional information.)	
Find out about health insurance if you will not have coverage under a spouse		If leaving full-time employment, make sure your coverage doesn't lapse.	
Apply for sales tax number	State tax department		
Get tax information, such as record keeping requirements, information on withholding taxes if you will have employees, information on hiring independent contractors, facts about estimating taxes, forms of organization, etc.	Local IRS office	Dial (800) 829–1040 for tax help and information. Ask what forms and information booklets would be useful to you, then order them by calling (800) 829–3676. One that you should definitely request is publication 454-A, *Your Business Tax Kit,* which includes several other publications most business owners need. Allow at least 2 weeks for delivery. If you don't want to wait, call the nearest IRS office and see if they have copies of the publication in stock. (See chapter 23 for information about tax laws that may affect you).	
Apply for employee identification number if you will have employees	IRS		

Table 2.3—*Continued*

Task	Contact	Notes	Date Done
Call Department of Labor to determine labor laws if you will have employees			
Find out about workers' compensation if you will have employees			
Open business bank account(s)			
Have business cards and stationery printed			
Place advertising			
Purchase equipment or supplies			
Call everyone you know and let them know you are in business			
Order inventory			
Order signage			
Order fixtures			
Have sales literature prepared			

3

Cash on the Line:
Connecting to Success
with a Telephone

Once upon a time, telephone lines carried only live voice conversations. Now they are being used to transmit computer data, speed copies of documents from coast to coast, search distant databases, retrieve prerecorded audio messages, and do dozens of other things that make money for someone, somewhere.

You, too, may be able to make money with your telephone. But to do so you will need to know how to distinguish true income-producing opportunities from the all-too-prevalent get-rich schemes designed to make someone else money at your expense. This chapter will help you gain a better understanding of what it really takes to turn your telephone into a money machine.

Q **How can I use the telephone to make money?**

You can make money either by offering a telephone-based service, by selling telephone services, or by using the telephone (usually in combination with computer or fax) to communicate with customers or an employer and deliver work to them.

Q **I've seen ads implying that for a few hundred dollars I can buy a 900 number and make several hundred dollars a day. Are these ads for real?**

Many of these ads are misleading at best. While there are legitimate ways to make money with 900-number information services, you are not going to be able to do it on an investment of just a few hundred dollars. Warns Robert Mastin, author of *900 Know-how: How to Succeed With Your Own 900 Number,* "There are a lot of snake-oil hucksters out there."

Q   How can I tell what is legitimate and what isn't?

Among the companies to be wary of are those that:

- Offer you the opportunity to share in the profits if you will advertise and promote their program.
- Pressure you to sign up *now,* before all available 900 numbers "run out."
- Imply you can get rich by owning a 900 line. A 900 number by itself is worth nothing to you. You must have a product and the money to advertise that product to make money.

Q   Are there any legitimate 900-number services?

Yes, there are many of them. Among the organizations and government agencies that have 900-number information services now or have used them in the past are: Dow Jones & Company, Microsoft, the New York World Trade Center, the Associated Press, the Michigan Department of Commerce, *Consumer Reports,* and the ABC TV network.

Among the types of services available through 900 numbers are up-to-the-minute stock quotes, software support, legal advice or faxed copies of legal forms, import/export leads, academic information, medical advice, and counseling for parents. You can also voice your opinion in TV polls or contribute to some fund-raising campaigns by using 900-number services.

Q   Are 900 numbers used frequently?

In 1991, more than 274 million calls were placed to 900 numbers, resulting in estimated revenues of approximately $975 million. *

* This figure, which comes from Strategic Telemedia, was published in the April/May 1992 issue of the Information Industry Association's *Voice Information Services Division Update.*

Q How do 900-number businesses work?

A 900-number business is simply a pay-per-call telephone information service. The 900 number is not, itself, a "business." Rather it provides a method for delivering a product and getting paid.

These services, according to the Information Industry Association,* generally are offered to consumers as a "team effort" by the following kinds of companies:

▶ An information provider who creates the information service (or sometimes an entertainment service) and is responsible for its content.

▶ A service bureau that provides a business message storage system to help the information provider handle the incoming calls. (Some information providers use their own message storage equipment instead of using a service bureau.)

▶ A long-distance carrier (phone company) that carries the 900 program (AT&T, MCI, or Sprint).

▶ The local phone company, which is responsible for the billing of the 900 services.

The information provider advertises the service (just as they would advertise any business) through whatever media they choose. Customers who want to use the service call the advertised 900 telephone number and obtain the information, incurring a fee that has been set by the information provider. At the end of the month, the local telephone company adds the 900-number charges to the customer's regular phone bill. The phone company takes its cut and distributes the balance of the collected fees back to the other players in the chain.

Q Haven't a lot of people been ripped off by calling 900 numbers?

There have been some con artists who have used the pay-per-call industry as a new way to work the same old scams that have plagued the mail order and telemarketing industries in the past. Among the advertised 900 numbers that have been most abusive have been services that advertise "guaranteed" credit, ways to

---

* The Information Industry Association (IIA) is a trade association for more than six hundred businesses involved with the creation, distribution, and use of information products, services, and technologies.

get out of debt, and even high-paying overseas jobs. Often the information re-trieved from such services is of little true value to the caller. In the past consumers often had no way of knowing in advance exactly how much it would cost to get the advertised information. Only when their phone bills arrived at the end of the month would they discover that the worthless information sometimes cost as much as $50 or more.

The industry also got a bad name in the past because of "adults only" call-in lines.

As a result, some federal and state regulations have already been put in place to regulate the industry and more may be forthcoming. In addition, the long dis-tance carriers now must approve advertising and content of 900 information ser-vices.

Q **Can small businesses really make money in the pay-per-call industry?**

It is possible for small and home businesses to make money with their own 900-number information services but not on a shoestring budget. Explains John Small, owner of Strategic Alliance Marketing, a Fort Worth, Texas, marketing and con-sulting firm, "The business can be small in size, but it can't be small in creativity or money. It takes promotion and advertising to make a 900-number service work."

Since 900 services have to be advertised heavily to succeed, money can also be made indirectly from 900-number businesses by small businesses in the advertising, copywriting, and video production fields.

Q **How much money do I need to start my own 900-number information service?**

Small, whose company uses 900 numbers to sell its own information services and also provides turnkey start-up services to other entrepreneurs, says the cost of turning an idea into a 900-number information product and test marketing it nor-mally runs somewhere between $2,500 and $10,000 depending on the media used to advertise the program. If the program is successful and you plan to continue it you should plan on having additional money available since it can take up to two months or more to collect your earnings from the incoming calls.

There is, of course, no guarantee that after spending that much money your information product will be a success. Thus, warns Small, you should start out with "at least ten thousand dollars that you don't have to see again, since there is risk involved."

Q **How do those costs break down? How much of it goes to buy the 900 number?**

You don't "buy" a 900 number. You (or the service bureau) are given access to a number and billed for usage of that number by your customers, much like you get billed when customers call you on an 800 number. You make money by charging your customers more than the phone company charges you.

Q **What kinds of costs will I incur?**

The costs you may have in running an information service on a 900 phone line are:

- The long-distance and local phone company charges for line use and billing (you get charged both per-minute charges and percent of total call charges, which together may come to about 70 cents per minute).
- Per-minute charges billed by your service bureau. Most service bureaus were charging 10 cents per minute in 1992, but some had fees of 45 cents per minute or more.
- A monthly minimum fee of about $300 to $500 from the service bureau.
- Set-up and programming charges from the service bureau, which could range from about $500 to several thousand dollars, depending on the complexity of your program and the service bureau you use.
- Other fees from the bureau for services such as caller ID to pick up caller's phone numbers and for recording addresses of callers and forwarding them to you.
- Your advertising costs, which may range from a minimum of $1,000 a month for local 900 information lines to as much as $10,000 to $15,000 a month if you advertise on a more widespread basis.

Q **Why does it cost so much to advertise the number?**

You have to create awareness of the number, and that means getting your advertising out to potential customers. If you have a service targeted at a particular audience you can use print ads or card decks or direct mail to keep costs down, but if you have a mass market product you will probably need to use television. To create enough awareness of your message and to get people to call, Small says, you will need to advertise three times a day every day for two to three weeks.

"At that point you know if you have a dog or something that can make some money because you have some call response," he says. "The next three to four weeks of advertising at the same frequency will start driving the numbers up. If they level off, get out of it. Cut your losses. You've either picked the wrong product, your market's wrong, or there's too much market saturation for the kind of product you have."

Q **How long does it take to turn the idea into a 900 service?**

Plan on 45 to 60 days to get the idea up and running on a 900 line.

Q **What do the service bureaus do?**

The service bureaus generally make arrangements with the long-distance carrier for access to 900 exchanges and provide the equipment necessary to receive calls and store and deliver your information product to callers. They also may receive the money from the phone company and then distribute it to you.

Q **Do service bureaus provide any marketing services?**

Service bureaus generally provide only the equipment and access to the phone lines, but there are marketing and consulting companies that can provide help with marketing.

Q **Wouldn't it cost me less if I didn't use a marketing or turnkey service?**

You would eliminate fees charged by the marketing firm; however, you still would have to allocate many thousands of dollars to get your program off the ground since the biggest expense is the advertising and promotion of the service.

Q **What should I look for in a service bureau?**

You will want a service bureau that can handle multiple incoming lines at once and that will make sure these lines will be up and running when your program is. If your service bureau has technical problems and calls can't get through, you lose money.

You should also find out who the bureau's clients are (ask for references and check them), what kinds of programs those customers run, if the bureau is financially stable, and what kind of capabilities they can make available to you. You should also ask about costs, of course.

Q **What kinds of services lend themselves to 900 phone numbers?**

Both John Small and Robert Mastin say information products that can be targeted at particular markets, time-sensitive information, and advice services that will bring repeat business are the most likely to succeed.

Q **How much money could I expect to make with a 900 number?**

If there is a market for the information you are selling through the 900 number you should be able to make two to three times the amount of money you spend to advertise the number, according to John Small.

Q **How much would I charge users for the call?**

You need to charge enough to cover your phone service charges and your advertising costs and make a profit. Typically that is $2 to $3 per minute, though certain programs such as opinion polling must be done at a lower amount (around $1 a minute) in order to attract callers.

Q **Can I use my own computer and voice mail system to handle incoming calls and avoid using a service bureau?**

It is not really practical to have calls come directly to you because of the sophisticated technology involved in handling multiple phone calls and delivering automated messages.

Q Can I put anything I want on the 900 number?

No. The content is regulated to some extent by the long-distance carriers and by federal and state regulations. Furthermore, you must provide actual information of value during the phone call. Generally this information consists of a pre-recorded announcement, an interactive menu of information (the most common), or a live person giving consulting or other advice. Not allowed in some states because of abuses in the past are job information and credit repair information. The Information Industry Association publishes a one-page guideline called *Standards of Practice for Voice Information Services* that discusses ethical conduct in regards to both the informational content and the advertising of voice services. You can get a copy by sending a stamped, self-addressed envelope to the Information Industry Association, 555 New Jersey Ave., NW, Suite 800, Washington, DC 20001.

Q What regulations affect 900 numbers?

Under current FCC regulations customers must be told as soon as they connect with a 900-number service what the charges will be and who the information provider is. They also must be given the option to hang up at the beginning of the call without getting billed. (The information provider has to foot the bill for all hang-ups.) Automated collect calls, line seizing, and generation of dual-tone, multifrequency tones are prohibited.

Consumers also have the option of disputing 900 charges to their phone numbers and cannot have their telephone service disconnected for refusing to pay a bill for a call to a 900 number. Businesses and consumers also have to be given the option by the phone company of having 900 numbers blocked (arranging it so they may not place calls to 900 numbers).

Different states have different regulations regarding the information that may be offered on a 900 number, and at least one state was trying to get legislation passed that would routinely block 900-number access from all phone lines, making it necessary for phone customers to specifically request access to 900 service.

The long-distance carriers and some of the service bureaus have regulations with which you must comply, too. AT&T, for instance, insists on seeing and approving advertising copy that will be used to promote a number as well as the actual information to be delivered once a caller connects with the number. At least one of the major service bureaus won't accept any information provider that will be using their lines for "adults only" material.

Q **What publications will give me more information about the industry?**

Among the publications that cover the telecommunications businesses are:

InfoText Magazine (34700 Coast Highway, Suite 308, Capistrano Beach, CA 92624, [714] 493–2434).

Inbound/Outbound (12 West 21st Street, New York, NY 10010, [212] 691–8215).

Teleconnect (12 West 21st Street, New York, NY 10010, [212] 691–8215).

Telemarketing (One Technology Plaza, Norwalk, CT 06854–9977, [800] 243–6002).

You may also want to read one of the following books:

900 Know-how: How to Succeed with Your Own 900 Number Business, by Robert Mastin (send $19.95 plus $3.00 postage and handling to Aegis Publishing Group, 796 Aquidneck Avenue, Newport, RI 02840, [401] 849–4200).

How to Start Your Own 900 Service by Claudia DuLude (IdealDial, 910 15th St., Suite 900, Denver, CO 80202, [800] 582–3425).

Q **Where can I find service bureaus?**

Here are a handful of service bureaus you might want to call. Many others can be found by looking through the ads in telecommunications and direct marketing magazines or by asking the long-distance carriers for recommendations.

IdealDial
910 15th Street, Suite 900
Denver, CO 80202
(800) 582–3425

Regal Communications, Inc.
1035 Camphill Road
Fort Washington, PA 19034
(800) 825–4900

West Interactive
9910 Maple Street
Omaha, NE 68134
(800) 841–9000

Q **What kinds of telephone-related businesses are there?**

You could sell telephone equipment (such as cellular phones) and services, reduced-rate long-distance services, telemarketing services, information services, or facsimile services. You could also sell advertising, publicity, or other support services to businesses in the telecommunications industry. The key to success is the same as it is in any industry: know the industry (or learn about it), then find a need and fill it.

Q **Is voice mail a fad?**

Voice mail is not a fad. It is used by large corporations and by local public libraries, as well as by small and one-person businesses and even home owners. It is a good way to let company employees communicate with one another when they are on the road, to reduce the volume of routine queries handled by bigger businesses, and to direct calls to the right department in a business.

Q **Is voice mail a good business to get into?**

It could be. Like any other business, however, you need to do your homework and determine if the business will work out for you.

Gerry Gollwitzer, owner of the Wexel Group, a business that provides telemarketing and other services to small businesses in the vicinity of Menomonee Falls, Wisconsin, suggests one way to determine if selling voice mailboxes is a good business for you: "Determine how many voice mailboxes you need to sell to make a decent living. If you want a three-thousand-dollar income per month, you will probably have to rent three hundred voice mailboxes a month. Every four minutes of messages takes up one megabyte of computer disk space. If you allow each of your three hundred voice mailboxes to store up to ten minutes of messages before being erased, you will need a seven-hundred-and-fifty megabyte hard drive just to store the voice mail messages."

(Obviously, you would also have to be able to sell three hundred voice mailboxes.)

Q **What should I know before starting a voice mail business?**

Among the things you should look into are:

 - who your customers will be
 - what they require in the way of automated phone services
 - how much they can afford to pay for the services
 - who your competitors are
 - what it will cost you to market and provide the service
 - how many sales you will have to make for the voice mail business to be profitable

Once you have this basic information you will also need to determine:

 - how many phone lines you will need
 - how many voice mailboxes you will have on the system
 - how much time will be allocated to each voice mailbox
 - what size hard drive you will need (a function of the previous two items)
 - how suitable your system will be for your customers needs (for instance, the first thing callers should hear when they get the voice mail system is the name of the company they are calling, not some menu telling them how to locate that company on the voice mail system)

Q **How much can I charge for a voice mailbox?**

Though fees will vary, you may not be able to get much more than $10 a month for a single voice mailbox. If you are selling to small businesses that have simple requirements, the amount you may be able to get might be even less, particularly if the local phone company in your area is offering low-cost voice mail options to business and residential customers.

> **Q** **What about those voice mail businesses you can buy? Are they worth it?**

Voice mail "turnkey" or "packaged" businesses may provide some hardware, software, and a plan to follow, but they will not put you into business. Only you can do that by going out and selling the service. You will also need to make sure the hardware that is provided as part of the package is adequate for the needs of a viable voice mail service. Some people who have bought turnkey voice mail systems have found they needed to upgrade the hardware and get more phone lines into the house/office in order to make the service marketable.

> **Q** **What about a facsimile service? Can I turn a fax machine into a money machine?**

Offering facsimile services is another way to bring in income. Offering the use of a fax machine to customers may bring in a few extra dollars here and there at an office supply store, secretarial service, or print shop. Specialized equipment that allows more sophisticated services can be used to bring in more substantial income if you know what services to sell and who to sell them to. For instance, faxback technology, a system that allows a person who wants to get information to call a special number and then have information automatically sent to his or her facsimile machine, is being used in a variety of ways to make money. Fax broadcasting (sending out faxes to multiple fax machines at once) is another service that has possibilities, particularly if used as an information delivery system rather than a way of distributing junk mail. (There are various regulations governing distribution of unsolicited advertising materials via fax.)

Among the potential drawbacks of services like these, however, is that repeat customers (and repeat customers are always the most profitable customers you can have), might decide they can save money by purchasing their own equipment after seeing how well yours works.

> **Q** **Could I make money running a bulletin board service or as a systems operator (sysop) on a national information service?**

If you have a good information product or service, you might be able to make some money, but few sysops can live on the earnings from their online information services. Sysops of private boards must pay for equipment, phone lines, advertising, repairs, and software to run the information service as well as whatever costs they incur to collect the information they make available to their customers. They make money only if they can get enough paying customers to cover all these costs and return a profit.

Sysops on the major online information services don't have to pay for mass storage equipment but must have a good information product that will attract a large mass market audience. Generally they are experts in their field and incur hard costs both in collecting information for their services and in promoting their services. Soft costs come in the form of many hours of work keeping the information online organized and doing a variety of administrative tasks. Income is usually derived in the form of royalty payments based on usage but is sometimes set as a flat fee or guarantee against royalties.

Q **Is selling cellular phone services a lucrative business to get into?**

There are three ways to make money selling cellular services:

▶ by being a direct sales representative for the cellular company
▶ by being a sales rep for an agent of a cellular company
▶ by being an agent of a cellular company

In any of the three cases you will need to plan on selling in volume since commissions on the initial sale will be relatively low (the agent may make less than $300 per sale and reps working for the agent may make only $50 per sale). Residuals on use of the service, when companies offer them, run only 2 percent to 5 percent.

To make a living, agents for cellular services often offer cellular as one of a mix of connectivity products. Other sources of revenue, says Henrik Rasmussen, the Carolinas district agent for Audiovox Corporation, are renting pagers for a paging company, selling accessories, and selling fax machines.

 Q **What about selling reduced rate long-distance phone services? Is that profitable?**

If you can locate customers with big long-distance phone bills and sell them on switching, you may be able to make 6 to 7 percent commission on the customers' actual bills. Thus if you bring in customers that do a total volume of $10,000 per month in phone calls, your commission would be $600 to $700 per month. Depending on what company you are selling for, you might have to bring in one or more new customers a month until you reach a certain dollar volume in order to collect your residuals. You will have some expenses for brochures, your car, getting leads, and so on.

Q **Could I make money purchasing my own coin-operated telephones and placing them in business establishments?**

Unless you get lucky enough to get an unusually good location, your average take per month will be about $20 per phone, says Jeff Michaels, one of the owners of Network Services Communication Corporation in Levittown, New York. Areas that do best for pay phones are bars and other busy locations where many people might normally be expected to make phone calls. Any money that is in the coin box gets split with the owner of the establishment in which you have placed the phone.

Q **What is a telecommuter?**

A telecommuter is an employee of a company who performs part or all of his or her work at home. Instead of commuting to the office in a car, the employee "commutes" via telephone, staying in touch with the people in the business by voice or computer. If the employee's work is normally prepared on a computer, it can be transferred from the employee's home computer directly to the company's computer over ordinary telephone lines with a modem.

Q **Do people telecommute every day of the week?**

It depends on the situation. In some jobs people work from home all of the time; other people work from home a few days a week or on a more occasional basis.

Q **What's the difference between a telecommuter and an independent contractor?**

Independent contractors are self-employed business people. They get no benefits such as sick pay, health insurance, or a pension plan from employers and are responsible for reporting and paying income tax and social security taxes (called self-employment tax when you are self-employed) directly to the IRS.

Most independent contractors work, or attempt to work, for more than one company. In fact, making one's services available to the general public is one of the criteria the IRS uses to distinguish independent contractors from employees, since they are treated differently for tax purposes.

Q   What kind of companies hire telecommuters?

According to a study of office staffing strategies published in 1992 by the Olsten Corporation,* 13 percent of businesses offer work-at-home options to their employees. These arrangements are most commonly offered in service businesses (20 percent) and in banking and finance (18 percent). Among other types of businesses where telecommuting opportunities exist or are being tested are insurance companies, telephone companies, and even state and federal government offices.

Q   How many people telecommute?

A study by LINK Resources Corporation put the number at 6.6 million in 1992, a 20 percent increase from the preceding year. The majority of the telecommuters were in management, sales, or were classified as "professionals" with the companies for whom they worked.

Q   Do businesses hire telecommuters as a way of keeping costs down?

No. In fact, telecommuting seems to be regarded more as an employee benefit than a work style. According to the Olsten study, alternative scheduling programs such as telecommuting are "employee-driven more than budget-driven." They are offered primarily as a way to attract and keep qualified workers. Companies that

---

* The study, *New Staffing Strategies for the 90s*, was based on input from human resource executives at 427 companies across the United States. The companies ranged in size from under 100 employees to more than 10,000 employees and sales of under $50 million to more than $500 million. Industry groups represented included manufacturing/construction; services (business services, consulting, etc.); banking/finance; retail/wholesale; public/nonprofit; insurance; utilities/transportation/communication; health care; and others.

offer telecommuting as an option have received increasing requests in recent years from employees who want to take advantage of that option.

Q **Do businesses advertise for telecommuters?**

Usually they don't. Most telecommuting jobs grow out of on-the-job work.

Q **How can I get my company to let me work at home?**

If the company doesn't have a formal policy, ask if you could work at home on a trial basis. Remind your supervisor that you could be more productive working from home since you will have fewer interruptions, and suggest they let you try working from home one or two days a week. Be sure you get your work done and keep in touch with the office during business hours. If the experiment is successful, consider asking the company to let you work at home more days a week.

Q **What are the drawbacks of being a telecommuter?**

There are a couple of disadvantages. First, you may lose contact with other staff members and run the risk of being passed over come promotion time. You may also find you miss the camaraderie of office work. Some people discover they dislike the peace and quiet of working at home and would much prefer being with other adults during the day or in a situation where things are "happening." Finally, working at home can be an expense. Employers usually do not supply the computer, fax, modem, or other equipment you may need. Furthermore, if you buy these items yourself and are employed by the company (rather than being an independent contractor), you cannot deduct their costs on your tax return.

Q **Is there any way I could deduct the cost of my computer and other equipment?**

If you go into business for yourself you may be able to deduct the cost of your equipment. Many people start off with their last employer as the first customer of their new business. You must be careful to set things up so you are truly independent, however, or you could lose your chance to take business deductions and the employer might get hit with a variety of penalties.

4.

Low-Cost Home Franchises, Business Packages, and Multilevel Marketing: Are They Any Good?

Sometimes it seems like the hottest business of the decade is the business of selling business opportunities.

Open any magazine aimed at small business owners and people who want to start businesses, and you will see page after page of ads promising to help you get started in allegedly lucrative businesses. You'll find ads for franchises that will put you into the "exploding" service industry, ads promising to send you "confidential reports" about some questionable new home business opportunity, and ads for franchises with familiar names like Dunkin' Donuts or Jiffy Lube.

Reading these ads is one way to answer the universal question, "What kind of business can I start?" But will purchasing the franchise or business plans or equipment advertised in such ads really lead to easy money?

Here are some tips and real-life experiences to help you decide.

Q **Is buying a franchise a good way to go into business?**

It can be. In 1990 over $600 billion in sales (about 34 percent of all retail sales) were made through franchised establishments. While not every franchise or every franchise owner is successful, franchising does reduce some of the risk of launching a new business by letting you copy a business concept someone else has already made successful.

56

Q **What specific benefits does a franchise offer?**

Depending on the franchise, among the benefits you might gain are:

- a business concept with a track record for success
- name recognition for the business
- management training
- access to proprietary methods and/or processes used in the business
- a ready-made business or marketing plan to follow
- ready-made ads, brochures, and other sales and marketing aids
- help with financing

Q **What are the disadvantages?**

The security you acquire by licensing someone else's business methods and practices has its price. Among the drawbacks of being a franchise are:

- Your start-up costs can be high.
- You will have to follow the franchisor's rules. That means you might have limitations placed on everything from what products and services you sell to what goes into ads, where you are allowed to sell, and even how your business is furnished.
- You will have to pay a percentage of your sales and/or a flat fee to the franchisor (company from which you purchase the franchise) each year.
- Your success is dependent in many respects on the talents, foresight, and stability of the franchisor.
- You will be locked into the terms of the contract with the franchisor whether your operation is successful or not.

Q **What should I look for in a franchise?**

First and foremost you want to look for a franchise that sells a product or service you would enjoy producing and selling. Your best bet is to find a franchise in an industry you know at least a little bit about. All too typical is the case of the Chicago car salesman who decided to change careers and go into business for himself. He bought a basement waterproofing franchise but then found the business boring. He wanted to sell it, but sales weren't as high as he had expected they would be and he had trouble finding a buyer. He was stuck paying off the franchise fee and working at a business he didn't enjoy.

Once you've pinned down some possibilities, you should get and carefully scrutinize a disclosure document called the Uniform Franchise Offering Circular (UFOC) for the franchise or franchises you are interested in. This disclosure document will give you the information you need to help you determine the answer to these and other important questions:

▶ How stable is the franchise and what is the background of its officers? (Any history of litigation or bankruptcy of the franchise or its officers is supposed to be included in the UFOC.)

▶ What will *all* your costs of purchase be? Advertising, training, inventory, insurance, and all other costs in addition to the franchise fee and royalties should be spelled out.

▶ How well established is the franchise? Have they been in business for many years or are they brand new? How many other franchises have they opened and where are they located?

▶ What kind of track record do they have? Have most of their franchisees been successful? Names and addresses of franchisees in your state should be provided before you sign any contract. Call the people on the list and ask about their experiences.

▶ What kind of training and support will they provide as part of your franchise fee?

▶ How close to your store can the franchisor let another franchisee set up shop?

▶ Will you be required to purchase supplies or products from the parent company? If so, compare your cost to the local retail prices of the same goods. There have been instances where the price from the franchise company for goods was *higher* than the price of the same goods in local retail stores. Selling anything under such conditions would be quite difficult.

▸ What do the contract terms say about ownership? Can you sell out to someone else if you wish? If you want to continue when the contract expires, will it be automatically renewed? Will you be able to convert your store into an independent operation if you should want to?

▸ Determine how disputes will be handled should they arise. Watch for clauses requiring arbitration in the franchisor's home state if it is different than yours. Should a dispute arise, you'd have to travel to that state for arbitration hearings.

▸ What criteria does the franchise use in selecting franchisees? Do they do any screening? Or, do they seem more interested in getting your franchise fee?

▸ Does the franchise use high-pressure sales techniques to get you to sign on the dotted line?

▸ Do you like the people you are dealing with?

▸ How big is the market for the franchise's products or services in your area and how much competition is there now?

Q **Will the franchise limit competition?**

The franchise will generally give you a territory in which you may operate and agree not to allow anyone else to open one of their franchises in your territory. However, they have no control on competing franchisors opening up a franchise in your territory (for example, if you own a PIP quick print franchise, a McPrint outlet may very well open across the street), and they have no power to keep independents with the same type of business from opening in your area.

Two other things you need to watch out for are the size of your territory and that any verbal territorial claims or promises actually get included in your final contract. No matter how helpful and friendly the company may be, when push comes to shove, the only thing that matters is what it says in the contract.

A franchisee for a company that sells products to a very specific niche market learned that lesson the hard way. He signed a contract with the franchise to open a store in a suburban East Coast community. His contract with the franchise stated that competing stores had to be located at least 7 miles away from one another. When he questioned whether this allowed proximity might hinder business, he was shown figures indicating that stores in a nearby city were profitable even though they were that close together and was also told the franchise company wasn't planning to open any other stores in his state for 3 years. Thus, they said, he would have plenty of opportunity to build his business and become established.

Less than a year later a second store from the same franchise company was opened in the area. The store was more than 7 miles away from the first one but close enough to seriously cut into the business. Warns the owner, "Buyer beware. A seven-mile territory in a densely populated city may be fine, but seven miles is nothing for some kinds of businesses in the suburbs. You wind up doing the advertising for the other store."

 Can I get copies of franchises' Uniform Franchise Offering Circulars (UFOCs) before I talk to any franchise management so I can compare several before calling a company?

There is a company called Frandata that can send most franchises' UFOCs to you for a fee. You can reach that company for information by calling or writing:

Frandata
1130 Connecticut Avenue, NW
Washington, DC 20036
(202) 659–8640

 What will it cost to buy a franchise?

Depending on which franchise you are interested in, your initial franchise fee could be as little as $1,000 or as much as $100,000 or more. On top of any initial fees will be other start-up costs, which could run from a few thousand dollars to $500,000 or more.

Q   **What's involved in running a franchise?**

Even if you will be able to hire other people, you yourself will need to know how to operate all phases of the business since you may need to train employees or to fill in for them when they are absent or if they leave. You will also need to be a good manager and salesperson and keep good records.

Q   **Can I avoid market research by buying a franchise?**

No. While the franchise company may help with site selection and other details, there is no substitute for doing your own research. Remember, a franchise isn't something you can walk away from easily if it doesn't work out. Therefore *before* you sign the franchise agreement, make sure you determine how many sales you will have to make to be profitable and whether your territory has the population and the demand to make it likely you can reach that sales figure even if a competitor opens.

Q   **Can I sell the franchise?**

Some franchises allow you to sell if you can find a buyer, and some don't. The UFOC will tell you what the franchise's regulations are regarding sale or transfer of your contract to anyone else.

Q   **Is there any place where I can get more information about franchising?**

The International Franchise Association has a catalog that includes various publications about franchising. For information about the association or to get a catalog, call or write:

International Franchise Association
1350 New York Avenue, NW
Washington, DC 20005
(202) 628–8000

In addition you can find information about franchising quite regularly in *Entrepreneur* magazine and in *Small Business Opportunities* magazine, both of which are sold on the newsstands.

Q Are there any inexpensive home franchises?

There are some franchises that can be run from home and which, therefore, may have lower start-up costs since you won't be required to build or rent space. But most of the low-cost home business opportunities you see advertised are either turnkey (also called "packaged") businesses or are multilevel marketing operations.

Q What's the difference between a turnkey business and a franchise?

When you buy a franchise, the relationship is ongoing. The franchisor is likely to have some say about the quality of the goods or services you sell and the methods you use to acquire the products or provide the service. They will also collect a royalty or other fee from you on an ongoing basis. In return they will give you guidance and training as well as name recognition.

A turnkey business generally does not come with the control or the support a franchise does. Sometimes the company who licenses the turnkey business to you may act as a service bureau. However, there is no requirement that you do business with them. Nor are there regulations requiring the turnkey company to give you a disclosure agreement like a franchise must.

Q How much does it cost to buy the turnkey computer businesses advertised in the magazines?

In 1991 and 1992 one company was charging approximately $10,000 to $12,000 for a package consisting of a microcomputer and other hardware for an entry-level telemarketing operation, plus business plans for approximately eight to ten businesses; ready-to-use ad slicks; telemarketing scripts; and sales literature. The businesses were things such as utility bill auditing, personalized children's books, scholarship search services, mortgage reduction plans, discounted long-distance services, and other products or services for which telemarketing could be used to generate sales leads. Five or six of these programs could be bought in packages without the computer for between $4,500 and $5,000.

Q **Are the turnkey computer businesses worth the money?**

It depends who you ask. One man from California claims a friend of his purchased a setup like this for $10,000 and got a computer he could have purchased elsewhere for $1,500, some shareware, several business concepts that didn't work (even though he followed the directions for marketing them), and 4 years' worth of second mortgage payments that are costing him approximately $470 a month.

People in other parts of the country have also reported difficulty making money using the business plans provided with their turnkey businesses. In some cases, they found that the equipment they received had limited capabilities and needed to be upgraded to work some of the plans they purchased. In other cases, they found that competition or costs made it impractical to work some of the purchased plans.

Still other people, though, are reasonably satisfied that the combination of business plans, hardware, software, and collateral material, such as sample ads and brochures, are worth the money.

Note:

Take the time to find out what laws or pending legislation might affect your business plans before investing in any telemarketing equipment. In response to consumer and business complaints about abusive marketing practices, federal and state laws have been enacted in recent years to regulate the use of telephone lines to deliver commercial messages. Among these laws is the Telephone Consumer Protection Act (TCPA) which was passed by Congress in 1991 to regulate automated telemarketing calls and unsolicited facsimile transmissions (junk-mail faxes). At the time of this writing a provision of that law that would limit the use of autodialers to place telemarketing calls to consumers was facing a legal challenge. If the challenge is overturned, however, use of autodialers to call residences to deliver prerecorded commercial messages would be prohibited unless there is prior consent for receiving such calls or unless there is an existing business relationship with the called party.

Other provisions of the TCPA require telemarketers to maintain in-house do-not-call lists, regulate the hours during which telemarketing calls (voice or automated) may be placed to homes, and ban the junk-mail fax transmissions. Prerecorded messages would have to identify the caller, give the caller's telephone number or address, and release the called party's line within five seconds after the called party has hung up.

Whether or not the challenge to the part of the law regulating the use of auto-dialers is successful, state and federal regulation of telephone marketing methods are a concern to telemarketers.

Q **Does anyone really make money from these turnkey businesses?**

A few people do. However, like any business, it takes time, hard work, and some trial and error to build the business and make it profitable.

Gerry Gollwitzer is the owner of a successful turnkey business. Gollwitzer was district sales manager for a large industrial chemical company until he purchased a turnkey computer business in 1990 and went into business for himself. After a year and a half of operating a turnkey business he was making a profit but "not yet enough to pay myself a decent wage."

Gollwitzer admits, "I thought it would have grown faster." He adds, however, that it was partly his own fault that it took longer than expected to start making money. Instead of focusing on one or two of the plans that came with his system, he tried to pursue several at the same time, diluting his efforts.

He also found he had to adapt and tailor the turnkey system somewhat. "You have to look at the capabilities of the system and see how they fit in," he says. You have to determine what people will buy in your part of the country and what you are comfortable selling. The system can generate leads, but you have to follow up on them and make the sale. "The bottom line is sales. You don't make any money until a sale is made."

Q **Is it mostly uneducated people and opportunists who lose money on business opportunities advertised in magazines?**

The amount of education one has seems to have little to do with who loses money or makes it. People who lose money in turnkey businesses or other business opportunities generally do so for one of these reasons:

▸ They have unrealistic expectations about how much time and effort they will have to put into selling the product or service to make it profitable.

▸ They have unrealistic expectations about how much money they can make from the business.

▸ They salivate on cue (much to copywriters' glee) to words like "easy," "confidential," "lucrative," and "profit," particularly if the ads also include five- or six-digit numbers preceded by dollar signs.

- ▶ They don't determine in advance if the product or service will sell, in what quantity it will sell, or what it will cost them to sell the product.
- ▶ They don't really like the product themselves or wouldn't buy it themselves at the price they have to charge.
- ▶ They discover after buying the business plans or package that the business will require selling and they hate selling.

Q **I've seen ads for scholarship search businesses that cost less than $500. Is this type of business a good one to get into?**

There probably are people who make money selling scholarship search services; however, many people who buy this particular type of packaged business wind up losing money. Although they do get instructions for conducting the business and a number to call to process the actual scholarship searches, people frequently report they have difficulty finding customers or that the cost of advertising makes it impossible to make money selling the service.

One of the reasons is that scholarship information is widely available, often at very low fees. In 1992, for instance, one university in New York was charging only $10 to run scholarship searches for students. Even if you don't have a college or university near you that offers this type of service, high schools or public libraries may. There may also be other home or small businesses trying to sell a similar service in your area.

Often, too, the cost of the advertising makes it impossible to provide the service at a reasonable price. Although some people figure they will convince PTAs or guidance offices to refer students to them, generally PTAs and schools will not cooperate.

All of that doesn't mean a scholarship search service couldn't work for you. It does mean, however, that you need to carefully evaluate whether or not the service will sell in your area of the country. To do that you should work out all your costs and get realistic estimates of how many people would buy the service. Ask students and their parents where they look for scholarship information and what they would be willing to pay for it. Ask libraries, high schools, and colleges in your area what scholarship services they make available and what they charge. Determine whether or not you can offer more assistance than they can. Check the actual costs of advertising and make realistic estimates of how many responses you might get (probably one-tenth of one percent of readers or listeners at best). Remember, too, that not all responses will turn into sales.

Consider the costs of delivering the material in a professional-looking format to your clients. Compare all your costs to what your research shows you could charge for the service and the number of sales you might realistically make. By doing this fact-gathering first, you can make an intelligent, informed decision about whether or not this particular business might be a good one for you to start in your location.

Warning: Don't be misled by claims of easy money or an unlimited potential market for scholarship search businesses. In 1992 the Federal Trade Commission (FTC) filed a lawsuit against one of the companies offering scholarship search businesses. The lawsuit claimed that the company deceived prospective purchasers of the business by misrepresenting potential earnings, response rates to direct mail solicitations, the number of existing business licensees, and the assistance and services licensees received. In addition, the FTC cited the company for the use of deceptive testimonials and endorsements.

Q **Is it possible to make thousands of dollars with little effort in my spare time like some of the business opportunity ads promise?**

It depends how much spare time you have. The two most important things to remember about opportunity advertising are:

1. **There's no such thing as a free lunch.**
2. **If it sounds too good to be true, it is.**

Remember, even though you may be able to process and fill orders in your spare time, you will still have to spend time finding customers and doing other routine business chores if you expect the business to be successful.

Q **What can I expect if I send for one of those blind ads that promise to tell me the secrets of getting rich?**

Many of them are reports on how to get credit cards or clean up bad credit ratings. Some of the credit clean-up statements either recommend or imply you should lie on applications, which is illegal. Others tell you how to make money in real estate deals or how to start chain letters. Certain kinds of chain letters are illegal as well. Often people send away for the materials out of curiosity or because the ad has a money-back guarantee and therefore somehow seems legitimate. It is probably the curiosity seekers that keep these advertisers in business.

Q **Don't the advertisers lose money if they offer a money-back guarantee and their program doesn't work?**

Not in practice. The guarantee is an advertising ploy that builds confidence and gets the reader to send in money. Most people never bother to send for their refund if they don't like the materials they get.

Q **How do I avoid frauds?**

There's no foolproof way to avoid scams; however, you can avoid many scams by steering clear of any business opportunity that:

- promises unrealistic profits
- promises you can become wealthy working a few hours a day in your spare time
- has agents or distributors that seem more interested in soliciting you than in selling products or services
- discourages or forbids you from contacting other investors, distributors, or licensees of the business
- requires an up-front payment before giving you any details of what the business entails
- claims no experience or skills are needed
- requires you to pay someone money to get at-home work
- makes you an agent for a company that you haven't thoroughly investigated

Be wary of travel agent opportunities. Entrepreneurs selling travel services as intermediaries have been sued by their customers when trips have fallen through. If you are considering becoming a sales rep for a travel company, check the company out thoroughly. If you have access to either Dow Jones News Retrieval or GEnie or CompuServe, you can search for back articles on travel fraud and get names of companies and their principals that are either currently under investigation for travel fraud or have been in the past. If you don't have access to these online services, your public library should be able to help you look for and retrieve information on travel fraud.

Q What is multilevel marketing?

Multilevel marketing (MLM) is a way of distributing and selling products and services through a chain of independent distributors rather than through traditional retail outlets.

Q How does multilevel marketing work?

Each distributor has two basic jobs: (1) to sell the company's products or services and (2) to recruit more distributors to sell the company's products or services.

Each new recruit a distributor brings into the organization is, in turn, encouraged to bring in their own recruits. The result is that an active distributor eventually develops a hierarchical substructure known as a downline that looks somewhat like an organization chart in a company with a lot of employees.

Each distributor gets sales commissions on his or her own direct product sales. He or she also makes a commission on the sales of the distributors in their downline. There are also likely to be certain bonuses available for reaching certain sales levels.

Since each distributor profits not only from his or her own sales but from sales of the downline, it is to the advantage of the distributor to guide and help those below to succeed.

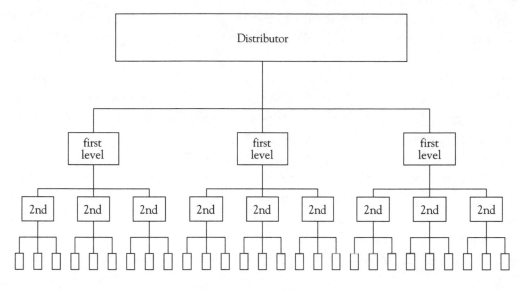

MLM Distributor Hierarchy

How do people get paid in MLM companies?

Compensation plans vary from one MLM company to another, but typically distributors' commissions or margins (a discount off the list price) depend on their sales volume and where they are in the distributor chain.

In some companies distributors earn a commission on their own sales (say, 10 percent) and a lesser commission on any sales made by people below them. They might make 7 percent on sales made by people they have recruited directly, 5 percent on sales made by the recruit's recruits, and so on. Thus if a level 3 recruit sold $50 worth of goods, she would make a $5.00 commission on the sale, the person immediately above her (the level 2 distributor in the chain and the one who directly recruited her) would make $3.50 commission on that sale, and the person at the top of the chain (the level 1 distributor) would make a $2.50 commission.

A margin or discount setup would work something like this: A consumer buys a product for $20 (the list price) from a level 3 distributor. The level 3 distributor gets that product from a level 2 distributor at 70 percent of the list price (a 30 percent discount, in other words) or $14. Thus, if he sells the product at list price he makes a $6 profit on the sale. The level 2 distributor in turn orders the product from the level 1 distributor at 60 percent of the list price ($12), making $2 on the sale of the product to the level 3 distributor. The top-level distributor buys the product direct from the company at 50 percent of the list ($10), making $2 on the sale of the item to the level 2 distributor. In reality, the level 3 distributor usually orders the product directly from the company; however, the commissions are structured as though each distributor in the chain had purchased the item from the distributor above.

Note that distributors at levels 2 and 1 did no selling in either scenario. They simply made money on the sales made by people in their downline. Had they made a direct sale they would have made more profit on it than the level 3 distributor made on his direct sale. (If level 1 sells the same $20 product directly to the consumer and gets the product for 50 percent of the list, he makes $10 for each product he sells compared to the $6 the third-level distributor makes.)

Q Is there a limit to how big a downline can get?

Yes. Different MLM companies set different rules about how many levels deep distributors will be paid. Some key the number of levels to the sales volume; others set the number of levels some other way. In addition the MLMs develop some kind of procedures (usually based on sales volume) that lets them break away or go direct—in other words, split off from the parent distributor chain and operate as the head of their own chain.

Q Getting paid for not working sounds too good to be true. Is it?

Ideally, that top-level distributor is also selling products as well as getting commissions from his or her downline. He or she is also supposed to be providing training and support services for the downline.

Unfortunately, things don't always work that way. In some MLM organizations new recruits are lured into joining (and buying products or sample cases) with promises of gaining financial independence and great wealth. All they will have to do to become financially secure, they are told, is to work a marketing plan that consists primarily of doing nothing but recruiting others to work the marketing plan.

Steve Bretzke, a distributor for Watkins, an MLM company that sells flavorings and related products, says that some MLM companies promise people they will be earning a $10,000 monthly income in 90 days. Since the cost of getting started is usually under $100, Bretzke says, "many people join before they have any idea what they have to do to succeed. Therefore, you see many dropouts."

Before dropping out, some recruits find they drop hundreds or thousands of dollars into the business, spending money on things like sample products they buy for their own use, meeting fees, transportation costs, promotional literature or catalogs they give out to prospects, and promotional tapes and books.

Q **Does anyone ever make money in MLM?**

Yes. Like almost any other industry or business the amount of money that can be made is usually proportional to the effort, time, commitment, and planning that goes into building the business.

Richard Suter, a CPA who specializes in taking start-up ventures public and who has done some work with MLM operations, says, "The ideal distributor is somebody who has the long view and the capital to back it up. They should have sales experience. Dealing with and overcoming rejection problems is the number one problem in all selling."

Bretzke, who says he just broke even the first year he was involved in MLM, agrees that the long view is important. He says it takes distributors about a year of working 10 to 15 hours a week to be able to make an income of about $1,000 a month. Where the real money is, he says, is in residual income, which can take 3 to 5 years of concentrated effort to build.

Q **What is network marketing?**

Network marketing is another name for multilevel marketing.

Q **What should I look for in an MLM company?**

The most important thing to look at is whether or not you like the products the company sells and would buy them yourself. People who don't believe in a product or service or think it is too high-priced will have a difficult time convincing anyone else to buy it.

Since your income will be dependent on residuals from future sales, you also need to look very carefully at the overall financial stability and the management ability of the company and its founders. Obtain Dun & Bradstreet or TRW credit reports about the company and try to determine if the founders have been involved in any litigation (perhaps in other MLM organizations) in the past. In addition, request the names of other distributors and ask about payment of commissions and what they think about the organization as a whole. Says Bretzke, "Since it will take three to five years or more to truly make any serious money in this business, you have got to be sure that the company will be there with you."

Another important consideration is the buyback policy, says Sharon Hayes, owner of Ergodynamix, a mailing list company in Montreal, Canada, that specializes in providing lists of MLM enthusiasts. "Buyback should be a minimum of 90 percent within one month for unopened goods that have an expiration date and three months for durable goods."

You should also steer clear of MLM businesses that make specific income claims. Says Hayes, "Ethical companies forbid any income claims and do not allow distributors to use anything other than company literature for this."

Q   Do they really teach multilevel marketing at Harvard?

According to the registrar's office at Harvard, the university does not teach multilevel marketing.

Q   How are MLMs different from illegal pyramid schemes?

The primary difference between a legitimate MLM company and a pyramid scheme is that an MLM company makes its money by selling products or services. In pyramid schemes that masquerade as MLMs, people coming into the organization pay money for the right to sell a product and the right to benefit by recruiting others into the organization. Selling the actual product or service, if it even exists, is incidental to recruiting.

Because of their emphasis on recruiting and other practices, some MLM companies that do sell products have been accused of illegal practices in various states. A few have been banned in some states. If you have any doubts about the legitimacy of an organization, check it out by calling your state attorney general's office or city consumer affairs office.

Q   How can I avoid the pyramid schemes?

There are a number of things you should do to steer clear of pyramid schemes and other scams:

▶ Watch out for claims of being able to make thousands of dollars a month within a very short time.

▶ Steer clear of any company that pressures you into buying substantial quantities of inventory either to join the organization or move up its ladder. If they don't buy back the inventory you can't sell (or if they go bankrupt), you will be out the amount you paid for the stock.

▶ Avoid any organization that requires any kind of significant investment to give you the "right" to bring other people into the organization.

▶ Watch out for investment or real estate management clubs where the money from the new investors winds up in the pockets of the earliest investors rather than being put into any actual real estate deals.

▶ Consider how much emphasis is placed on selling the product or service. If the emphasis is entirely on recruiting, the operation may be a pyramid scheme disguising itself as an MLM opportunity.

Q **Where can I find other people to ask about the company or the opportunity?**

Excellent sources of information are the home office and small business areas of any of the online computer information services. If you don't have a computer and modem, try asking people in networking or professional associations to which you belong if they know anyone who has heard of or has bought into the plan or business you are interested in. Try to get names and numbers and call the people and ask their opinions. Also check the public library for information, the attorney general's office, and the Better Business Bureau in the area the company is located.

Q **There seem to be more scams than real business opportunities out there. How can I find a business to start without getting ripped off?**

Thoroughly investigate any business opportunity, turnkey business, or franchise you are considering before getting involved. Make sure you can answer each of these questions affirmatively:

- Do I personally like the product or service?
- Would I buy this product or service at the price I will have to charge?
- Would I be satisfied with the quality of this product or service?
- Do I trust the people selling the opportunity, the turnkey business, or franchise?
- Have I had an attorney review the terms of the contract if I have to lay out much money?
- Do I know exactly what I will be getting for my money and what I won't get?
- Have I called or contacted others who bought this business or plan and asked if they were satisfied?
- Will I enjoy doing whatever is necessary to sell the product or service?
- Will I enjoy this line of work?

In addition, make sure you gather the *facts* to answer all of these questions:

- Who will buy this product? (Be specific.)
- Where will I find these people?
- What, specifically, are they looking for when they buy this type of product or service? (Don't guess. Call prospects and ask!)
- How many potential customers are there in the area in which I will be marketing the product or service?
- How many sales will I have to make to be profitable?
- What will it cost me to make those sales?
- Does the product or service lend itself to repeat customers?

5.

Mail Order Riches:
Are They for Real?

For years, mail order has been touted as the easy road to riches—the ideal way for anyone with little money and little time to start a business that will stuff their mailboxes with dollars.

With industry figures showing that businesses and consumers purchase more than $175 billion in goods through the mail each year, it would appear that there is big money to be made in mail order. Yet one can't help wondering if mail order businesses are really as easy to start as some advertisements, articles, and books suggest. Has anyone ever made much money with a shoestring mail order business? And, if they have in the past, is it still possible to make money in mail order now?

 What is mail order?

Mail order, as the term is being used in this book, is selling or delivering merchandise through the mails. For very small businesses on tight budgets, that usually means selling through small advertisements in print publications or selling through a catalog mailed to people who have previously bought from the company. Mail order may be your only way of selling products, or it could be an additional sales outlet.

 What kind of products are suitable for mail order?

Almost anything can be sold by mail. Consumers and businesses buy everything from pens and pencils to furniture, computers, expensive collectibles, and stereo systems through the mail.

What you need to consider isn't so much the *kind* of things that could be sold by mail but rather the products that would be *practical for you* to sell as a small business. The cost of ads, catalogs, business stationery, postage, and packaging materials, can add up quickly. Thus, it is often best for small businesses to focus on products that:

- are targeted at a well-defined market
- do not break easily
- can be sold for a markup that will cover all costs and allow for some profit
- have a big enough market to make the effort worthwhile
- have a market you can afford to reach
- can be adequately described or depicted without using full-color photographs

Q **How will I know what products will sell well?**

The secret is to identify a need and a market. "Too many people get involved in mail order without doing enough research," says Steven Reed, vice president of marketing and sales for American Supply International, Inc., a company that sells groceries and household supplies to people in the U.S. Foreign Service. "Although you can sell anything by mail," Reed says, "you really have to understand your customers' needs and then find the products to fill those needs."

Reed started American Supply International with his wife, Brenda, in 1990 because he and Brenda had had trouble getting products they wanted when he was stationed overseas in the foreign service. The couple spent 6 months researching what products they could get and resell at a profit. Then, they launched American Supply International with an investment of $250 to photocopy a catalog Steve created on his Atari computer. The couple sent the catalog to overseas embassies and were in business shortly afterward when their first order came in from Uganda. By the summer of 1992 the company was grossing more than $20,000 a month in sales and had been moved out of the Reed's home and into a warehouse location.

Q **But how can I spot needs if my background isn't unusual?**

"Watch, listen, and think," says Reed. "Start thinking of people as belonging to specific market segments . . . mothers with children, the elderly, college students, et cetera. Think of what these specific markets may need that could be sent through the mail."

Q **Where do I find products to sell?**

You can find the products anywhere. In some cases, you may actually manufacture the products yourself. Everything from gingerbread cookies to ink have been literally cooked up in entrepreneurs' kitchens and then marketed by mail.

Products you don't manufacture yourself can often be found in nearby warehouse outlets, manufacturing companies, from distributors, and advertised in trade magazines and in classified ads in newspapers like the *Wall Street Journal* or the *New York Times*. Industry trade shows are another excellent source of ideas for new products to sell. If you know what you want to sell and can't locate a manufacturer or distributor, look up the product in *The Thomas Register of North American Manufacturers* (available at libraries or in online databases). Call the manufacturer and ask for names of distributors. Look in the public library for other directories of manufacturers as well.

Q **How do I get a good price on items for resale?**

The way to get the best prices is to shop around and/or to negotiate. Reed and his wife found they could get the best prices on some items at the Price Club, which is a warehouse buying club for small business owners and for members of certain unions. Other goods in their catalog come from wholesalers or other suppliers.

Q **How do I determine what to charge?**

This is where your research comes in. You should have a pretty good fix on how much your customers are willing to pay for the convenience of getting the goods you want to sell through the mail. You should also know what all your expenses will be to advertise, purchase, and deliver that product. While many people in mail order say you should sell merchandise for at least four times what it costs you to buy or produce it, the actual amount depends more on what the market will bear. In some instances, you may only be able to mark up a product 50 percent, but if you can sell it in quantity to customers who will make many repeat purchases, that markup may be sufficient for profit. With other types of products you may be able to mark up your prices tenfold because your costs are extremely low and/or people can't get what you sell any other way.

Q   **What kind of catalog do I need? Does it have to be in color?**

The type of catalog you need will depend on your product. If the products are items people are familiar with or that can be described adequately in a few words or sentences, a neat list of items, perhaps with a few simple drawings included to break up the gray look of the type, may be all that's needed. If you are selling clothing or anything that people normally want to see up close before ordering, you will need photographs in your catalog. If people are going to want to see the color of your product, you will need color photos in your catalog, which will add considerably to your printing costs.

Q   **Can I print a catalog on my home computer?**

If you have a laser printer or an inkjet printer that produces good clear type with no "jaggies," you could print out master pages (called camera-ready copy). The quality of the type would be better if you output your finished work on an imagesetter at a service bureau, but if you can't find a service bureau or don't want the added expense, you can get away with using output from a good computer printer. If you need more than just a handful of catalogs, it will be cheaper and faster to bring the master pages to a copy center or a quick printer. Photocopies can cost as little as 3 to 4 cents a page, depending on where you live.

Q   **How many items do I need to sell?**

It depends on what your customers want to buy and what you can provide for them. Often companies start out with just a handful of products and describe them on a single flier. Gradually, however, they add to their list of offerings. The Reeds, for instance, now offer approximately 3,000 items in their catalog. Steve Richardson, a New York entrepreneur who has a part-time business selling adult stories via mail order, includes close to 500 titles in his catalog.

Q **Suppose I only have one or two items to sell. Is there any other way to sell them through mail order?**

If you are the manufacturer, you might be able to get a large catalog company to include your item or items in their catalog if you can prove that you can meet orders and deliver a professionally packaged, quality item. If you can't get into the large catalogs yourself, you might be able to find a sales representative who could get your items into a major catalog. Still another option is to get together with several vendors who sell different products but target the same market and do a cooperative mailing or advertisement. You might also be able to find people who sell to your market who would be willing to place inserts or small coupons advertising your product in their products.

Q **Can I really make money with little classified ads?**

Yes, you can use little classified ads to bring in business and make money. There are people right now making anywhere from a few hundred dollars to $40,000 or more a year in their spare time from mail order businesses they have started with classified ads.

Q **A lot of people say they've placed classified ads and never made a cent. What's the secret to making them work?**

The secret to making money with classified ads is to plan on creating a *line of products* and to use classified advertisements as one relatively inexpensive way to find customers for that line. In effect, the advertising buys the customer and you make your money through multiple sales to that customer.

Don't plan on selling anything expensive directly through classified ads. Generally the best things to offer in classified ads are free literature or a very low-cost product. Products that are most likely to sell directly from a classified ad are those priced under $3. When you fill the order or request for information, you send the customer a catalog or sales literature describing other merchandise you have for sale.

Don't expect to be swamped with orders or inquiries from a single ad. Depending on the publication in which you advertise, you will be lucky to get one-tenth of one percent of the advertised circulation to respond. A good response from a classified ad in a carefully chosen publication may be as few as forty to fifty inquiries. You should plan on using the income from your initial sales to pay for additional advertising, thus allowing you to build a customer list little by little.

Plan on advertising repeatedly and in multiple publications. Initially, you will want to test your ad and product in only one or two publications to see if you get any response. If you get enough inquiries to indicate an interest in what you are selling, then you will need to advertise regularly in several publications.

Expect to spend several years building the business. Even if you happen to have the money to take out big ads in a lot of publications all at once, it generally is not advisable to do so. Being new to mail order and new to business you could easily make any number of mistakes. Typical mail order mistakes involve the choice of products to sell, the price at which to sell them, the publications in which to advertise, the time of year to advertise, or even the wording in the ad. (One budding entrepreneur was selling an inexpensive item and forgot to include the price of the item in the classified ad!) Starting small means mistakes will be small.

Plan on increasing the size of your ads as you begin to know what sells and what doesn't. Once you start to get some customers and income as a result of your classified ads, you will want to try using small display ads to attract more attention and bring in more customers. If budget is a consideration, test a small display ad for a short time before agreeing to run it for several months. You will want to be sure the increase in customers will be worth the extra expense.

Plan on doing direct mailings in addition to classified advertising. In addition to responding to advertisements, profitable mail order companies also send out mailings several times a year to people who have purchased from them or responded to ads in the past. These mailings remind customers about the company's products and announce new items that are available.

 Tip: Remember that profits depend on satisfied customers and repeat sales. The best source of new business in mail order is always sales to old customers. It is therefore essential to treat the customer as though he or she were your best friend. That means shipping merchandise promptly and offering no-questions-asked refunds or replacement if a customer is dissatisfied or claims an item was damaged or lost in the mail.

Q **Should I wait until checks clear to ship merchandise?**

Since most customers want their purchases to arrive as quickly as possible, many vendors do not wait until checks clear unless the amounts involved are very large or they have some reason to be suspicious. That is taking a risk, of course, but it is a risk some vendors feel is warranted if the average dollar amount of orders is small, or if they provide goods people can easily purchase elsewhere.

Q **How do I go about accepting credit cards?**

You will need to apply for merchant status through a bank or an independent sales organization authorized to grant merchant status to vendors. Getting merchant status can be a difficult and frustrating process for mail order vendors, and having merchant status can be fraught with danger if you sell expensive items. The problems of obtaining merchant status and accepting credit cards are discussed in detail in chapter 18.

Q **Can I make money selling booklets by mail?**

People do make money selling small booklets and reports by mail. In fact, booklets and special reports can be ideal mail order products because they are lightweight, don't break, and can often be sold for many times your production and mailing costs. However, to make money, your booklets will need to contain in-demand information that appears unique and that can be targeted to specialized audiences. Chances are you won't be able to support yourself on the income; however, you may be able to make a satisfactory part-time income selling information by mail.

Q **Why is targeting so important? Isn't it better to have a big market?**

People today are bombarded with print and broadcast advertising. As a result, they tend to tune out noise advertising—which is anything they are not interested in hearing about or reading about at the moment. The way to avoid being noise advertising is to put your ads in places your customers are likely to search when they want a specific kind of product. Thus, while your potential market for herbs or recipes for making wine might be any adult, the people most likely to buy those items are more likely to look for them in a publication like *Mother Earth News* than in the classified section of *Success* or the *New York Times*.

Q **What about chain letters that sell recipes or booklets—do they work?**

People who try these chain letters invariably report little or no response to their mailings. Thus they wind up throwing away all the money they spent on paper, envelopes, labels (or list rental), and postage.

The only people who might possibly make money on any of these chain letters are the mailing-list companies that are often named in the letters. These companies often specialize in renting names of opportunity seekers. They may be referred to in letters as a source for fresh, hot, or quality mailing lists that will increase the response to your mailing or make it easier (by supplying you with preprinted labels) to mail out hundreds of copies of the chain letters.

Q **Are such chain letters legal?**

Some chain letters claim to be legal because they sell a product or service. Nevertheless, the United States Postal Service, in a booklet called *A Consumer's Guide to Postal Crime Prevention*, has the following to say about chain letters:

> *Don't waste your money . . . chain letters are a form of lottery and may violate federal mail fraud laws. The same three elements that apply to lotteries (payment, prize, and chance) also make these schemes illegal.*

Q **Should I rent a mailing list and send everyone on the mailing list a catalog or brochure describing my products?**

You have to work out the mathematics to decide whether the cost of the mailing list rental, the postage, and the preparation of a direct mail package would bring you enough new customers and potential repeat customers to be worthwhile. If you have a clear picture of your target market (for example, all chemical engineers with IBM computers or 25-year-old males who like water sports) and can find an appropriate mailing list to rent, you may get a 1 to 2 percent response rate to your mailing. The 1 to 2 percent figure is about average for a targeted mailing that is not to already-existing customers of a company. Your actual response rate, depending on the product, what actually goes into the mailing, and many other factors, could be much higher or lower.

If you think you can make a profit on a 1 to 2 percent response rate and won't go broke if you try and don't make a profit, do the mailing. (You may have to order a minimum of 5,000 names. Ask ahead of time if you want to rent fewer than that.)

Tip: If you are on a tight budget and can't afford to take a chance sending out 5,000 brochures in the mail, try building your own small mailing list if you sell to businesses. Often buying guides in trade magazines will list contact information for companies. You could also call businesses you think might be potential customers and ask who is responsible for purchasing what you sell. You may also be able to swap customer lists with other small, noncompeting businesses. If your small list draws enough responses, then consider renting a larger mailing list.

Response rates on residential mailing lists will be much, much lower. One-tenth of one percent or less is a typical response to mailings sent to all people in a neighborhood.

Q What laws do I need to know about?

Most of the laws that affect mail order businesses are the same as those affecting any business selling any product. Your advertising can't be deceptive or purposely misleading, and you may need to be concerned about product liability, warranties, and the legality of selling your products.

You should also be aware that you can't ship unordered merchandise and bill customers for it. You must be able to deliver what you have advertised within the time you state in your ads or within 30 days of the time you receive orders if no time is stated in the ad. If there is a delay due to some unforeseen circumstance, you have to notify the customer and offer to refund his or her money.

Q Do I have to collect tax on out-of-state mail order sales?

At the time this book was written you were not required to collect sales tax on out-of-state purchases unless your business had a physical presence (office) in the state in which a sale was made.

Q How do I ship orders?

You can ship orders using either the United States Postal Service or any private shipping service. It is important to find out ahead of time how the merchandise should be packaged for safe shipment. There are any number of packaging companies that can supply boxes, tapes, cardboard envelopes, or other packaging supplies for shipping.

Tip: Not all products can be shipped to all locations by mail. Be sure to check with the U.S. Postal Service or any other shippers you plan to use. You should also call the Department of Commerce to determine whether there are any regulations restricting the sale or shipping of your merchandise to any foreign countries.

Q What is drop shipping?

Drop shipping is an arrangement in which you take orders for a company that manufactures or supplies one or more products your customers want. You send the orders to the suppliers along with shipping labels (usually), and then the manufacturer or supplier sends the product to the customer. You don't need to retain inventory or do any actual shipping, but you also don't have much control over when the product is shipped or how it is shipped, which can be a problem if a customer claims never to have gotten a product or that it arrived damaged.

What about those mail order companies that say you can make money selling their products to other customers. Does anyone ever make money that way?

You would need to evaluate whether or not the products are unique and of sufficiently good quality to sell. You also need to consider whether the discounted prices they offer will allow you to make a profit after you pay for necessary mailings and promotional materials. Finally you need to consider whether you have a sincere interest in selling the type of merchandise the company offers. One entrepreneur keeps up his membership in one of these organizations because it allows him to buy gifts at a discount. He has never sold the items by mail but instead has successfully sold the merchandise at flea markets and to small stores. Others, however, have never made money as an agent for this type of company.

 Will I have to spend a lot of time running a mail order business?

In the beginning you can run a small mail order business in your spare time from home, but as it starts to become profitable and generate a lot of customers you will find that your spare-time business is taking up 30 or 40 hours each week.

6.

Creating Your Own
Business Opportunities

Some people spend months or years dreaming about being self-employed and waiting for the right opportunity to arise. Others think they see the opportunity bandwagon passing by and jump on it without considering where it is going, what it will cost, or whether or not they'll really enjoy the ride.

As you can imagine, neither approach to starting a business is particularly successful. To build a profitable business you have to learn the business and then put yourself in the driver's seat and forge ahead. Here is a brief look at what it takes to create a variety of businesses.

Q **What do I need to start a word processing or secretarial service?**

Word processing businesses are among the easiest to start, but due to competition, it may take time and effort to get the business going.

To get started you will need a microcomputer, word processing software, a laser printer or other type of printer that will print smoothly formed numbers and letters. You will need business stationery and other office supplies. You may also need an impact printer (one that has pins or a wheel that actually strikes a platen) with a mechanism (called a tractor feed) for pulling continuous form computer paper and labels through the printer. (Continuous form paper is the paper that has holes along the sides allowing it to be fed through a printer continuously and perforations that enable it to be separated into single sheets after printing.)

A dedicated word processor (a computerized typewriter that only does word processing and has built-in programming) is not a good substitute for a computer and often will be no easier to learn to use than a word processing program on a microcomputer.

If you are working in a storefront location rather than from home, at some point you might want to add copy machine and fax services for your customers. A photocopy machine is always handy for your own use, too, but probably shouldn't be purchased until after you can pay for it from the business profits.

Once you buy and learn to use equipment and software, your toughest job is going to be attracting a steady stream of customers. You may be able to get started by making a lot of phone calls and using personal contacts, but sooner or later most secretarial services find they need to use some form of print advertising. That advertising may be a small display ad in the Yellow Pages (an ad that's an inch or so big on the page, for instance) or an ad that appears regularly in the classified section of weekly newspapers or shoppers. Others find they do well by targeting a niche market and advertising in publications bought by that special market. Someone who likes to type academic papers might advertise in college or university newspapers, for instance, while someone who wants to do typing or transcription for medical or legal professionals would want to advertise in local journals or newsletters that lawyers or doctors in the area read. Advertising won't work miracles, however, and it also has to be frequent to pay off.

Pricing of the actual services you perform will need to be competitive. Depending upon where you live, the price may run from $12 to $20 an hour for word processing. Typesetting, resume typing, and related work, if you have the software and experience to do a good job, can usually be billed at a higher rate. You do have to check the going rates in your area and keep an eye on costs to stay competitive.

Once you find customers, it is important to provide quality work. Joan Kumpitsch, who ran the Johnstown, New York, company J.V.K. & Associates for 16 years before merging it with her son's printing company, R.J. Litho, advises, "Start small enough and do what you do well. You can always add services, but if you start with your sights set too high and end up doing a shoddy or mediocre job, you'll soon be out of business. One bad job or one that is done poorly can cost you several new ones."

Q **What does it take to start a money-making newsletter?**

To publish a successful newsletter you need to start out with a very clear focus of who your potential customers are and what kind of information you can provide for them that is different from what they are now getting from other sources. Once you know the focus you will need to decide:

- *Who will write the articles for each issue?* Will you do the writing yourself? Pay free-lancers to write? Hire a writer? Will you have enough information to publish regularly and keep readers interested?

- *What format will you use?* Will the newsletter be set up with two or three columns of type on a page and include pictures or artwork to break up the type? Or, will it be more in a letter format like the *Kiplinger Washington Letter?* Will it be 8½-by-11 inches in size or bigger or smaller?

- *How many pages will the newsletter be?* The newsletter will need to be long enough to make your subscribers feel they are getting their money's worth without being so long you can't fill every issue. You'll want to consider postage costs, too, in planning the size of the newsletter.

- *Will you accept advertising?* Most newsletters don't accept advertising, but some publications that call themselves newsletters do. Your decision will affect subscription prices and the length, style, and possibly the content of the publication.

- *How will you market the newsletter?* How do you plan to get subscribers? Will you advertise? Will you do direct mailings? Will you post samples of the newsletter on electronic bulletin boards? What will marketing cost? Could you publish and continue marketing if you got less than one percent response to your initial marketing efforts? Even though your newsletter may be the best around in your field, and you target your market carefully, your response could be as low as one percent or even lower.

- *What will you charge for subscriptions?* Pricing will need to be based on a realistic estimate of all your costs for getting all issues to the customer, the profit you need to make over that amount of time, and how much customers will be willing to pay for your publication.

▸ *How many subscriptions will you need to break even?* How many to make a profit on all your costs? Don't forget to figure in the costs of marketing, postage, and phone calls along with your other costs. You need realistic figures to determine pricing—and whether or not to proceed with the publication.

▸ *How much time are you willing to devote to the newsletter?* Unless you have money to hire people to write, edit, typeset, and design the publication, the newsletter is likely to consume every spare minute of your time. Are you willing to devote that kind of energy to it?

▸ *How long a turnaround time do you need to allow?* Remember to determine how much time it will take from the time you write and do layouts for a newsletter until you can get it printed, folded, mailed, and actually delivered to the reader.

▸ *Can you afford to market and publish the newsletter for months without a profit?* Be realistic. Work out all the figures before deciding whether to go ahead with the project. Remember, marketing will have to be an ongoing effort, not a one-time event. You will have to plan for the expenses of printing newsletters, printing sales and marketing literature, and mailing both, as well as the costs of doing mailings to get subscription renewals.

▸ *Do you have the skills to do any writing, editing, layout, or design you plan?* Computer equipment greatly simplifies some of these chores but only if you have the basic writing, editing, and production skills plus experience using a computer and page-layout (desktop publishing) software. If you don't have this background, the going will be rough with or without a computer.

▸ *Do you have a method for tracking subscribers and expiration dates, printing labels, and mailing renewals?* You should have all those details worked out in advance. Don't wait to figure out how to use your database until subscriptions start coming in. Get it all set up in advance or have someone who is experienced do it for you.

Q How can I make money as a free-lance writer?

There are many different ways to make money as a free-lance writer. People who write magazine articles and books often start out writing for publications in their spare time. Some have full-time jobs as writers in industry; others are independent contractors who write advertising copy, do publicity for business, write technical documentation, or do other writing chores to keep up a steady income. Those who just write books and magazine articles or short stories usually have years of experience as writers and frequently have several books in print.

If you are just starting out, it helps to have a specialty and to realize that you may have to do some writing for very little pay just to get published. Once you get published you will, ideally, be able to use copies of published clips plus good ideas and writing skills to get better-paying assignments.

You will also have to consider the market when you write. You may be the world's greatest writer, but if few people besides you are interested in the subject matter of your article, story, or book, you won't get any traditional publishing companies or magazines to publish it.

Q What about self-publishing books? Can I make money doing that?

You probably won't get rich but you can make some money self-publishing your books if you have a clear target market, can write well, and put a lot of effort into marketing and promoting your book.

Neil Tarvin, owner of Garrett Press, Ltd., a Tulsa, Oklahoma, company that helps self-publishers get their work into print, agrees that self-publishers need to be able to write, to deal with people in graphics and printing industries, and to market their work. But, he says, "above all it takes a great deal of commitment. You will be spending time and money at every step of the process, and you simply can't let down on any of them."

Careful planning is essential if you want to make a profit. You need to carefully choose a subject based on who you can sell the book to. The better you can determine who will buy the book and what specific channels you can use to reach potential customers, the more likely your success at self-publishing. "Nonfiction that can be targeted to a specific group of people is the best to self-publish," says Tarvin. "Mass-market books are difficult for self-publishers because the distribution system that large publishers have is just not available to self-publishers."

You also have to watch costs. Production costs can be kept to a minimum, he says, if you learn to negotiate. "Most people think printing prices are carved in concrete and that a price is a price," says Tarvin. "But just knowing that the business is 'feast or famine' can save many hundreds of dollars. Get a bid from a printer during his 'famine' phase, and you'll save an easy twenty percent. Negotiate a little, and you can boost that savings to thirty percent or better. Make a deal with a typesetter to input your own copy. Or, desktop publish and have a service bureau 'play out' the type for you on a phototypesetter. A two-hundred-page book, soft cover, five and a half by eight and a half inches, will probably run about four dollars each to print in lots of five hundred at standard prices. Negotiating and creativity can cut your cost to $2.50 to $3.25 each. Photos and drawings, et cetera, will add to those costs."

Q   Can I do my own printing and production with a laser printer and binding equipment?

Some people do that, but your book may not look as professional as some customers will expect, and, therefore, you may not be able to sell it for very much. By the time you add in the cost of the laser printout or good photocopies of laser printouts, the binding materials and cover stock, plus your time to prepare books, your costs might wind up being higher than if you paid to have the books professionally printed and bound.

Q   I've got a computer. Would desktop publishing be a good business to start?

People who create successful desktop publishing businesses often work in advertising or graphic arts for many years before launching their own business. That's because desktop publishing really isn't a business. Instead, the term means using a computer and computer software as a tool to simplify some production chores in the creation of print publications, slides, and multimedia works. If you have experience doing typesetting or commercial art and want to start your own service, it is almost imperative to have desktop publishing tools available to you.

If you have no experience in typesetting, commercial art, or related fields, however, buying a computer and desktop publishing software is not going to put you into business overnight as a desktop publisher. Typesetting, layout, and design all require special skills and training. While these skills can be learned, it takes time to acquire the basic manual skills and hands-on experience needed to know how to create professional-looking documents. In addition, you will also need to spend time learning to use page-layout and art programs. These programs are quite sophisticated, and as a result, have quite a steep learning curve.

If you think you would enjoy using a computer to do typesetting and commercial design work, you should get the training before investing in the equipment. Training is offered in night courses at two-year colleges and technical schools and, sometimes, in adult education classes at high schools.

Q Can I make money screen printing T-shirts?

Screen printing T-shirts and other garments has proven to be a lucrative business for some entrepreneurs. There are companies that started out as home businesses and within a half-dozen years were taking orders for thousands of shirts at a time and were grossing several million dollars a year. There are also businesses that start in basements or small storefronts and never do much more than break even, if they do that well.

Q Can I get started in screen printing at home without spending a lot of money?

The start-up cost depends on the capabilities you want and whether you can locate used equipment to buy. You can operate out of your basement or garage (if zoning laws don't prohibit it), but your production will be small compared to that of larger screen-printing shops.

"If you're content to do one-color designs with water-based ink, and if you're handy at carpentry, a couple hundred dollars will get you started," says screen printer Ray Dittmeier, who is in charge of production for T-Shirt Designs in Kentucky. He adds, however, that "the guy with the real shop can print more elaborate designs with more colors. He can work faster and more efficiently. For all but the simplest designs, he can probably produce a noticeably better print." Although you may be able to price your screen-printing service lower than the person with better equipment, you will need to screen a lot of shirts to make enough money to support yourself. Says Dittmeier, "You can't go out and be a salesman *and* do the production work. There just isn't enough time, no matter how dedicated you are."

Q How long does it take to screen print a T-shirt?

To some extent it depends on the equipment. Dittmeier says that in his shop, the easiest job (black ink on a light-colored shirt) can be done at the rate of about 12 dozen an hour, but something like a six-color design on a black shirt can slow down the work to only "a couple of dozen or fewer" an hour. That's important, he adds, because "you have to have some idea of how long a particular job is going to take in order to price it properly."

Many companies that started as basement operations were run by husband-and-wife teams. They expanded and bought equipment and hired employees as they could pay for it out of the business. You can buy blanks (plain white or colored shirts) from any distributor for about $2.50 each and up, depending on the quality and quantity of shirts you buy.

Q Who buys printed T-shirts?

Printed T-shirts are purchased by a wide variety of businesses and individuals. Businesses often purchase screen-printed T-shirts for their employees to wear on the job. Churches, schools, civic groups, sports teams, restaurants, and even radio stations or banks are all potential customers, too. The screen printers who make it big, however, are those who go after and get orders from large businesses, universities, and national catalog companies, and those who become licensed to print major sport team logos.

T-shirts aren't the only items these companies screen print. Most see themselves as being in the screen-printing business rather than the T-shirt business. T-shirts, because of stiff competition, may make up only 20 to 40 percent of their business. The bulk of their business often comes from screen printing other types of items, such as baseball caps, sweatshirts, jackets, and other apparel, as well as advertising specialties that are not garments. In fact, one screen printer shifted his emphasis from screen printing T-shirts to screen printing with inks that contain silver—and conduct electricity—onto electronic membranes used in the touch panels of photocopiers and other electronic goods.

Q **Can I make money just selling the T-shirts without doing the screen printing myself?**

Yes, there are people who do that, and as Dittmeier indicates, it can benefit the screen-printing shops, too. These entrepreneurs get the orders, buy the shirts themselves (to keep costs down), and then bring the shirts to the screen printer for printing. If you are good at sales and have a good screen printer who can fill the orders quickly and competently, you can make money just handling the sales.

Q **What's the difference between screen-printing companies that make a lot of money and those that don't?**

Among the factors that seem to work against screen printers who don't do well are competition, undercapitalization, lack of equipment, lack of time, or the inability to reach wholesalers or buyers who can give out large jobs. The businesses that are successful in this field generally are those that were started by at least two people who were able to expand their company gradually, using profits to buy new equipment, move to bigger quarters, and hire staff—eventually enabling them to take on large orders from major corporations.

Q **What does it take to make it as a consultant?**

The keys to success as a consultant are knowing your industry inside and out, taking the time to know what your client wants, and delivering what your client wants in a professional way. James A. Smith, a Chicago resident who has worked as an independent consultant to radio stations for more than 11 years, says that in his field, a consultant needs "an understanding of how radio stations operate, particularly within a given format and a given market size." The needs of a country music station in Wisconsin are obviously going to be different from those of a rock music station in Detroit.

To make money as a consultant, Smith says, you need to do the following: "(1) keep the customer satisfied; (2) remember you are just advising others how to do things, you are not in control; (3) agree in advance on the goals, expectations, and methods of measuring the success of your work; (4) don't try to change too much or too little [in the client's operation]; (5) don't bite off more than you can chew or let yourself stagnate in a changing field."

<table><tr><td>Q</td></tr></table> **How do you put those precepts into practice?**

Whether you are in radio consulting, management consulting, computer consulting, or any other kind of consulting, the way to put theory into practice is to first be an expert in what you do and then to bend over backward to satisfy the client.

José Kirchner, a corporate consultant and human resources trainer in Carmichael, California, describes this scenario as being typical of the kind of effort needed to create a workshop series for one of his clients:

I get a request for a workshop such as a series of five two-hour briefings/workshops on sexual harassment. The target audience is supervisors and managers of all departments. They hired me because word of mouth in a neighboring city said I'd do it right, and their Employee Assistance Program uses me as a trainer—a lot!

I contact the program manager for their Employee Assistance Program (EAP). He tells me the supervisors do not utilize the EAP or its management consultants for corrective actions to the extent other city governments do. He wants me to clarify the role of management consultants and how they can be of help in a case of possible sexual harassment—early on, before it actually become sexual harassment, if possible.

Contact with the personnel director will tell me a bit more about what is going on: Is there a policy? Have there been incidents? What are the attitudes? Is there a particular work area where this has been a problem? Is there anything he wants me to cover specifically? Does he agree with my proposed approach?

I will also contact the Health, Safety, and Training Officer to get more specific information on each department and possible contacts in each.

Then I will fine-tune my presentation, create an outline, and add or delete transparencies, which are the main focus points for the audience. I then prepare some handouts and send them for preparation and distribution.

After the first workshop, I will consult a bit more, especially with the HST Officer, and make any necessary revisions. At the end of the series, I will meet with her and with the personnel director, then give feedback to the training director and program manager at the EAP. All of my contacts are annotated in my client database. I may also prepare written recommendations and a summary. And all participants fill out a one-page program evaluation, which I review and turn over to the personnel director.

Obviously, the specific tasks a consultant will need to perform will differ depending on the type of consulting job. Overall, however, it is this kind of client contact and client focus that is required to establish a consulting practice and develop it into a profitable business.

Q **How long does it take to build up a good business as a consultant?**

Once you have established a track record for solving problems, it will take a year or more to establish a business. Things may be lean at first, but if you continually promote yourself, are good at what you do, and are professional in the way you work, your reputation and business will grow.

Q **What is an information broker?**

An information broker is someone who makes money searching for and analyzing and/or organizing information for customers. Much of the work is done using microcomputers to access electronic databases, but in many instances, computer searches are used to get bibliographic citations only. Actual copies of documents must be retrieved from other sources.

Q **What do I have to do to be an information broker?**

If you are starting out on your own, you will need to be:

▶ *An experienced researcher.* You must know where to look for various types of information. Many information researchers have a degree in library science or extensive library research experience.

▶ *An experienced computer database user.* Computerized databases make it easy to find everything from chemical abstracts, stock quotes, and verdicts in precedent-setting law suits to background information on companies or people in the news, statistics, and demographics. The fees for searching some specialized databases can be hundreds of dollars an hour, however, so it is imperative to know which databases to use and how to use them efficiently. Several of the major electronic database services such as Dow Jones News Retrieval and Dialog hold training courses at various locations throughout the country.

- *An educator.* Barbara Quint, editor of *Database Searcher* magazine, explains that people who aren't professional researchers may not realize how much information is available to them. "Half the job of any professional searcher is educating customers about the nature of the information revolution," she says.

- *A good communicator.* You have to find out exactly what your customers need and how they want to use the information and then deliver the information in the format they expect. Sometimes that requires writing reports or analyzing data.

- *A good salesperson.* You will have to market your services and show potential customers the benefits of using you to find and deliver the information they need.

Q Does an information broker just resell information they get from online services?

No. An information broker helps clients solve problems or answers questions by doing research for them. As an information broker you are really an intermediary who gets paid for your research skills and gets reimbursed for any costs (the online time) incurred in doing clients' research.

Q Who buys the services of information brokers?

The majority of customers will be small businesses that can't afford to have their own in-house research library. Typical clients include attorneys, public relations executives, consultants, or any other business or individual likely to need a lot of varied information and need it in a hurry.

What does it take to get started as an information broker besides research skills?

You should know what kinds of questions you are good at answering and have people who can attest to your search skills, says Quint, who runs her own information broker service as well as editing *Database Searcher* magazine. "Information brokering involves a lot of trust, so word-of-mouth advertising means a lot."

In addition, you will need a computer and often a facsimile machine, as well as business stationery. If you are going to start out full-time, you should plan on having at least enough capital to go for six months without making any money and should know in advance what kinds of businesses you will target as clients. You can also work part-time on your own, or as an independent contractor for larger, established information search firms.

Anyone serious about working as an information broker should also consider joining the Association of Independent Information Professionals (AIIP), since members of the organization are entitled to significant discounts on some of the major database services used by information researchers. In addition, those who are experienced information brokers may also want to be listed in *The Burwell Directory of Information Brokers*. The directory lists information brokers from throughout the United States and from more than forty other countries. There is no fee to be listed in the directory; however, you do have to fill out an application form and actually be in business to be listed in the directory.

Information about joining AIIP and about getting listed in the Burwell Directory is available by contacting:

Burwell Enterprises, Inc.
3724 FM 1960 West, Suite 214
Houston, TX 77068
Phone: (713) 537–9051
Fax: (713) 537–8332

The Association of Independent Information Professionals is a volunteer organization whose officers change yearly. Burwell Enterprises is the volunteer who sends out membership information for the AIIP each year.

 How much can I make as an information broker?

Independent information brokers charge an average of $50 to $65 an hour plus expenses for searches. If a company needs consulting services as well, the fee may be over $100 an hour. Some information brokers with computer database programming skills branch out into setting up databases for their clients.

Q **Where can I get more information about the field?**

The best book for people who want to get started in this field is *The Information Brokers Handbook,* by Sue Rugge and Alfred Glossbrenner (New York: Windcrest–McGraw-Hill, 1992).

Among the trade publications of interest to people in the industry are:

Database Searcher, Computers and Libraries, CD-ROM World, and *Library Software Review,* all published by:

Meckler Publishing
11 Ferry Lane West
Westport, CT 06880
(203) 226–6967

Online, Database, and *CD-ROM Professional,* all published by:

Online, Inc.
462 Danbury Road
Wilton, CT
06897–2126
(203) 761–1466

Link Up and *Information Today,* both published by:

Learned Information
143 Old Marlton Pike
Medford, NJ 08055
(609) 654–4888

Q **What do I need to do to start a travel agency?**

To start your own travel agency you will need to have experience working for a travel agency. You will also need to post a bond with the Airlines Reporting Corporation (ARC), comply with state laws, and get adequate business insurance, something that is difficult to do if you don't have experience as a travel agent. In most cases you have to have a retail location to be a travel agency.

You can also work as an outside sales representative for a travel agency and split commissions with the agency (they do the ticketing and are responsible for all the red tape; you just sell). You must be extremely careful in selecting agencies or companies to do this work for, however. If the company doesn't actually deliver the tickets or the quality of service your customers paid for, you will be sued by the customers. In addition, depending on your state laws, you may not be allowed to sell travel services without a license, even if you are acting as a salesperson for another company.

If you do work as an outside agent, the usual arrangement of fees is a fifty-fifty split, says James Van, owner of EventNet, a company in Portland, Maine, that specializes in concert trips and other niche travel services. "The outside agent generally does all the legwork, such as bookings, selling, and some paperwork. The finalized itinerary is submitted to the agency, who then takes over the reservation and prints the necessary documents."

Van, who started his own business after gaining experience and making contacts putting together promotions for a radio station, warns against ads that claim to be able to put people in business instantaneously as travel agents. "The only way to legally run a full-service travel agency is through affiliation with an ARC-approved agency or by becoming the owner of one. Consult with a lawyer, the local Better Business Bureau, and the consumer affairs division in your state before signing on with any company promising you can be a travel agent."

Q Can I make money selling at flea markets?

If you go about it in the right way you can. John Hunter, who runs Tools-N-Stuff, a company that sells tools and other items for automobiles, makes his entire income by selling his wares at flea markets. One of the tricks of the trade, he says, is knowing your products and learning where and how to buy your goods. Your prices should be a little lower than those in retail stores—10 percent or lower works, Hunter says. But, the real secret he says is selling items that are hard to find at any price in retail stores.

Another key to running a profitable flea-market business is to have a wide variety of items in low to medium price ranges so you have something available for everyone. Hunter usually sets out about 500 different items, many of which are priced at $5 or less. These will help attract traffic to the booth. The small sales add up and "keep you from just sitting there all day watching people walk by."

Items you choose should not be prone to fading in the sun and should be attractively displayed. You also need to be equipped to quickly cover everything with plastic and secure the plastic with clips in case of rain. At flea markets that have open-air booths as well as indoor booths, the outdoor vendors often do better than the indoor vendors. In fact, Hunter says, some who have indoor booths rent space outdoors as well.

Hunter, who travels around the country "doing" flea markets, suggests looking in *Thomas's Register of Manufacturers* for names of companies that manufacture products you want to sell, going to trade shows, and looking for items to sell in *Closeout News*.

The biggest mistake people make in working flea markets, he says, is not being businesslike. You have to get necessary licenses and comply with the tax laws, and you also have to plan. "You can't do things halfheartedly. You have to run it like a business." If you are businesslike, he says, you should be able to gross at least $400 to $500 every day you sell.

Q   How can I make money in crafts?

There are a variety of ways you can make money in crafts, but for many businesses that sell handcrafts, the profit is low compared to the time expended. The trick to increasing profits is to have items that cost little to make and that can be made quickly. Selling other people's crafts on consignment, selling craft supplies, and selling your own original patterns are other ways to add to craft income.

If you develop a unique product or design that proves extremely popular and that could be mass produced, you might be able to make money licensing your design to large manufacturers.

Q   Can I run an industrial business from home?

Yes, if zoning laws don't prevent you from working at home and if you can comply with any EPA regulations that might apply to your business. Chemical distributorships, gold-plating operations, and even machine shops have been run or started in garages and basements of people all over the country. You could also start an industrial consulting practice if you have experience. You would need to be a registered professional engineer and be fairly well known in industrial circles. "Advertising for this business just doesn't work," says industrial engineer Lew Merrick, owner of Tangent Engineering in Lynnwood, Washington. "People don't look in the Yellow Pages for an engineer—they call up a couple of friends and ask for recommendations."

Q **I speak Spanish and French fluently. Could I get work as a translator?**

Possibly, but you should know it takes more than the ability to speak a foreign language fluently to make money as a translator.

Q **What kind of qualifications would I need?**

Gabe Bokor, owner of Accurapid Translation Services, Inc., in Poughkeepsie, New York, says "Some technical background and experience in specific technical fields is as important as perfect writing skills. A very good understanding of both the source and the target language is necessary, too, so that idioms and ideas are translated without losing their original meanings." You will also need some computer skills and access to a computer, modem, fax, and appropriate dictionaries.

Q **Where would I find translating work?**

Translators get work either directly from client companies or through agencies or bureaus.

Q **How much would I charge for translating?**

The amount you charge will depend on where you got the work (through a bureau or directly from the client), what language you are translating to and from, and how technical the work is that you are translating. Fees recommended by the American Translators' Association range from about 9.5 to 13.5 cents per word (the latter for experienced translators dealing directly with clients). Some technical translators make quite good free-lance incomes; others don't. Failure may result from the lack of industry knowledge, an overabundance of translators, or poor skills.

Q **Where can I find names of trade publications and trade associations?**

Visit your public library and look in the reference section for *The Encyclopedia of Associations*, published by Gale Research, and *Ulrich's International Periodicals Directory*, published by R.R. Bowker. The reference librarian will be able to show you how to use these references and may be able to point you to directories of newsletters or other directories of trade associations or publications that can give you the information you want.

While at the public library, you may want to dig up industry statistics by reading back magazine or newspaper articles about the field. The newspaper and magazine indices (available at most libraries) will help you locate these articles. Many libraries now have the newspaper and magazine indices on computer, making it fast and easy to search out articles, and some now have articles on CD-ROM disks rather than on microfilm. The library staff can help you learn how to use these tools if you are unfamiliar with them.

Q **How do I find my niche?**

The secret is to start with what you know or with what you like. Learn everything you can about whatever that "thing" is. You can learn on the job or in your spare time, but learn all there is to know about the product, the service, the market, and the business end. Then, before you start your business, plan it all out in advance. Realize you will have to work hard and be committed to making the business successful and that in almost all cases it will take anywhere from one to five years or even more to build a successful business. Take a close look at any overnight success and you will discover many years of training and hard work went into positioning the business or the individual to be in the right place with the right product or service at the right time.

II.

Pulling
the Pieces
Together

7.

Planning: Your
Personal Road Map to
Success

If you are like many people who start and run very small businesses, writing a business plan sounds like a task you really don't have to do, or at least one you don't have to do this week, or this month . . . After all, you know what you want to do with your business, right? You are going to sell your product or service and make money. The way you are going to do that is all in your head. Why take the time to write it down when there are so many other things to do? The answer has to do with focus, realism, and achieving your dreams.

Q **What is a business plan and what is it used for?**

A business plan is an operational guide to your business. It should be used to define the scope of your business, the goals you establish for the business, the methods you will use to reach those goals, and the potential profitability of your business.

It can also be used as a yardstick to measure your progress toward your goals, as a reference to keep you from veering away from your goals, and as a communications tool to give bankers and investors the information they need if you are looking for a business loan or private funding.

Q   **Who needs a business plan?**

Anyone who wants to start or run a business successfully needs some type of plan. After all, building a business isn't much different than building anything else: there are a lot of pieces to put together and a lot of details that need to be coordinated. If you were trying to erect a building you would need to follow some kind of plan, whether the building was a toolshed in your backyard or a skyscraper in a big city.

Q   **How can a business plan help me if I'm already running a successful homebased business?**

Once you've got the business up and running, a business plan serves as your road map to success. By periodically comparing where you are with where you want to go in the business, you can keep yourself on course, and if you spot problems developing, make necessary changes in either methods or your ultimate goals before little problems turn into big ones.

Q   **How elaborate does the plan need to be?**

The amount of detail that goes into your business plan should depend on what you stand to gain or lose in your business.

If you are going to turn your favorite hobby into a part-time business and won't have to spend more than a couple hundred dollars to do so, your business plan could be just a page or two of notes. You'd want to sketch out what you will sell, how you will sell it, how you will price it, and what start-up steps (getting permits and licenses, business stationery, insurance, and so on) you will need to take.

Considerably more thought and research should go into your plans, however, if any of the following circumstances apply:

▸ you will be spending a significant amount of money to launch the business
▸ you will be quitting a full-time job to start a business

- you will be starting the business because you *need* an income and hope it will replace the job you can't find or don't want to get[*]
- you will be devoting a significant amount of time to the business, which you might be able to use in more profitable ways
- you will be expanding an already profitable homebased or other small business

Q **What goes into a formal business plan?**

If you are doing a formal plan to present to a bank or to investors, you will want to include all of these elements:

- A *brief title page* or cover sheet containing a date and the business name, address, and phone number.

- A *table of contents* for the plan.

- An *introduction*, often called an executive summary. This is a brief overview of the pages that follow. It describes the purpose of the plan and summarizes the key elements in the body of the plan so investors, bankers, and others who read the plan can tell at a glance what the business does and how it is or will become profitable.

- A *history of the company*, including details of when it was founded, who founded the company, where it is located, what kind of business the company is in, and what the objectives of the company are.

- A *description of the products or services* the company sells and why they appeal to customers.

---

[*] The reason for creating a detailed business plan in this case is because it will help you evaluate business opportunities from a rational point of view rather than an emotional one. When money is tight and jobs are scarce, fear of the future and worry make one want to grasp at anything that sounds like it could help. Unfortunately, however, many of the opportunities advertised in publications or passed along by well-meaning friends either are not worth pursuing or take considerably more money to pursue profitably than originally thought. Careful planning can help you steer around the pitfalls.

▶ *A description of the market* for what you sell. This section should show who your customers are, how many of them there are, and why they will want to buy your products or services. It should discuss who your competitors are and how what you sell is superior or different from what the competitors sell. It should also analyze industry or market trends and how they might affect the size of the market.

▶ *A description of how you will sell the product or service.* You can have the world's biggest market, but if you don't have an affordable way of selling to that market you won't make a cent.

▶ *An operational plan.* How will you produce or acquire what you sell? How will you protect your ideas or processes? How will you deliver the product or service?

▶ *A description of the management and organization of the business.* Who is involved? What talents do they have? What strengths and weaknesses do they bring to the company? Can they handle finance, sales, marketing, technical aspects? Do you have the right "mix" for success? Resumes should be included for the key executives involved in the business. What business structure (regular corporation, S corporation, partnership, etc.) is being used to run the business? How will investors (if the plan is to attract investors) make their profits?

▶ *The financial plan.* This section should include sales projections (how much do you expect to sell over what time period?), cost estimates, and details about how you expect to finance operations and what assumptions you have made to arrive at sales and other projections. (In other words, what basis do you have for thinking you'll sell 50,000 widgets a month? Is the figure based on results of test marketing? feedback from focus groups? demographic information?) You'll also need past and projected cash flow statements, income statements, and balance sheets. Financial ratios showing assets-to-liabilities, debt-to-equity, and rate of turnover of inventory and receivables may also be required depending on the scope of your business and who will be reviewing your plan.

110

What should go into a business plan if I'm not looking for a loan or investors?

If you will be investing a significant amount of money or time in your venture, you should create a business plan that at minimum puts the following information down on paper:

▶ *What business am I in?* The answer to this question should dictate the focus for all your operations. For instance, are you in the business of selling dried floral arrangements or decorative home accessories? Do you have a word processing business, a resume service, or a secretarial service? If you offer several different products or services, how do they fit together? What do they have in common? You should be able to summarize the nature of your business in a sentence or two. If you can't do that, your business isn't likely to have the focus it needs for growth and success.

▶ *Who are my customers and what do they want to buy?* Even though you aren't looking for a loan or investors, you still need to gather facts about your market so you can make realistic sales forecasts.

▶ *How will I sell my products or services?* Many homebased entrepreneurs get so engrossed in developing their ideas that they forget to determine how they are going to *sell* their products or services and what it will cost them to make those sales. Typical is the person who pulls thousands of dollars out of savings to buy the equipment necessary to run a business, then discovers that newspaper ads cost more than he thought and that he doesn't have enough money left to run ads long enough to have them do any good. The time to make such discoveries is *before* you sink thousands of dollars into setting up your operation, not afterward.

▶ *What will all of my expenses be?* One of the biggest mistakes made by people who start homebased and other very small businesses is not calculating all of their costs. Production and advertising expenses are only part of the costs you will incur. Even if you work from home you will still have to buy supplies (for instance, just printing out or photocopying a single page of text can cost you anywhere from about 2 to 5 cents, depending on the cost of

111

ink and the type of paper you are using). You will also pay for business cards, letterhead and envelopes, equipment, repairs, gas (if you travel to your customers), professional fees, taxes, insurance, and so on.

▸ *At what point will I make a profit?* The point of being in business is to make a profit. You must determine how many sales you need to make at what price to make the kind of profit you want or need from the business. You also need to ascertain how long it might take you to reach that level of profit so you can determine if you have enough money to live on and support the business until it does become profitable.

Q **Why do I need to put the business plan in writing if I don't want a loan?**

Putting your plans on paper will help you succeed by forcing you to give direction to your business activities. Writing down your plans will make you set specific goals and make realistic and informed decisions about what methods you will use to reach your business goals and what your costs and profits are likely to be.

Q **What is a marketing plan?**

A marketing plan shows how your product relates to the market. It considers what you will sell, the number of potential customers, the strategies you will use to reach those customers, the percentage of customers you will be able to sell to, and how you will get them to buy your products or services instead of those of your competitors.

Q **When do I need a marketing plan?**

You should develop a marketing plan when you start a business and revise it periodically to adapt to changing market conditions. By doing this, you can keep your business in tune with the needs of your customers.

Q **What factors should I look at when preparing a marketing plan?**

The specifics will vary somewhat according to the nature of your business, but in general, you should attempt to get answers to as many of the following questions as possible:

- What products and services are you selling (planning to sell)?
- Who (specifically) will buy these products and services?

  - How old are your typical customers?
  - Are they male or female?
  - Do they belong to any specific ethnic group?
  - Do they share any occupational characteristics?
  - What is their income level?
  - What is their education level?
  - What other common characteristics do they share?

- Will businesses buy what you sell?
- Which types of businesses can use your products or services?

  - Businesses that provide services?
  - Businesses in a particular industry?
  - Manufacturers?
  - Government agencies?
  - Educational institutions?
  - Nonprofit organizations?
  - Warehouse operations?
  - Contractors?
  - Retailers?
  - Others?

- Where are your customers located? (In your city? county? state? nationwide or worldwide?)
- How many potential customers are there in your market area (how big is your market)?
- What are the annual sales in this industry?
- Are sales in this industry (or for this product) on the rise, stable, or on the way down?
- What percentage of the market or how many sales will you have to make to be profitable? (Will you need to sell 50,000 bagels a week? If so, are there enough potential customers who will buy from you to reach that goal?)

‣ How will your customers use your products or services?

‣ What do the customers expect or prefer when they buy your type of product or service?

‣ How are they getting this product or service now?

‣ How will your product or service benefit them?

‣ How frequently will they buy what you sell?

‣ How can you reach them to tell them what you sell?

- Will you advertise?
- Where will you advertise? (Newspapers, trade publications, Yellow Pages, direct mail, TV, or radio?)
- Will you have a sales force or use independent sales agents, a sales representative, wholesalers, distributors?
- How might you generate publicity?
- How can you get word-of-mouth publicity or advertising?

‣ How will you get the actual products or services to customers?

‣ What commissions or fees will you have to pay distributors, wholesalers, sales agents, or others who sell for you?

‣ Who is your competition? (Consider the answer to this question carefully since there can be some surprising answers. The competition for your typesetting service, for instance, may not only be the typesetter five blocks away from you. It may also be the computer store selling desktop publishing systems to businesses who want to do their own in-house typesetting.)

‣ How does your product or service measure up against what the competition offers? Is the quality the same, better, or not as good?

‣ What are your competitive advantages and disadvantages? Some factors to consider:

accuracy	customized service
attention to detail	durability
availability of the product	ingredients
availability of consumables	method of delivery
availability of replacement parts	name brand
better guarantee	portability

price of consumable supplies	speed of delivery
price of the product or service	styling
recyclable (or made of recyclable materials)	versatility
	weight
safety	years in business
size	

- Who are your key suppliers?
- What will you do if they go out of business, raise their prices, or stop selling what you buy from them?
- What new products or services could you reasonably expect to add on and sell to the same customers in the future?
- Where will your business be located?
- If you need retail space, will you be in an area that your customers frequent? If not, how will you convince them to come to you?
- If you are going to work alone, how will you market the product or service and produce it, too? How will you split up your time effectively?
- How could you cope if a strong competitor entered your market?
- Can you meet potential demand for the product or service?
- What problems or obstacles could you run into?

Q How do I make realistic sales forecasts?

You start out by getting industry statistics if possible. Trade associations, trade magazines, and newspapers all may have information on the total volume of sales in an industry and how this year's sales compare with last year's sales.

You may be able to get some information about the size and location of your market through the same sources. Demographic information available from the U.S. Department of Labor, the Bureau of Census, the U.S. Department of Commerce, and local or regional economic development agencies can also be extremely valuable.

Other ways you can get the facts you need to predict sales include:

- Using industry averagers to calculate response rates to different advertising and sales methods.

- Asking distributors, wholesalers, or sales representatives or agents what their experience has been with similar products or services.
- Getting circulation figures (or audience size) for the media you plan to use for advertising.
- Calling other advertisers who use or have used that media in the past and asking what their response rates have been.
- Surveying your potential customers (in person, by mail, or on the phone) to find out what they buy, how much of it they buy, what they like or don't like about what they buy now, and what it will take to get them to switch to your product(s) or services.

Q **How do I estimate advertising and publicity costs?**

To estimate advertising costs, you will need to get rate cards and quotes from the various media you want to use. You will need to determine how frequently you can afford to advertise, what size ad you want (or how much air time if you will be advertising in radio or TV), and how frequently you will need to advertise. Find out what it will cost to produce the ad. (Will you pay someone to do the graphics for you? Will a small newspaper or weekly shopper do the ad for you? Will an ad agency work for you only on the commission it gets for placing an ad, or will it also charge a fee? Will you have to pay photographers or anyone else?) If you are going to use direct mail for advertising, you will also need to determine printing and postage costs.

The cost of publicity will depend on what lengths you plan to go to publicize your business. If you are only going to send out a couple of press releases and make a few phone calls the costs will be negligible. If you are going to send out press kits and photos to a multitude of editors and make a lot of follow-up calls, calculate the costs of preparing and printing the press kits, postage costs, and the phone call charges.

Q **What are income statements?**

An income statement is sometimes called a profit and loss statement or an operating statement. It shows your total sales minus your cost of goods sold and your operating expenses over some specific time frame, usually a year or a period of years. (See Table 7.1.)

Table 7.1: Income Statement

Date: _____

	Jan	Feb	Mar	Apr	May	June	July	Aug	Sept	Oct	Nov	Dec	Total
REVENUE													
Gross sales													
Returns, or discounts													
NET SALES													
(gross sales minus returns)													
COST OF GOODS SOLD													
Materials													
Labor													
Overhead													
GROSS PROFIT													
(net sales minus cost of sales)													
OPERATING EXPENSES													
Selling expenses													
Advertising													
Commissions													
Administrative expenses													
Salaries													
Payroll taxes													
Insurance													

Table 7.1—*Continued*

Date: _____

	Jan	Feb	Mar	Apr	May	June	July	Aug	Sept	Oct	Nov	Dec	Total
Administrative expenses (*cont'd*)													
Rent													
Utilities													
Telephone													
Professional svcs.													
Real estate taxes													
Repairs													
Maintenance													
Postage													
Supplies													
Licenses													
Interest													
TOTAL EXPENSES													
NET OPERATING PROFIT (gross income minus expenses)													
ESTIMATED INCOME TAX													
ESTIMATED AFTER-TAX PROFIT													

Q **What are cash flow projections?**

Cash flow projections are predictions about where the cash will come from and how it will be spent in a given time period or business cycle. It differs from an income statement in that it shows the movement of cash through a company instead of focusing on sales or profits. (See Table 7.2.)

Table 7.2: Cash Flow Statement / Projection

Projected Annual Cash Flow

	First Year
CASH ON HAND (beginning cash balance)	_____
CASH RECEIPTS	
Cash sales	_____
Receivables collected	_____
Earned interest	_____
Loan proceeds	_____
Investor equity	_____
TOTAL CASH RECEIPTS	_____
TOTAL CASH (cash on hand plus total receipts)	_____
CASH PAID OUT	
Purchases	_____
Operating expenses	_____
Administrative expenses	_____
Loan principal payments	_____
Capital purchases	_____
Income taxes paid	_____
Other	_____
TOTAL CASH PAID OUT	_____
ENDING CASH BALANCE	_____

What is a balance sheet?

A balance sheet is a summary showing what you own, what you owe, and what your net worth is. (See Table 7.3.)

Table 7.3: Balance Sheet

Assets

CURRENT ASSETS
Cash _____
Accounts receivable _____
Inventory _____
Other _____
TOTAL CURRENT ASSETS _____

FIXED ASSETS
Equipment, machinery _____
Land, buildings _____
Other fixed assets _____
Less depreciation _____
TOTAL VALUE FIXED ASSETS _____

OTHER ASSETS _____

TOTAL ASSETS _____

Liabilities and Equity

CURRENT LIABILITIES
Accounts payable _____
Bank loans and other
short-term loans _____
Taxes payable _____
TOTAL CURRENT LIABILITIES _____

LONG-TERM DEBTS _____
OWNER'S EQUITY _____

TOTAL LIABILITIES PLUS OWNER'S EQUITY
(should equal total assets) _____

Q **Where can I get an example of a finished business plan?**

There are numerous books available in bookstores and libraries that contain simple business plans and formats you can follow. There are also a variety of computer programs available through the large mail order companies, and even some shareware (software you try before buying) available on online services and private computer bulletin boards. The software business plan templates are handy because they contain either programming or templates for popular spreadsheets that can speed up some of the projections you may need to make.

Q **Are the computer templates for business plans good enough to use if I'm looking for funding or investors?**

They are a starting point. You will need to add detail and knowledge about your business and should have your accountant look over your plan—and poke holes in it so you can rework it—before you present the plan to bankers and investors.

Q **Are there other sources of help for writing a business plan?**

Small Business Development Centers (see page 476), Service Corps of Retired Executives (SCORE) offices (see page 473), the Small Business Administration Office (see page 473), and local government offices for small businesses often offer free or low-cost help for entrepreneurs trying to write business plans. They will *not* write the plan for you or gather the information you need to put into the plan (and you shouldn't expect them to!), but provided they have the staff, they will help you figure out how to put it all together.

8.

Pricing What You Sell

Major corporations spend millions of dollars each year to determine what to charge for their goods and services. Typically, they'll do extensive market research, plug collected data into spreadsheets only an M.B.A. could love, and then test market the product at different prices in different geographic locations to determine what selling price will produce the most profits.

Small businesses don't have the time, money, or patience to conduct such extensive studies. So how do successful small businesses determine what to charge? More importantly, how can *you* come up with the right price for what you sell? Here is a collection of questions and answers to help you set prices that are both competitive and profitable.

 What's so difficult about setting prices? Can't I just charge more than it costs me to buy or make what I sell, or a little less than what everyone else charges?

It doesn't take much seat-of-the-pants logic to realize the best selling price for a product or service should be a price that falls above costs and at or slightly below competitors' prices. But here's the rub: business owners who try to slide by on this logic often overlook some important variables. Among them:

▸ The amount it costs you to buy or make a product or service is often only a small part of what it costs to sell that product or service. If your prices don't allow for all the other costs of doing business, you could lose money on every sale.

▸ Neither production costs nor competitors' prices predict whether anyone will buy the product or service from you.

▸ Buying decisions are rarely made on the basis of logic alone. In fact, customers sometimes equate quality with price. If your prices are too low, they may suspect your goods or services are inferior in quality and not buy.

Q **What should be considered in pricing a product or service?**

No matter what you sell, your pricing strategy should be based on these fundamental principles:

▸ In addition to what it costs to make or buy what you sell, your minimum price must take into consideration marketing expenses, operating expenses, labor costs, the amount of profit you want to make, and income and self-employment taxes.

▸ The price you can get for any product or service depends on the amount of money customers are willing to pay or expect to pay.

▸ There must be a large enough market to allow you to sell profitably over a long period of time. If there isn't a market for your product or service, it won't sell at any price.

Q **Other than a few supplies, what expenses do small service businesses have?**

Service businesses normally don't have to spend large sums to purchase production materials or inventory, but they can have fairly significant daily operating expenses. Even a one-person service business is likely to have many of the following expenses:

▸ purchase price and maintenance cost of a computer, photocopier, printers, cameras, tools, answering machine, fax, or other equipment

- telephone line and usage charges
- upgrades to equipment and additional computer software needed to meet customer requirements
- business stationery (business cards, letterhead, envelopes)
- supplies such as notepads, computer diskettes, file folders, printer ribbons, toner cartridges, mailing labels, photocopy supplies, film, art supplies, etc.
- file cabinets, desks, chairs, bookcases, and other office furniture
- cost of trade magazine subscriptions
- cost of membership in professional associations
- client entertainment costs
- sales and marketing literature preparation and printing
- postage and/or express mail and delivery services
- appropriate business insurance (fire & theft, personal liability, errors & omissions and, if you have employees, state compensation insurance)
- your salary (as the owner)
- cost of benefits you'd get as an employee (health and disability insurance, pension plan, etc.)
- federal, state, and city income taxes
- self-employment taxes
- cost of legal, accounting, and other professional services
- nonbillable time

If you have or take on employees, in addition to the cost of their salaries and any benefits you offer, you will have to allow for workers' compensation, employers' share of social security benefits, extra office overhead expenses, and benefits.

 What is nonbillable time?

Nonbillable time is the time you spend doing work you can't charge your customers for. Typically such work includes writing proposals; making business contacts; answering customer questions; doing your own filing, typing, and bookkeeping; and learning to use new computer programs.

 Why is nonbillable time considered an expense?

In a service business, earnings are tied to the number of hours devoted to income-producing work. In some small service businesses one-third or more of the total working hours each week may be spent doing work that can't be billed to any client. In fact, it's not unusual for the owner of a one-person business to work from early in the morning until late at night without directly producing a cent of income.

Under such circumstances, time is a commodity with a significant value. For instance, assume you work a total of 40 hours a week in your service business and on an average you make about $25 an hour on time spent on client work. If you spend 10 hours a week doing nonbillable jobs, you have only 30 hours a week left for paid client work. Thus you are losing $250 a week in sales (the 10 nonbillable hours times $25 an hour). If you normally charge $50 an hour for your time, those 10 hours of nonbillable time will cost you a whopping $500 each week.

Q **How can I factor the cost of nonbillable time into my fees?**

Calculate what your expenses will be for a month. This figure should include a salary for yourself, plus all other expenses including loan payments, if any, allowances for equipment upgrades and repairs, and so on (see list on pages 123–124). Add in an amount for profit. (Your own salary is not profit. Profit is what the business makes over and above your salary and all other expenses.)

Multiply this figure by 12 to determine what the gross yearly income of the business should be. Then divide the gross yearly income by 48 to determine the amount of money the business will need to make per week. (The reason for using 48 instead of 52 is to allow 4 weeks for vacation time, holidays, and sick days.)

Once you determine the amount of money you need to earn per week, divide that amount by your billable hours. If you plan to work 40 hours a week but will spend 10 of them on your own accounting chores or other nonbillable work, divide the weekly gross income needs by 30 to get the hourly fee you should charge.

For example, if you determine you need to bring in $5,000 per month to cover your salary and other business expenses, here's how you would calculate hourly fees:

$5,000 (monthly income) × 12 (months) = $60,000 (gross yearly income)
$60,000 (gross yearly income) ÷ 48 (weeks) = $1,250 (per week)
$1,250 (per week) ÷ 30 (hours) = $41.66 (per hour)

What are typical overhead costs for small offices?

There's no such thing as a "typical" overhead figure; however, one medium-sized commercial printing company in the Southeast came up with the following figures after prorating all of its expenses to determine an average cost per employee in their desktop publishing (DTP) department. Note that what the average employee made in salary (payroll) was only about one-fourth of the company's total cost per employee.

Depreciation	7,000
Insurance	289
Property tax	253
Occupancy cost	6,824
Payroll	16,640
FICA & unemployment	1,520
Benefits	965
Maintenance (service contract)	1,200
Direct supplies	800
General factory (allocation of general factory costs)	11,156
Administration and overhead expenses	20,157
TOTAL	$66,804

Calculating allowances for vacation, holidays, and sick days, the company figured this average worker worked 1,864 hours during the year at an average efficiency of 75 percent, which reduced the billable hours for the year to 1,398, making their *cost* for this average employee $47.79 per hour. They added only about 20 percent to that cost to come up with the hourly billing rate ($55) for the DTP employees, since they made their profit from printing the work that the DTP department produced. If all of their income had been derived from DTP operations, they would have had to mark up their costs much more in order to be profitable.

What about independent sales representatives, distributors, agents, and others who work on commission only? How do they make sure they'll make enough to cover expenses and make a profit?

If your business will be some type of agency, brokerage, or distributorship, the commission you can charge will have to conform closely to industry standards. The way to make this type of business profitable is to know your industry inside and out, maintain close contacts with buyers or purchasing agents, and have top-notch sales skills. Whether you plan to be a print broker, distributor for industrial filters, or a literary agent, you need a good handle on:

- which companies are buying what type of products
- how much they are paying for them
- who makes the buying decisions
- how many sales you can realistically expect to make
- how long it will take you to make the sale
- what it will cost you to make the sale
- how long it will be from the time the sale is made until the time you collect your fee
- what the likelihood of repeat sales is

Since the amount of money you make will be limited to the commissions you make on each sale, add your estimated expenses and the after-expense income you want to achieve, then choose clients whose goods or services will sell at high enough prices and/or in sufficient quantity to produce the income you want to achieve.

 How can I make accurate sales or cost estimates if I've never run my own business or been involved in marketing products or services?

Here are several ways to get the information you need to predict sales and costs:

- Talk to other business owners. Find out what they charge, and ask how much they spend per year on marketing, advertising, office overhead, etc. At the end of this chapter you will find a list of typical fees charged by different types of businesses. The fees will offer you some guidance, but you should try to get information about prices in your part of the country as well.

▶ Contact industry or trade associations and ask if the association has literature that will help you determine what business expenses you may incur and what the going rates are for the general type of product or service you plan to sell.

▶ If you own a modem, sign up for one or more of the commercial online information networks. All have forums or special-interest groups where owners of small and homebased businesses network with one another. You'll find many of these people will readily share information about pricing and business expenses.

▶ If you are starting a one-person service business and aren't sure what to charge, read employment ads and call several employment agencies to determine what hourly salary you might expect if you were to provide your service as an employee in someone else's business. Consider tripling the salary figure to allow for benefits you'd get as an employee, office overhead, and profit.

▶ Gauge your fees according to what other service providers charge you. For instance, if local services in your area charge an average of $50 an hour for labor (car repair, computer repair, etc.) consider setting your prices in the same range.

▶ If possible, run the business part-time on a small scale, keeping accurate records of all expenses and income. Also keep track of how much time it takes you to complete work or make sales and how long it takes you to collect from your customers. Review this information once a quarter and make any necessary adjustments in your fees.

▶ If you sell a product, comparison shop. Check prices of similar products in retail stores, discount stores, shopping clubs, warehouses, and mail order catalogs.

▸ Test market your product or service. Advertise it in one publication or do a small mailing to test your response rate.

Q Is it better to charge for a service by the hour or the job?

There is no "better way" to charge. In fact, there will be some instances when you charge by the hour, others where you charge by the job, and perhaps still other times where you work on a retainer basis, or get a "per head" fee (for teaching seminars, for instance), a contingency fee, commission (on sales or placement), or royalties.

▸ *Charge by the hour* if the job is one where the customer is likely to make changes in the job specifications while you are working on the project. Here's the type of situation you need to be wary of: A copywriter, after spending half a day at a client's office getting all the information he needed to write the copy for a brochure and sales letter for one of the company's new products, spent the better part of a second day writing the material. Then, before he had a chance to deliver the assignment, he got a call from the company's marketing manager who informed him the company had decided the mailing should include a limited-time offer for a large discount on the product. The entire mailing had to be redesigned and rewritten. Had the writer quoted a flat rate on that job he would have lost at least one full day's earnings.

▸ *Charge by the job* if the client won't agree to an hourly rate. Or, if you know how long it will take you to do a certain type of job (such as write a publicity release), it is often more profitable to charge by the job. For instance, if the going rate for writing a short publicity release is $150, and you can write the release in an hour, it's obviously better to state a flat fee of $150 for writing the release than it would be to charge $50 or $75 an hour for your work.

Tip: Sometimes charging by the job is advisable to avoid raised eyebrows and questions about why your rates are so high. If the client has no idea how long it takes to write a press release, the flat fee of $150 might well be immensely more acceptable to your client than a stated fee of $75 dollars an hour.

Tip: On corporate or other projects where many changes are likely, due to either a difficult client or the need for approvals from multiple department heads in a company, at each phase of a project have someone at the company "sign off" on the work (sign a piece of paper approving the work and authorizing the next step or acceptance). This will allow you to bill for changes made at a later stage (and perhaps help keep you from being held responsible for errors) that should have been made in early stages of the project.

Q **What problems are associated with charging by the job?**

The main problem with a per-job or per-page rate is that a job can look deceptively easy (a directory with relatively few words per page, for instance) but can turn out to be extremely time-consuming, particularly if the client is difficult to work with. The way to solve the problem is to spell out very clearly (in writing) what you will do for the project rate and what services or changes in the project will carry an additional fee.

Q **How do you know how long it will take to do a job?**

You learn that from experience. If you don't have experience, you may be able to get the information one of these ways:

▸ *Ask other people in the same line of work.* Be sure to give enough detail about the job so people can give accurate advice. Don't just say you have a directory to typeset for a university, for instance; give details, such as "there are ten entries on a page, the name is in bold type, with all related information for the entry indented. The number of lines varies from three to five."

▶ *Do one small part of the job and time yourself.* Then estimate the total job time.

▶ *Consider not taking the job* or doing the job for free if you are just starting out in a business and have little experience in the industry. In other words, don't bill customers for the time it takes you to learn your trade.

Q **What about retainer agreements? How do they work?**

A retainer can be a lump sum used as a type of secured credit against which you draw as you do work for the client, or it can be a regular monthly fee paid to you to guarantee the availability of your services when the client needs them. Generally the amount of money paid on retainer is based on your normal hourly rate.

Q **How do contingency fees work?**

When you work on a contingency arrangement, you get paid only if the outcome of your endeavors is successful. The actual payment is usually a percentage, such as the percentage of a settlement an attorney wins for his or her client, but it can be a flat fee, too.

Q **How high can I set my fees without pricing myself right out of business?**

To answer that question, you'll have to find out what the going rates are for the type of service you perform. In addition to the nature of the service, your experience, geographic location, competitors, and the clients you target all will have an effect on the maximum rate you can charge without losing worthwhile customers.

Q **How do I find out what the going rates are?**

The best advice on that score comes from Roy Bernstein, president of Demand Research Corporation, a Chicago-based company that conducts market research studies for major corporations. Advises Bernstein: "Instead of diddling around with formal market research, the small business owner should get out in the marketplace and go nose to nose with a few air-breathing clients." In other words, get out and talk to the people you want as customers. Find out what they want to buy, how much they are willing to pay for it, and where they are buying similar services now.

Q What if no one is selling a product or service like mine?

Bernstein's advice for introducing new concepts is to "be innovative and non-traditional." Instead of trying to explain how a new product or service will benefit your prospects, show them. That's what Lewis Lehr, chairman of 3M, did when Post-it Notes were developed. To test the acceptability of the notes in real-life corporate settings, Lehr had his secretary send samples of the product to the secretaries of a few dozen CEOs at other Fortune 500 companies. As a result of that test, you now pay premium prices for tiny squares of notepaper.

Q How do I get up the nerve to ask for high fees?

Knowing what you ought to charge is one thing; actually asking for your fee and holding out for it is quite another. Here are a few tricks you can use to bolster your self-confidence and determination.

▶ Pretend you are selling the product or service for someone other than yourself. You are less likely to take it personally if a client rejects you because of high fees (or any other reason).

▶ Calculate how much it costs you and your family to live for a year. Add in an amount to allow for your business expenses. Now divide that figure by 1,920 (average number of working hours in a year). This will be the bare minimum you have to charge just to keep your head above water.

▶ Make a list of your personal goals (for example, the new house, expensive sports car, vacation condo, etc.). Imagine yourself enjoying them, then put a dollar amount next to each goal, and set a reasonable date for reaching the goals. Each time you are asked to quote a fee, think of your quote as moving you one step closer to your goals.

▶ Consider how much money the client saves by buying your services instead of hiring a staff member to do the work. By hiring you on an as-needed basis, the client avoids overstaffing, reduces the need for additional office equipment and space, and saves on expenses such as unemployment insurance, compensation, Social Security, health care plans, and other benefits.

Q **Should I ever donate my services or charge very low fees to get my foot in the door?**

If you are just starting a new business and have no experience in the field, donating your services or charging low fees can be beneficial. It can help you gain the experience you need and can be a good way to build a portfolio and references to attract higher paying clients.

Additionally, if you are new in a community or want to build goodwill for your business, it may be beneficial to donate products or services to key community organizations or projects. Before accepting charity work, however, consider carefully whether it is something you really want to do, whether you will benefit from the work, and whether you will actually have the time or financial capacity to see the project through to its conclusion. If you already have all the work you can do or have no particular interest in the charity, learn to say no. Otherwise you will find yourself spending a great deal of time doing work that doesn't benefit you in any way.

Q **Should I charge friends and family?**

That's always a touchy question. When you are just starting out, you may want to do work for friends and family for free to build up credentials, but once you have been in business long enough to have steady customers, you may not have time to do work for free.

If you can't afford the time, you should make clear to friends and family that you are in business and must make money to be profitable. If they don't understand, consider it their problem and not yours. Don't get involved in lengthy disputes. Just say you'd like to help them out but have commitments to paying customers that prevent you from doing so.

Q **Should I charge all customers the same fee?**

In fairness you should charge everyone the same rate. In reality, however, many small service businesses alter their fees somewhat according to who the customer is, how much the customer can afford to spend, and how badly they want the customer's future business.

 Tip: If you charge different clients different fees for similar work, get them to agree in writing not to disclose your fees to other individuals or companies. You might also tell a client that the low fee you are charging is a special rate because you value their business, enjoy working with their staff, etc.

Q **Should I charge for travel time?**

Some businesses charge for travel time, and others don't. Those that do charge reason that the time they spend traveling is time they can't spend on other income-producing activities. You will need to decide what's right for you based on what others in your field do, how badly you want any individual customer, and how much time you will spend traveling for that customer. If you do opt to bill for travel time, be sure your customers are aware of that fact before you start work on any project for them. A written explanation of all your fees presented to the client before you start a project will go a long way toward avoiding billing misunderstandings after you've completed the work.

Q **How much should I charge for travel time?**

Travel time is usually billed at either the full hourly rate or one-half the hourly rate.

Q **Should I undercut the competition?**

If you have many competitors and you are not known, you may have to charge a little less than your competitors to make a name for yourself. Some people who run service businesses say being faster and better is an attractive benefit to their prospects. Others say underpricing can backfire. One disc jockey, for instance, lost a sale when he quoted a price $600 lower than one of his competitors. The client felt the lower price reflected a lower level of professionalism. Others have found that increasing their prices considerably increased their number of clients.

 Tip: One strategy that works well for many one- or two-person businesses is to start at a price a little below what the competition charges (if that price is profitable) and then gradually raise prices, eliminating marginally profitable customers as the business grows.

Q What costs are associated with selling products?

Following is a list of some of the expenses you may expect when you sell products. The list is not all-inclusive, since no two businesses are likely to incur all the same costs. It will, however, help you determine what costs should be factored into your selling price.

- wholesale price of products you will resell
- price you pay for materials and supplies used to manufacture the product
- outside manufacturing costs you may incur (for instance, to have dies or molds made or have a product produced to your specifications)
- machinery and tools needed to produce the product
- preparation and production of instruction manuals (writing, design, typesetting, printing, and binding costs)
- preparation and production of other items shipped with the product
- packaging (box, Styrofoam filler, shrink wrapping)
- package design cost
- licensing fees or royalties
- cost of warranty cards and registration cards (including business reply postage) included with the product
- cost of sales brochures, press kits, and other marketing materials
- advertising, copywriting, printing, duplication, or other services you may need to purchase
- labor costs (*your own* plus that of any employees)

- employee benefits, such as vacation time, sick leave, pension plans, insurance (again, don't forget to calculate in an amount for benefits for yourself)
- employer share of FICA (and your own self-employment tax if the business is not incorporated)
- state unemployment and compensation insurance costs for employees
- trade show expenses
- publicity expense
- mailing costs
- mailing list rental costs
- office overhead (rent, maintenance, phones, and other utilities, equipment, equipment repairs/service contracts, office supplies, etc.)
- business insurance and product liability insurance
- legal and accounting fees

Q **How do I determine the best selling price for products?**

Here are several methods to help you decide what to charge for your products.

Base the selling price on cost per unit: *

1. Estimate how many sales of the individual product (number of units) you will make within 3 to 6 months or some other given time frame.
2. Add up all the business costs you will incur to produce and sell the product and run the business during that time frame.
3. Divide the total expected costs by the expected number of sales. This will tell you what your costs are per sale (unit cost).
4. Determine the profit you want to make on each sale (per unit) and add the profit (plus an allowance for income and self-employment taxes) to the unit cost. This will give you the minimum price you will need to get for each product to cover your costs and provide a profit. If you sell directly to your customers this would also be the minimum selling price.

* The cost per unit method works well for many small software companies, such as Survivor Software, a company that sells Macintosh accounting software. Mike Farmer, Survivor Software's CEO, says, "As a rough estimate you can figure the final product will have to have a retail price of twice your per-unit cost."

5. Determine what discounts you will need to offer distributors or others and any commissions you will need to pay to independent sales representatives. (Distributor discounts are figured as a percentage of a *product's retail list price.* Thus if the list price of a widget is $2, and the distributors in your industry expected a 50 percent discount off the list price, the actual amount of the discount would be 50 percent of $2, or $1. Sales representatives' commissions are generally calculated on the selling price, not the retail list price.)
6. Add the discount and/or commission amount to the total cost per unit to arrive at a retail price.
7. Compare the price you determine with the list prices of similar products or products aimed at a similar market. If your price seems much higher, go back and look for ways to reduce your costs.

Decide on a retail price and work backward from the expected retail price, subtracting distributor or other discounts, sales commissions, and your profit. This will give you a cost per unit. If you can't manufacture the product at this cost per unit, change the retail price and work out the figures again.

Calculate your break-even point. You don't need to be a mathematician to calculate break-even points. The break-even point is simply the number of sales you need to make at a given price to cover your costs. To determine break-even points, you divide your total costs by the selling price of the item. Your answer represents the number of products you have to sell at the stated price to pay back your costs (break even). If the number of sales you will need is larger than what you might realistically expect to achieve in a reasonable time, look for ways to lower your costs, or consider raising your price per unit.

If you can't easily produce your product in volume, if there is only a very limited market for what you sell, or if you have only a shoestring budget and can market to only a small fraction of your potential market, you will want to shoot for higher selling prices to achieve a lower break-even point.

For example, suppose you make decorative wooden wall plaques and sell them once a month at craft shows. This is a sideline business, and you can make only about thirty plaques a month at a total cost to you of $360. To calculate your break-even point (the number of plaques you would have to sell just to pay your costs), you would take one or more possible selling prices and divide the selling price into the total cost figure. Your results might look like this:

Break-Even Point Calculation

Your Total Cost	Selling Price	Number of Sales to Break Even
$360	$12	30
$360	$15	25
$360	$18	20
$360	$20	18
$360	$24	15
$360	$30	12

Looking at the figures, you would immediately see that at $12 per plaque you would have to sell every single one just to pay back your costs, and that to make a decent profit, you would have to price the plaques at the upper dollar amounts. If you frequent craft shows (and you should if you expect to sell at them), you will have some idea about whether or not items similar to yours sell in the higher price ranges. If they typically don't sell for much more than $15, you will have to decide whether it's worth your while to make and sell the plaques.

Q **How do I find out what my competitors are charging?**

If you aren't sure what your competitors are charging, either call and ask for prices and product literature; go to retail stores or other sales outlets and price similar products; look through catalogs, magazines, and newspaper ads (don't forget the classified section); or call or contact potential customers and do a survey to find out where they now buy what you plan to sell and how much they pay for it.

Q **What should I do if my price estimates indicate that I will need to charge more than my competitors?**

Basically you have four options:

- *Look for ways to cut costs.* Consider using less expensive materials, different manufacturing methods, cheaper labor, or cutting overhead expenses.

- *Target the cream of the crop (skimming method).* Look for ways you can add value to your product or imply added value (better grade of materials used in manufacture, more capabilities than competitor's products, etc.), and target your product at the top end of the market. You will need to know the market for your product well enough to make a good estimate about how many sales you could make at premium prices. Multiply the selling price by the expected number of sales, and compare to the cost of sales.

- *Consider different distribution methods.* Calculate the cost and possible effects of different distribution methods. Would the additional volume a distributor could achieve offset the discounts or the commissions you'd have to give and allow you to sell the product at a lower price? Might independent sales representatives have more industry contacts and thus be able to sell your product or service to more customers who are willing to pay a premium price for what you sell? Could you reduce costs and retail price by selling the product through direct mailings?

- *Don't manufacture or sell the product.* While a particular product may catch your fancy, it's pointless to make or sell a product if your figures suggest you can't manufacture or sell it at a competitive price or in sufficient quantity to be profitable.

Q What's the going rate?

Following is a list of typical fees charged for a variety of jobs. The figures are based on the stated fees from businesses in various parts of the country and are only presented as a rough guide. In general, even if you quote a flat fee for a job, the fee should be based on what your hourly rate is and should take into consideration overhead costs, benefits, and profit.

Most of the price figures are given in ranges. If you live in an area where salaries and cost of living are relatively low, where there is a lot of competition for your product or service, and where people can't afford to pay small businesses high fees, the fees you can charge are likely to fall in the low end of the range. The same is true if you have limited experience in a field.

If you are highly experienced and work for companies located in a major metropolitan area with a relatively high cost of living, you should be able to command fees in the higher ranges. In fact, the way pricing works in the "real world" is that many businesses start out working at low fees for small businesses, and as their skill in businesses and their reputation grows, they work their way up the ladder both in terms of the size of companies for which they do work and the fees they charge for that work.

GOING RATES

Accountants (CPA): $75 to $125 an hour and up. An accounting firm will generally bill its staff out at different rates depending on their experience.

Advertising/marketing copywriting: $35 to $75 per hour and up, with a markup of 17.65% on other services purchased for the client.

Advertising sales commission, newspaper: 15 to 20 percent of the dollar amount of the ad.

Artist's representatives or agents: 25 percent commission.

Authors' agents: 15 percent commission.

Attorney fees: $75 to $300 an hour plus expenses, depending on experience, reputation, and specialty.

Bookkeeping and payroll services: $25 to $30 an hour and up.

Brochure writing: $200 to $800 for writing a two-fold sales brochure. Generally, the bigger the company, the bigger the fee.

Catalog copywriting: $15 to $25 per item in the catalog and up, depending on the type of catalog, length of copy, etc.

Commercial art design fees: $50 to $100 per hour or more for skilled commercial artists; higher fees are generally paid by larger clients.

Computer consulting without programming: $35 to $50 per hour for setting up small microcomputer systems with off-the-shelf software, setting up batch files, backing up, and troubleshooting. Some consultants, however, were getting only $15 to $25 per hour in the Southeast in 1992.

Computer programming, systems analysis: $50 to $100 an hour.

Computer training: $25 to $40 per person per product covered; or, $25 to $40 per hour for tutoring, staff training, etc.

Consulting, marketing/advertising: up to $100 per hour or higher for experienced consultants in major metropolitan areas.

Contracting, estimating interior jobs: depending on the job and the location, approximately three times the cost of materials, or by the running foot (example: one experienced New York City contractor was charging $300 a running foot in 1991 for kitchen remodeling).

Data entry: by individuals working at home, $6 to $12 an hour; billing rate for data entry from a secretarial service can go up to $30. Typesetting may be higher. See typesetting and desktop publishing prices.

Desktop publishing production: $30 to $40 per hour for typesetting and layout or $25 to $30 and up per page depending on complexity.

Desktop publishing consulting: $350 to $1,000 per day, depending on qualifications and experience.

Direct mail package, writing: $1,500 to $2,000 for a four-page letter, brochure, and reply card.

Graphic design, agency billing rates: $50 to $125 per hour.

Letters: to type generic letter and print multiple copies, no merge, $.20 to $.30 per page.

Letters: to type a generic letter and customize by merging with customer addresses, $1.50 per letter.

Mailing list data entry: $.25 per record for records that are 3 to 4 lines in length, sorted by zip code.

Mailing labels (printed out from entered list): $.075 per label

Mailing list update: billed at hourly rate.

Mail order products: at least four times the costs for any item. Some people set $19.99 to $29.99 as a minimum price for a product they find profitable to sell via mail.

Manufacturer's representative: 5 to 25 percent commission or more, depending on industry and the point in the distribution chain. Sales reps who are also dealers selling to the end-user and reps who assume all marketing costs might get considerably more than 25 percent, while someone who reps the product to distributors might only get as little as 2 to 3 percent commission, depending on the industry practices.

Medical claims processing: fees that were actually being received in 1991–1992 by companies doing medical claims processing ranged from as low as 35 cents per claim to 5 percent of the cash brought in. However, many doctors were having their own staffs do the data entry and claims processing. In 1992, Medicare, Medicaid, and Champus were not charging doctors to accept the claims electronically; Medicare and Medicaid were providing the data entry and processing software free of charge to doctors. *

---

* John Rigdon, a computer VAR who is familiar with claims processing and has written software for it, warns, "To my way of thinking, this means that the claims processing business is being squeezed to the point that the future is very limited. There'll always be some doctors who will use a service agency, but it's not the golden egg some folks have touted."

Newsletters: a single newsletter written and sold to multiple companies (such as health and wellness newsletters distributed by the chiropractors), $800 to $1,000 per thousand, imprinted with logo of the company ordering the newsletter.

Newsletter writing for large corporations (such as an internal or external company newsletter): up to $1,000 or more for a four-page newsletter, research material provided. The exact fee will depend on the company, the nature of the publication, the geographic location, and the writer's negotiating skills.

Newsletter production: *see* desktop publishing prices.

Product fact sheets, writing: $120 to $300 and up.

Photography, brochures, catalogs: $150 to $500 per shot.

Photography, presentation slides: $55 to $100 per shot.

Public relations: $40 to $150 per hour; press releases $150 to $300 for 1 to 3 pages.

Research for corporate newsletters: $25 to $40 an hour.

Resumes, writing: $35 to $75 per page.

Resumes, typesetting: $30 to $45 per page.

Resume, storage: $5 per resume.

Resumes, extra printouts: $1 per page or $20 per 25 pages. Blank sheets $.10 a page; blank envelopes $.25 each.

Retainer agreements: Retainer agreements are usually figured by multiplying the normal hourly billing rate times the number of hours the client company wants set aside for its work. Some retainers paid in the Northeast:

- $1,700 per month plus expenses for 20 hours of work as a retainer to handle advertising for a company with $20 million in annual sales. Any hours over 20 in any given month are billed at an additional fee whether all hours have been used in preceding months or not.
- $1,000 per month plus expenses for computer consulting and trouble-shooting for a graphic arts firm with a network of three computers, a laser printer, and an image setter.
- Retainer for legal research: full expected cost of the research (held in escrow, with charges deducted from escrow account as incurred).

Sales letters, writing: $100 to $500 per page, with highest figures going to seasoned professionals in direct mail.

Tax preparation: tax preparers who are not CPAs often charge by the form, charging about $25 to fill out Form 1040, using the client's figures, and $5 to $15 for each additional form. Bookkeeping or other services and electronic filing are extra. Tax preparation at accounting firms is billed by the hourly billing rate of the person assigned to do the return.

Training seminars: $50 to $90 "per head" or a flat fee, which can run from $500 to $2,000 or more a day, depending on the instructor's reputation. Minimum fee of $300 for short sessions is not unusual.

Trademark search: by an attorney, with opinion about the availability of the trademark, $200 to $500, with higher fees for searches for unregistered marks. (Preparation of trademark application is extra.)

Translation: agencies charge their customers approximately $.085 to $.13 per word, depending on the client, the language being translated from and to, and the technical difficulty of the work.

Typesetting: $25 to $50 an hour; $30 to $45 per page; one-page flier is $30 to $45; standard letterhead (typeface and logo chosen from sample book) is $15.

Writing, books: depending on the publisher, the experience of the writer, the number of previously published works, etc., $2,500 to $15,000 and up, as an advance against royalties.

Writing, articles: $.02 per word to $1.00 per word and up. Most established writers try to get a minimum of $.50 to $.60 a word, unless the article can be written very quickly. Pay of $.35 a word for a 1,000-word article can work out to over $100 an hour if it only takes three hours to write and research the piece.

Writing, technical: $35 to $60 per hour and up. *

 Tip: When estimating the time to write a manual or other kind of technical book for a corporation, multiply the time you think it ought to take by 150 percent. Then multiply that figure by your hourly rate. This allows for jobs that take much longer than expected.

* For additional information on writers' fees, see *Writer's Market*, by Writer's Digest Books. This reference is published annually and should be available in your public library.

9.

Money: What
You'll Need and
Where to Get It

What does it take to turn your business plans and ideas into a viable business? The answer, in most cases, is money. The amount of money and the time at which that money needs to be invested will vary from one small business to another.

For instance, some businesses start out with only a small investment on the part of the owner and are either kept small or are expanded slowly using the profits of the business to finance growth. Other businesses start out small and then turn to outside lenders or investors for money to expand. Still others need hundreds of thousands or even millions of dollars to launch their businesses and require sophisticated management skills as well as investors with deep pockets.

The bigger the investment required to launch or run a business, the bigger the risk to the owner. Thus, your own willingness and financial ability to accept risk will be a determining factor in the kind of business you start and its eventual size. This chapter presents some of the financing options you may want to consider at various stages in your business.

Q **How much do I need to start a business?**

You need enough money to acquire or produce what you sell, market and deliver the product or service to the customer, keep the business running, and keep your personal bills paid until the business is profitable. If you are starting a service

146

business and will run it in your spare time or if you have a spouse who has a full-time job that will cover all your living expenses and health insurance costs, you might be able to start your business with as little as $200 to $300—or possibly even less. If the business you are starting will require you to purchase expensive equipment, machinery, inventory, raw materials or rent space, hire employees, make significant outlays for advertising or promotion, and/or quit a job that you now rely on to pay your bills, you will need significantly more money to start the venture.

The best way to determine exactly how much money you will need to start your business is to use a worksheet similar to Table 9.1 on pages 148–149 to estimate your one-time start-up expenses and the regularly monthly costs of doing business. Because it can take time to get your first customers (and collect from them if you have to bill them), you should plan on having at least enough money to cover start-up expenses and three months of operational expenses.

Q **Where do I get the money to start a business?**

Most people get the money to start a business from their personal savings, by taking out personal loans or second mortgages on their homes, and/or by using charge cards to pay for equipment or supplies. Equipment leases and vendor credit may be possible, too. Family and friends or other private investors are also common sources of start-up funds. Sometimes the amount of cash actually needed to start a business can be reduced by bartering or by working out some type of business deal with other individuals or businesses.

On rare occasions a manufacturer, supplier, or even a successful entrepreneur provides some start-up funds, equipment, building, or space. This type of opportunity is one you can't really search out, however. What usually happens is that someone with money or equipment spots a bright, industrious, inquisitive employee and figures that the employee has what it takes to build a new business or take over an existing one.

Q **What kind of deals could be used in place of money to help start a business?**

One type of deal is a sweat equity arrangement, which is basically an exchange of work for ownership in the start-up company. In other words, one person agrees

Table 9.1: Start-up Expenses Estimate

Use the list of start-up expenses below as a guideline to estimate how much money you will need to start your business.

One-Time Expenses	Cost
Permits	$
Licenses	$
Copyright registrations	$
Patent(s) (initial costs)	$
Trademark(s) (initial costs)	$
One-time legal & professional fees	$
Deposits (telephone, utilities, rent)	$
Grand opening advertising & publicity cost	$
Starting inventory	$
Other one-time expenses	$
TOTAL A: ONE-TIME EXPENSES	$

Monthly Expenses	Monthly Cost
Raw materials and parts	$
Supplies	$
Inventory	$
Shipping costs	$
Telephone	$
Equipment	$
Office furniture	$
Rent	$
Utilities (other than phone)	$
Fixtures	$
Display cases	$
Interior or exterior redecoration	$
Signs (inside or outside)	$
Property & general liability insurance	$
Errors & omissions insurance	$
Product liability insurance	$
Business auto/truck insurance	$
Letterhead, envelopes, business cards	$
Sales literature (brochures, fliers, etc.)	$

148

Table 9.1—*Continued*

Advertisements (production costs)	$	_____
Advertisements (media charges)	$	_____
Mailing list rental	$	_____
Publicity expense	$	_____
Postage for direct mail or publicity	$	_____
Employee salaries	$	_____
Employee FICA, worker's compensation, etc.	$	_____
Owner's draw (what you need to live on)	$	_____
Health insurance	$	_____
Other expenses	$	_____
TOTAL MONTHLY EXPENSES	$	_____
Multiply by 3 to get:	×	3
TOTAL B: MONTHLY EXPENSES FOR THREE MONTHS	$	_____
Add Total A and Total B to get:		
MINIMUM REQUIRED FOR START-UP	$	_____

to work for free or at a lower salary than normal and, in exchange, gets partial ownership of the business. A different type of arrangement, also beneficial, is one in which an existing business provides certain services for free for a start-up in exchange for a guarantee of future work if the start-up is successful.

Ben Mandell, an entrepreneur who has built several successful businesses, used this technique to produce the pilots he needed for a new TV game show he wanted to produce called "I've Got a Crush." Mandell, who was expecting to spend $300,000 to launch the show, explains, "A big part of the budget is for studio rental. I can pitch my show to the studio and get a lower rate for the pilots with an express written understanding that I will shoot 130 shows at their studio [and pay their daily studio fee] if and when the show is sold. I have a producer I have worked with before. . . . He will produce the pilot at no cost to me until the show is sold. If the show is sold, he will produce 130 shows the first season." Mandell worked out similar deals with other suppliers.

 Will the bank give me a loan to start a business?

Getting a bank loan to start a business can be extremely difficult. Banks are very conservative and are often reluctant to deal with start-up businesses, particularly if the owner has little or no experience running a business. If you have a good business plan and a good credit history, you may be able to find a bank willing to work with you, though you may have to shop around for the right bank. If you can't get a business loan you may be able to get a personal loan or a home equity loan or line of credit. (A line of credit is an agreed-upon amount of money you can borrow when needed.)

Q **How does a bank decide whether or not to approve a business loan?**

The bank will want to know how much money you are requesting, how you will use the money, and how you will be able to repay it. They need assurance that you and any other owners have the management experience and commitment necessary to run the business. They'll expect you and any other principal owners to have invested a significant amount of your own money in the business. Generally banks will expect the owner(s) to have an investment in the business equal to between one-third and one-half the amount of the loan requested.

The way to present all this information to banks is by preparing a loan proposal that includes these elements:

- business name and address
- name, address, and Social Security number of each owner of the business
- exact amount of the loan
- purpose of the loan
- financial statements for the last three years, or if the business is just starting, projections of financial data for three years
- business tax returns for the last three years if available
- tax returns and financial statements for each of the business owners for the last three years
- information about the company's market (how large it is, if the market is growing, who the typical customer is, how your business meets customers' needs)
- business profiles of the owners of the company, indicating management experience, special industry knowledge, skills, education, accomplishments

150

- an indication of what collateral the owner(s) is willing to pledge as security for the loan (collateral is any asset the bank could take over to get its money back if you can't pay off the loan, such as cash, stocks, real estate, and inventory)

Q **What kinds of bank loans are available to businesses?**

The two general types of loans are short-term loans and long-term loans. A short-term loan is one that has a term (the time from when you get the loan until when it has to be paid back) that is usually one to six months but can be up to one year. Usually short-term loans are made to cover temporary or seasonal financial needs.

Long-term loans are usually made for terms longer than one year. Generally these loans are for major purchases, business expansion, or purchase of equipment or real estate. You will usually have to pledge some kind of collateral to get a long-term loan.

Q **What is a secured loan?**

A secured loan is a loan for which you have pledged assets as collateral (or security). If you can't pay, the bank takes over whatever assets you have pledged to pay off the loan.

Q **What is a revolving line of credit?**

A revolving line of credit works something like bank credit cards. You are granted a certain amount of credit, you may use it up to that amount, pay it off, use it up again, etc.

Q **What is a personal guarantee?**

A personal guarantee is a legal document that makes you liable for the debts of your business. You may be asked to sign a personal guarantee for small loans for which you don't pledge collateral, for business leases, and in some other circumstances. If the business defaults on the loan and you have signed a personal guarantee for the loan, the lender can force you to sell personal assets to make good on the loan if you don't have the cash to repay it.

Q **What is receivables financing?**

Receivables financing (also called accounts receivable financing) is short-term financing used to provide companies with a source of cash between the time they sell a product and when they get paid for it. The business pledges the accounts receivable (outstanding bills) as collateral for the loan. If the business doesn't pay back the loan, the lender makes arrangements to have customers of the business pay their bills to the bank instead of to the business.

Q **What is factoring?**

Factoring is the outright purchase of accounts receivable (as opposed to lending against them). The business sells the receivables at a discount, getting, say $70 for every $100 in receivables it is owed. The factor may take over the collection function. The factor used to bear all the risk. Nowadays, however, the factor may have recourse back to the company that originated the sale.

Q **What is inventory financing?**

Inventory financing is a loan used to bridge the gap between the time a company has to make an outlay for raw materials or inventory and the time the raw materials can be turned into products and sold. Although inventory financing may be used in conjunction with receivables financing (to gear up for seasonal sales, for instance) it is more individualized than receivables financing.

"Some lenders will advance only on raw materials and finished product but not on work in process," explains Larry J. Bister, chief financial officer of Crest Converters, Inc., in Milwaukee, Wisconsin. "Some lend only on raw materials. Most lenders want to make sure that any advances against finished product are only against newly created inventory—they don't want to be stuck with merchandise that is old and has no commercial value."

Q **How do I get vendors to extend credit to me?**

Often all you have to do is ask or say "Bill me." Other times, you may have to promise future business in return for the extension of immediate credit.

Q What are financials?

Financials are the income statements, balance sheets, and other financial data you prepare for your business plan.

Q Can I get a loan from the Small Business Administration?

Most Small Business Administration (SBA) loans are guaranteed loans. You get them by applying for a loan through a regular bank. If you don't qualify for a regular bank loan but have a good business plan and are creditworthy, you might qualify for an SBA guaranteed loan. These loans guarantee the bank that the government will pay a percentage of the loan if the business defaults on the payments. The amount guaranteed is between 75 and 90 percent of the loan amount, depending on the circumstances and size of the loan.

Although guarantees are available for businesses that banks normally consider too new or risky to qualify for traditional business loans, you still must have a good business plan showing how you propose to repay the loan and will still need to put up collateral to secure the loan.

If you don't qualify for an SBA guaranteed loan but do meet certain other very specific criteria, you might qualify for one of the very few direct loans the SBA makes. These are generally available only for Vietnam veterans, disabled veterans, handicapped individuals, businesses owned by low-income individuals, and businesses in high unemployment areas. In addition, a pilot program launched in 1992 in thirty-five cities in the country was making very small direct loans to very small and homebased businesses that might not otherwise qualify for business loans. Whether the program will be continued or not will depend on the availability of funding and the results of the pilot program.

Q Does the SBA offer any other kinds of loans or financial assistance to small businesses?

There are several other types of financial assistance available through the SBA that can be of value to growing small businesses. Among them:

▶ *The contract loan program.* This program offers short-term lines of credit used to finance labor and materials to perform a specific contract (hence the name *contract loan*). To qualify, a business must have been in business for at least 12 months and must provide a specific product or service under an assignable contract.

▸ *The surety bond guarantee program.* Under this program, the SBA guarantees a bid or performance bond, which may be required to get construction contracts, allowing the small business to qualify for the bond it might not otherwise get. (A bond is a guarantee that work will be performed or completed. If the company being bonded can't complete the project, the bonding company has to step in and complete the contract work or pay any losses caused by default on the contract.)

▸ *Disaster loans.* Loans to help small businesses recover from disasters such as earthquakes or hurricanes.

▸ *Export Revolving Line of Credit program (ERLC).* This program offers revolving lines of credit for small businesses that export their products overseas.

The SBA also licenses and provides some of the funding for certain venture capital firms. These firms are known as Small Business Investment Companies (SBICs) and Minority Enterprise Small Business Investment Companies (MESBICs). Apple Computers, Federal Express, and Nike are examples of the types and sizes of businesses that have received SBIC funding in the past.

Q   Where can I get more information about financial assistance from the SBA?

To find out more about these and other SBA financial assistance programs, call the nearest SBA office. You will find the number listed in the blue pages of your phone book under the federal government listings. You can also call the SBA answer desk at (800) 827–5722 and use the automated answering system to get a prerecorded message giving the phone number of the nearest SBA office to you. A list of SBA regional offices is on pages 474–476.

Q   Are there other government organizations that will help my business get a loan?

Depending on the nature of your business and its ownership, you may also be able to get help from numerous other federal or state agencies. Among them: the Export-Import Bank, the Department of Housing and Urban Development, the Department of Agriculture, and the Department of Commerce (see pages 471–473). Generally, none of the agencies will toss money your way just because you think you've got a hot idea for a new business. But they may have loan programs available that will help your business expand and grow or secure certain types of contracts.

You also should investigate state sources of funding. Look in the state government office listings in the phone book for phone numbers of departments with names like economic development or industrial development. Call and ask if your state has any funding programs available that would help your type of business. You may also be able to get this information from a local Small Business Development Center (see page 476), a Service Corps of Retired Executives office (see page 473), or an SBA office (see page 474). Women and minority business offices (state, city, or federal) are still another source of information (see pages 482 and 492).

Finally, don't ignore management help available from regional, state, or federal government sources. The training sessions and one-on-one counseling often provided by government sponsored organizations can provide needed consulting and other help at low or no cost.

Q **Will the government give me a grant to start a business?**

Chances are you've seen classified ads in newspapers that claim you can get "Free Government Money for Your Business," or something similar. What you need to realize is that while there *is* grant money available from government and other sources, no one is going to give you a grant just because you want to start a business. In fact, rarely does anyone get a grant to *start* a new venture. Grant money that is available is generally awarded for the development of some service that benefits the public or is given to companies that have developed or have the facilities to develop a product or service needed by the government.

Q **Where can I find out what government grants are available?**

The *Federal Register* is one source of information about grants. It is published on weekdays by the federal government and contains a variety of announcements, including announcements of grants. You can either subscribe to the *Federal Register* or can find it at large public or college libraries. Since the subscription fee is $195, you probably will want to read the publication at the library until you see if it would benefit you to get it on a regular basis.

Another source of information about federal grants is the Catalog of Federal Domestic Assistance (CFDA), which is published yearly by the government. This publication is available in some large public libraries and college libraries. Computerized searches are also possible from certain locations in some states. For information about the CFDA, contact:

Federal Domestic Assistance Catalog
General Services Administration
300 7th Street, SW
Washington, DC 20407
(202) 708–5082

Finally, your state or city might have grant money available either directly from their own coffers or, more likely, through federal grant programs that are administered locally. The federal government gives grant money to the state or local government; the local government is responsible for handing out that grant money to deserving local businesses that apply for it.

Your state may have one office designated as a clearing house for information about grants. In New York State, for instance, the Assembly Speaker's Office publishes a newsletter called the *Grants Action Newsletter*, which lists available state grants and includes brief summaries of some federal grants that are open. A state (or city) office of small businesses, department of economic development, or department of industrial development should be able to point you toward sources of grant information in your state or region.

Q **Are there any other sources of government money for small business?**

A program called the Small Business Innovation Research program offers small businesses funding to do research for various federal agencies. These research projects are announced quarterly in the *SBIR Pre-Solicitation Announcement*. In fiscal year 1991, federal agencies participating in the SBIR program made 3,341 awards to small businesses, funding research projects totaling $483.1 million.

Q How does the Innovation Research program work?

Congress created the Small Business Innovation Research (SBIR) program in 1982 to encourage small businesses to do technological research for the government and to encourage the commercialization of research done for the government.

Federal agencies that participate in the SBIR program select certain research topics for funding and then publish a list of those topics in the *SBIR Pre-Solicitation Announcement* which is published quarterly. Businesses interested in doing research on any of the announced topics contact the appropriate agency for the complete solicitation, which gives more specific information about the type of research desired. If the business still wants to apply for funding after reading the solicitation, they submit a formal proposal showing how their company would handle the research project.

Q How do the agencies choose which proposal will receive the award?

Your proposal will be considered along with any others received. If several companies submit suitable proposals for the same project, the best will be selected for the award. If none of the proposals for a particular project are acceptable no award is made. Among the criteria the Department of Defense uses to judge proposals are these:

‣ scientific and technical quality of the proposal
‣ relevance to the topic description (with emphasis on the innovation and originality of the proposal)
‣ qualifications of the principal investigator and other key personnel
‣ adequacy of equipment or facilities
‣ anticipated benefits of the research

Among the reasons proposals get rejected are:

‣ they don't conform to the instructions listed in the Proposal Preparation Instructions and Requirements section (which is included in each SBIR solicitation)
‣ they don't match the needs specified in the solicitation

> ◗ the company doesn't appear to have the stability or experience to complete the project

Q **How much money would I get if I received an SBIR award?**

There are two levels of awards, Phase I and Phase II. Phase I awards are made in amounts up to $100,000, with work on the project being started and completed within a six-month period. Phase II awards are for up to $750,000. You cannot apply for a Phase II award unless you received Phase I funding for the same project.

Q **How can I get the *SBIR Pre-Solicitation Announcement?***

Contact the SBA Office of Innovation, Research, and Technology and ask to be put on the mailing list for the *SBA/SBIR Pre-Solicitation Announcement*. The address is:

Office of Innovation, Research, and Technology
U.S. Small Business Administration
409 3rd Street, SW, 8th fl.
Washington, DC 20416
(202) 205–7777

Q **Once I get a business going and see I need more cash, how can I get it?**

The traditional ways include getting bank loans, inventory or receivables financing, a contract loan (if available), funding from family or friends or a second or even a third mortgage on your house. You could also take a partner or limited partner (a general partner usually works in the business with you while a limited partner usually just puts up money) or incorporate and seek investors who will give you money in exchange for equity (ownership) in your company.

Q **What is venture capital?**

Venture capital is money invested in a business in return for partial ownership. Generally, venture capital is used to fund high-risk businesses that show the potential for high profit (for example, $50 million in sales within 5 to 8 years). Venture capital firms make their profits by selling shares of stock of the successful ventures to the general public.

Q **What do venture capitalists look for?**

In addition to a product or service that has the potential for rapid growth, venture capitalists want to see a management team that has the ability to take the business concept and make it work. If you want to start a business in an industry you know nothing about, if you have no experience running businesses, or if you want to run the business on your own, don't waste postage sending business plans to venture capitalists.

Q **How much money do venture capitalists usually invest?**

There's no set amount; however, most are looking to invest at least a half a million dollars since companies requiring less than that amount are likely not to have the potential to become large enough and profitable enough to make the investment pay off.

Q **Will venture capitalists give me cash to start a business?**

Although some venture capital firms do provide seed money (start-up funds) for some businesses, most of the time venture capital isn't invested until there is an available track record indicating the business is successful and has potential for growth. However, you might find start-up funds from one or more local "angels" (small investors, also known as informal venture capitalists). It is usually through these private investors that new businesses raise enough money to get a business going or to do initial development work.

Q **Where do I find these "angels"?**

The angels often come from your personal contacts—friends, family, professional references. Some people also advertise for investors in the business opportunity section of newspapers. If you plan to advertise for investors, it would be advisable to consult your attorney first to avoid running amuck of laws governing the advertising of investment opportunities in your state. (These laws are often called blue-sky laws). One way some entrepreneurs try to avoid hassle over investment advertising laws is to advertise for a partner and include phrases in the ad such as "substantial equity position for the right partner."

 Where do I find venture capitalists?

There are several routes you can follow. One is to attend venture capital club meetings in your area. These can help you make connections and learn what venture capitalists and angels expect from you.

To find out about such groups near you, call for contact information:

Association of Venture Clubs
265 East 100 South, Suite 300
P. O. Box 3358
Salt Lake City, UT 84110–3358
(801) 364–1100

Other potential ways to locate investors are through attorneys, accountants, colleges and universities that teach business, Service Corps of Retired Executives (SCORE) offices, Small Business Development Centers (SBDCs), or SBA offices. In addition, there are directories of venture capital firms that describe the speciality of each firm, the size of the investments the firm usually makes, and other pertinent information.

Such directories are available at large public libraries. You can also get a microcomputer program called VenCap that lets you search electronically for this information if you have an IBM PC or compatible computer. For information about VenCap and current pricing, contact:

AI Research Corporation
2003 St. Julien Court
Mountain View, CA 94043
(415) 852–9140

 Does it matter which venture capital firm I contact?

Yes. Venture capital firms usually specialize in particular industries. If you are looking for money for a bio-tech company, it is a waste of time and postage to send your business plan to venture capitalists that specialize in entertainment.

Q. **What should I do to contact these firms? Do I call? Go to their offices?**

The best way to contact venture capital firms is to get a reference to the firm or investor through your banker, a venture capital club, or some other source. If you can't find anyone to make a reference and don't meet anyone through your own networkings, call firms listed in directories and ask to speak to whoever handles your type of business. If interest is expressed, find out whether the contact prefers to see the plan first or would be open to having you present the plan in a personal interview.

Q. **How else can I find investors?**

There are also people who "rep" a plan (find investors for you through contacts they have). Expect to pay a fee to such representatives (as much as 5 percent of the money raised), but this fee should come out of the money raised; you shouldn't have to pay any up-front fees except, perhaps, for travel, mailings, and similar out-of-pocket expenses your representative may incur. These people are often called financial consultants. You may be able to find them through business brokers or through private networking.

Q. **What will investors expect in return for money they invest?**

Investors will expect some degree of ownership and a way to get their money out of the business after a set period of time. The amount of ownership you would have to give up will vary with what you are bringing into the business in the way of experience, money, value of the business at the time of financing, and so on. If you have a great idea but no management team, the venture firm might want to hand-pick people to run the company. The investors will generally plan on getting their money back by selling their shares of the business to others through public or private stock offerings.

10.
Making It Legal

You're honest, hard-working, and you report all the income from your home business. So you don't have to worry about lawsuits, right?

Wrong!

No matter how small your business is, it is likely to be governed by a complex web of local, state, and federal laws. Some of these laws are designed to protect your customers, suppliers, creditors, and employees from being harmed by your business or its activities. Others protect you from competitors, suppliers, and even your clients. Still others exist (as municipal servants will invariably tell you) because "that's the way it's done" or because "that's what the law says."

Typical of this type of law is a statute in a New York State township requiring individuals who want to start a home business to get a building permit, have the home office inspected by a town building inspector, and get a certificate of occupancy for the "office" even if they will be working at the dining room table, won't be making physical changes to the home, and won't be having customers come to the house.

Q **What do I have to do to make my business legal?**

The regulations with which you'll need to comply in order to be legal vary according to what you do and where your business is located, but typically, with a

162

business owned and operated by one individual who has no employees (sole proprietorship), you will need to follow some or all of these steps:

- ▶ Register your business name and get a certificate of doing business under an assumed name (commonly called a DBA). In some states you are required to register your business name whether you are operating under an assumed name or not.
- ▶ Publish your intention to do business in an official notice (required in some but not all states).
- ▶ Get required permits and licenses (these will be in addition to the DBA certificate).
- ▶ Comply with zoning regulations, regulations regarding signs on your business property, environmental protection laws (if any apply to your business), licensing laws, etc.
- ▶ Make arrangements to collect state sales tax if you sell taxable products or services.
- ▶ Keep accurate income and expense records and report your income to the IRS and state tax authorities.
- ▶ Pay owed income taxes and self-employment tax quarterly.
- ▶ Meet any specific bonding or insurance regulations your locality or state has instituted for your type of business.

Depending on the nature of your business you might also have to comply with noise codes, sanitation regulations, laws governing placement and size of signs, or other laws. If you add employees you will also have to comply with all applicable state and federal labor laws.

Q **Are there any laws that could prevent me from starting a home business?**

Unfortunately there could be. Despite the millions of people who work at home, many communities have zoning or other regulations prohibiting home businesses. Although the intent of such laws may be to maintain property values and prevent a residential neighborhood from turning into a little Main Street, most home businesses generate less neighborhood traffic and far less noise than the average car- or truck-driving suburban teenager.

Other laws or regulations might also interfere with your work-at-home plans, including labor laws, health codes, and licensing requirements. The only way you will know for sure what rules affect you is to ask appropriate local agencies and officials.

Q Why don't communities change the outdated laws?

Many communities are attempting to change the laws, but often change does not come easily. Municipalities may be caught in an intractable situation involving residents who want the change, residents who fear the change, and residents who howl "not fair" because their type of business will not be included among those deemed acceptable for home pursuit.

The resulting battle can be time-consuming and costly. The town of Southold in New York was sued after it implemented a zoning law change that allowed certain types of home businesses. The citizen who filed the suit (and won) claimed the new law was illegal because the town had not first done an environmental impact study. As a result, the town had to do the environmental study, schedule and hold new hearings, and then vote on the law a second time—a process that took many months.

Q Are the laws the same throughout a state?

No, zoning laws are established locally, often at the township, city, or village level. Furthermore, each town or village decides for itself what types of home businesses it will allow. Thus in one community you might be able to run a home business that has up to two employees while in another community the same business might be restricted from having any employees. In still another community you might be able to have a homebased business if you are a fisherman or carpenter but not if you are a real estate agent or insurance broker.

Q Don't a lot of home businesses just ignore zoning laws?

Many people do operate businesses in violation of zoning regulations. In some communities, there is no attempt to enforce the regulations unless a resident complains and forces officials to close down the illegal home business. In fact, according to a report in the *Chicago Tribune*, there was one community in Illinois where

164

two trustees of an Illinois town had to excuse themselves from discussions of a proposed zoning law that would legalize home businesses. The reason? Each of the trustees had a homebased business.

You cannot assume, however, that it is OK for you to disregard local law because *some* town boards don't enforce regulations and *some* people get away with operating on the sly. If there are laws prohibiting your type of home business, it will only take one complaint to plunge you into a pot of legal hot water.

Q **Who would complain?**

Neighbors are generally the source of such complaints. A neighbor may not like seeing your truck parked in the street, may think your equipment interferes with TV reception, or may not like it that you wear a single earring or your son has shoulder-length hair. The motivation for the complaint doesn't matter; if you are in violation of the law and a complaint is filed, town officials have to follow established procedures to deal with the complaint.

Even if your neighbors wouldn't complain, someone outside the immediate neighborhood might. Under the heading of "life isn't fair" comes an incident where zoning officials were alerted to an illegal home business after a postal carrier made a comment to his supervisor about the volume of mail going to one home on his route.

Q **What would happen if someone did file a complaint?**

Usually you would be forced to stop running the business from your home and could be fined, and even possibly put in jail, if you continue to violate the ordinance. Fines can be as high as $75 to $100 a day or more.

Q **Is there anything I can do if town officials say I can't run a business from my home or apartment?**

If your business creates no traffic, noise, odor, or other neighborhood disturbances you might consider trying to get the laws changed. Many communities are beginning to realize their laws are antiquated and need to be updated.

If you don't want to try to change the law, you might want to try to get a variance. A variance is a license allowing you to do something that is contrary to the general law.

Enterprising individuals sometimes tackle the problem in other ways, too. A woman in Florida who raised plants as a hobby decided to turn her hobby into a business by selling plants at a flea market. She applied for and got a state nursery license, but when she applied for a business certificate from the town, she was told by town officials she couldn't run a business from her home and would be prosecuted if she accepted any money for her plants.

Infuriated, the woman wrote a letter to the town licensing agency and sent copies to county officials. In the letter she compared her business to that of an Avon representative who stores and sorts inventory at home but actually sells the product and delivers it to clients away from the home. She added that if she were denied the right to run her business from home, she would make every possible effort to see that Avon representatives and other people who did similar work would also be denied the right to work at home. The woman got her business license.

Still another tactic was used by Bernadine and Joe Foley, founders of Westchester Book Composition, Inc., when town officials told them they would have to stop operating their business from a garage on their property. They realized it was only a matter of time until Westchester Book would outgrow the converted garage, but they weren't quite ready to move. So they challenged the zoning law in court. "The town couldn't force us to stop operating the business while we were contesting the suit," explains Joe Foley. "It cost us thousands of dollars in legal fees and eventually we lost," adds Bernadine, "but it bought us the time we needed to get ready for the move."

Q How do I find out about zoning laws?

To find out what the zoning laws are in your community, look in the blue pages of your phone book (the government listings), and find the number of your town or city zoning board or building department. If you can't find a phone number for either of these departments, call the main administration number for the town and ask where to get the information.

Describe the type of business you want to start and the nature of the location from which you'd like to operate (home, main street, building in an area that appears to be a mixture of residences and offices, etc.). Ask what laws might apply to that type of business and if any special permits or licenses will be needed. If you don't want to give away your identity, call anonymously. If you want to be sure to maintain your anonymity and you live in a community where the phone company is selling caller identification services, make your call from a pay phone. (Caller identification systems allow people who are receiving a call to see the phone number of the person making the call.)

Q If a business was operated on the property before I bought it, will I be able to run a business there, too?

Not necessarily. If the property is in a residential area, the people before you might have been operating illegally or might have had a special use permit that won't apply to your business. Other factors can also come into play. In Southern California, a horse breeder ran afoul of zoning laws after buying a ranch because he had twenty-nine horses on the ranch, and the zoning laws only permitted twenty-one. The only way you will know for sure is to check the zoning laws or have an attorney do it for you.

Q Where do I find out about state and federal laws affecting my business?

Local offices of the Small Business Administration (SBA), the Service Corps of Retired Executives (SCORE), or the Small Business Development Corporation (SBDC) in your area may be able to provide the information you need or tell you where to get it (see appendix 2). Look in the blue pages of your phone book under federal government for SBA and SCORE locations near you, or call the SBA automated information system at (800) 827–5722 for the location of the nearest office. If there are any SBDCs in your area they will be under the state listings rather than the federal government listings. Still another possible source of information will be colleges or universities in your region that have small business or entrepreneurial courses or majors.

Q Should I use my own name or a business name?

Many people operate under their own name at least during the start-up phase of their business. Doing so lets them avoid having to open a separate bank account for the business. While this works for some businesses, others find telling people to make checks out to them personally makes the business look small and unprofessional.

Q **Can I add "and Associates" or "and Company" to my real name without having to register it as a business name?**

Adding words to or changing your legal name in any way makes it a fictitious name and will most likely subject you to registration requirements.

Q **What happens if I don't register my business name?**

Most banks will not cash checks made out to your business name unless you have given them a copy of your DBA. Thus, if you don't register your business name and a customer gives you a check made out to that name, you either have to return the check and ask for a new one or register the name and get the DBA before cashing the check. If you try to register the business name and someone is already using a confusingly similar name, you may not be allowed to register your chosen name.

Q **What will it cost to register my business name and get the licenses I need?**

Usually the cost of a DBA is relatively insignificant. Fees quoted from different parts of the country range from $10 to $60. Fees you may have to pay for other permits, licenses, or bonds can be steep, however, running to hundreds or maybe even thousands of dollars, depending on the nature of your business.

Q **What do I have to do to register the business name?**

You should go to the county or city clerk's office and search the records to see if there is any other business in your area using the name you want to use. If no other business is using that name, you will fill out a form, sign it, get it notarized, and pay a fee. In a few states, sole proprietorships and partnerships are registered at the state level rather than local. (Corporations are always registered at the state level often through the Department of State.)

Q **What can I do if someone else *is* using the name?**

Often, the only thing you can do is choose another name. To avoid wasting time, it would be a good idea to check local phone books to see if anyone is using the business name you want before you go to register the name and to have several alternatives in mind if the name you prefer turns out to be already in use.

Q **Can I use any name that isn't registered in the local area?**

There may be companies that operate regionally that have trademarks or prior use rights to a name, which would bar you from using that name even though it is not registered locally. You couldn't call your local computer company Apple Computer, for instance, even if Apple Computer has not registered its name in your locality. You might be able to register Apple Stationery, Apple Chair Company, or other names that combined the word *apple* with something unrelated to computers.

Q **What happens if I do accidentally use another business's name?**

If the business sells in your area and has prior use rights to the name, they could force you to stop using the business name. You would then have to alert your customers, change your stationery, change your phone listings and business cards, and so on.

Q **How can I find out if businesses outside my immediate area are using the name I want to use?**

If you have access to a computer and modem and subscribe to online information services, the easiest and fastest way to check is to search several electronic databases for the name you want to use. Dialog, GEnie, and CompuServe all offer trademark and trade name databases as well as electronic versions of *Thomas's Register* and other business directories. If you don't have access to a computer and modem, or can't afford the search fees, ask the reference librarian at your public library to help you find the appropriate print references.

Q **Do I really have to go to all that trouble?**

Like so many other things in business, it's a judgment call. If you will be operating only in a small local area, and could, if you had to, change your name without a tremendous loss of money or customers, you may want to skip the national name search and just search for similar names in use in your area. If you proceed this way, you must realize that if some company based in another region is using the name as trademark or trade name and moves into your area, they might be able to force you to stop using the name.

Q **When do I register a business name?**

The time to register your business name is as soon as you are sure you are going to go into business and decide on a business name. You wouldn't want to go to the trouble and expense of getting business stationery, opening a bank account in the business name, and advertising the name if you won't be allowed to register it.

Q **Do I have to register in every county, state, and city I plan to do business in?**

If you only maintain an office in one location and do not physically travel from place to place selling merchandise, you probably will not be required to register your name in any place other than your own county, city, or state. For instance, if you live in Kansas and have a mail order business that advertises in a national publication, you would not be required to register your business name in every state in which you have customers. (Even though you may not be required to register your business name in other states or localities, you might find it beneficial to register your business name as a trademark either in one or more states or nationally to prevent other companies from using a business name like yours to sell similar goods. See chapter 20 for additional information on trademarks.)

Things work differently, however, if you are a flea-market vendor or craftsperson who travels from place to place selling goods. In such cases, you may be considered to have a physical presence (which is called *nexus*) in each locality in which you set up a booth or rent a table to sell your goods. You may therefore be required to register your business, get a license, and to collect and remit local sales taxes. If you are unsure of the requirements, show promoters and other vendors should be able to tell you what to do and whom to contact. *

If you have offices in several counties or states you may be required to register in those areas. If you operate as a corporation you have to register as a foreign corporation in any state you have offices in other than the state in which the corporation secures its charter.

Q How do I sign up to collect sales tax?

If your state collects a sales tax, call the state tax department and ask for information about getting a sales tax number, also called sales tax permit, resale number, or resale permit.

Q Do I have to pay sales tax on items I buy for the business?

What is taxable and what isn't taxable varies from state to state, but generally, if you buy taxable items that will be consumed in operating your business (say, paper or toner cartridges) you either have to pay the sales tax on them when you purchase them, or, if you use your reseller's number to avoid paying tax at the time of purchase you will have to pay a use tax for using the items. The use tax will be equal to the sales tax you would have paid. The difference is that you will send it in at the same time you send in sales taxes you have collected on items you have sold to your customers.

On the other hand, if you are purchasing something that will be used to make a product you will sell (a hard drive that you will be installing in a computer system you build from scratch for a client, for example), you do not have to pay sales or use tax on the purchase if you have a sales tax number. The reason is that sales taxes in the United States are paid by the consumer, not the manufacturer. **

---

*Some flea-market vendors and craftspeople ignore the local laws and do not register with the appropriate officials or collect sales tax. Although some get away with it, breaking the law is never advisable. Furthermore, state and local officials often roam through many of the larger flea markets and crafts shows spot-checking for licenses and collection of sales taxes.

**In certain countries manufacturers may encounter a value-added tax. With a value-added tax the manufacturer *does* pay a tax on the goods and supplies used in manufacturing the product. The cost of that tax is added onto the other costs in determining the final price of the product to the consumer. (If the item would cost $100 and the company had to pay taxes equal to $5 for goods used in the manufacture of the item, the purchase price would be $105.)

Q **Do I have to have an attorney to start a business?**

You aren't required to have an attorney to start a business, and many businesses do not have legal help getting started. If your business is regulated by local, state, or federal authorities, if you will be writing or accepting contracts involving significant sums of money, or if you will be operating as a partnership or corporation, it is highly advisable to consult with an attorney. The money you spend up front to make sure things are set up properly and in your best interests can save you hundreds of thousands of dollars and much aggravation in the future.

11.
Who Owns the Business?

Many people think about starting a business the same way they would think about starting to paint the house, starting a new career, or starting any other big project: they think about *doing something* rather than *owning* something. Yet, when you start a business, in the eyes of the law you become a business owner and have to choose a form of business ownership. The form of ownership you choose has important legal, financial, tax, and marketing implications.

Q **What forms of ownership are there?**

There are three primary forms of business ownership:

- sole proprietorship (you are the only owner)
- partnership (two or more parties join together in the business, splitting up the work load, profits, and financing of the business however they wish)
- corporation (a legal entity, which under law has a "life" of its own separate from any individual who owns the corporation)

Q **What are the advantages of a sole proprietorship?**

A sole proprietorship is the easiest form of business to set up and run. Here are a few of the reasons why:

▸ *You make all the decisions.* You alone can decide what to sell and how to sell it, when to expand the business and when to pull back, when to look for financing, when to buy new equipment, when and how long to work, and when to take the day off—without having to justify your decision to anyone.

▸ *You can take money out of the business easily.* Although it is not advisable, you don't even have to maintain a separate bank account for a sole proprietorship. As long as you keep accurate records of income and expenses, you could run it out of your personal checkbook.

▸ *You can use losses to offset other income* on your personal tax return.

▸ *Start-up costs are relatively low.* You generally have less paperwork and fewer regulations with which to comply as a sole proprietor than you do with other forms of business.

Q Are there any disadvantages of operating as a sole proprietor?

Virtually every book and magazine article discussing what form of business a business owner should choose will tell you the biggest disadvantage of a sole proprietorship is that you have unlimited liability for the actions of your business. In other words, *you are personally responsible for all business debts and actions and could lose your personal assets if the business goes bankrupt or gets sued.*

But also remember that *as the owner of any small business, you are likely to take the same risk no matter what form of business you start.* Contrary to what you may read in books and how-to articles, incorporating a very small business does not automatically protect you from liability for the company's debts or actions.*

---

* Unfortunately, you will still find many books and articles and even an occasional individual with a degree in law or accounting stating that incorporating shields personal assets from liability. What they don't bother to explain, or perhaps never really investigate, is how that protection comes about or how it changes with the size of the business. See page 181 for additional information.

Other disadvantages of a sole proprietorship include:

▶ *There is no continuity of ownership.* Usually when the owner of a sole proprietorship dies, the business comes to an end. While you could train someone to take over the business and make arrangements to pass on the business to a family member should you die, there may be no one in your family who has the interest or ability to carry on without you.

▶ *Financing your business may be more difficult.* Banks and other lenders may be reluctant to loan your unincorporated business money.

▶ *Fringe benefits you can give yourself are quite limited.* The amount you can put tax-free into pension plans and the deductibility of health insurance premiums are both limited, for instance.

▶ *Getting and keeping good employees* may be difficult as the company grows.

Q **How does a partnership work?**

A partnership lets two or more people (or in some cases businesses) work together to achieve a common goal. There are different kinds of partnerships, but each partnerships must have at least one general partner. (In most very small business partnerships, each partner is a general partner.) The partners share in the profits and the work according to an agreed arrangement. Each general partner can act on behalf of the partnership, doing anything necessary to run the business (hire employees, sign contracts, make purchases, etc.).

Q **What are the advantages of a partnership?**

The chief advantages of a partnership are:

▶ *It lets you pool resources* with others to build a larger, more profitable business.

▶ *It is easy for the partners to take money out of the business.* This is one of the reasons many professional practices use a partnership format.

175

▸ *The life of a partnership can be easily limited* to suit your needs. Thus a partnership can be formed for a specific project or to achieve a specific objective and can then be dissolved.

▸ *It may allow you to bring needed capital into the business* to finance long-term projects or growth.

▸ *You may have lower costs and fewer legal regulations* than you would running the business as a corporation.

▸ *The partnership itself does not pay income tax.* All profits and losses get passed along to the individual partners.

Q **What are the disadvantages of operating a partnership?**

Disadvantages of running your business as a partnership include:

▸ *Partners don't always get along.* Frequent causes of disagreements are disputes over work loads (who is doing how much); spending (one partner thinks the other is a penny pincher and the other thinks the first is a spendthrift); and methods of operation.

▸ *Each general partner is liable for the actions of all the other general partners.* Thus, if your partner leases a new Mercedes in the partnership name and then skips town with the car, the partnership—and you personally as a partner—would be responsible for paying for the car. The same holds true if your partner commits the partnership to any contract or does anything illegal in the partnership's name.

▸ *You may incur more legal fees* with a partnership than with a sole proprietorship. Although it isn't always done, it is in your best interest to have a formal partnership agreement with your partners and to have the agreement drawn up by an attorney, or at least reviewed by one. If you don't have a formal partnership agreement and the partnership ends, you are likely to end up with even more legal fees to untangle disputes over partnership debts and assets.

▶ *Changes in ownership* mean the partnership technically comes to an end (dissolves); if a partner is bought out or a new partner is added, however, the business can continue.

▶ *Fringe benefits,* as with sole proprietorships, are limited compared to those available with regular corporations.

Q **Does my spouse automatically own part of my business?**

Depending on the state laws where you live, your spouse may automatically have a legal interest in your business and be entitled to a share of the business if you divorce. This holds true even for partnerships. (The partner's spouse may have a legal interest in the partnership even if he or she has never been involved in the operation of the partnership.)

Q **What happens if my spouse and I get divorced?**

Depending on where you live and what precautions you have taken, you might have to "buy out" your spouse's interest in the business as part of a divorce settlement, even if the spouse never has worked in the business.

Q **I'm thinking about going into business with a friend. Are we both sole proprietors?**

According to the Uniform Partnership Act (UPA), which is a body of law that establishes basic guidelines for partnerships,* a partnership is "an association of two or more persons to carry on as co-owners of a business." If you and your friend work together in the business you would be considered partners, whether you formally agree to be partners or not. That means you would each be bound by all the rights and responsibilities and liabilities of a formal partnership arrangement. Thus, it would be advisable to have a formal partnership agreement with your friend.

Q **Why do we need a partnership agreement?**

*The Uniform Partnership Act (UPA) has been adopted with some variations by all states except Louisiana.

While you and your partner may be the best of friends now, it is very easy for misunderstandings to develop in a partnership, just like it is easy for misunderstandings to develop in any agreement that isn't written down. Several psychologists who were also good friends learned this lesson the hard way. They agreed to open a jointly run practice. They were advised to have a formal partnership agreement, but since they were all "experts" in dealing with human relationships, they decided it wouldn't be necessary. Less than a year later their joint effort ended, leaving them engaged in bitter and expensive legal disputes over ownership of partnership property and responsibility for various debts.

Q **What should a partnership agreement cover?**

Among the basic points that should be explained in the agreement are:

- the name of the partnership
- the function or purpose of the partnership
- the duration of the partnership
- the duties and extent of authority of each partner
- the number and kinds of partners (limited, general, silent, etc.)
- the method for admitting new partners
- the method for dissolving the partnership should the partners be unable to work together
- the contributions (money, labor, equipment, etc.) of each partner to the partnership
- the method for dividing profits and losses
- how the books will be kept
- how property used in the partnership will be owned
- the method to be used to resolve disputes
- how absences from the business or disability will be handled
- what buy-out procedures should be followed in the event that a partner should leave the partnership or die

Q **What happens if we don't have a partnership agreement?**

If you don't have a partnership agreement and your partnership breaks up, you have no way of proving any verbal agreements about who contributed what to the partnership or whether anything contributed to the partnership became partnership property or remained the property of the original owner. Thus any business equipment you brought into the partnership (your computer system, scanner, and laser printer, for example) could be considered partnership property that has to be sold to pay the partnership's debts or split up between the partners.

Q Do we need an attorney to write the partnership agreement?

It is advisable to have an attorney to draw up the partnership agreement.

Q Are there partners who just contribute money and don't get involved with the business at all?

Yes. Usually that kind of arrangement is set up as a limited partnership and specifically spells out when and how and under what terms the investor(s) will get back their money. It is frequently used for financing small businesses. Limited partners are not liable for debts or actions of the partnership; the most they can lose is the amount they invest.

Q How does a corporation differ from a partnership?

A corporation is a legal "person." In other words, it has an identity that is distinct and separate from the individuals who own the corporation. Like a real person, the corporation is legally entitled to enter into contracts, conduct business, own property, lend or borrow money, and so on.

Q What are the advantages of incorporating?

The primary benefits of operating under a corporate form generally revolve around tax and marketing considerations and ease of attracting investors. In real life, while the benefits of incorporation may technically be available to a business of any size, in practice, very small businesses may gain little or no benefit by incorporating until they have employees or can reap tax benefits by incorporating.

That said, these are the potential benefits of the corporate form of business:

- You may be able to raise capital more easily as a corporation than as a sole proprietor; however, there are no guarantees.[*]
- It may be easier to transfer ownership in a corporation than it is in a sole proprietorship or a partnership.
- Under some circumstances your tax rate might be lower.
- If you have employees, incorporation may protect your personal assets if an employee does something that causes the company to be sued.
- You may be able to give yourself more company-paid fringe benefits as an employee of your corporation.
- You may be able to get and keep good employees by offering them stock in the company.
- You may gain estate-planning benefits.
- You might find incorporation preferable to a partnership if you will be going into business with one or more other people.

Q **What are the disadvantages of incorporating?**

Among the disadvantages of incorporating are:

- *Your cost of doing business usually increases* due to added fees you have to pay.
- *The amount of paperwork you have to do increases* because of legal record-keeping requirements.
- *You may be subject to "double" taxation,* having your profits taxed once at the corporate level and once again as an individual.
- *The IRS could limit your salary as an employee of your own corporation* to an amount it considers reasonable and treat amounts above the "reasonable" salary to be dividends.
- *Your personal finances must be kept completely separate from the corporation's finances.* Thus, you can't dip into the corporate bank account if you come up a little short on personal cash for the week.
- *Closing the corporation's doors* permanently can be somewhat complicated and costly.

[*]Banks are going to look for the same thing whether you are incorporated or not: your ability to repay a loan. Being incorporated may make it appear you are more serious about running your business. However, incorporation in no way assures that you will be able to find people to buy shares of the business.

Q **Doesn't the corporate form of business protect your personal assets?**

No, it won't necessarily protect your personal assets. Here's why:

Even though you, as a shareholder of your own corporation, may not be responsible for the debts of the corporation (since the corporation is a separate "person"), there is nothing to prevent someone from suing you personally for actions you performed. For instance, suppose you personally created an ad campaign for your corporation criticizing a competitor. The competitor views the campaign as malicious and untrue and decides to sue. They might sue your corporation and you, personally, as the creator of the ad. While you would not be liable for any settlement the corporation has to pay as a result of the suit, your personal assets could be attached to pay off any judgment the competitor won in its case against you the individual.

In addition, even though you might not technically be liable for the corporation's debts, if you owned a very small corporation, chances are you would have to dig into your own personal bankroll to come up with the money to fight the lawsuit.

Thus incorporation does not necessarily prevent liability problems. One important step you can take to help protect your assets against loss is to obtain adequate liability insurance (business property, professional errors and omissions, and product liability).

The other fallacy about incorporation is that somehow it protects you from paying off any bad debts the corporation incurs. But things rarely work that way. While you are not automatically responsible for the corporation's debts the way you would be responsible for your sole proprietorship or partnership debts, *rarely will you be able to get a loan for a new small corporation unless you sign a personal guarantee, which means that you, personally, will have to pay back the loan if the corporation defaults.* You may also have to sign personal guarantees on building or equipment lease agreements.

Q **How old do you have to be to incorporate?**

The minimum age ranges from 18 to 21 depending on the state.

Q **Can I start a corporation with only one person?**

Most states allow you to start a corporation with only one shareholder.

Q When is it a good idea to incorporate?

A good accountant who is used to dealing with small business tax matters can advise you whether or not to incorporate. In general, he or she should help you evaluate whether business growth or other individual business circumstances indicate that incorporating is likely to benefit you by doing any of these things:

- cut your tax bill
- give you better fringe benefits
- increase the amount of money you can put tax free into your pension plan
- make your company appear bigger than it is
- allow you to retain money in the corporation to meet some specific need
- allow for smooth transfer of ownership
- make it possible to expand the business by bringing in investors

Q I've heard it's a good idea to incorporate in Delaware, because of tax breaks and other benefits. Is this true?

As a small business with just a few shareholder-employees, the easiest and best place to incorporate is usually within your own state. Although Delaware may offer some tax breaks and potentially more statutory protection from liability for corporate directors than your own state, for a small corporation the advantages are likely to be outweighed by the disadvantages. For instance, you will have to appoint someone in Delaware to be an agent for your corporation (there are companies in Delaware that do this); you will have to pay an annual franchise (corporate) tax to the state of Delaware; and if you incorporate in Delaware but do business in another state (the state where you live, for instance), you will have to file an application in your home state to do business as a foreign corporation and will then have to pay a franchise fee as well as income taxes in your home state.

Q What will it cost to incorporate in my own state?

The actual fees charged to incorporate may be anywhere from under $50 to a few hundred dollars, depending on what state you live in. Attorney's fees, if you use an attorney to incorporate your business, can run from $400 or $500 to close to $1,000 or more depending on where you are located and how much work the attorney has to do for you.

Q Should I incorporate to get investors?

If you have people who want to invest, incorporation is one way to set things up so they might be able to get their money out later. (A limited partnership might also accomplish your goals.) But incorporating won't automatically bring you investors.

Q What kinds of corporations are there?

There are two basic forms of corporations: regular corporations (called C corporations) and S corporations (formerly called subchapter S corporations). Small corporations often organize under the S format. Another term associated with corporations is "close" or "closed" (or sometimes, "closely held"). This refers to a corporation that is owned by a few private individuals rather than having its shares available to the general public.

Q What's the difference between C corporations and S corporations?

The main difference that is of concern to small businesses is the way profits and losses are handled. In a regular corporation the profits are taxed to the corporation and losses absorbed by it. In an S corporation, profits and losses are passed through to the shareholder and taxed at the shareholder's tax rate.

Q Which type is best?

The answer depends on the individual circumstances of your business. If the shareholder's personal tax rate is lower than the corporate tax rate, an S corporation may be preferable. Businesses subject to the alternative minimum tax may find the regular corporate status preferable since the alternate minimum rate is lower for corporations than for individuals.

Q What types of businesses does the IRS consider personal service corporations?

Corporations offering services primarily in the fields of accounting, actuarial science, architecture, engineering, health, law, the performing arts, and consulting are considered personal service corporations. Writers, artists, and sales agents do not fall into this classification.

Q Do I need an attorney or accountant to incorporate?

Technically you could incorporate without outside help, but it is not advisable. Because of the complexity of corporate law, you should get help and advice from an accountant and/or attorney. But not just *any* accountant or attorney. Look for one who has experience dealing with small corporations. Nadine Keilholz, publisher of *Sweepstakes Update* newsletter, learned that lesson the hard way. Explains Nadine,

> Before we incorporated, all we had to worry about was a quarterly state sales tax form and payment and a Schedule C along with our personal federal filing. As soon as we incorporated, I started getting forms I'd never heard of, from taxing authorities I didn't even know existed. I was buried up to my ears in 940s, 941s, state unemployment taxes, state intangibles taxes (on the value of stock), and about twenty other things. It seemed that every week I got two or three new forms to fill out. And that doesn't even count the environmental impact statements and other nontax-related things.
>
> Unfortunately, the accountant we had been using was fine for personal taxes and a small personal business—but after about two years, when I started getting notices from the IRS, FICA, the state of Florida, et cetera, that we had unfiled returns and unpaid taxes, I found out that he didn't know how to handle a corporation.

The problem, Keilholz eventually discovered, was that although the accountant had actually mailed in their tax forms and checks for payment, he hadn't submitted the proper transmittal forms with the returns. "All that money was sitting there with the IRS instead of having been forwarded to FICA, or with one state agency instead of having been sent on to another."

Keilholz has since found another accountant and says "the peace of mind of just being able to throw all of our receipts, our check register, and the myriad forms that we receive each month into an envelope and send them to him and know that it'll be done—and done right—are well worth his fee."

Q **How do I keep corporate minutes?**

There are companies that sell incorporation kits with fill-in-the-blank forms you can use to record corporate minutes (which are a record of shareholders' meetings). These kits generally have sample articles of incorporation, bylaws, notices of meetings, stock ledgers, and transfer ledgers (for recording names and addresses of stockholders), and bank stock certificates. A kit put out by a company called E-Z Legal Forms is available for under $15 at discount office supply stores.

Q **When is it advantageous to form a nonprofit corporation?**

Nonprofit corporations may offer certain tax advantages to corporations formed for charitable or other kinds of work. They may be eligible for certain grants, research money, reduced postage costs, and other benefits. Directors and executives of the corporation can be paid decent salaries and get reimbursed for expenses. The rules covering nonprofits are even more complex than those covering C or S corporations and should be discussed with an attorney or accountant familiar with nonprofit management concerns.

Q **How do I choose a board of directors?**

Your board of directors will generally be responsible for determining corporate policy and deciding how to conduct the business. The directors are elected by your stockholders; the corporate officers are chosen by the directors. Thus, if you are the only stockholder, you might appoint yourself director, then, as director, appoint yourself, or whoever else you choose, to each of the corporate officer positions required by law in your state (generally, president, vice president, and treasurer), unless your state requires different people hold those positions or requires corporations to have more than one director.

The bigger you grow your business, the more important your choice of directors. If you are looking for outside capital, investors are likely to want to see that your directors and officers are qualified to run the business. If you should have the type of business capable of attracting venture capital, the investors may also become directors.

Q **Can I start the business as a sole proprietor and incorporate later?**

Yes. In fact, it is often advisable to do that since a sole proprietorship is the easiest form of business to start. You simply run the business as a sole proprietorship until it grows big enough to warrant the time and expense of incorporating.

Q Can I switch back and forth between a regular corporation and an S corporation?

You must incorporate first as a regular (C) corporation. Then, if the shareholders agree to do so, you may elect S corporation status. If you choose to terminate S status for tax or other reasons, you can do so at any time. However, once you have terminated your S status you may not elect it again for 5 years.

Q Is there any other way of working with someone else?

If you don't want to form a partnership or corporation, the only other ways to work with other people are to hire them as employees or retain them under an independent contractor or subcontractor agreement. In either case, though, the individuals are just working in return for money.

12.

What Equipment and Supplies Do I Need to Get Started?

Whenever I meet someone who says they have an office in their basement I conjure up images of the first home office I ever saw. It was my father's workshop—a tiny area off to one side of the basement steps that was furnished with an old, scarred workbench and a beat-up metal stool. There, under the glare of a single, bare lightbulb, my father would spend his evenings changing vacuum tubes in TV chassis and trying to coax the broken-down sets back into working order for the people who had asked him to do the repairs.

Television sets and technology have changed a lot since then. And so have the equipment and supply needs of many home offices and away-from-home small businesses. Some businesses today couldn't exist without one or more microcomputers; others feel the world will crash in around them if their facsimile machine or their modem breaks down. But many business owners function quite well with nothing more high-tech than a telephone and a file box.

The variety of equipment available today can make it quite confusing at times to know just what to buy. Generally, if you remember to let the business dictate what equipment you need rather than your emotions, you'll make the right choices. Here, though, are some guidelines to help you determine what you may need when you are starting out.

 Can I work at the kitchen table?

One of the great things about working for yourself is you can work anywhere you find convenient. That means you could work at the kitchen table, the dining room table, the coffee table, or the backyard picnic table. In fact, if the work that needs to be done requires nothing more than a paper, pencil, and your imagination you could plop your body into an oversized tire tube and work while you cool your heels in the backyard swimming pool. What you should consider in choosing a permanent spot to work is how you will keep your work materials organized so they are always together. If you don't want to make space for a formal office in your home, buy an inexpensive file box that will let you keep all your papers and notes together in an orderly fashion.

Q Do I need to get business cards?

Business cards are one of the least costly and most helpful promotional tools. The card tells people what you do and puts that information in a format they can easily store in a wallet, copy into a phone directory, or file in a card directory so they can have your name and number the next time they need what you sell. Thus, you should get business cards and get in the habit of handing them out to everyone you possibly can.

Q Do I need to give myself a title on my business card?

If you are trying to give people the impression your company is bigger than a one- or two-person business, or if you like titles, you can give yourself a title, such as president. If you don't like titles and don't have to impress anyone, you don't have to use a title. The name of your business and your name, address, and phone number should be all you need to include.

Q Do I need business stationery?

Business stationery is another essential. Even if you don't often write business letters, there may be times when you need to write to suppliers or customers. If you want your letters to look professional and important, you need letterhead stationery and envelopes printed with your business name.

If you don't think you will need business stationery often, have just a small quantity printed. After seeing how long it takes to use it up, you can reorder a larger quantity if appropriate. Don't wait until the day before you need the stationery, however. It can take a week to two weeks for a printer to print a job.

Q **Do I need expensive business stationery?**

The type of business you run will dictate how impressive your business stationery needs to be. If you run a simple service business and get customers because of your efficiency and your reasonable prices, expensive-looking stationery would be a poor choice. Customers would be likely to equate expensive-looking stationery with an expensive service.

If you are in a business where you are expected to be dignified and highly professional, however, you will need to use the best quality paper you can afford.

Your printer should have samples of different papers, stationery designs, and type styles available. He or she may also have books of pictures or symbols you could use if you want artwork on the letterhead, business card, and envelope. You can also purchase stationery by mail from several different companies. These companies all have catalogs showing available designs.

Important Note: Be sure whatever paper supplies or forms you buy work with your printer, word processor, or typewriter before ordering in large quantities. Certain papers are too thick to feed through your printer or photocopier, some make the ink from an inkjet printer look blurry or smudge easily; some won't accept the ink from a laser printer properly (the ink will crack when the paper is folded or will smudge). If you use a laser printer, watch out for raised ink letterhead and envelopes. Many raised inks melt from the heat of laser printers.

Many printers and mail order houses are reasonably knowledgeable about what paper works with what printers and are more than happy to help you make the right choice. Be sure to tell them what kind of equipment you will be using, and if there is any question about what will work, ask them to give or send you a couple of sheets of paper to test.

Q **What about order forms? Where do I get them?**

Order forms, sales call forms, invoice forms, purchase order forms, estimate forms, and even specialty labels can all be ordered with your name printed on them from a local print shop or by mail. They can be purchased as loose sheets or as continuous forms for computer printers that have a tractor feed mechanism (a gear with teeth that catches the holes in computer paper and pulls the paper through the machine).

If you just need forms occasionally and don't want to buy printed forms, you can get packages of forms that have a space to type in your name and address at most office supply stores. Or, if you have a computer, you may be able to use either a word processor, page layout program, or a database program to print out forms as you need them.

A few of the mail order companies that will print forms and stationery are:

Moore Business Products
P. O. Box 5000
Vernon Hills, IL 60061
(800) 323–6230

New England Business Service, Inc. (NEBS)
500 Main Street
Groton, MA 01471
(800) 225–6380

Paper Direct
205 Chubb Avenue
Lyndhurst, NJ 07071
(800) 272–7377

Streamliners
5 Pleasant View Drive
P. O. Box 480
Mechanicsburg, PA 17055
(800) 233–1177

If you need to purchase cardboard envelopes (for disk mailers, for instance) one company that can supply them imprinted or blank is:

Mail Safe
4340 W. 47th Street
Chicago, IL 60632
(800) 848–6552 or (312) 523–6000

Q How much business stationery and how many forms should I buy?

If you have no way of estimating how many letters you will write or how many orders you will get, order the minimum quantities of stationery at the start. For a home business, five hundred letterheads and envelopes will be sufficient unless you are planning to do a large personalized mailing. (In that case order enough stationery to do the mailing as well as a few hundred pieces for routine mail.) Although you can get quantity discounts, there's no point buying and having to find a suitable storage place for a few thousand letterheads and envelopes if it will take you 2 or 3 years to use up that many. If you need order forms and invoices, you might want to use the packaged ones from an office supply store and fill in your business name until you determine how many forms you will need each month.

Q Can I make my own stationery on a laser printer?

You could in a pinch, but it isn't advisable. Even if you are artistic and good at designing stationery, what you produce on a laser printer just won't have the crispness that comes with professional typesetting. What most desktop publishers do when they design letterhead is use the laser printout as a proof copy to see if the design looks the way they want, and when it does, they send the computer file to a service bureau that prints out the work on image setters, which produce much sharper type than laser printers.

Not only will you get better-looking letterhead by having it typeset professionally, you may wind up paying less when you add up the cost of your laser toner (the ink), paper, and the wear and tear on your printer.

Q Do I need a separate phone line if I work at home?

Unless you live alone it is advisable to have a separate telephone line for your business. Having the separate line will let you always answer the phone with a business greeting and will prevent ten-year-old Johnny from picking up an extension and trying to dial a friend's home while you are trying to land a new customer. Equally important, having the separate line makes it much simpler to track business phone expenses for your tax records.

Q **If I run my business from home will I have to get a business phone line?**

Whether you will need a commercial phone line instead of a residential line will depend on your local telephone company rules. In some localities, you only are required to get a business (commercial) line if you want a listing in the yellow pages. In other parts of the country, other rules apply. Call the business office of your local telephone company or the utilities commission of your state to find out what the rules are.

Q **Should I get an 800 number?**

Some small businesses find that having an 800 number for orders boosts sales, and others find they get few extra calls on their 800 line. Since it is possible to get 800 service for around $20 a month plus calls, it may be worthwhile. One software developer says his monthly 800 costs are under $90, a price that is more than made up, he feels, by the extra orders he gets.

Q **Should I get an answering machine?**

You need some way for customers to leave you messages when there is no one in your office to take calls. The options available are:

▶ an answering machine
▶ an answering service
▶ your own in-house voice mail system
▶ voice mail purchased from a private vendor or from the phone company

A *conventional answering machine* is the least expensive option. You can get a reliable answering machine in discount stores for under $50 if you watch for sales. While you can get machines with all sorts of bells and whistles, the useful features are a voice-activated message recording system (this makes the machine keep recording as long as the caller keeps talking) and beeperless remote call-in (which lets you call the machine from any touch-tone phone to retrieve messages or even change the message). Other features you may find useful are the ability to turn off the answering machine from an extension phone (handy when the answering machine is downstairs and someone picks up the upstairs extension), the ability to answer two lines, automatic time and date stamping, and the ability to choose your own call-retrieval code (the three digit number you punch in to retrieve messages from a phone when you are away from the office).

Answering services that use live operators to take calls are preferred by some businesses—particularly those who must be notified of emergency situations. Some people who have used answering services complain, however, about messages being incomplete or that the operators don't get the right phone numbers or forget to give them the messages. Thus, if you plan to use an answering service with live operators it would be a good idea to ask other business people in your community which service is the best to use.

Your own microcomputer-based voice mail system can be handy if you have an IBM or compatible microcomputer system and enough storage space and power to handle the voice messaging system. These computer-based voice mail systems work—as far as the caller is concerned—just like the voice mail systems they hear when they call large corporations. In other words, they get a menu of choices such as "Press one to leave a message; press two to place an order; press three for customer support; . . ." You can even program the systems to call-forward incoming calls to another number if you want. The main disadvantage of these systems is they take up a lot of disk space. Computer programmers and others who have to keep up with the latest computer technology sometimes dedicate their outdated PCs to voice mail functions.

Commercial voice mail systems are offered by some local telephone companies. Paging services often offer a voice mail option that will call your beeper when messages have been left for you in voice mail.

Q Is call waiting a good service to get?

Call waiting—which signals you that there is another call coming in and lets you put the first caller on hold while you see who the second caller is—may be convenient for you, but it can be annoying or even insulting to your customers. If you don't want to miss messages while you are on the telephone, consider using the telephone company's voice mail service, if available, instead of call waiting.

The phone company's voice mail would pick up if your line is busy and allow callers to leave a message without disturbing the call in progress.

In addition, if you use a computer to receive or send data over telephone lines, the call-waiting signal interferes with and disconnects the computer call. If you do decide to get call waiting, find out if there are ways to temporarily disable it if you use your computer on your phone line. This feature is not available in all communities.

Q   How do I choose a photocopier?

The best way to choose a copier is to make a list of all the ways you expect to use it. Consider not only your present needs but how you expect to use the copier in the next year or two. Here are some needs to consider:

 ▸ How many copies will you make at once?
 ▸ How many copies do you expect to make every month?
 ▸ How frequently will you need to copy multipage documents?
 ▸ How often will you need to collate multipage documents?
 ▸ What size are the originals, and will you often need to enlarge or reduce them?
 ▸ Will you want to photocopy both sides of a page onto the front and back of a single sheet of paper?
 ▸ Are you going to be photocopying photographs?
 ▸ Will you need to photocopy onto both legal- and letter-sized paper frequently?
 ▸ How much space do you have available for the photocopier?
 ▸ Will you need to photocopy onto card stock? Overhead transparencies?

Compare this list of needs to the photocopier equipment available at local discount stores, superstores or shopping clubs, and office equipment dealers, comparing features and prices of various units. Be sure to ask about the price of consumable supplies such as toner. The inexpensive personal photocopiers may cost significantly more per page to run than the more expensive office copiers. To get the best buy you will need to compare all your costs.

In addition to the price of the copier, consider how much paper you can put in paper trays at one time, how many paper trays the unit will work with (if any), whether you can add collating equipment later on if you will need it. Be sure to find out about power requirements, too. The photocopier may draw so much power that it will require its own separate electrical line.

If you have any special uses intended for the copier (for instance, copying onto card stock, onto papers with rough or textured surfaces, or copying photographs), test the copier with the actual work you want to do. Look at the quality and speed of the output. If space is at a premium in your office, note whether the top of the copier unit (called the platen) slides back and forth during copying or is stationery, and if it slides back and forth, how much room it needs to operate.

Finally, ask about guarantees, maintenance, and service agreements. If you will be using the machine daily or if it is very heavy, you are likely to want someone to come to your office to service the unit, so ask if a service contract is available and what it costs.

Q Do I need a facsimile machine?

Facsimile (fax) machines could probably be best described as instant mail machines: they are used to send or receive all sorts of printed documents, orders, and letters from one location to another almost instantly. If your business will require such instant mail you will need a fax machine.

If you only need to send or receive faxes occasionally, you should be able to find a local fax service instead of buying a fax machine. Copy centers, quick print shops, secretarial services, libraries, and even office supply stores often have fax service available. In addition, most online information services also have fax services available that let you send a text message to any fax location in the world that the online service reaches.

If you need to send or receive more than a few faxes, however, you will probably want to get your own fax or fax-modem for your computer. Prices advertised by discount stores for stand-alone fax machines suitable for small offices start as low as $300 and go up to around $1,700 to $1,800 for plain-paper fax machines.

Q What kind of fax machine should I get?

There are two broad categories of fax equipment: stand-alone fax machines and fax boards or modems that work with microcomputers. With a stand-alone machine, you feed printed or handwritten pages into the machine, which scans the documents and converts them to a format that can be sent out over telephone lines to another machine. When you use a fax/modem you use a combination of computer software and hardware to send documents that are stored in your computer to a receiving fax machine. Incoming faxes are received into your computer and can be printed out, or with the proper software, converted to a format you can put in a word processor and edit.

Which type of fax you should purchase depends on how you will use it and on your preferences. Here are various questions and options you should consider in making your decision:

▶ Where will you get the documents you need to send out? Are they already printed documents such as contract forms or letters printed on your letter-head? Are they formatted documents or drawings that are stored in your computer?

▶ Will you need to send photos or drawings via fax?

▶ Will you need to send copies of handwritten documents or printed documents that have handwritten notations on them?

▶ What size documents will you send or receive? Standard letter size or bigger?

▶ What will you have to do with a document after you get it via fax? Will you need to just look at it and discard it? File it and store it for any length of time? Will you need to get the document into your computer to work on it?

▶ How often will you need to send or receive fax documents?

▶ Does the fax machine need to have a sheet feeder or a way to automatically send multiple pages?

▶ If you are considering a fax/modem for your computer, do you have a scanner available that will allow you to scan graphics and text into your computer if you need to fax something like a newsletter or contract you get in the mail to someone else?

‣ How fast will you want the machine to transmit documents?

‣ How will you enter the phone numbers of receiving fax machines? If you have a computer, can you transfer names and addresses automatically from your database software to your fax modem software?

‣ Will you need to send a single fax to multiple machines (called broadcasting), or will you only be sending faxes to one machine at a time? If you will want to broadcast faxes to the same numbers repeatedly (all your regular customers, for instance, or a group of publications to which you regularly send press releases), will the software let you set up group lists and automatically send out a fax to each number on the list when you choose the group name? Or will you have to select each number separately?

‣ If you are using a fax/modem can you launch the software from within any application?

Q **Can I use a plain-paper fax as a photocopier?**

Since the ink used in plain-paper fax machines won't fade or deteriorate the way copies printed using thermal fax paper do, you could use a plain-paper fax to make permanent copies of documents printed on loose sheets of paper. However, if you will need to make more than an occasional photocopy, using the plain-paper fax as a substitute copier isn't going to be practical. The copying process is far too slow and you will only be able to copy documents printed on loose sheets of paper. Furthermore, if the fax/copier breaks down you will lose both the fax and the photocopier until the unit can be repaired. Finally, if cost is a factor, you may be able to get the two separate machines (fax and photocopier) for less than the price of the combined unit.

Q **Should I buy a typewriter, a word processor, or a computer?**

If you are going to be using the machine for business, you should probably buy either a dedicated word processor or a computer and printer. The benefit of the computer is that it will allow you to do more than just type documents when you are ready to do more. The dedicated word processor will probably be less expensive and might be easier to learn how to use.

In addition, if you will be doing any kind of written or graphic work for other companies you will probably need a computer. Many companies expect you to have the ability to store documents so you can make minor changes and reprint them, or to even transmit work back and forth to them on disk, through electronic mail systems or through direct computer-to-computer modem hookup. Even if you wouldn't be required to do any of these things, you are likely to need a computer to be competitive if you sell to businesses or if you have to manage a large inventory or customer list.

Furthermore, once you have a number of customers, you may find a computer helpful to handle your accounting; maintain customer lists, parts lists, and price lists; do financial planning and estimating; type your own routine correspondence; and perform any chore that involves mathematical computations, or repetitive typing, or graphic arts.

 What kind of computer should I buy?

To choose a computer you need to start by considering two things:

▶ what functions you want the computer to perform (word processing, accounting, financial forecasting, graphics, etc.)
▶ what computer capabilities the majority of your potential customers expect you to have

Economy and ease of use are important, too, but not as important as being compatible with the computer hardware and software your customers are likely to use.

If your business isn't one that requires you to have hardware and software compatible with the computers your customers use, base your choice of a computer on what software (computer programs) is available to handle the tasks you want to perform. A computer, after all, is only a processor that sits and waits for instructions about what to process and what methods and procedures to use. The software gives it those instructions.

How do I find out which software programs are right for my business?

The best way to find the right software is to read reviews in recent computer magazines and trade magazines. Among the computer magazines you might want to look at are *Computer Shopper, MacUser, PC/Computing, Byte, MacWorld,* and *Home Office Computing.* Your public library should have back issues of at least several of these publications.

You may also want to ask friends who are knowledgeable about computers for suggestions. Be aware, however, that their favorite computer and programs might not be right for your business needs. Computer-user groups, if there are any large ones near you, are another valuable source of information.

Once you have an idea of what software programs would be appropriate, look at how much computer memory those programs require. Many programs today require a lot of computer memory to function properly. A computer that has 4 or more megabytes of memory, or one that will allow you to expand the memory at a later date, would be preferable, if your budget allows.

Note: The memory a computer uses to process work is called RAM, which stands for random access memory. This memory gets turned on and off and is not used to store data or programs permanently. Programs and data are stored on a disk when not in use and get loaded into memory only when they are needed. A reasonable analogy would be a mixing bowl. Each time you use it, you would get out the ingredients from a storage closet (or refrigerator) and "load" them into the bowl. The amount of ingredients you can put in the bowl at any one time will be limited by the size of the bowl. The bigger the bowl, the larger the volume of ingredients it will hold. The bigger the computer memory, the more data and program instructions it can work with at one time.

Q **Could I use a notebook computer instead of a regular desktop model?**

Yes. Most of today's notebook-sized portable computers are extremely powerful, and most have ports (sockets) that will let you attach a full-sized keyboard and a full-sized color monitor if you wish to do so. (Some notebooks these days have color displays.) You will pay more for a notebook computer than you will for a comparable desktop model, but if you travel a lot, the notebook would be a good choice.

Q What should I look for in a notebook computer?

Jeff Chasalow, manager of internal audit support for Beneficial Finance Corporation, was given the task of selecting the laptops the company's auditors would take on the road. The criteria he used in late 1992 to select notebook computers were:

▶ *Price*
▶ *Weight:* under 6 pounds including the AC adaptor is desirable.
▶ *Dimensions:* briefcase-size is preferable.
▶ *Processor and speed:* at least an 80386 processor and a minimum speed of 16 MHz (megahertz).
▶ *Display:* is the display comfortable to look at and easy to read?
▶ *Memory:* at least 2 megabytes; 4 would be better if Microsoft Windows will be used.
▶ *Hard disk size and speed:* at least a 60 to 80 megabyte hard drive with a seek time of no more than 28 milliseconds. (Seek time is the average time it takes to locate a file on a disk.)
▶ *Internal modem:* does the laptop have one or can it be added?
▶ *Floppy drive:* 3½-inch, high-density drive.
▶ *Keyboard:* comfortable and convenient to type on.

Q What kind of printer should I get to go with the computer?

Before you decide what type of printer to get, you will need to know what kinds of documents you plan to print out. If you have to print out any multipart forms, you will need an impact printer, which has a mechanism that produces an image by hitting an inked ribbon that then hits the page. Impact printers you can buy today are usually dot matrix printers. They are the printers that use conventional-looking computer paper (the kind with the holes along the edges).

Laser printers and inkjet printers (which often get the most attention in computer magazines) are not impact printers and therefore won't produce an impression on the second or third sheets of multipart forms.

In addition to whether or not you have to print multipart forms, you need to consider:

▶ *The speed of the printer.* Find out how long the printer takes to accept and print a single page of text, a single page of graphics, and multiple copies of a single page. A printer that prints only one page per minute will be inadequate for your needs if you have many pages to print in a short time.

▶ *The quality of the image the printer produces.* The quality of the image depends partly on something called resolution or dots per inch (dpi) and partly on the way the characters (fonts) are generated. PostScript-compatible printers are generally considered to be the most versatile and produce the best graphic images for personal printers. (PostScript is a computer language that enables the computer to send font and graphics commands to the printer.) These printers also have the widest range of quality fonts (type styles) available. If you plan to use a computer for desktop publishing, you should plan on getting a PostScript-compatible printer.

▶ *The cost and availability of the ribbons or ink cartridges.* Find out the cost of the cartridge or ribbon and the number of pages you can expect to print with each cartridge or ribbon. An ink cartridge that costs $17.98 but only prints 300 pages will cost you about $.06 per page for ink. A cartridge for a different type of printer that costs $100 but prints out 3,000 pages would be about half that amount per page. Be sure the cartridge or ribbons for the printer you select are widely available in stores or mail order outlets. You may also want to find out if refilled cartridges cost less than new ones.

▶ *The way documents are queued up for printing.* Some printers will let you queue up a number of files at one time to print and let you use the computer for something else while the printer churns out the pages. Other printers make you wait until the printer is finished printing to move on to other tasks. Often you can get a software spooler that will allow you to work and print at the same time but that will increase your costs.

▶ *The amount of noise the printer makes.* Some dot matrix printers make a racket, which is not only annoying while you work but could keep children or your spouse awake if you work when they are trying to sleep.

▶ *Portability.* Will you be traveling? Will you need to print documents while you are traveling? If so, you might want to look at the printers designed to fit in briefcases, at least as a backup printer. They probably aren't going to be suitable as your primary printer, however.

▶ *The number of sheets of paper that can be stacked in the printer at once.* Less important, perhaps, than all the other considerations, but it is annoying to send a document to print and then return expecting it to be finished only to find a message on your screen saying the printer is out of paper.

▶ *The printer's ability to handle heavy paper and/or envelopes.* Printers vary in their ability to print on thick paper and envelopes. Envelopes are of particular importance to test. Some printers, even though they claim to be able to handle envelopes, just don't do a good job. Either the method of feeding the envelopes is slow and laborious, or the printer twists the envelope so printing is skewed, or it can crunch the corners or leave black ink smudges. If at all possible test the printer you want to buy with the type of envelopes you will be using.

▶ *Color.* Will you want to add impact to overhead transparencies, special reports, or other documents you print in small quantity? If so, you might want to consider getting one of the less expensive color printers on the market. Hewlett Packard makes color inkjet printers that work with Macintosh and IBM-compatible computers and let you print in full color at a reasonable price. (The printer can be found for around $700 and the multicolor ink cartridge can be purchased for about $30.) The printer is not a substitute for regular printing, but it is good for occasional color touches consultants and others may want to add to client work. Color Postscript-compatible printers are available, too, but because of the cost, they are suitable at this point primarily for advertising agencies and designers who need color proofs (samples) of work before having it printed.

▶ *Budget.* If you are just starting out and the optimum printer is too expensive, consider possible alternatives. You might be able to use a less expensive printer now and bring certain jobs to a service bureau. Or, perhaps you could make do with a slower printer until the profits from your business allow you to buy a second, faster printer. If you are going to produce work on a regular basis, sooner or later you will need backup equipment so you can continue to work if something breaks down. The less expensive printer you buy today could be your backup printer tomorrow.

Q **What will it cost me to buy a computer?**

You can buy IBM-compatible computers that are powerful enough for small business needs for as little as $1,000—and sometimes less. If you require speed and a lot of memory, you will probably pay closer to $2,000. Printers can be purchased for as little as about $350 and up. PostScript-compatible printers start at about $1,200. Monitors (the computer screen) aren't always part of the price, so be sure you know exactly what you are getting for your money.

Q **Can I save money by purchasing a computer or printer from a mail order catalog or discount store?**

Discount stores and mail order companies can save you money, but may not offer as much customer support as you'd like. Getting service if the computer or printer breaks down can be a problem, too, if you buy at discount stores or through the mail. Often you will have to pack up the device and mail it away to be fixed if there is a problem. Even if you pay extra for overnight mail to and from the repair center, it can take a minimum of three days to get your computer back when you have to mail it away for repairs. That can play havoc with your deadlines if you rely on the computer or printer to produce work for your customers. Some discount chains and mail order companies do offer on-site service, however. If you will need the computer every day, it would be wise to look for such offers.

 Tip: Don't assume that all retail stores fix computers and printers on-site or in their own repair centers. Ask to be sure. Some stores will take in repairs, but then turn around and send

out the computer for repair. When this happens, you may
wind up having to wait a week or even longer to get your
computer back.

Tip: Be wary of buying closeouts. If the company that manufactured the computer or printer stops supporting it or goes
out of business you may be unable to find parts or consumable supplies when needed.

Q What is a modem and do I need one?

A modem converts computer data so it can be transmitted over the telephone
lines. It lets you send information stored inside your computer to other computers
that have modems.

Having a modem can be very useful since it lets you connect with many different individuals and business resources to get information, exchange electronic
mail, get product support, and to do business.

Q How can a small business benefit by using online information services?

Online information services allow you to:

▶ Get tips on solving problems from other business owners in online conferences and bulletin boards.

▶ Find low-cost business software (called shareware) that you can try before
you buy. Not only does shareware help prevent you from making costly
software mistakes (most commercial software isn't returnable), but you will
also find that there are some shareware programs available that are better
than any commercial programs.

▶ Get the latest news sent directly to your electronic mailbox with an electronic news-clipping service. This lets you track competitors, new products,
or just follow subjects of interest.

- Gain valuable how-to information in online libraries.

- Get shareware artwork to use in publications.

- Access stock reports.

- Get product support from software and hardware manufacturers.

- Find out what experiences other people have had with hardware or software you want to buy. Often you'll get more insight and get the information sooner than you would from magazine reviews.

- Discuss tax laws, business laws, computer problems, marketing concerns, and almost any business concern with experts.*

- Make your name known by sharing your expertise with others in public online bulletin boards. Most bulletin boards do not want you to advertise, but your name does get known and people may contact and hire you if you share your expertise with others.

- Search for trademarks and patents, manufacturers, and even old newspaper or magazine articles online. Several of the services have extensive database capabilities that let you quickly find information that could take you hours and hours to locate in the public library.

- Get financial information about public companies.

- Make travel reservations.

- Get the names, addresses, phone numbers, and fax numbers of senators and congresspeople from your state.

---

* Attorneys, accountants, and other professionals online cannot give you specific advice, but they can and do provide general information that can help you understand issues and solve problems.

▸ Put your business name, contact information, and a brief description of what you do in a searchable online database where businesses and individuals can find it when they need what you sell. *

▸ Get help learning how to sell to the government.

▸ Order needed business products, services, or software online.

Q   What commercial online services are there?

Among the major online information services are GEnie, America Online, CompuServe, Prodigy, Dow Jones News Retrieval, Delphi, Dialog, and Apple-Link.

Q   Are there any other gadgets I'll need?

If you get a computer system, you should be sure to get a *surge protector* or an *uninterruptible power supply*. The surge protector is the least expensive and offers some protection to your equipment against power spikes (too much power) that sometimes come through lines. A power spike can destroy your computer circuitry, so protection is well worth paying for. If you have a lot of very important data on your system or have very expensive computer equipment, you will probably want to price the uninterruptible power supplies.

Whichever you get, it is still a good idea to unplug the computer in a thunderstorm. Nothing can survive a lightning hit. You should also unhook the modem from the computer during a storm since telephone lines can carry damaging power surges if hit by lightning.

Also useful are the wrist rests that are designed to help avoid carpal tunnel syndrome, foot rests, a well-made office chair designed to offer back support and a work surface that is the right height for you. An adjustable copy holder, if you do a lot of typing, and a device that holds the computer monitor (computer screen) and lets you adjust it to a comfortable viewing height and distance are good to have if you will be working for long periods of time.

---

* This database is the Business Resource Directory, which is available on the GEnie service. Readers of this book who don't have a modem and would like to be included in that database should send a self-addressed, stamped envelope to: The National Small Business Network, P.O. Box 223, Centereach, NY 11720.

III.

The Brass Tacks:
Finding Customers,
Getting Paid

13.

How to Find Customers
for What You Sell

Anyone can start a business. But to stay in business, you need a steady stream of customers who buy what you sell.

Finding those customers sometimes seems like a difficult, time-consuming, and expensive task. But it doesn't have to be. Although you may never learn to love sales and marketing (which is what finding customers is all about), you can learn to do it effectively and economically. Here are answers to some of the most frequently asked questions about how to win customers for your small business.

Q **Is there any secret to marketing products?**

The secret of successful marketing is to realize marketing requires you to do four things:

1. Get the word about your products and services out to as many potential customers as you can.
2. Remind those potential customers frequently about what you do.
3. Persuade them to buy from you rather than from the competitor.
4. Deliver a top-notch product with top-notch support so your customers will give you repeat business and refer new customers to you.

Q **How do most small businesses get their customers?**

Results of a survey completed by more than nine hundred visitors to the Home Office/Small Business RoundTable on the GEnie service in 1992 show that the majority of small and homebased businesses (54 percent) get most of their customers through word-of-mouth advertising. The second leading source of customers for the same group of people was networking (16 percent).

Q **What is word-of-mouth advertising?**

Word-of-mouth advertising is what happens when one person tells another about what you do. If the word of mouth is a glowing testimonial or even a neutral "I know someone who does that," it can bring customers your way. It will also make people more responsive to your ads or calls because they will have already heard positive things about your company. On the other hand, if the word of mouth is negative—if a customer complains you didn't satisfy their needs, screwed up a job, or didn't respond to their calls, word-of-mouth advertising will drive customers away.

Q **What is networking?**

Networking is making business contacts. It is you telling other people what you do. The contacts you make may be directly with potential customers, or they may be with individuals who will give you leads or refer customers to you. Your networking contacts may also be with people who can provide valuable information that will help you improve your business or gain industry knowledge.

Networking is what you do every time you:

- give someone you meet a business card
- shake hands and introduce yourself to others at chamber of commerce or professional association meetings
- participate in a formal or informal sales lead exchange group
- flip pancakes at the Lion's Club breakfast
- accept a seat on the board of a nonprofit organization
- exchange tips and business information with noncompeting businesses

- ▶ attend the professional association dinner dance
- ▶ introduce yourself to the person sitting next to you on the airplane or standing in line ahead of you at the bank
- ▶ offer to answer another business's questions
- ▶ ask another business person for suggestions or about experience in some particular matter
- ▶ donate a prize for a holiday bazaar

Q How does networking lead to new business?

Networking can boost business in several ways. One of its most important functions is to make your name familiar to prospective customers. If someone has met you or heard about your company from a friend they are likely to place more trust in you than they would place in a stranger. This, incidentally, is the reason people buy name brands products instead of less expensive house brands, even though the house brands may have identical ingredients.

Networking puts contact information in the hands of potential customers. When you give people you meet your business card and they put it in their wallet or briefcase, you are making it easy for them to contact you. Even if a prospect loses your business card, he or she may remember your business name after meeting you and be able to get in touch with you by looking your name up in the phone book or calling information.

A single networking contact can, at times, give your business a tremendous, long-lasting boost. Barbara Robbie, owner of Belle of the Ball, a formal gown rental service in East Setauket, New York, was at a private party when she happened to meet a woman who was responsible for planning the annual spring fashion show at a local church. When Robbie described her unique business—renting out wedding party and prom gowns—she was asked if she would like to put on the show at the church that year.

Robbie accepted the invitation and then asked women from the church and girls from a local high school to model her gowns at the show. The models publicized the show to all their friends and the church publicized it in the weekly bulletin distributed among parishioners. On the night of the show, close to four hundred women and teenage girls packed into the church basement for the event. Robbie got dozens of new customers directly from the show and continued to get referrals and business from people who had attended the show for several years afterward. The church benefited, too: the fashion show proved to be one of the most successful fund-raisers it had that year.

Q **Won't people get annoyed if I talk about my business all the time?**

A little common sense goes a long way. For instance, no one really wants to "talk business" at social gatherings, but when a group of strangers happens to be seated at the same table or be standing in the same corner of the room at a cocktail party, it's natural for people to ask one another what they do for a living. If you are asked, there's nothing wrong with briefly stating what you do and sounding excited about it.

Many business functions are held specifically to allow business people to network. Others combine networking with association meetings. Such functions generally set aside a half hour or so for networking before the actual meeting takes place. The most difficult thing about networking at this type of meeting can be finding a way to shake hands with a new acquaintance and exchange business cards without spilling your drink.

Q **Is handing out business cards at business gatherings all I have to do to network and get new customers?**

Usually people who build the most contacts through networking are those who become actively involved in two or three organizations in which they have a sincere interest and which are somewhat related to their business. People who just show up to push their products and services and have little concern for the organization or little interest in what other members of the organization do are usually seen as opportunists and don't get much business tossed their way. Those who actively participate in a group, regularly attend meetings, contribute thoughts, and if needed, pitch in and help plan events, maintain membership lists, or even move chairs, or serve the organization in some other way are the ones most likely to land business.

Q **How else can I build business through networking?**

Asking for help when you need it can sometimes be extremely effective. Many successful business people like being mentors to business owners who are just starting out. They will offer information, leads, and contacts to help a new business owner get off the ground. You can tap into this network through associations and business groups. Sometimes all it takes is to ask if anyone has any experience handling a problem that puzzles you.

Paul Mayer, author of several widely used shareware programs for IBM and compatible microcomputers, says his shareware sales were languishing along at one or two a month until he joined the Association of Shareware Professionals and learned about marketing shareware. A few years after joining the association, he was able to quit his full-time job and earn his living entirely from his shareware sales.

Be aware, though, that people don't like to be used. Don't expect people to do things for you that you could easily do yourself. And do remember to thank friends for their help. If you abuse people's generosity they will remember, and like negative word of mouth, the memory will wind up driving customers away rather than attracting them.

Q **What other ways do home and small businesses find customers?**

Home and small businesses find customers in every imaginable way. Here are just a few:

- sending out personalized or mass mailings
- getting listed in the Yellow Pages and other directories
- using sales representatives
- calling prospects on the phone
- making personal visits to prospects' offices or homes
- using print or broadcast advertising
- exhibiting at and attending trade shows
- bidding on contracts from government organizations
- getting publicity in trade or other media
- speaking at meetings, on panels, etc.
- partnering with large corporations or becoming a certified developer, trainer, etc.
- participating in cooperative advertising programs with major manufacturers
- doing cooperative advertising with noncompeting small businesses

- getting products "advertised" in (included in) large mail order house catalogs
- subcontracting or free-lancing for larger businesses in the same field
- getting major distributors to take on and sell products
- getting products reviewed in publications
- getting certified by regulatory agencies
- being a member of one or more professional societies
- hanging up a sign in an area where business signs are permitted
- displaying wares (flowers, vegetables, antiques) on lawns, on sidewalks, or any other way visible to passersby
- selling at flea markets
- selling at juried craft shows
- selling products on consignment
- giving lessons (art, pottery, etc.) in a store or home and selling related products and supplies
- having an open house to sell products
- offering people free merchandise if they agree to host a "party" for their friends at which you sell your merchandise
- sending promotional newsletters to targeted customers
- getting work shown at galleries, banks, or restaurants
- having the business name professionally lettered onto the business car or van
- exchanging mailing lists with businesses that sell to the same customers but don't compete with you
- selling to federal, state, or local governments

Q Will networking and word-of-mouth advertising be enough to get customers or should I advertise, too?

Some small businesses never use traditional advertising; others would have few customers if they didn't advertise. Generally, businesses that sell consumer goods and services and require a high volume of sales tend to be the ones that benefit most from traditional advertising. Businesses that sell creative or consulting services to other businesses tend to benefit the least from traditional advertising.

Thus, car repair, catering, resume preparation, rental services, tutoring services, pizza parlors, hair and nail care salons, appliance parts stores, and similar businesses usually need to advertise regularly using the Yellow Pages, newspapers, magazines, TV, radio, or community mailers. Businesses selling creative services (writing or art work, for instance), consulting services, programming services, or similar intangible services to businesses generally derive little benefit from traditional advertising, though they sometimes do well with direct mail.

Still other businesses find that their customers come from a combination of paid advertising and word of mouth. Barbara Robbie got the first customers for Belle of the Ball by placing a very small ad in a popular weekly newspaper for 4 weeks as a trial. That ad brought her inquiries and customers, so she repeated the ad, and then she placed the same ad in a second weekly newspaper in the same community. Although she believes that most of her customers now come from word-of-mouth advertising and repeat business, she not only continues to advertise to maintain visibility but, as business income permits, gradually expands the number of newspapers (and thus the number of towns and villages) in which she advertises. As a result, her shop now draws customers from both Suffolk and Nassau counties on Long Island and, occasionally, from New York City as well.

Robbie's method of gradually expanding advertising efforts is probably the best way for most small businesses to approach advertising, whether they are using print, broadcast, direct mail, or any other advertising methods. It not only keeps a business from making expensive advertising mistakes when it can least afford to but it also allows the business to expand at a pace the owner can control and handle.

Q **How do I find my first customer?**

Usually you find your first customers the same way you will find the rest of your customers: through personal contacts, ads, mailings, and so on. If you've researched your market before going into business, finding likely prospects for what you sell should be relatively easy. What some new businesses have trouble doing, however, is converting prospects to customers; in other words, convincing potential customers to actually purchase goods or services. Most often that difficulty occurs because the owner lacks self-confidence or dislikes selling.

Q **I always feel uneasy about pressuring people to buy from me if they don't want to. How can I overcome this problem?**

To overcome the problem, you need to think about sales in a different way. A good salesperson never pressures anyone into buying anything. Instead he or she *helps the prospect make a decision* that will solve a problem or achieve some kind of desirable benefit.

Thus, to overcome any dislike or fear of selling you may have, you must:

▶ *Believe in your product or service.* Would you buy what you plan to sell at the price you plan to charge and be satisfied with the quality of the product or service? If you can't immediately say "Yes!" don't expect to be able to convince many customers that your products or services are worth buying.

▶ *Know how the product or service helps customers.* Your customers don't really care whether you are starting a business or that you need their business. All they care about is how well your products or services match their needs. Demonstrate how your goods fill real needs, how your services solve the customer's real problems or help the customer achieve some goal, and your products or services will almost sell themselves.

▶ *Learn not to take rejection personally.* Many times people are afraid to go out and sell their products because they fear personal rejection. They worry prospects won't want to talk to them, will complain about the call or visit, will slam the phone down, or won't like the product or service. Although such concerns are natural, you shouldn't let negative responses to your sales efforts get you down. No matter what you sell, there will always be people who don't want or need your product. No matter how good it may be, only a tiny percentage of people who hear about it (through calls, contacts, ads, or any other method) are going to be willing to buy and buy today. The rest are simply not going to be interested. Some may even be rude. You have to learn to roll with the punches.

▶ *Make sure you have capabilities to meet customers needs.* Don't try to sell your services as a consultant, programmer, desktop publisher, auto mechanic, dressmaker, copywriter, or anything else unless you have the experience in the field. Without experience you will find it very difficult to convince people to buy from you. Your inexperience might also result in monetary loss or personal injury to your customer. If that were to happen, you could get sued. If you want to start a business in a field you know little about, get experience or hands-on training before you look for customers. Go to work for some other business, take training courses, volunteer your services to friends or community groups, or do whatever else may be necessary to build experience on your own time and at your own expense. Once you have the training and experience and can prove (to yourself as well as to potential customers) that you can do the work you say you can, selling will be much easier.

▶ *Don't sell yourself short.* If you are experienced and good at what you do, don't let the competition scare you off. If your research has shown there is room in the market for both you and your competitor, market to your strengths and don't worry too much about the competitor, even if they are much bigger or more widely known than your company. Your small size may actually be a hidden advantage if it lets you offer customers more personalized service or attention to details than your competitor can.

Q **How else can I convince customers to buy?**

There are a slew of techniques salespeople use, but the most important techniques for the small business person to remember are these:

▶ Qualify your prospect. Make sure he or she can afford what you sell and has the authority to make the purchase decision. You don't want to spend hours demonstrating your product to the manager of the marketing department if he or she doesn't make the buying decisions, or have any influence on them, for your type of product or service.

▶ Know what objections you are likely to hear and have answers ready to meet them.

▶ Know your product and your competitors inside and out.

▶ Give the customer a small sample of a product to test.

▶ Don't knock the competitor. Sell your product's benefits instead.

▸ Learn to ask for the order. Once you've interested a prospect in your product or service, ask them for an order. If you don't, he or she may just buy from your competitor instead of you. Tricks of the trade that make it easier to get the order are to ask what color the customer wants or when he or she needs the product delivered or the work completed. For products or consumer items, asking how the customer would like to pay for the product can work, too.

▸ Think of the word *no* as meaning "I need more information."

▸ Don't exaggerate. Have facts to support all your claims.

▸ Encourage your prospect to ask you questions and talk about his or her specific needs. Then explain how the feature of your product or service can meet those needs.

Q **Is there any way to make word-of-mouth advertising happen?**

The way to get positive word of mouth to circulate is to have a good product or service and bend over backward to please your customer. Calling customers to make sure they are satisfied with the product or service a short time after you've done the job is a good image builder and gives you an opportunity to ask for repeat business and/or referrals. When you get a referral, follow it up, using the name of the person who gave you the lead.

Q **Can I post ads on electronic bulletin boards and commercial information services?**

Most commercial online services have classified advertising sections where you can place ads. If you are using GEnie, you can also place a directory-style listing for your business, products, or services in the Business Resource Directory, which is a searchable database of small businesses and of resources for business.

Another option is to put promotional newsletters, how-to articles, reviews, and shareware programming in electronic libraries online. If your information is valuable and demonstrates your knowledge or expertise in some way, this kind of advertising can bring you customers. Make sure to include a resource box telling people what your business does and how to reach you.

Be aware, however, that most online services discourage or forbid advertising in the electronic bulletin boards because the bulletin boards are intended as forums for discussion of issues and ideas. Most mass market online services also forbid or discourage users from sending unsolicited advertising through electronic mail, too, since customers don't like to get junk electronic mail. If you are unsure what the policies of a particular service are, there should be some type of policy statement available online. If you can't find it, most services have an electronic mailbox set up for feedback (complaints or questions about the service). In addition, almost any sysop (forum manager) online should be able to answer general policy questions.

Q **Do those little magnets, pencils, and other advertising specialties help?**

Like business cards, they are a good way to get people to remember your name and phone number. Another excellent tool for helping prospects remember you when they need you is to have Rolodex-type cards made up with your business name. The little tab on the card could have either your name printed or the nature of your business (printer, delivery service, etc.).

Q **Should I solicit business from a company I used to work for?**

Former employers frequently are the first customers of a new business. They are easy to sell to because they know what you can do from experience working with you.

Q **Can I solicit business from a former employer's customers?**

It depends on the circumstances. If you signed a noncompete agreement (an agreement preventing you from competing with the employer), or if the employer regards their customer list as a trade secret and you copied the list, you could be sued if you solicit business from the former employer's customers. If you haven't stolen a customer list and never signed a noncompete agreement, you might try calling some of those contacts or sending out an announcement that you are now in business for yourself.

Q Can a home business use sales agents or distributors?

If you can get a sales representative to take on your product or service, and if the sales agent is efficient, the relationship can be very beneficial since it will let you concentrate on producing the product or service while the sales rep concentrates on selling it.

Q How can I find a good sales agent?

The best way is to ask the stores you would like to see your products sold in or companies you would like to have sell your products which manufacturer representatives they order products from. If you have friends or business acquaintances who sell to the same market you do and use sales representatives, ask them for recommendations, too. Finally, you could ask around at industry trade shows about good sales reps.

Q What do I need to do to convince an agent to represent me?

You will have to have a good quality product or service and often a line of products. You will also need to show you will be able to fill orders if the rep gets your product into a popular catalog or store and that you can handle the paperwork professionally. If you can't deliver the goods or don't handle the paperwork professionally, it will hurt the sales representative's reputation and ability to make good deals in the future; hence, good reps are often very choosy about the companies with which they deal.

Q Should I tell customers I am homebased?

It depends on who the customer is. Huge department store distributors or mail order companies may not want to deal with homebased businesses because they fear they may not have the resources to meet customers' needs. Your best bet, usually, is not to volunteer information about being homebased. But if asked, don't deny it either.

Q Can a small business sell to the federal or state government?

Yes. The federal and state governments have programs to encourage small businesses to bid on contracts or seek work as subcontractors on government work. Among them are small business seminars, procurement (jobs) fairs, and outreach programs through community development organizations. The U.S. Air Force maintains a RoundTable on the GEnie service to help small businesses learn about procurement opportunities and how to deal with government red tape.

Q What does the government buy?

The government buys everything from food to computers to sophisticated electronic surveillance equipment. In fiscal year 1992 the Department of Defense (DoD), alone purchased more than $117.1 billion in goods and services. Of that amount, almost $24 billion in contracts was awarded to small businesses. In addition DoD prime contractors awarded small businesses another $18.2 billion in subcontracts.

Q Can a home business or a one-person business sell to the government?

Home businesses that have the experience and capabilities do sell products and services to the government. The government, like any other customer, is primarily interested in a company's ability to perform the contract and meet deadlines.

Q Is there a lot of red tape?

Yes, there usually is. In fact, the red tape is the leading deterrent to most small businesses who want to sell to the government. You generally can get some help dealing with the red tape through local offices of federal or state agencies or at Small Business Administration branch offices (see page 474).

Q How do I find out what the government wants to buy?

One way to find out what the government is buying is to read the *Commerce Business Daily (CBD)*. The *CBD* lists notices of proposed government procurement actions, contract awards, sales of government property, and other important procurement information. It is published every business day and contains approximately five hundred to a thousand notices each day. Each notice appears in the

CBD only once. All federal procurement offices are required to place notices in the *CBD* about proposed procurement actions over $25,000 and contract awards over $25,000 that are likely to result in the award of any subcontracts. These notices are organized into categories to make it easier to find the ones that might apply to your particular business. The *CBD* is available in print and electronically. The subscription prices for printed copies are $321 per year for first-class mail delivery or $275 per year for bulk-mail delivery. You can order a subscription by calling or writing:

Superintendent of Documents
Washington, DC 20402-9325
(202) 783–3238

If you have a computer and modem, the *CBD* can be downloaded in full or by individual service and supply code listing from the Air Force Small Business RoundTable library on the GEnie service. You do not have to subscribe to the *CBD* to download it from GEnie; it can be downloaded the same way any other file online can be downloaded.

You can get information about procurements that aren't published in the *CBD* by contacting local branch offices of government offices directly. Ask to have your name placed on bid lists and find out if there is a bulletin board (the traditional kind or an electronic bulletin board) you should read to find out about proposed procurements (purchases). It might also be a good idea to ask about possible sub-contracting opportunities with prime contractors in your vicinity. Other sources of information that may be good leads to government contracts are cable TV, local newspapers, and state agencies.

Q **What's a prime contractor?**

A prime contractor is the contractor that has responsibility for a project.

Q **What are the benefits of subcontracting?**

Subcontracting work from prime government contractors gives small businesses the opportunity to participate in (and profit from) federal contracts by doing part of the work on big contracts. It is simply an indirect way of doing business with the government.

Q How do I find lists of prime contractors?

The Department of Defense and other agencies maintain lists of prime contractors. You can often get these lists at local government procurement opportunity fairs, through local branch offices of government agencies and through city, county, or regional economic or industrial development offices. Many of these offices have people specially designated to help small businesses wade through the red tape of selling to the government. If you have no previous experience working with the government, this help can be very useful, even if you will be subcontracting work from a prime contractor.

Q Will my business benefit by exhibiting at trade shows?

Small companies that can afford the expense of the booth space, product literature, hotel accommodations, shipping costs for displays, and so on can benefit from exhibiting in trade shows if they have a product that works, is professionally packaged, and is ready to ship or be sold in quantity to customers at the show and afterward.

Q What do you need to stand out in a trade show?

You don't have to have the fanciest booth in the hall, but you do need a neat and attractive display in a good location for the booth to pay off. You also need to have the booth staffed. Empty booths with literature on the table but no one to explain it or demonstrate the product aren't going to bring in much business.

You will also need to have a sufficient amount of professional-looking literature to hand out. If you don't have literature or if it looks like it was done by Aunt Tillie on her 9-pin dot matrix printer that needed a new ribbon, you aren't going to make many sales or impress many people.

In addition to the literature you have available at your booth, you should have press kits made up to hand out to members of the press or other important contacts who attend the show. Find out, too, if the show has a press room, and if so, if you can leave stacks of your press kits there for members of the press to pick up. That may get your literature to people who might not find your booth on the show floor.

Giveaways and gimmicks to attract passersby to your booth are useful, too. The giveaway doesn't have to be terribly expensive: samples of your product given away as contest prizes periodically during the show, T-shirts with your company name on them given away after each demonstration of your product(s), or even something as simple as a bowl of wrapped candies can attract people to your booth.

Q **How do I decide which shows to go to?**

Try to check out a show's history. Ask other vendors in your industry which shows have been most productive for them and which shows least productive. Ask which attract the most attendees and the most important contacts. Sometimes direct sale of your product from a booth isn't as important as the contacts you may make with businesses, distributors, or sales representatives who can help you bring in more business.

Q **Is there any way to take advantage of trade shows without spending too much money for literature and booth space?**

If your company is too small or new to comfortably afford its own booth at a trade show, you may benefit by helping someone else out in his or her booth, sharing a booth with another company, or simply attending the show and introducing yourself to large companies and distributors who could be useful contacts for you.

Q **Can you go as an attendee and hand out fliers?**

Doing that is frowned on (understandably) by vendors who have paid to work at the show. Bring business cards, introduce yourself, and hand out business cards, but leave your sales literature in your hotel room or home unless you are sharing a booth with another company.

14.

Publicity:

An Almost-Free Ride

How can you get word about your product or services out to your customers if you can't afford to advertise extensively? One way is through free publicity in newspapers, magazines, or on broadcast media. Here are tips and hints on how to get various types of publicity and on how to get the most mileage out of any publicity you do get.

Q   What is publicity?

Publicity is making people aware of your business name and what you do. Usually that means getting the media to talk or write about you or what you do. The media can be television, radio, newspapers, magazines, or even books and newsletters. It may be local, regional, national, or specialized, such as a trade magazine. The nature of your business and what you sell will usually dictate which media will consider what you do newsworthy.

Q   Does publicity work as well as paid advertising?

Favorable publicity often brings in more sales than advertising does. The reason: people tend to believe what they read in editorial copy more than they believe claims in ads. Thus, if you get positive publicity, your product gains a testimonial, and your business gains credibility in the eyes of your customers.

On the flip side of the coin, you have no way of controlling what the press says about your product or service. If they don't like it and publish something negative about it, you may lose sales.

Q How do I get publicity?

The way to get publicity is to *seek* it. You have to telephone and send press releases to appropriate editors, reporters, and broadcasters and tell them what you do and why they should write or talk about you. Rarely will they discover you on their own.

Q How do I find editors to contact?

First, make a list of publications and broadcast media your customers are likely to read. If you sell locally, include only the local newspapers, radio, and cable TV. If you sell on a more widespread basis, you'll want to include trade publications in your field and perhaps the mass media or large regional newspapers and popular magazines that cater to your customers' needs.

Once you have this list, call each publication or broadcast station and ask who covers the type of information you want them to publish.

Sometimes your call will be put through to an editor or reporter. Other times you will just be given the name of an editor or reporter to whom you can send a release. If you aren't sure about the spelling of the name, ask the receptionist to spell it for you. Editors and writers don't like to see their names misspelled.

If you do get to talk to an editor or writer, tell him or her briefly what you want to publicize, and answer any questions he or she may have. If you are asked to send or fax a press release, do so immediately. It would be a good idea to mark the release, "Here's the release you asked me to send," or something similar. Hundreds of pieces of paper cross an editor's desk every week. Your note on the release can help keep it from getting buried and forgotten.

Q Is there any way to contact many editors at one time?

Try to get a wire service to cover your story. Two to contact are:

Associated Press
50 Rockefeller Plaza, 4th fl.
New York, NY 10020
(212) 621–1500

Reuters
1700 Broadway
New York, NY 10019
(212) 603–3300

If your products or services are aimed at computer users or involve computers in any way, another wire service to which you might send your information is Newsbytes. Newsbytes distributes computer news to several of the major online computer information services. You can reach Newsbytes online by sending electronic mail to the address Newsbytes on most online information services. You can also write or call Newsbytes at one of these addresses:

Wendy Woods, Editor in Chief
Newsbytes
822 Arkansas Street
San Francisco, CA 94107
Phone: (415) 550–7334
Fax: (415) 648–2550

Ian Stokell, Managing Editor
Newsbytes
12467 Lake Wildwood Dr.
Penn Valley, CA 95946
Phone: (916) 432–9569
Fax: (916) 432–9568

If your business is big enough, another option is to subscribe to the PR Newswire. This is a membership news service that distributes company press releases and publicity stories to media throughout the country or to only selected media contacts. The PR Newswire has a $75 annual membership fee. You also have to pay a fee for each release distributed. For additional pricing and membership information contact PR Newswire at:

PR Newswire
150 East 58th Street, 31st fl.
New York, NY 10155

Q   How do I get editors to actually write an article or talk about my product or service?

You have to have an interesting story or a "hook." The fact that you sell cellular telephones is neither exciting nor newsworthy. But if you tell a reporter about the interesting or new way your customers are using your portable cellular phone, you might make the news and get your company name in the press.

You also must know which media would be interested in the story you are presenting. "The major mistake people make is to propose stories that are not appropriate for the publication," says Ron Roel, deputy business editor of *Newsday* and *New York Newsday.* "Be familiar with the publications you are trying to pitch the story to. Know what kinds of stories they print, what the length is. Show that you have done some research and you have a particular reason to call about a particular story, not that you just want someone to write about you."

Q   There's nothing particularly newsworthy about what I do. Should I just forget about getting publicity?

Not necessarily. If there is nothing truly new or newsworthy about your product, consider making news happen. One or several of these "gimmicks" might work well for your business:

▸ Conduct a survey about something related to your product or service. Send out a release announcing the survey and a second one announcing the results.

▸ Hold a contest. Send a press release out to announce the contest and another to announce the winners.

▸ Write a booklet about something related to your business and give it away free. Send a press release out to announce the free booklet.

- Conduct a free seminar or training class related to what you do. Send out a release to announce the seminar.
- Donate your product or service to a nonprofit organization that can use it. *Have the nonprofit organization send out the press release.* (They may have more name recognition and clout with the press than you do.)
- Tie your product or service to a trend and publicize the trend, showing how people are jumping on the bandwagon by using what you sell.

In addition, local publications or trade publications might also publish an article about you if you are doing something for the first time or have released a brand new product.

Q How do you write a press release?

Put whatever facts you think will most interest the editor (your hook) in the very first sentence of the news release. The rest of the first paragraph should provide a little more detail, appealing directly to the editor's readers.

If the editor gets to the end of the first paragraph and doesn't know why the release is important, your information is not going to get used. Therefore, it is often *not* a good idea to start out your release with either your name or the name of your company. An opening paragraph like the following one, for instance, is not going to do much to spark anyone's attention.*

> *George Anderson today announced the expansion of Anderson Widgets into the home gadget market. A leading seller of squeak-free garage door mechanisms, Anderson Widgets will begin selling automated stereo controls for home use this fall.*

Even if George Anderson or Anderson's Widgets were well-known in the community or industry, the information sounds humdrum and unimportant. Who really cares what Anderson is going to add to his line this fall?

Change that ho-hum first paragraph to one that emphasizes customers' needs, and the release becomes interesting:

---

* Large corporations often publish releases that start very much like this. They sometimes get their information used simply because the corporation, by virtue of its size, is newsworthy. Small businesses have to prove their newsworthiness to get mention by the press.

Relief is just around the corner for parents who are tired of screaming at their offspring to turn down the stereo volume. Thanks to a new remote control device that can be hooked up to any stereo system, parents soon will be able to turn down the boom-box volume from anywhere in the house.

The new gadget, introduced at a trade show today by Anderson Widgets, will . . .

The paragraphs after the lead paragraph should give the editor any other important facts about your news. Be sure they include all the who, what, where, why, when, and how information that a news story normally contains. The release should be brief (about two to three double-spaced typed or typeset pages) but complete enough so the editor could write a paragraph or two without having to call you for additional information. The easier you make the editor's job, the more chance you have of getting publicized.

Q **Is there any special format I should use?**

You should follow these basic conventions in preparing your release:

- Use conventional typefaces and sizes. The editor wants information, not samples of your desktop publishing prowess.
- Type or print* your release on standard, 8½-by-11-inch letterhead stationery. Don't use any kind of erasable bond paper, and don't use ink that smudges when wet. If you don't have letterhead, type in the name, address, and phone number of your organization at the top of the page.
- If you wish, type "News Release" at the top of the page or just under your company name and address.
- Skip down a line or two and type "Release date:" followed by the date or "For Immediate Release" to tell the editor when to run the story. (A specific release date is generally used only if you don't want the information released before a particular date.)
- Skip another line and type "Contact:" followed by the names of one or

---

* "Print" refers to using a computer printer, not printing by hand. If you don't have a good typewriter or good electronic printer, have a commercial or quick printer typeset the releases or pay someone to produce them on their computer equipment if you need only a handful printed.

more people (often this will be you) the editor should call if additional information is needed.

▶ Skip another line and write a headline that describes and summarizes the importance of the release. Usually this will be a variation of the material you have in the first paragraph of the release. Use bold-faced type for the headline if you can.

▶ Skip one line and start your release by typing a dateline. A dateline is a notation about the city and state from which your release is being issued and often the date the release was issued. If you will be mailing your release (rather than faxing it), you might want to leave the date out of the dateline. That way, if your release is late getting out or gets stalled in the mail, it won't look outdated when it hits the editor's desk.

See a sample of how the release might look below.

Sample Press Release

ANDERSON WIDGETS, INC.   **NEWS RELEASE**
123 4th Street
Hauppauge, NY 11788

For Immediate Release
Contact: G. T. Anderson
             (516) 987-6543

NEW DEVICE INTRODUCED BY ANDERSON WIDGETS CONTROLS STEREO VOLUME FROM ANY ROOM

Hauppauge, NY—April 29, 1993—Relief is just around the corner for parents who are tired of screaming at their offspring to turn down the stereo volume. Thanks to a new remote control device that can be hooked up to any stereo system, parents soon will be able to turn down the boom-box volume from anywhere in the house.

    The new gadget, introduced at a trade show today by Anderson Widgets, will . . .

Q Do I send identical releases to all editors?

You could do that, but often it pays to change the headline and the first paragraph slightly to tailor the release for different audiences or markets. For instance, if news about the remote volume-controller for stereos was going out to local media, the headline might be changed to read "Hauppauge Manufacturer Develops Remote Control Device for Stereos." The copy (text) would be adjusted slightly to get the local angle in near the top of the release, too.

Q Is a press release the best way to get publicity?

The press release works best when used in conjunction with personal calls to editors or reporters. What often happens is that you alert the editor to the story in your phone call, and then if they are interested, they will tell you, "Send me a release," or "Send me some information." The personal contact isn't essential, but often it does help get your release and story noticed.

Q Do I just send the release and forget about it?

Usually it is best to follow up on the release by calling the editor or reporter a few days after you think a release should have arrived.

Q Don't editors get mad at all these calls?

Some editors get annoyed at phone calls. If you encounter an editor who doesn't want phone calls, be sure to make a notation on your contact list so you don't accidentally phone the next time you are sending out a release. Many, however, welcome them, provided you keep the following guidelines in mind:

▸ Keep the call brief. Reporters and editors very often must meet hourly deadlines. (Radio news personnel may be trying to squeeze in the conversation with you before the next broadcast goes on the air.) Your call will not be welcomed if you ramble and don't get right to the point.

▸ It's a good idea to outline in advance what you want to cover in your talk and to gather together any facts the reporter might ask for so you don't have to look them up or call back.

▸ Don't make a pest of yourself. Call only if you have news or information they may want.

▸ Never complain about a story the reporter did or about not getting publicity.

▸ If you have to call to correct an error the reporter made in a story, be polite and *never* make it sound like you think he or she made a mistake. No one likes to be told they did something wrong, particularly if they think they were doing you a favor by giving you publicity. Besides, the error could have occurred in production.

▸ If your contact seems rushed or says it is a bad time to talk to him or her, don't keep talking! Ask when a better time might be and call back then.

Q **How far ahead of time should I send a release?**

The date you should send out the release varies with the type of media. Announcements of dated events should go out to newspapers, radio, and local TV stations about 2 to 4 weeks before the event. (It is a good idea to call the individual newspaper or broadcast station and ask how far ahead they want to get the releases.)

The lead time (time to allow) on magazines is 4 to 6 months for editorial copy. (Seasonal and some specialty magazines may be longer.)

Q **Will the editor publish the press release as I wrote it?**

In some small publications and in some trade publications, press releases are used as written. Usually, however, editors or reporters will select facts from the release and rewrite the information to suit their needs.

Q **How often should I send out press releases?**

Send out press releases as often as you have something newsworthy to publicize! The more frequently editors read your name, the more likely they are to remember having seen it before and to give credibility to what you have to say.

Q **Should I send a photograph?**

Sending a photograph is a good idea for all media, except radio of course.

The reason a photo can be useful to newspapers and magazines is that they need "art" (to an editor, anything other than text) to break up the text and make the paper appear more readable. If there is a toss-up between two equally acceptable stories, and the editor is looking for some art to break up the page the story will be on, the story that came with the photo may get chosen over the one that didn't.

One problem, however, is that any photos you send out need to be good quality and should be 5-by-7-inch, or larger, black-and-white prints or color slides. Since there is no guarantee your photo or your release will be used, you will need to decide whether the extra cost of sending a photograph is practical, especially if you are only sending an individual release.

Q **What kind of photo should I send? Should it be a picture of me or the building my shop is in?**

A "head shot" (picture of you from the shoulders up) might be appropriate to send out if you have won an award, are writing a column, trying to get seminar or speech engagements, or are sending information about your business to TV stations. But usually what you should send out is a human interest picture showing how people benefit or enjoy what you sell.

Q **What about video news releases? Are they practical for small businesses to send out?**

If you are a very small business, the answer is probably no. TV newsrooms still get and read conventional news releases and will send their own reporter out to shoot a story if the story is sufficiently newsworthy and if it requires footage.

Q **What is a press kit and do I need one?**

A press kit (also known as a media kit) is a packet containing information about your company and its products or services. The purpose of the packet is to make it easy for reporters or others to find facts about you. It also makes it easy for you to respond to "send me something" inquiries.

From a practical point of view, whether or not you need a press kit will depend on how polished an image your customers or the media expect your type of business to present. If you are a small, one- or two-person operation, only sell locally, or get most of your business from word-of-mouth recommendations, you probably won't benefit by putting together a full-blown press kit. But as your business grows, or if your type of business requires you to present a polished, expensive "face" to the media and others, you may benefit by having press kits on hand and ready to pop in the mail.

Q **What goes into a press kit?**

The materials are generally enclosed in a good quality pocket folder. Often the name of the business is printed on the folder, but if you need to keep costs down, you might consider having stickers printed with your company name and applying the stickers to quality off-the-shelf folders. This "trick" works so effectively that Ziff Communications Company used it for their press kits at the PC Expo in New York City in 1992. Information about one of their product lines, Ziff Buyer's Market, a searchable online database of computer products, went into a plain glossy white folder and had a big blue circular sticker with the logo pasted on the upper right-hand corner of the folder. Information about ZiffNet went into the same kind of white folder but had a red label with the ZiffNet logo positioned in the right-hand corner.

Inside the folder you would put whichever of these items is appropriate for your business:

- an overview of the product or service
- current press release(s) about your products and services
- fact sheets with product specifications
- explanations of the technology involved if it is not widely understood
- photos of the product in use
- examples of how to use the product

- photos of what the purchaser will be able to produce using the product or service
- explanations of how to use the product if warranted
- company history
- testimonials
- copies of past publicity
- frequently asked questions and the answers
- background information about the principals if appropriate
- photo of the principle if appropriate
- your business card

Q How do I get reporters to quote me in stories instead of my competitors?

Become an expert on your industry. Then, when there's an event happening that you know about, call reporters and let them know you have information they may be able to use.

"Reporters don't have time to sit down and get to know you. Get in on a specific story. Let the reporter know you have something to say," advises *Newsday*'s Ron Roel. Make sure, he says, that you are available, easy to reach, and can explain things simply. "Too often experts get wrapped up in jargon and can't speak in less than a paragraph, making it hard to get the two-line quote that is often needed. Think in 'print bites.'"

Q How else can I get my company name mentioned in publications?

One of the best ways to get mentioned in publications is to write articles and get the articles published. If you are a consultant to a particular industry, for instance, try your hand at writing how-to articles on subjects related to what you do. A computer consultant might write a brief piece on how to choose a computer consultant, for instance, and submit it to the trade magazines that cater to the kind of customers he or she writes programs for.

Q How do I get invited to speak at association meetings or conferences?

If you are not well-known enough for conference planners to seek you out, seek them out. Call and tell them what expertise you have or how your knowledge will be of interest to people attending their meetings.

Q   **Will I get paid for speaking?**

If you are seeking to publicize a product or service or yourself, you probably won't get paid. On the other hand, if an organization thinks you will make a good draw for them, then you may get paid anywhere from a small honorarium to thousands of dollars for your time.

Q   **How can I get more mileage out of speeches?**

There are dozens of ways to leverage your speech or panel participation into sales. Here are a few:

▸ If your speaking engagement is to publicize an event, be sure to have enough handouts about the event for all who might be there.

▸ Have sales brochures and business cards available for attendees to pick up.

▸ Use the speaking engagement as still another opportunity to get press coverage by sending out an announcement about your participation in the event.

▸ If you are publicizing a book, either have copies with you or have a form people can mail in to get the book.

▸ Add a line about your speaking engagements to your resume, capabilities brochure, or other information you send out to prospective customers. It adds credibility to your claims of being an expert.

Q   **What other ways are there to publicize my business?**

There are probably as many low-cost ways to publicize a business as there are independent small businesses. If you think about what publicity really is—getting other people to talk about your business—you will think of dozens of ways to get publicity for your business. Many involve networking with other business owners or simply getting out and talking to potential customers. Here are some ideas that may work in your business:

▶ Make sure your business card gets into as many hands as possible. It is your calling card, the way people will remember who you are and what you do.

▶ Consider having an extra set of business cards made up in the form of Rolodex cards. If your potential customers can put your number directly into their Rolodex, they will see your name every time they flip past that part of the alphabet.

▶ Join the same associations, the local chamber of commerce, or other organizations to which your customers are likely to belong. Introduce yourself to people you meet and give them your business card. If you have sufficient expertise, offer to be a speaker at a future meeting. If you have time and sincere interest in the organization, offer to help with its projects. You can make both good business contacts and good friends that way.

▶ Make photocopies of any publicity you get and send it out with sales letters or other literature you mail to prospects.

▶ Do the monthly newsletter for an organization to which you belong. (This gets time-consuming, so be sure you have the skills and the time before offering.)

Q **Will it cost me anything to get publicity?**

Publicity is free in the sense that you don't pay media for space or air time as you would if you advertise. It is not a totally free ride, however. You still incur costs for printing and mailing releases, phone calls, product literature, and press kits you have to mail out, and it will take a considerable amount of your time to publicize your business on a regular basis. Still, publicity could be one of the most economical ways to spread the word about what you sell.

15.

Advertising Basics

If you ask a dozen small business owners about the value of traditional advertising, you are likely to get a dozen different answers. The owner of the limousine service will tell you he couldn't stay in business if he didn't run ads in the local papers; the person who runs the resume service may tell you newspaper ads don't bring many responses, but advertising in the Yellow Pages does. One computer programmer may tell you paid advertising is a waste of money, while another will tell you the ads she placed in trade magazines allowed her to expand her business from a little homebased operation to a company that now employs twenty-five people.

Q What businesses should use paid advertising?

You should consider using paid advertising if you sell products or services that: you can market to people with very specific interests (for instance, all hobbyists who have an interest in tole painting); need little explaining; must be sold to many customers to be profitable; or are traditionally advertised in newspapers, weekly shoppers, the Yellow Pages, or on TV or radio.

Q Are there any businesses that shouldn't use paid advertising?

Paid advertising may not be a good use of your money if you can only work for one or two customers at a time, if you are a consultant, if you sell creative services like writing or custom design, if your product or service needs a lot of explaining, or if no one else in your line of work advertises. In these cases the only type of paid advertising that might be worth considering would be ads or listings in trade directories or specialized trade publications.

Q **Is there any good way to determine whether or not I should advertise?**

One yardstick is whether or not your competition advertises. If the competition advertises, you probably should, too. And, you should advertise in the same publications the competition uses since your customers will expect to look in those publications for ads for your type of product.

Q **Where should I put paid advertising?**

There are numerous places you could advertise your products or service. You need to determine which places will help you reach the most number of likely buyers at the lowest cost. Among the places you may want to consider are:

- Regular or classified advertisements in daily newspapers, newsstand magazines, and weekly newspapers.
- Ads in weekly "shoppers." These publications consist of almost all advertising and have little or no editorial content. They may be mailed or tossed on driveways or stoops and contain ads for plumbers, garage sales, hair salons, tire dealers, etc.
- Regular or classified advertisements in trade publications or special-interest publications.
- Listings or advertisements in the Yellow Pages.
- Listings or ads in trade directories.
- Ads in card decks, which are ads printed on index-sized cards and mailed to subscribers of certain magazines or people who are known to buy a certain type of product or service through the mail.
- Radio ads.
- Network and cable TV ads.
- Inserts in weekly papers or shoppers.

- Classified advertising sections of commercial and private computer information services. *
- Ads on the back of theater programs or church bulletins.
- Coupon books or envelopes mailed to homeowners by a local mail service.

Q Why does paid advertising work for some businesses and not for others?

Advertising is not an exact science. Response to advertising is affected by the words and pictures used in an ad, the location of an ad in a publication, and the business owner's skill at choosing the right media. The weather, the time of year, what's on a page next to an ad, or what comes on before or after a commercial on TV or radio all can have an effect on advertising response rates, too. Thus, to some extent, finding what works and what doesn't is a matter of trial and error for every business.

Q Advertising is expensive. Is there any way to avoid wasting a lot of money on ads that don't work?

There is no way to completely avoid advertising mistakes and no way to ensure that every ad you place will be a success. In fact, some may not bring in enough responses to pay for themselves.

You can minimize the risk of costly error, however, if you remember these seven secrets of successful homebased and small business advertisers:

1. Know the purpose of your ad.
2. Set a budget.
3. Make realistic estimates of the number of responses you will get to ads.
4. Know how many responses you will need to break even on your advertising costs.
5. Choose a target market and then put your ad in media aimed at that market.

---

* **Important:** Classified advertising or other kinds of ads that have no general information content usually need to be posted in a special advertising section, not in the regular message area of services. Shareware and informative text articles, sample newsletters, and other text files containing real information as well as a plug for a company's products or services can usually be put in electronic libraries. Be aware, however, that almost no commercial or private electronic service allows opportunity chain letters.

6. Test on a small scale before launching an expensive large-scale ad campaign.
7. Expand the number and/or size of ads little by little, building on your successes, learning from the mistakes.

Q **Isn't the purpose of all ads to sell?**

Yes, but different ads sell in different ways. Advertising can be used to sell in any one of these four ways:

▶ build name recognition (so the customer remembers the product or service and looks for it in the future when the need arises)
▶ get inquiries that are followed up by sales calls or by sending sales literature
▶ sell products directly by getting people to call or send away for a product
▶ get customers to come to a shop or restaurant

Generally, the more expensive a product or the smaller the ad the less likely it is that customers will buy directly from an ad. If you want to sell a product directly from an ad, you will need one that's large enough to give the prospective customer enough details to make a purchase decision. If you can only afford small ads, you will need to have sales literature made up to hand out to people who ask about your product or service.

Q **How do you target ads to specific markets?**

Different media appeal to different types of people for different reasons. Putting the ad where a lot of people will see it isn't necessarily as important as putting it where the *right kind* of people will see it. Place your ad where people who have a known interest or need in the type of product or services you sell will find the ad and respond to it.

For instance, an ad for candle-making supplies is likely to draw far more responses in *Crafts* magazine than it is in *Computer Shopper*. Although people who use computers might also make candles, they would never look in a computer magazine to find out about candle-making supplies. Similarly, while someone who

242

makes candles or designs patterns may well use a computer, they aren't going to look for ads for drawing software or computer clip art in *Crafts* magazine.

Q **What do I need to know about my customers to choose the right advertising media?**

You need to know as much as you possibly can about customers' buying habits and interests. How old are they? Where do they live? Where do they shop? Where do they look for your type of product or service? Do they normally buy what you sell through the mail? What kind of publication are they likely to look in when they want information about what you sell? A phone book? A special interest or trade magazine? The ads in the Sunday newspaper or the weekly shopper?

Q **How many responses do magazine ads get?**

Advertising in the kind of magazines you see on the newsstands generates far fewer responses than most people imagine. Although response rates vary greatly, experienced marketers often find that a well-written ad placed in carefully chosen publications will get a response of about one-tenth of one percent of the media's audience—or less.

If the ad or the publication isn't right for the audience or what is being sold, the response rate can dip much lower. One entrepreneur placed an ad for a $39 item in a magazine that had a circulation of 600,000. The ad asked people to send for more information, rather than to place an order. He got only seventy-two inquiries, and although he immediately responded to each inquiry by mailing out a package of literature, only three out of the seventy-two people who responded to the ad actually bought his product. Needless to say, he didn't repeat his ad.

Q **Why do businesses advertise if the response rate is so low?**

Advertising is a numbers game. Some businesses can make a profit on a low response rate. Suppose, for instance, you spend $2,600 to purchase a full-page ad in a publication that reaches 250,000 people who are likely prospects for what you sell. You are charging $19.95 for your product and get 250 orders (a response rate of one tenth of one percent, or .001), totaling $4,987.50 in sales ($19.95 × 250).

Each product costs you $5.80, a price that includes manufacturing, packaging, and shipping costs. Thus, filling the orders would cost you $1,450 (250 × $5.80).

Your total costs would be: *$2,600 + $1,450 = $4,050*

Your cost per customer would be: *$4,050 ÷ 250 = $16.20*

Your profit would be: *$4,987.50 − 4,040.00 = $947.50*

While $947 isn't going to make you unbelievably wealthy, if the ad brings in approximately the same number of responses every month, that one product would give you a profit of more than $11,000 over the course of a year.

Furthermore, people who use mail order to sell goods rarely have just one product. They have a line of products and use their ads partly to "buy" the customer, since every person who responds to one ad is a likely customer for other products a company sells. Most companies find that they make most of their profits by making repeat sales to their existing customers. Once they start to accumulate a lot of names, they also make money by renting their customer lists to noncompeting companies.

You must be able to afford to experiment, however. If either your ad or the publication is off target, you may get few or no responses to the ad.

Q   **Should I experiment with classified ads in magazines to save money?**

Many businesses use classified ads in magazines to get new customers since the cost of these ads is much less than the cost of display (big) ads. But usually they use classified ads as a way to get inquiries, rather than a way to sell products directly. Since classified ads are too small to carry much information, people usually won't buy anything priced at much more than about $3 from such an ad.

Another drawback is that a classified ad may get fewer inquiries than a display ad, and your total cost per order is going to be higher because you have to send sales literature (or make a sales call) to follow up on the inquiries.

If the ad costs you $125 and you get seventy-five inquiries and send out a package of sales literature that costs you $1.00 each (including postage), your cost per inquiry will be $200 ($125 + $75). If four people who get your follow-up mailing actually buy your $19.95 product, you will take in only $79.80 ($19.95 × 4).* If the manufacturing of each product costs $5.80, your cost of filling those orders will be $23.20 ($5.80 × 4). Your total cost for getting the ad, responding to inquiries, and filling orders will have been $223.20, or $55.80 per customer. Thus, you would have lost $143.40 on that one ad. If, however, you sold each of those four customers another $100 in merchandise over the next year, you would—in the long run—make money as a result of running the original ad.

Q **Does advertising in newspapers work the same way?**

Newspaper advertising is harder to target than ads in magazines since newspapers are sold to a much more varied audience than are most magazines. In addition, newspapers generally aren't kept around as long as magazines, though people occasionally do clip ads from newspapers and save them for several months.

You can target potential customers through a particular newspaper or weekly shopper by choosing certain distribution areas. Weekly shoppers, and even some large dailies, will sell advertising by region, charging varying fees depending on the number of people in each region and the total number of regions in which you want your ad to circulate. Weekly newspapers sometimes are put out by a publishing company that allows you to buy advertising more or less the same way—you pay one rate for one publication, another if you add a second weekly, and so on.

In choosing newspapers in which to advertise, think about the demographics of the distribution area. If you are selling in-ground swimming pool maintenance services, most of your customers are likely to be affluent, so you would want to be sure to advertise in publications distributed to affluent areas.

Not all products sell well from newspaper ads. An ad for direct store delivery software might do well in a magazine aimed at retailers, but the same retailers might not see or respond to that ad in your local newspaper.

Q **Can I tell from one ad whether or not I should continue my advertising?**

Running one ad isn't really a good way to determine whether or not you should advertise. All you can learn from the response to a single ad is whether that one

---

* Four responses in seventy-five would be a little over 5 percent. Although some people claim they get as many as 25 percent to actually buy the product from follow-up literature, most people usually get between 5 and 10 percent.

ad worked in the media you chose. For instance, one woman who wanted to start a one-person cleaning service put a small ad in the smaller of two weekly newspapers in a well-to-do community on Long Island, New York. She got no responses to the ad. She tried the identical ad in the competing newspaper and got all the customers she could handle.

The same thing could happen to you. Or, if the ad doesn't bring as many responses as you'd like, it could be that the ad doesn't have a good headline, doesn't make clear what you sell (a very common problem when people try to be creative when writing their ads), isn't in the right media to reach potential clients, or neglects to give a phone number. People who are most successful at advertising track responses and test different ads, changing one thing in an ad at a time (either the headline, copy, media in which they advertise, etc.), until they are satisfied they are getting the best possible results.

Because of the number of advertisements competing for readers' attention, potential customers may gloss over your ad the first few times they see or hear it. Experienced advertisers say customers often need to encounter your ad or hear your name a minimum of six to nine times before they pay much attention to it. Furthermore, a prospect might not want your service this week, but might need it three months from now. If he sees your name in an ad now and then sees it again in three months, you will seem somehow familiar to him and therefore more trustworthy than someone whose name he hasn't seen before. He may call you instead of a competitor.

Of course, a lack of initial response could really mean you shouldn't bother advertising.

Q **Should I advertise in the classified sections of newspapers?**

Certain kinds of businesses gain a lot of benefit from classified ads or small display ads in the classified section of publications. Many people turn directly to the classified ad section when they are ready to buy a product or service. That means you don't have to sell them on buying the product or service; you just have to convince them to buy from you.

One indicator of whether you should advertise in the classified section of a particular publication is if it has a classified heading, such as "plumbing" or "music," that seems appropriate for what you sell. If you find such a heading and see that many people advertise under it regularly, you can probably figure readers look for that type of product or service in that paper.

The most successful classified ads in newspapers and weekly shoppers tend to be those for services people can't do themselves or don't want to do themselves, or for products or services they can't find anywhere else. Usually plumbers, electricians, those who repair appliances, tutors, cleaning services, rental services, and the like do well with this type of small ad.

Q What should I put in my ad?

What goes into an ad will depend somewhat on the size and nature of the ad; however, whether you are placing a full-page ad or a small classified ad, it should:

- get the reader's attention;
- make clear what is being sold;
- build interest and desire for what is being sold; and
- tell the reader what action to take and persuade the reader to take that action.

You should also be sure the ad:

- states how the reader can contact you;
- states the name of the product or service; and
- includes your business phone number and, preferably, your address, too. If you don't want to give out your address in an ad that has your phone number in it, at least include the town if the publication circulates throughout several towns.

Q Do I need an ad agency?

You probably do not need an advertising agency to create ads for local media until you've been in business for a while and are spending $50,000 or more a year on advertising. Newspapers, weekly shoppers, and even some radio and TV stations will offer some help and advice if you are creating ads for use in their publications or on their stations. Although a good advertising agency might be able to produce better results, your business may not be big enough to interest them. As your business grows, however, you may want to look into getting ad agency help. If you just need someone to create a brochure or other product literature, you might want to use a free-lance commercial artist rather than an ad agency.

Q How can I judge how well ads are working?

If you are running several different ads at one time you will need to ask people where they got your name or code ads in some way so you know which ads produced how many responses. Otherwise you have no way of determining which ads are working for you and which aren't, which should be continued and which dropped.

If you are using coupons in your ads, you can put a distinct number or letter in tiny print in a corner of each coupon to indicate which publication the coupon came from. If people will be responding to you by mail, you could key the responses to the publication by changing something noncrucial in the mailing address or adding something like "Suite 5" or "Dept. A" to your mailing address. You might also key an ad by using or not using your middle initial or using a nickname. For instance, if I had three classified ads running for the same product in three different publications, one might say to reply to Janet Attard; another to J. Attard, and another to Jan Attard.

Q How do I track them?

You need to keep a list showing which ads people responded to in which publications. If you have a computer you can keep this list in a database or a spreadsheet program for easy sorting. When you only have a few orders it may seem silly to do this, but as your business grows, you will need to know exactly which ads and which media produced the most orders so you can plan your advertising to get the most mileage for the least money.

Q How often do I have to advertise?

If your testing shows advertising does bring you customers, then you will probably want to advertise on a regular basis unless your business is seasonal. How often "on a regular basis" is will depend in part on your budget and in part on the media in which you advertise. If weekly publications bring you good results, however, you should probably advertise every week. If you are advertising in a daily publication, you may want to pick certain days of the week to advertise and always run your ads on those days so prospects know to look for your name and number on those days.

Q Should I advertise on radio or TV?

You will need to compare the costs and results of TV advertising to that of other media. TV advertising must be repeated several times a day for several weeks in order to be effective. It also needs to be aired at a time customers are likely to see or hear ads and respond to them. A tuxedo rental store in one town, for instance, did well with TV advertising right around prom time.

Q Should I get a listing or ad in the Yellow Pages?

Some businesses get many customers from their Yellow Pages ads or listings, and others get no calls. To decide whether or not you should use the Yellow Pages, you need to consider carefully where your customers look for your type of product or service. You should also consider whether there is a clear-cut heading under which to put your ads. If there isn't, you might not get many customers from your listing.

If your service or product can be easily depicted in a small picture or if you can add some kind of textual information that will build confidence (for instance, "board certified"), then a display ad might be worthwhile. If you are just starting out, however, you may want to make the ad small. If it is successful, consider getting a slightly larger ad the next year, as long as you can be sure the ad will stay on the same page with other listings for your type of business.

Q Will color help in the Yellow Pages ad?

Opinions differ on how effective color is in a Yellow Pages ad. Some people say it increases response and some say it doesn't. One of the problems with using color in your ad is that the salespeople may have talked everyone else into buying an ad with a color border, too—so yours won't stand out.

Q Do I need to offer a money-back guarantee?

It is a good idea to offer a money-back guarantee for at least two reasons: it builds customer confidence and it can help lower your chargeback rate if you accept credit cards. Often customers won't buy from a store or a mail merchant unless they can return merchandise for a full refund if they aren't satisfied. Although there will always be some who take advantage of money-back guarantees and attempt to return a product after using it, the majority of customers are honest, and the goodwill you create by offering the guarantee will usually outweigh any losses due to people returning goods they've broken, copied, and so on.

Q **Do I need to be able to accept charge cards?**

Being able to accept charge cards as payment can boost sales. However, it can also increase your costs and risks. Securing merchant status may be difficult, too. See chapter 18 for additional information.

Q **Should I use special offers?**

Special offers can increase your response rate and help you determine which media gets responses. However, special offers can also bring out the tire kickers and freebie hunters, too. You need to test special offers to see which attracts the most paying customers. If you use a special offer, make sure it has a cut-off date or people will be pulling out the coupon or ad for months to come and demanding your product at the special rate. Also, if your cut-off date is at 9 P.M. Friday, don't be surprised if a lot of people wait until 8:30 P.M. on Friday to order or to walk into your store.

Q **What kind of special offers can I use that won't cost a lot?**

Discounts on products work well (the need to offer discounts should be considered when developing your pricing strategies), free information, and giveaways of inexpensive items, such as balloons, markers, pens, and magnets, may be useful in certain circumstances. For kids, free samples of your product or a free trial period are typical types of promotions.

Q **Can I say my product is better than that of the competition?**

The only safe way to indicate that your product is better than the competitor's is with indisputable facts. Size, weight, retail price, and number of pieces, for example, could be compared without problem to show your product's benefits over that of the competitor. But if you say your competitor's products are ugly or shoddy, you could be setting yourself up for a costly lawsuit. The same is true if you say your products are healthier or longer-lasting if you don't have hard facts to back up your claims.

Q   Should I advertise in card decks?

Card decks can bring your sales message to a large group of potential customers at once (typically 100,000 prospects), and the prospects can be well targeted, such as all readers of a particular trade magazine. Response rates are low—typically one-tenth of one percent—though they may be higher or lower depending on how well your items match your target audience. As with mail order ads in magazines, however, there are companies that can make a profit despite the low response rate. Those companies seem to be ones with high-ticket products, products that lead to repeat sales, and products that are one of a line of products sold by the company who places the ad. If you only have one product to sell, it is probably unwise to try to use card deck advertising unless the product sells for at least $40 or $50 or more and you will be following up leads from the card deck with sales calls or additional literature.

Q   How do I get into card decks?

Many magazines do card deck mailings periodically. In addition most card decks you receive will contain contact information for the publisher of the deck. Thus, if you see a deck that seems to be addressed to your target market, just call the publisher of the deck and ask for their rate card. You can also find the names of card deck publishers in directories available in the library. *Standard Rate and Data Service* directories are among the ones that list card deck publishers.

Q   Are there any ways to cut the high costs of advertising?

Here are several ways you may be able to cut costs:

▶ Barter your product or service for space or air time. (Barter is taxable. Ask your accountant about tax implications.)

▶ Ask for a lower rate than the one advertised on an advertiser's rate card—the rates may be printed in black-and-white but aren't necessarily carved in stone.

▶ Ask about remnant space, which is space left that hasn't been sold at the time a publication is ready to go to print. If you have your ad ready to go, you may be able to purchase the remnant space for much less than the price of the space listed on the rate card.

▶ If you sell retail products, ask manufacturers about cooperative advertising programs. These can reduce your advertising costs.

▶ Do cooperative advertising with other small businesses. You may be able to advertise in their catalogs or have your product literature inserted into their merchandise packages in return for inserting theirs in with mailings going out to your customers.

▶ Trade lists with other noncompeting businesses, or trade your list for ad space or air time.

▶ Rent out the mailing list you accumulate to bring in extra income.

▶ Send an ad or a catalog of products along with every order you fill to encourage additional sales. The ad or catalog rides free with the order if it doesn't increase the shipping weight enough to raise the cost of shipping.

▶ Tack up business cards in stores, beauty shops, print shops, universities, and other public places if appropriate.

▶ Post computer shareware or text files with contact information in electronic libraries on commercial services and private bulletin boards. If you don't have a modem or don't have access to these online services, you can get people to upload your shareware and files for a fee.

- Send disks with your shareware to companies that sell shareware through catalogs.

- Consider placing inserts in weekly shoppers rather than doing a residential mailing.

- Consider doing small direct mail campaigns instead of advertising if you don't need to sell to a lot of people at once.

- Have your business card or other business information printed on a Rolodex card and mail the cards to your customers and prospects.

16.

Mail Profits: Using the Mail to Build Your Business

Each day the United States Postal Service collects, processes, and delivers approximately 550 million pieces of mail. A large percentage of that volume is made up of business mail designed to get new customers or make repeat sales to existing customers. Here are tips on how you can use the mail to bring in business.

Q **How can businesses use the mail to market their products or services?**

There are probably as many ways to use the mail as a marketing tool as there are ways for you to communicate with prospects and customers. Here are just a few ideas:

▶ send out traditional direct mail packages (several pieces of sales literature in one package—typically a letter, brochure, and response card or return envelope aimed at getting the prospect to place an order immediately)

▶ send out sales letters designed to get the prospect to call and make an appointment to talk to you about some product or service you sell

▶ send out a newsletter to prospects to demonstrate your expertise and drum up sales for your business

▸ send out invitations to an open house or other event designed to drum up business

▸ send reminders about services people need to purchase periodically (oil change or health checkups, for instance)

▸ send a package of coupons for items in your retail store to people in your local area

▸ send catalogs listing new and old products

Q **What kind of response does direct mail get?**

Most mailers are satisfied if a mailing to a rented list of targeted prospects gets a one percent response (in other words, if one person out of a hundred responds to the mailing). That figure goes down to one-tenth of one percent or less if the list you mail to is a residential mailing list (rather than a list of people who share a specific interest). It goes up—often to 5 percent or more—if you are mailing to a list of customers who have purchased from you in the past.

With a mailing, as with advertising, response rates are important for planning and estimating; however, what really matters is the cost of getting the customer and the long-term profitability of the customer. If you are selling one item by mail, you will need to look closely at how many responses you will need to make a profit in order to determine if the mailing is worth doing.

Q **Is it less expensive to use the mail to get customers than it is to advertise in magazines or newspapers?**

It depends on what kind of mailing you are doing. If you are trying to sell products that compete with commercial items, and you will be mailing out expensive sales literature, you could easily spend as much to reach five thousand people with a direct mail piece as you would spend to put an ad in a publication reaching tens of thousands or even hundreds of thousands of people. However, your mailing might have a better chance of being seen and read than an ad would, thereby getting more responses and orders.

If you are a free-lancer or a small service business that sells to other businesses, you could send out a simple sales letter to a hand-picked list of fifty or one hundred likely prospects for less than $50 and possibly land one or more clients who will give you thousands of dollars worth of work.

Q **Is one mailing enough to get new customers?**

Often, no. Just like with ads, people have to see your mailings many times before ordering from you. Some mail marketers prepare a series of six or seven different letters and mailings and automatically send out a different letter in the series every few weeks until the customer buys, or until they reach the end of the series of letters. Each successive mailing brings in new customers that the preceding mailings didn't attract.

Q **Where do I get mailing lists?**

You can get mailing lists from companies called mailing list brokers. You can also get lists directly from some magazines and associations, or you can create your own lists from contacts in your industry or by calling companies likely to need your product or services and asking for the name of the purchasing agent, a department head, or whoever would be responsible for making purchasing decisions. Among the companies that rent mailing lists are:

American Business Information, Inc.
5711 So. 86th Circle
Omaha, NE 68127
Phone: (402) 593–4593
Fax: (402) 331–6681

Compilers Plus
466 Main Street
New Rochelle, NY 10801
Phone: (800) 431–2914; in New York: (914) 633–5240
Fax: (914) 633–5261

Edith Roman Associates
875 Avenue of the Americas
New York, NY 10001
(800) 223–2194, in New York: (212) 695–3836

You can find many others in the Yellow Pages of your phone book or in the *Standard Rates & Data Services (SRDS)* directories available in your public library.

Q **What kinds of lists can I get?**

There are two broad categories of mailing lists: compiled lists and response lists. Compiled lists are created by getting names, addresses, and phone numbers from phone books, industry listings, and government lists of business names. Each name on the list may be verified by a phone call and, in some cases, names of contacts (if a business) can be added to the compiled information.

A response list is a list of people who have responded to some appeal—a mail order ad, a subscription offer, etc. These lists generally cost more and produce better responses than a compiled list.

Q **How often can you use a mailing list you get from a mailing list broker?**

It depends on the company and the list and on the form in which you buy it. It used to be that you could only rent mailing lists for one-time use. Now, however, you can purchase some lists on computer disk or magnetic tape and use the list as often as you want within the time frame specified in your agreement with the mailing list company. Compilers Plus, for example, will sell you compiled lists on either disk or magnetic tape and allow you unlimited use of the list for a year. Response lists generally aren't available on diskettes.

Q **How does the list broker know if you reuse the list?**

List are "seeded" with names of people who get and track mailings to prevent unauthorized reuse of lists.

Q **What does it cost to buy or rent a mailing list?**

The base prices for compiled lists average about $50 per thousand names to rent for one-time use. The fee to purchase a compiled list may be about double the rental fee. There may also be a flat fee added to the price to put the data in disk format you can use.

The base price for response lists generally ranges from $75 to $125 per thousand names. Usually response lists can only be rented for one-time use.

On top of the base prices for compiled or rented lists, you normally pay extra for selecting names by zip code and for pressure sensitive (self-sticking) labels. You also pay extra if you want phone numbers in addition to addresses or if you want names and titles of contact people at various organizations.

In many cases there are minimum fees or a minimum number of names you must rent at once. One company, for instance, has a minimum fee of $95 for a compiled list and a minimum order of five thousand names for response lists.

Q How do I choose a list?

You choose a list that matches as closely as possible the characteristics of your customers or expected customers. For instance, you might be able to get a list of all female executives who have purchased some type of mail order product in the last six months. If you can describe your typical customer to the list broker, he or she should be able to help you identify and get the best list for your needs. You could also compile your own list from your knowledge of an industry or from the local phone book.

Q What's a house list?

A house list is the list of your own customers. If you sell a line of products or the type of service that is needed periodically, your house list will often produce more customers than any other list.

Q How important is it to have the name of a person on the mailing?

Usually you will get a better response if you address your mailings to particular people. A letter addressed to a "Occupant" or "Sales Manager" or "President" or "Purchasing Agent" immediately tells the recipient that what is inside is an ad from a business or individual they don't know. That makes that letter less important to read. Overworked businesspeople and home owners who don't like getting junk mail often will throw out such letters without ever opening them.

Q What should I put in a mailing to find new customers?

It is usually best to include a sales letter, brochure, and a response card or return envelope. Some people just send out a brochure or a sales letter, but using both gives you more opportunity to explain what you sell and show the recipient of your mailing the benefits of your product or service.

Q How do I write a sales letter?

The purpose of a sales letter is to sell—in other words, to convince someone to take some specific action, such as order a product, call you for an appointment, visit your store—and to take that action immediately.

Although that might seem obvious, many small business owners send out sales letters that don't sell. A typical letter reads something like this:

We are pleased to announce the opening of the George Jones Bookkeeping Service. The service, which is designed to help small businesses meet their bookkeeping needs, uses the latest computer equipment to store all customer records. You can reach us from 9 A.M. to 5 P.M. at 555–1234.

The problem with a letter like that is that the recipient really doesn't care that *you* have opened a bookkeeping service or anything else. What might interest them, maybe enough to call you, is information about what your service will do for them. Tell them how you can save them time, minimize errors, or perhaps help them reduce their income tax bills by making sure they have all the records they need to take all the deductions they are entitled to—then you are much more likely to catch their attention and attract their business.

Q How do I write a brochure?

Use the brochure as an expansion of your sales letter. The brochure should give further details about your product or service, but it should still *sell*, not tell. The cover of the brochure should highlight the key benefit of your product or service, and the text and headlines inside the brochure should build on that benefit and add one or two additional reasons to buy or call you immediately. Finally, the brochure or a separate response card should ask for the order or the phone call and, if possible, give the recipient an incentive to do what you have asked immediately. That incentive might be a discount for ordering before a certain date, a free gift for calling within the next 5 days, or something similar.

Be sure the brochure includes your business name, address, and phone number in several places. You also need to make sure people who see the brochure for the first time can immediately tell what the brochure is all about and what you want them to do. Studies have shown that you have between 3 and 7 seconds to capture a prospect's attention with your mailing piece. If the prospect can't figure out what you are selling or why it should interest him or her, your brochure will wind up in the garbage.

One good way to test the clarity of your brochure is to have someone who knows nothing about your business read the brochure and tell you what he or she thinks the brochure says. If the person can immediately tell you what you are offering and why it's a good idea to buy what you are selling, then your brochure probably will accomplish your goals. If there are questions about what you are selling or about the information in the brochure, you probably have not conveyed your sales message as well as you could have. In that case, consider rewriting the brochure or have a professional help you write it.

Q **Do I need pictures in my brochure?**

Photographs or drawings can be useful in your brochure if they help get your sales message across. If the pictures are just there to satisfy your ego or sense of pride, they probably don't belong. You may be thrilled about the new building you are moving into; your customers probably don't care, however. Thus, including a picture of your new building is likely to be a waste of space and money, since it costs extra to put a photo in a brochure.

Q **What kind of information should go in a brochure?**

You will want to make sure your brochure includes all the main features of your product or service and that it expresses those features as benefits. For instance, instead of saying your database software stores customer data, you'd talk about how the software saves time by automatically printing customer addresses on shipping labels or improves cash flow by making it easy to spot overdue accounts.

In addition to features, you would want to include facts, statistics, and perhaps testimonials that would help the reader make a decision to call or place an order.

If you are using the brochure to make a special offer, the nature of your offer and how the recipient can take advantage of it, as well as a cut-off date for the offer, should be very clear.

Q **How do I get testimonials?**

Satisfied customers will often write or call you and tell you how great they think your product or service is. These people, if asked, often don't mind letting you include their comments about your product or service in your sales literature. You should get a signed statement from them indicating you have their permission to use their comments in your sales literature.

Q **Can I make up testimonials?**

No. That is a violation of truth-in-advertising laws.

Q **Can I rent my mailing list to other companies?**

Renting mailing lists is a good source of extra income for many companies; however, you will usually need to have at least 5,000 to 10,000 names for your list to be rentable. The information also will need to be current and accurate. If your information is much more than 6 or 9 months old, it may have too many address or name changes (for business contacts) to be useful to others.

Q **Do I need a bulk mail permit from the post office to send out mailings?**

Mail permits let you take discounts on large mailings if your mailings meet certain post office specifications. These specifications include the number of pieces mailed at one time, the uniformity of the pieces mailed, the destination of the mail, and the method of sorting, bundling, and depositing the mail at the post office. Since you have to pay a one-time permit fee plus an additional annual fee for each class of mail for which you want discount rates, you will need to be mailing at least several thousand pieces of mail each year in batches of at least two hundred to make getting a permit worthwhile. (At this writing the one-time fee and the annual fee are each $75.)

If you are going to use a letter shop to prepare your mailings, they should be able to send out your mailings using their permit.

Q **Should I use first-class mail or third-class?**

That depends partly on your budget, partly on how soon you need the mail to arrive, and partly on whether you want your mail to look like a letter rather than an ad so that it will get opened. If you are mailing a piece that must reach everyone on the list by a certain date, and that date is a week or two away, or if you want your mailing to look like a regular letter, use first-class mail. Sending the mailing third class immediately alerts recipients that it is not a personal letter. In addition, third class gets sent only after all other mail goes out. If a post office is particularly busy, as it is during certain times of the year, third-class mail sits on the side until someone has time to get to it. That means it can sometimes take more than two weeks for third-class mail to reach its destination. A brochure urging readers to visit your trade show booth isn't going to do any good if your customers get it a week and a half after the trade show is over.

Q **How can I make my mailing stand out among all the other junk mail people get?**

One way to make your letter stand out is to use real stamps on it rather than using a meter. Using a lot of small denomination stamps instead of one first-class mail stamp may make it stand out, too. Still another way to make your mail stand out and get people to open it is to put a message on the outside of the envelope telling people that the contents will benefit them or save them money.

17.

Getting Paid

One of the biggest drawbacks of being your own boss is you no longer collect a paycheck at the end of the week. Instead, unless you run a cash business, you are likely to have to wait weeks or even months to collect for work you've done or products you've delivered.

Sometimes such delays are unavoidable. It may be standard practice for a particular company or most of the companies in a particular industry to take 60 to 90 days or longer to pay. Other times, though, your customers will give your bills low priority because money is tight or because you are a small business and unlikely to damage their credit rating or be much of a pest if they pay you late or don't pay you at all.

Regardless of the circumstances, unusual or unexpected delays in payment can put a crimp into your business and gray hairs on your head, particularly if you have a payroll to meet or a family to feed, clothe, and shelter. The strategies in this chapter should help you avoid some common collection pitfalls.

Q **How long could it take to collect from customers?**

If you don't get paid at the time products or services are delivered, it can take anywhere from a few weeks to 90 days or more to collect on your invoices. While some companies pay within 10 to 30 days of delivery of work or a product, it is not unusual for payment to take 45 to 60 days from the time your invoice reaches your customers. In some industries, or with some individual companies, you can expect to wait 90 days or more for payment.

Q When should I consider a payment late?

Consider a payment late if it does not arrive within about 10 days of the time you would normally expect it to arrive. For instance, if a business normally pays in 30 days, you should have payment in hand within 40 days of the date you mailed the invoice.

Q What should I do if I don't get paid on time?

If you sell to businesses, call your contact at the company and make sure they got your invoice and that the invoice has been signed off and forwarded to the accounting department for payment. If you sell to consumers, send out a friendly reminder asking if the customer has misplaced or overlooked the bill.

Q What should I do if the customer says they never received the invoice or that they mailed the check?

Although there are some businesses that will use such ploys to delay payment, occasionally invoices, checks, and mail do get lost or misplaced. As long as the loss is an isolated incident, the best thing to do is give the client the benefit of the doubt. Send a new invoice if the client tells you the invoice has been lost. If accounting says the check has been cut, ask them to see when it was mailed. If the company is local and more than a week has elapsed since the check was supposedly mailed, ask them put a stop payment on the old check and issue you a new one. If you suspect the company is not being honest about mailing the check, tell them you will stop by in person and pick it up.

Q What can be done to speed collection?

In some types of businesses there may be nothing you can do except to plan ahead for the delay in payment. This is one reason accountants and experienced business owners warn neophytes not to quit a job to start a business unless they have or can raise enough cash to cover business and living expenses for 6 to 12 months. But for many businesses one or more of these suggestions may help.

- Discuss payment terms before the work is done. Be sure you and the customer are each clear about when payment will be expected.

- Ask who should get your invoice when the work is done. It may or may not be the person who assigns you work. If your invoice is misdirected, payment is likely to be delayed.

- Put everything in writing. If you don't have a formal contract with your customers, summarize details of any verbal discussions in a letter (commonly called a letter of agreement), and send it to the customer. The letter should include enough details about prices, delivery, and payment to avoid disputes later on about your fee, what you are supposed to do for that fee, when you are supposed to do it, and when and how much you should be paid.

- If the customer has the right to accept or reject work, make sure any contracts or letters of agreement specify a time frame within which the customer must make that decision. If you don't, the customer could hang on to your work and/or delay payment for months just by neither accepting nor rejecting what you've delivered.

- Consider retainer arrangements with some or all of your customers if it is customary in your field. These can be set up on a per job basis or on a long-term basis. If the retainer gives the customer a certain number of hours of your time each week or month, make sure the contract is worded so that your customer can't "save up" (carry over) unused time. Otherwise you could get stuck with two or more customers each demanding at the same time that you make good on the time you "owe" them and do their projects immediately despite other commitments you have made.

- Get part or all of your money up front. If you can't get the entire fee in advance, arrange for progress payments for the balance. Set up the arrangement so you have covered all costs and at least some of your profit before you finish a job or deliver the final product. That way if the company stalls, "loses" the invoice for your final payment, runs into a cash flow problem of its own, or decides not to pay you for any reason, the loss will be minimal.

Dirty Tricks Warning: From time to time you will run into a business that has no intention of playing fair with small business vendors. Such businesses are often surprisingly large and regularly chisel vendors or subcontractors out of anything from a few dollars here and there to a few hundred dollars, knowing full well the small vendor won't do much more than raise an eyebrow or kick a tire because (a) the amount is too small to be worth pursuing legally, or (b) their business is too important for the small vendors to jeopardize by insisting on full payment. If you run into one of these businesses, you basically have three choices:

- make a fuss and risk losing the client
- waste your time and money going to court and, later, trying to collect on any judgment you are awarded
- swallow pride, your tongue, and a little gall, and accept the lower fee as yet another cost of doing business

Unfortunately, the last option is usually the most practical from a purely business point of view since it wastes the least amount of time and money—which is why the bigger company knows it is likely to get away with its tactics.

- If you are working for a federal or state government agency or a prime contractor to a government agency, ask if they have a program to pay small businesses within 30 days. If they do, find out what you have to do to be part of that program.

- If you are working for other businesses, consider offering a discount for payment within 10 days. A common discount is 2 percent for payment within 10 days.

Dirty Tricks Warning: If you offer a discount for early payment, you will find some companies will take the full 30 days or more to pay and then still take the discount. You can argue with them, insist on payment, or ignore the "mistake." What you do will probably depend on whether or not you want to do business with the company in the future.

- Send out invoices as soon as jobs are finished. The sooner your invoices go out, the sooner they are likely to be paid. If you deal with businesses that run payables only once or twice a month, and your invoice reaches accounting the day after the company ran payables, your invoice could take 15 to 30 days longer than it should have to get paid.

- Look into the possibility of getting merchant status and accepting credit cards. If you are approved, depending on your agreement with the company, you will usually get paid by the credit card company within 2 days to 2 weeks.

- Decide, based on industry norms and your experience with individual vendors, how long it should take to get paid. Any time you do not receive payment within the time limit you set, send out a reminder or overdue notice immediately. Follow up with repeat notices at regular intervals until you get paid. The longer you wait to collect on late accounts, the harder it may be to collect.

- Be persistent if you have trouble collecting. The adage about the squeaky wheel getting the grease holds just as true for collecting from accounts as it does for other situations.

- If possible, don't start a new job for a company until you get paid for the previous one.

- If you sell to businesses and have a computer and modem, consider checking the credit rating of potential business clients by searching the TRW Business Credit Profiles available on Dialog and through gateways to Dialog from GEnie and other computer online information services. TRW Business Credit Profiles contain more than 2.5 million company listings and can be searched quickly by entering a company name and, if desired, city and state information. If there are any matches for your search, you will get a list of companies that match search terms you keyed in. If the company you want information about is on the list, you can get a full credit report displayed immediately on your screen. This report will contain, if known, the company name, address, sales, employees, ownership, credit history, and the number of credit inquires made in the past 9 months.

Q **What does it cost to get a business credit report online?**

You pay the regular hourly service charges ($6 an hour during nonprime time on GEnie at modem speeds up to 2,400 baud) plus a surcharge for use of the TRW credit reports. The surcharges are as follows:

No-Hit Search	$1.25	(no matches for your search terms found)
Initial Company Search	$7.50	(each set of up to five company names)
Full Company Record	$29.00	

Since the search and retrieval can be done in just a few minutes, the cost for getting a business credit record this way can be under $40.

Q **I've done a lot of work for a company that always seems pleased with my work and pays on time. Now, they are more than two months late paying me and won't return my phone calls. Could it be they were displeased with the last two projects I did for them?**

When a customer who appears to be pleased with your work stops paying on time and won't talk to you about the problem, there is good reason to suspect the company is having a cash flow problem and that the missing payments are a result of their cash crunch, not the quality of your work.

Q **What can I do to get them to pay me?**

This is always a difficult situation for a very small business. On one hand, if the customer is big and has provided a lot of business in the past, you may not want to lose their future business. Thus, you may not want to be too aggressive in your collection efforts. On the other hand, you can't stay in business if you don't get paid for your work in a reasonable amount of time. If you are a free-lancer or a very small business, very late payment for just one or two large jobs can affect your ability to pay your own bills if you don't have much spare cash.

Therefore, the first thing you have to do is decide whether you want to keep this customer's business and if the business is worth keeping. If you sell to businesses rather than consumers, one thing that may help you decide if a customer's business is worth keeping is to talk to other business owners who sell to the same company. Find out what their experiences have been with the company.* Trade or business associations are a good place to make such contacts. If you start hearing things like "They do that to everyone" or if you learn several other suppliers or free-lancers have stopped doing business with the company, you may well want to consider crossing the company off your customer list. Networking with other business owners can also help you avoid losses and payment delays by alerting you in advance to companies that are known to be slow or late payers.

If the business is worth keeping, about the best you can do is send statements with polite reminders of the unpaid bill each month and continue to try to reach your contact at the company. If you do succeed in reaching your contact, try to find out the reason for the holdup. If the company is having cash flow problems, suggest they pay you part of the outstanding balance every 2 weeks until the invoice is paid.

If you don't want to deal with the customer in the future, send a series of firm (but not threatening) collection letters. Phone call reminders may also help pry money loose from the company. If the company doesn't respond to your letters or calls, you might consider suing them in small claims court if the amount involved is within the limits set in your region. Occasionally you will find that a company will pay what it owes shortly before the day they are told to appear in court.

---

*You have to be careful that you don't say anything that could be considered libelous or slanderous by the client company. For instance, you don't want to imply the company is about to go bankrupt or never pays its bills to anyone. You could mention the company seems to be taking a long time paying you, and ask others if they know how long the company usually takes and/or what their experiences with the company have been.

Q **What should I do if the customer keeps calling me but isn't paying?**

Basically, you have only four choices:

▸ Thank them for thinking of you but tell them you can't ship merchandise or start new projects for them until they pay part or all of what they owe you.
▸ Refuse to do business with them at all.
▸ Ship goods on a COD basis or get up-front payment for services.
▸ Take the order or the job and add it to their bill—and risk having their cash flow problem become yours.

Q **I don't want to be bothered going to court because of the amount of time it will take. Would it do any good to just send a letter telling the company I'll sue if they don't pay?**

No, you can't do that. Threatening to sue a company (or a consumer) when you have no intention of doing so could cause you to be sued yourself. If you are unsure of what you can and can't do to legally collect from your customers, ask an attorney for advice. For a relatively small fee, you could save yourself a bundle if the advice prevents you from getting sued or helps you collect debts.

Q **Should I sue if I can't sue in small claims court?**

That's another sticky situation for very small businesses. Unfortunately, in some cases, despite the loss of the income, the most practical thing to do is accept the loss and go about your business. Unless the company owes you a lot of money and you could recoup your costs of suing, legal and court costs and the time you have to devote to the lawsuit may make it impractical for you to sue. Your best bet in a situation like this is to ask your attorney for advice and consider all possible outcomes before making your decision. Remember, too, that should you win and your customer can't pay, your victory will be a very expensive one.

Q **The company claims I didn't do part of the job so they aren't going to pay me. What can I do?**

The first thing you should do is sit down and talk to your contact at the company to determine the cause of the misunderstanding. If you had a contract to perform the work, ask them to pinpoint how the company thinks you failed to live up to your responsibilities. If the problem revolves around a misunderstanding over terms in the contract or over the nature of the work to be delivered, see if you can work out an equitable solution. If not, discuss whether the company might make partial payment (if you are willing to accept partial payment) in settlement of the contract.

If you can't work out your differences, you will have to sue the company if you want to collect the money you are owed. If the amount is larger than the maximum claim allowed in small claims court, the cost of your legal fees might make the lawsuit impractical to pursue. Thus, if you can reach any kind of compromise with the company, you are likely to come out ahead. (You will also learn, albeit the hard way, to make sure your contracts let the customer know exactly what you will and won't do for your fee.)

Q   Do I have to have a written contract with my customers to get paid?

Under something known as the Uniform Commercial Code (UCC), contracts for the sale of goods worth $500 or more must be in writing to be legally enforceable. (Items you can move or ship are generally considered "goods.") Although personal services and goods valued under $500 are not covered by that law, it is always a good idea to get contracts in writing. Without a written document there is generally no way to prove whose version is correct if a dispute arises.

Q   How should I go about notifying people that their account is past due?

It would be a good idea to develop a series of letters notifying the customer of the past due amount and requesting payment. Each of these letters should be slightly more emphatic than the previous one about the importance of paying the past due amount *now.*

If you send out computer-generated statements, the reminder could be printed directly on the statement instead of being mailed as a separate letter. If you use multipart forms, an alternative to a form letter might be to put a sticker saying essentially the same thing as the form letter on a copy of the original bill and mail it to the customer. Still another alternative (a little less friendly, though) is to send the customer a copy of the original bill and using a rubber stamp, mark it "Past Due."

Q **Are there any regulations about what I can and can't do to collect bills?**

The Fair Debt Collection Practices Act set down a number of guidelines governing the collection of consumer debt by third-party bill collectors. While the provisions of the act may not apply to you unless you retain a collection agency to collect outstanding consumer bills, you would still be wise to abide by the provisions of the act.

Among the actions you should avoid are:

▸ making threats
▸ using harassing or abusive language
▸ accusing the debtor of being a liar or deadbeat
▸ making the debtor's name known publicly (reporting late or defaulted payments to credit bureaus, is not illegal, however)
▸ making false, misleading, or deceptive statements about what will happen if the debtor doesn't pay (such as saying you will sue if you have no intentions of doing so)
▸ implying that the originator (person who is requesting payment) of a collection letter is an attorney if he or she is not
▸ making a collection letter look like a telegram
▸ implying that the debtor has committed a crime
▸ making dunning calls more frequently than once a week
▸ making calls at very early or very late hours (after 8 P.M. is considered very late for dunning calls in some states)
▸ calling a consumer who is a debtor at work if his or her employer forbids it

Q **What should I say in past due notices?**

The first reminder should be very polite, suggesting the customer has merely forgotten or misplaced the bill. The tone should be friendly and indicate you assume the customer will pay it immediately now that he or she has been reminded. It might read something like this:

Dear Mr. Southard,

Bills sometimes get misplaced or overlooked, and we have not yet received your payment for our invoice #1234 dated April 25. Please check your records, and if payment has not gone out, mail a check today.

If a check was recently mailed, please disregard this notice. Thank you for your attention to this matter. We appreciate your business.

Sincerely,

If you don't get payment within two weeks of sending the first reminder, send a second notice. This second notice should be worded a little more strongly than the first. In addition, it should also ask the customer to call you if there is any problem related to the bill. This may flush out customers who aren't paying because they dispute a charge or aren't satisfied and those who might need to pay the bill in stages instead of all at once.

Dear Mr. Southard,

We have not yet received your payment of $230 for invoice #1234 that was mailed to you on April 25. Would you please take a minute to check your records now and forward payment so we may bring your account up to date? If there is some problem with your bill that you would like to discuss with us, please don't hesitate to call.

Thank you for your immediate attention to this matter.

Sincerely,

The third letter should be a little firmer.

Dear Mr. Southard,

We still have not received your check for $230 for invoice #1234 dated April 25. Since you have not questioned previous statements we assume our records are correct. To pre-

serve your credit privileges, please forward us your check for $230 today so that we may bring your seriously overdue account up to date. If you cannot pay the full amount at this time, please call our main office to work out a payment method you can abide by.

Thank you for your speedy cooperation in this matter.

The fourth letter should specify what you will do if you do not receive payment by a specific date. You must be very careful not to make such letters threatening or to misrepresent what you will do. Don't say you will report the customer to credit bureaus or sue unless you plan to do those things, and don't say or imply anything that could otherwise be construed as threatening. To be sure your collection letters don't violate any laws, it would be a good idea to have an attorney review and approve them. Here is a sample of what your fourth letter might look like:

Dear Mr. Southard:

Over the last two months we have sent you several reminders about your overdue payment of $230 for invoice #1234. At this time, your bill is still unpaid.

Please remit your payment of $230 within 5 days to prevent further collection action.

Sincerely,

Q **Can I send postcards instead of letters to alert people to past-due accounts?**

No. By law, there can be no marks or visible indication referring to collection efforts on anything you put in the mail. If you use envelopes with see-through windows allowing the address to show through, make sure nothing about late payments shows through the envelope window.

Q **How should I handle phone calls to collect money owed me?**

Collection phone calls should pretty much follow the procedures described for letters. The one thing you will need to do, however, is make sure at the outset that you have reached the right individual. Even if the person's last name is unusual, you could have phoned the wrong person, particularly if you looked up their phone number in a telephone book. As noted in the list of collection practices to avoid, you also should avoid making your calls at unusual hours.

Q **Does it pay to use a collection agency?**

Most people do not like to be contacted by collection agencies, and some will pay up when they see their account has been turned over to one for collection. Additionally, the agency may be more persistent and routine in its collection efforts than you are. However, a collection agency doesn't have any methods available to it that you don't. They can't threaten, harass, or mislead the customer into paying the debt, and they have no legal means of forcing payment. Nothing short of a court order can force your customers to pay up.

Q **What do collection agencies charge?**

Collection agency fees range from one-third to one-half the amount collected. Be sure you know in advance all the fees you will be charged. For instance, will you have to pay a fee for each letter the agency mails on your behalf or just give the agency a percentage of the amount collected?

Q **A customer owes me a lot of money and seems to have skipped town. Is there any way I could track this person down and collect?**

If the amount owed is significant, you might want to consider hiring a private investigator to do the search.

Q **My customer is from out of state. Where do I file the lawsuit?**

In most cases you have to file suit for collection in the legal jurisdiction where the customer is located.

18.
The Charge Card Dilemma

In January 1992, VISA International issued a report saying its services had "evolved from a credit card company into a full-service consumer-payment system." The report also indicated that "the company's goal in the coming years is to become the preferred consumer-payment system for virtually every type of consumer transaction."

While those claims and predictions might seem grandiose, in the United States alone general-purpose credit cards are already used to purchase $250 billion in goods and services annually. Furthermore, the goods and services that can be purchased on a credit card now include not only items such as equipment, clothing, travel, and miscellaneous supplies but also food and medical and dental services.

As a result, any business that sells consumer goods and services or that sells goods and services frequently charged on corporate credit cards is at a disadvantage if they cannot accept credit cards. As Dennis Mulgannon, owner of Maxwell Street Pizza in Hemet, California, puts it:

The more I sell the more I make. . . . Because I am so much like everybody else, I need to place myself so that I can sell more than the guy down the street. . . . Or, if I cannot beat them I have to at least join the "me too" club. Accepting credit cards falls into the "me too" category.

As convenient as it may be for people to charge purchases on credit cards, the widespread use of credit cards presents three major problems for small businesses:

▶ They have extreme difficulty in finding a bank or other reputable credit card processor willing to grant merchant status* so they can accept credit cards.

▶ They are easy prey for unscrupulous salespeople and con artists who either charge exorbitant fees for finding a source of merchant status for the business or just take hefty application fees and disappear.

▶ Very small businesses are at risk for catastrophic losses if they are hit by a rash of charges on stolen credit cards.

Although there are no guarantees, by arming yourself with the facts in this chapter you stand a good chance of avoiding the pitfalls in obtaining merchant status and processing charge sales.

Q **Won't it cut into my profits if I accept charge cards?**

Accepting credit cards will increase your cost of doing business since you will have to pay the credit card company a percent of each sale and are likely to also have to pay an additional flat transaction fee plus some flat monthly charges. Thus, if you have a very low profit margin, you may want to increase your prices overall to offset the credit card fees. You may find, however, that your sales volume and the dollar amount of each sale increases more than enough to offset the fees you pay the credit card company. In addition, if you have been used to billing customers and waiting 30 or more days for payment, letting customers charge purchases could reduce your billing costs and improve cash flow. You shouldn't expect to clear up outstanding bills by gaining merchant status, however. It is against credit card company rules to let customers charge unpaid bills to their cards. Only new purchases can be charged.

Merchant status is the term used to indicate a business is authorized to accept credit cards in payment for goods and services. A business with merchant status will have the charges processed through their merchant account with a bank or other credit card processor. Credit card companies and banks use the term *merchant* to denote any business that accepts credit cards.

Finally, keep in mind that after achieving merchant status, some businesses find little improvement in sales, and a few actually lose money due to credit card fraud or consumer abuse.

Q How long does it take for the credit card company to pay me when I accept charge cards?

How soon you get your money will depend on whether funds are transferred to you electronically, held for a time against possible chargebacks, or mailed to you in a paper check. Generally, however, you can expect to get paid in 2 to 14 days.

Q How do I go about accepting credit cards?

To accept credit cards, you will have to apply for merchant status (also called a merchant account) through a bank or other financial institution, an authorized independent sales organization (ISO), or the credit card company itself for certain cards. Once you are granted merchant status, you will need to buy or rent a device for imprinting or electronically processing the credit cards.

Q Do I need a separate merchant account for each credit card I want to accept?

American Express and some other credit card companies require separate accounts, but VISA, MasterCard, and Diner's Club can often be processed through a single merchant account. The company or financial institution giving you the merchant account will be able to tell you which cards you'll be able to accept on your account.

Q Where do I go to apply for merchant status?

If you have been in business for two years or more, your business is not homebased, and you don't sell mail order, you may be able to get merchant status through the bank with which you normally do business. If you are a small mail order company, run a homebased business, are new in business, or operate certain types of businesses, your regular bank may turn down your request for merchant status, or not even be willing to talk to you about it.

Can I get merchant status without going through a bank?

You don't have to get merchant status directly through a bank, but getting merchant status elsewhere may not be any easier. The owner of a homebased mail order company in New York says he called "every single bank and S & L" listed in the burough of Queens and then called "all the places that advertise in the Sunday *New York Times.*" These calls, he says, produced one of three results: "Either they said they won't deal with mail order and/or homebased businesses, or they quoted me outrageous prices, or they insisted that they had to come down to my home and explain the whole service to me and then give me a price."

 Why is it so difficult to get merchant status? Don't the banks or other companies want my business?

Banks want business, but they don't want risky business, and home businesses, new businesses, and mail order operations all look like high-risk operations to credit card processors. Here's why: Federal laws give credit card users broad protection against unauthorized use and unfair credit practices. * As a result of these laws, credit card issuers act as intermediaries in disputes between the consumer and the merchant. If a consumer claims they did not make a purchase or that a purchased item was inferior and the merchant won't replace it or refund their money, the credit card company refunds the cardholder's money in most cases and charges back (bills) the merchant for the amount of the refund. While merchants are supposed to be given a chance to prove the purchase was actually made or the goods were satisfactory, merchants say that doesn't always happen.

If the merchant is very small (as homebased operations often are), the company may not be financially able to make good on chargebacks, particularly if they are hit with someone buying merchandise with one or more stolen credit cards. If they go bankrupt (or simply close their doors and disappear, as some fraudulent businesses do), the credit card issuer has to absorb the loss. In addition, under VISA regulations, if the percentage of VISA chargebacks to a merchant account goes over one percent, the merchant bank may face stiff fines or possible loss of their ability to process VISA cards.

---

* The Truth in Lending Act and the Fair Credit Billing Act both contain regulations affecting credit card use and billing.

Q Why do banks object to giving legitimate mail order businesses merchant status?

Mail order businesses are particularly risky from the credit card processor's point of view because the company selling the merchandise never sees the customer, does not get the customer's signature at the time of the sale, and has no way of determining for sure that the person calling in the order is actually the owner of the card. "Any time you don't have an imprint of the card (or the electronic equivalent) and a signature, you take a one hundred percent risk on the sale," says Tim Pfeiffer. Pfeiffer is in charge of MIS functions for Teleflora CreditLine, the merchant services division of Teleflora Incorporated, a company known to many people because of its floral wire services. He also worked in the company's customer support division.

Q Are there any other circumstances that might prevent me from getting merchant status?

Credit card processors are not going to want to give you merchant status if you have a bankruptcy on your records, tax liens in effect, or accounts that have been written off by a lender.

Q No bank will grant me merchant status. What should I do?

One option is to leverage your way up the credit card status ladder. North Carolina entrepreneur Ben Mandell, who turned a single one-hour photo shop into a successful chain with more than thirty locations, suggests starting with American Express, which has less stringent requirements than some other companies that grant merchant status. "Tell them you want to establish a merchant account," he says, then after you get it, "approach Discover Card and tell them the same thing." Wait a few weeks after you get merchant status with Discover Card services, Mandell says, "then call back and tell them you also want to process VISA and MasterCard."

Q Is there any more direct way to get a merchant account for VISA or MasterCard?

There are numerous companies called independent sales organizations (ISOs) that are authorized by credit card companies to serve as intermediaries between merchant banks (banks that process credit cards) and businesses that want to accept charge cards from their customers. As the word sales implies, these companies *sell* credit card processing services and within certain limits can sell their services for whatever the market will bear. Many also sell, lease, or rent credit card processing terminals and provide other services such as check verification services.

 I've heard stories about business owners paying steep applications and other fees and sometimes still not getting merchant status. Does that happen a lot?

Unfortunately, merchant status is sometimes so difficult to get that the small merchant becomes easy prey for opportunistic and unscrupulous salespeople.

"I swear these people blow into town with the wind," says Dennis Mulgannon, the California pizzeria owner. Mulgannon had wanted to accept credit cards in his restaurant but was turned down by his bank because his business was too new. But then one day, he says, "this guy comes into the store and asks to see the owner. He says he can get me not only merchant status but also an electronic reader and printer.

"Well, I saw the clouds part and heard the Mormon Tabernacle choir singing the *Hallelujah Chorus*. But it must have been just a recording. . . . Three hundred dollars and four weeks later I was 'regretfully informed' that I'd need to reapply after I had been in business longer."

When Mulgannon asked about the partial refund he had been promised if his application wasn't approved, he was told, "We are mailing it today." A week later, when the refund hadn't arrived, the response he got was, "Oh, we are so sorry for the mix-up." A week after that, says Mulgannon, the only response was the telephone company's recording, "We're sorry. The number you have reached is no longer in service. . . ."

Mulgannon was understandably furious. But not long after the first salesperson disappeared, Mulgannon says, "this other guy blows in the door. Did I learn my lesson? Did I? No! I *wanted* merchant status. This new guy wants money, so I start sorting my payables list through my mind and decide that if my kids want to eat, they are going to have to go out and get jobs. Hey, I am looking at the future. . . .

I plunked down my fee, filled out the application. He took Polaroid pictures of the business. . . ."

But this application didn't pan out either. Eventually Mulgannon did get merchant status and without losing any more application fees. "I just flat-out told the last guy that he was not getting so much as a penny until I was approved, and the equipment was up and running."

Unfortunately, Mulgannon's story isn't unusual. Nor is it the only way unsuspecting business owners get "taken" in their quest for merchant status.

Some sales agents actually do come through with a merchant account but then charge exorbitant transaction fees, monthly fees, and/or equipment fees. Some business owners are actually talked into paying discount rates as high as 8 percent on each transaction *plus* an additional flat fee of $1.25 per transaction. Many get talked into signing noncancellable contracts requiring them to pay $3,000 to $4,000 for equipment they could purchase or lease elsewhere for less than $1,000.

Q **How much should I expect to pay to apply for merchant status?**

Fees will vary by how new or risky your business seems to the credit card processor and which cards you are processing. In late spring of 1992, application fees were running, on the average, from $100 to $300, but some sales agents were charging over $700 to take an application for merchant status in 1992. Some ISOs were also suggesting merchants alert them ahead of time if they think there might be a reason (such as a bad credit history) the processing company might turn them down. Says Teleflora's Tim Pfeiffer, "We are not interested in declining applications at $100 apiece and will be happy to discuss your situation ahead of time." But, he adds, once you actually do submit an application, the fee Teleflora charges ($100 in June 1992) will not be refunded if your application is turned down since the company has to order credit reports and incurs other expenses to process the application.

Q **Why is there such a large discrepancy in fees?**

ISOs have to order and pay for credit reports on applicants and have to pay employees to review applications and credit reports. Thus, they often charge an application fee to cover these costs and to discourage applications from people who have little real interest in achieving merchant status or who know they are unlikely to get merchant status because they have many delinquent accounts or have defaulted on loans.

However, since an ISO's actual costs to process an application should be well under a $100, fees much over $100 are likely to include a fair amount of profit being made on the application process itself. Much of that profit is likely to go to the independent sales agent rather than to the company the sales agent represents. In such instances, the salesperson's goal may to be to take as many applications as possible so he or she can make as much money as possible, regardless of whether or not the ISO is actually likely to approve the applications.

 How much should it cost to buy or rent the terminals to process the cards?

Fees vary with the type of terminal, but average prices for the special electronic terminals used to process credit card purchases range from under $500 to approximately $700. Printers that work with the terminals are about the same price. According to one industry insider, sales agents often make a profit on terminal sales or leases as well as on application fees; thus again, the higher the fee the more the sales agent may be making on the equipment.

 What kind of fees should I expect to pay on each sale?

Discount fees (the percentage of each sale the credit card processor takes out before giving you your money) ranging from 2.25 to 3.25 percent are common. However, some ISOs charge discount fees as high as 6 to 8 percent. The per transaction fees from ISOs with the lower discount fees were averaging 20 to 25 cents; agents selling higher-priced services were charging up to $1.25 for each transaction. Fees from the better ISOs depended somewhat on volume and choices of payment method, too. Companies that had a high volume of transactions and/or were willing to wait 2 weeks to receive their money from the ISO were able to get slightly lower fees than low-volume businesses that opted for 2-day electronic deposit of funds.

Many ISOs were charging monthly minimums or a flat monthly fee and chargeback fees. If you have a printer that ties into your terminal you will also have to pay the cost of the special paper and ink cartridge or ribbon, which you may have to purchase through the company renting the machines.

Some processors require merchants to have reserve accounts (money set aside to cover chargebacks), and some were demanding the option to be able to electronically withdraw funds from the merchant's bank account as well as to deposit them so chargebacks could be immediately collected from the merchant.

One other thing to watch out for are exceptionally low discount fees, which are occasionally used to get merchants to sign up, and then, after they do, the discount fee or other charges go up significantly.

Q Is it ever worth paying much higher than normal fees?

Certain kinds of businesses find it particularly difficult to get merchant status because of the nature of the product or service they sell. One ISO mentioned not dealing with limousine services, escort services, or companies selling "adult" products. Another mentioned not accepting multilevel marketing companies, businesses selling water filtration devices, and certain kinds of telemarketing services because they tended to either disappear or have a high customer dissatisfaction rate, and therefore a high chargeback rate. In addition, many ISOs won't grant merchant status to a small business if the owner has a poor personal credit history.

If you fall into any of these categories you may have to pay high rates to find a third-party processor willing to take on the risk of your business. However, you shouldn't be willing to do so until you have first approached several other sources for merchant status. What one company won't accept, another may. Additionally, what your bank considers a poor credit history may not be considered "that bad" (as one ISO representative put it) to a third-party processor.

Finally, be aware that paying a lot of money to someone who promises to get you merchant status does not assure they will deliver. As mentioned above there are independent sales agents whose only goal is to take applications. There are also some that require a high application fee and, instead of getting you your own merchant account, try to hook you up with a fulfillment company. The owner of a homebased software company in California paid $750 to a sales agent who said his fee was refundable. What he provided for the software company was not the merchant account the owner wanted but a fulfillment service that wanted to charge several hundred dollars a month in shelf fees to store product inventory and process orders. The company also wanted the authorization to withdraw money at any time for any reason from his bank account.

Couldn't I avoid all these hassles by having a friend process my charges for me with his number and giving him a percent of each sale?

No. This practice is forbidden by credit card companies because of the potential for fraud. Even though your operation may be totally legal, if the credit card company discovers what's going on, your friend could lose merchant status.

Generally only two kinds of companies want to have their cards processed this way: (1) those that can't qualify for merchant status on their own because their business is risky and (2) fraudulent businesses. The way the latter type operates is that a con artist will pose as a new merchant and will make contact with existing merchants in town, saying how difficult it is to get merchant status, and offer the other merchants a percentage of each charged sale. The con artist will then submit phony orders, duplicate orders, or advertise some kind of bargain and have the calls go to the established merchants. He or she collects the money from the merchant, then skips town before the scam is discovered. The result: the helpful merchant has to make good on all the chargebacks to his or her merchant account.

On the flip side, once you do achieve merchant status in your own name, you should never let anyone talk you into processing their charges through your merchant account.

 How does having another merchant process your charges differ from what an ISO does or from what a fulfillment service does?

The primary difference is that the bankcard company knows about the arrangement and has authorized the company to act as a third-party processor or to take orders. If you are unsure whether a company is legitimately able to process charges for you, ask whose name will be on the bill the customer receives. If it is the other company's name and they do not store your inventory and ship your product to the customer, you would be wise to try to get the name of their merchant bank and verify through the bank that the company does have authorization to process charges for other merchants.

 Is there any good way for a new or homebased business to get merchant status?

Teleflora's Tim Pfeiffer recommends you start with your own bank, since some banks in some communities will work with small and homebased businesses if the business owner has a long-standing relationship with the bank. If the bank can't grant you merchant status, says Pfeiffer, ask them if they can recommend a third-party processor who will.

If the bank can't refer you to anyone, ask other business owners in your area who their merchant card processor is and what their experiences have been with the company. Other good sources of information may be associations or business groups to which you belong. The Direct Mail Association, the Association of Shareware Professionals, and some local chambers of commerce are just a few of the groups that are able to suggest reputable third-party processors to their members.

Be aware, however, that if you are a brand-new homebased business, you may have a great deal of trouble getting merchant status.

Finally, many business people who have had bad experiences with some third-party processors advise that you be sure to get copies of, read, and understand every paper you will have to sign. Watch out for hidden processing fees, shelf fees, extra monthly fees, and noncancellable (and generally lengthy) equipment leases. Also be wary of salespeople who will sign forms saying they have inspected your premises when they have never set foot on your property or in your place of business.

 I really don't know any business people in my community, and I don't belong to any associations. Where else can I get names of companies offering merchant status?

If none of your local contacts can help you, you may want to contact one of the bankcard companies or third-party processors listed below. Each of these companies has some restrictions, and each has different fee structures and requirements. Make sure you read and understand all details of any agreement you sign with these or other companies.

Charge Card Companies

American Express
Merchant Services Division

1661 East Camelback Street, Suite 300

Phoenix, AZ 85016

(800) 528–5200

(Press 0 when you hear the recording)

Discover Card Services

P.O. Box 28541

Columbus, OH 43228-0541

(800) 347–6673

Bank

Indiana National Bank

Merchant Services Division

1 Indiana Square

Indianapolis, IN 46266

(317) 266–6000

(The bank indicated it was offering merchant status only to Indiana businesses and a few businesses in the gift basket and software industries out of state.)

Independent Sales Organizations (ISOs)

Card Acceptance Corporation

9393 Activity Road, Suite D

San Diego, CA 92126

(619) 530–1770

Teleflora CreditLine

12233 West Olympic Boulevard

Los Angeles, CA 90064

(800) 325–4849

(310) 826–5253, for Teleflora main switchboard

U.S. Merchant Services

9 East 41st Street

New York, NY 10017

(212) 818–1807

Litle & Company
54 Stiles Road
Salem, NH 03079
(603) 893–9333
(Note: Litle & Company will not consider home businesses but will consider direct marketers and mail order companies that are not homebased.)

The above list is by no means exclusive. It consists only of companies that were recommended by associations or were mentioned favorably by business owners who were using the services, were willing to answer questions about their policies over the phone, and indicated a willingness to work with very small, homebased and/or mail order businesses.

There were a few other companies I called that didn't appear very interested in answering questions over the phone—at least not after I'd tell them that I wasn't interested in obtaining merchant status for myself. One of those was an ISO that markets its services extensively and aggressively. (A 21-year-old was contacted by this company so soon after he had registered his business name that he hadn't even gotten his sales tax number issued to him by the state!) Each time I called this particular company, an operator wanted to put me through immediately to a sales agent. When I explained that I merely wanted information, I was transferred to a company executive's office, and asked to leave a message. The executive never called back. As it turns out, many business owners have had bad experiences with this particular company. Typical complaints have mentioned numerous hidden charges, exorbitant fees for equipment, noncancellable 4-year contracts, outright lies, failure to return copies of signed agreements, and difficulty in locating a real address or phone number for the company headquarters. One merchant actually had to close a bank account because one of the agreements he had to sign to get merchant status gave the ISO authority to make withdrawals from his account and they appeared to be making withdrawals for services he had never agreed to purchase. This company has agents selling all over the United States. It reportedly operated under another name a few years ago, shut down operations under that name due to its bad reputation and reopened under a new name—using the same shady practices as it had in the past.

Unfortunately, companies that use questionable practices such as this are likely to remain a problem for as long as merchants need to accept credit cards. To avoid falling into the traps such companies set, take the time to investigate various ways to obtain merchant status. Compare what various ISOs have to offer, and don't deal with any company that won't answer all your questions and provide you copies of agreements it expects you to sign. Go over all contracts and agreements carefully making sure you understand every word in them. Your best bet would be to have an attorney review the contracts before you sign them. Finally, be sure to ask other merchants what rates and fees they are charged for processing cards and what bank or ISO they deal with. Compare what you are being offered with their experiences, and proceed with care.

Q **Are there any dangers in accepting credit cards?**

The biggest danger is getting hit by crooks who are buying goods with stolen credit cards, stolen credit card numbers, or counterfeit credit cards. By law, the credit card holder is liable for only the first $50 in losses if their card is lost or stolen, or if someone gets their number and makes unauthorized purchases to their account. All purchases above that amount, once the unauthorized use is discovered, get charged back to the merchants, who have to cover the loss even though they shipped the merchandise.

Q **How can that happen? If I ship the merchandise, and it hasn't been returned, why should I absorb the loss?**

The merchant is always responsible for verifying that the person using a credit card is legally authorized to do so. You are supposed to compare the signature on the credit card to the signature on the sales slip at the time of purchase to verify the person using the card is the person to whom it belongs. You are also supposed to compare the number imprinted on the card to the number that shows up when a card is passed through an electronic verification terminal, since there are some counterfeit cards being used that have one number printed on the card and a different number encoded into the magnetic data strip on the back of the card.

If you are taking orders over the telephone, it is impossible to verify a signature or match numbers in this way. You have no way of knowing if the caller is the actual owner of the credit card and authorized to use it or if he or she is using a stolen card or has obtained the number fraudulently. Until the person to whom the card was issued discovers the loss or unauthorized use of the card and reports it, all charges are likely to go through up to the limit of the card. But once the cardholder discovers the unauthorized charges and challenges them, all the unauthorized purchases will be charged back to each merchant who accepted the card in payment for sales.

Q How much would I stand to lose?

The amounts can be substantial if you sell high-priced merchandise or if you sell the kind of products people order in quantity. California business owner John Ferguson, whose small company takes orders over the telephone and then ships merchandise to customers, had to borrow from friends and family to make good on $14,000 worth of fraudulent charges made on stolen cards. He implemented procedures to screen out possible fraudulent orders and during the following year refused to ship $25,000 in orders that seemed suspicious. Says Ferguson, "I don't believe I have refused any legitimate sales. If I had, the customer would have called to complain that they never received their order and not one has."

Q Is there any way to tell if an order placed over the phone is legitimate or not?

Based on his experiences, Ferguson says people ordering goods on stolen credit cards often share some of these characteristics:

- They will usually be placing large orders.
- They might request/insist their order be shipped by overnight delivery. This is so they know exactly when the package arrives (UPS guarantees 10:30 A.M. delivery) so they can be waiting to pick it up.
- They don't seem to care what the cost is. They want the item at any price.
- They hesitate to give you a daytime phone number.
- They request the item be shipped to an alternate address than the one listed for the cardholder.

Q What should I do if an order does sound suspicious?

Under any of the above circumstances you should be particularly cautious and do everything possible to ascertain the person ordering the merchandise is actually the cardholder.

These tips, though not infallible, may help you decide if an order is legitimate:

- Get a complete name, address, and phone number of the cardholder. Then, verify the information you are given by calling the merchant bank or using whatever other address verification system is in place through the ISO that processes your charges. If the address you were given doesn't match the address of the cardholder, don't ship.

- Only ship to the address of the cardholder. People ordering with a stolen card generally request the merchandise be shipped to a vacant house or apartment. (Some shipping companies leave packages at the door if no one is home.)

- A person using a stolen card won't give you their real phone number. Find an excuse to call the customer back, using the phone number he or she gave you, and ask to speak to the cardholder. If you can't reach the cardholder, don't ship the merchandise.

- Look up the address and phone number of any local orders in the phone book.

- If the address and phone number check out but you still have doubts, ship the merchandise AOD (acknowledgment of delivery) or certified mail. That way, you get a signature back that may help you fight your bank if the customer has signed but claims to never have received the merchandise.

- Hold on to signed sales slips and orders for at least a year.

- Send a reminder letter to people when you ship an item telling them the item has been shipped and when they can expect it to appear on their bill. This type of letter can reduce complaints and chargebacks from people who simply forget what they ordered or from whom.

Q **How does a chargeback differ from a return, from the bank's point of view?**

A customer who wants to return something goes to the merchant, and the merchant issues the credit. A chargeback is when the customer can't get satisfaction or when there has been unauthorized use of the account, and the customer complains to the credit card company. The credit card company then refunds the money to the customer, and in turn has to get the money back from the merchant. Too many chargebacks could cause a merchant to lose merchant status.

Q **A friend told me he has a fulfillment service that lets him use their 800 number and their merchant account to take customer orders. Is this OK to do?**

If the company is a legitimate fulfillment service and stocks and ships merchandise for you, the benefits of their order-taking services and your ability to give your customers the option of paying with a credit card may be worthwhile—if you can afford the cost.

If the company is going to take orders, bill the customer under *their name*, and then send the orders to you to fill, your best bet would be to contact someone in authority at the card issuer or merchant bank and make sure that company is authorized to process your charges.

Q **A salesperson told me people are starting to use their automatic teller machine (ATM) cards like credit cards and that if I can't get merchant status for my home business, I should get the equipment to accept ATM card transactions. Is this true?**

ATM cards are starting to be used as debit cards (as opposed to credit cards) to purchase goods and services. What happens when someone uses one of these cards is that the money for a purchase is withdrawn (debited) electronically from their account at the time of the purchase and transferred to the merchant's account. Due to the immediacy of the transaction, the ATM cards are used as a substitute for cash, rather than allowing the customer to postpone paying for the purchase until the end of the month (or later), as they would with a conventional credit card.

Whether or not ATM cards will catch on among consumers as an alternative to paying for goods and services with cash remains to be seen. But whether they do or not, being able to accept an ATM card is not likely to be an adequate substitute to being able to accept charge cards, since many people who use charge cards do so because they can delay payment or because they know the charge card company will refund their money if they have a problem with the merchandise that can't be resolved with the merchant.

Q **What kinds of charges are associated with the use of these cards?**

Merchants are usually charged a flat fee for each transaction, usually in the neighborhood of 10 to 50 cents, and usually do not have any discount fees. Since there is no loan made (as there is, in effect, with a traditional charge purchase), there are fewer restrictions on the use of these cards. On the minus side for card-holders, the cardholder is responsible for the first $500 in losses if someone steals their card and discovers what the personal identification number (PIN) is. Credit-card holders are only liable for the first $50.

IV.

The
Business Side
of Business

19.

Your Business and
the Law

If you are like most small business owners, you don't ever expect to become involved in a lawsuit. However, whether you sign a $30,000 contract to remove asbestos from a school building or sneeze and scare the cat (who leaps up off the windowsill and spills your open bottle of Yoo Hoo onto the turn-of-the-century heirloom family Bible you were restoring for a customer), as a businessperson, your actions have potential legal consequences.

While there is no way to anticipate or avoid all possible legal entanglements, you can learn to steer clear of some common pitfalls. This chapter should help you get through the school of hard knocks with fewer bruises.

Q **Does every business need an attorney?**

In a word, yes. While it isn't practical for a small business to call in an attorney to dot every *i* or cross every *t* in every business transaction, sooner or later every small business can benefit from an attorney's advice.

Q **When do I need an attorney?**

Kent Seitzinger, a California attorney who frequently worked with small business clients before accepting a position as senior litigation attorney for the CIGNA Corporation, says:

The easy answer is [to retain an attorney] before a problem ever arises. In law, as in most endeavors, the proverbial ounce of prevention is worth a pound of cure. Translated into the legal arena, what this typically means is that you can pay an attorney a few hundred dollars to advise you before entering into a matter or pay the attorney several thousand dollars to help bail you out later on.

Therefore, among the times when your business should seek an attorney's advice are:

- when a contract must be signed and the terms or clauses in the contract are difficult to understand
- any time you sign a contract for a significant sum of money or that obligates you to do something over a lengthy period of time
- any time you buy a business or franchise
- when you need to structure an agreement to discourage employees from starting their own businesses to compete with yours
- any time you are sued or are threatened with a lawsuit
- when you have an invention to protect
- when you form a partnership or corporation

Q. How can I find a good attorney?

The best way to find an attorney is through a referral, whether you get the referral from another business owner or through an industry association to which you belong. Although your sister's husband's uncle might be a great divorce attorney, he or she may not be the best person to represent you when your client claims your rewiring job was responsible for the fire in his office.

If you don't know anyone who can refer you to a business attorney, you might try calling the local chamber of commerce, rotary, or a local industrial association in your area and asking for referrals. If you can't get a specific referral from one of these groups, call the local bar association, or look in the Yellow Pages of your phone book. If you want to get biographical information about an attorney you see in the Yellow Pages, go to the public library and look him or her up in the *Martindale-Hubbell Law Directory.*

Q. How do I know an attorney is the right one for me?

298

An attorney is no different from any other person you hire. You must be able to communicate with him or her, and he or she must have the background and experience to handle the work you need done. Ideally, your attorney should have experience handling matters for other businesses with similar legal needs and problems to those of your business. To determine how closely the attorney's experience and personality mesh with your needs and preferences, ask the attorney questions like these:

- Is there a charge for an initial consultation?
- What is your background and experience?
- What type of clients do you have?
- Do you have a specialty?
- How big are the businesses you typically serve?
- What do you charge?
- How much experience do you have with————?
- Are you the person that will do most of the work, or will a paralegal or someone else be involved?
- Could the legal fees exceed any settlement costs?*

Q **How much does it cost to hire an attorney?**

You may pay anywhere from $75 an hour to $300 an hour or perhaps more for legal help. Geographic location, experience of the attorney, and area of specialization will all influence the fee. Depending on the situation, you may have to pay the attorney a retainer up-front to take your case. This money is held in an account, and the attorney takes his or her fee and costs out of this account as the work progresses. If you are paying an hourly fee, get an estimate in advance of what the total costs may be and how long the legal work may take or how long it is likely to take for the case to come to trial.

In some instances, an attorney may work on a contingency basis. In this case he or she will take a percentage of the settlement (what you win). The contingency fee will generally be at least 25 percent and often higher.

Q **Is there any way to keep legal fees down?**

---

* In Minnesota, two law firms claimed $208,733.67 in legal expenses for representing four clients. They won the case for the clients, but by law, the maximum damages their clients were entitled to were $750 each for a total of $3,000.

If the work you need done is routine, consider reading up on the subject before you talk to the attorney. Always do whatever preliminary work you can. You might do a preliminary trademark or trade name search, for instance, before retaining a trademark attorney. Another way to keep costs down is to use boilerplate contracts for some jobs. The boilerplate could be either one created initially by your attorney or one adapted from an industry-standard contract. If you adapt a standard contract, have the attorney look it over to see if it needs any changes to fit your individual circumstances.

If you are being sued or will be suing another party, collect and organize all the pertinent data or documents that may be necessary to put together your case. If your attorney will need industry statistics, information on government regulations affecting your business, or other information you have or know where to get quickly, let the attorney know and gather the information yourself, rather than have the law firm do the research. Remember, the less time the attorney spends on your behalf, the lower your bill will be. While the value of your own time always has to be considered, chances are if you are running a small business your hourly billing rate is going to be a lot lower than the attorney's. Furthermore, you may have more knowledge of your industry and be able to hunt down the facts or pertinent regulations more quickly than the attorney could.

If you have to call the attorney for anything, gather all your facts and list the points you want to cover in the call before you lift the receiver. When you reach the attorney, get right to the point. Since attorneys bill for phone time, the less time you spend on the phone, the lower your bill will be.

Q **When should I ask customers to sign a contract?**

You should have a written agreement with your customers whenever the amounts of money or work involved will be substantial. A written agreement is also advisable whenever you want to avoid misunderstandings about the terms of a sale or agreement.

Oral contracts are enforceable up to one year only if you are selling services and only when the amount of the sale is $500 or less if you are selling goods. Whichever you sell and regardless of the amount, it can be extremely difficult to prove who agreed to do what if you don't have a written contract.

Q What should I do if my customer and I agree to a deal over the telephone?

You should put the details of the oral discussion into a letter confirming the deal and send the letter to your customer. That way you and the customer both have something to refer to in case a dispute develops about what was agreed to. Be sure the letter includes everything you discussed, including details of the job, fees, and due dates.

Q A supplier sent me a letter summarizing details of a deal we had discussed, but he seems to have left out a couple of points I thought we agreed on. What should I do?

Let the supplier know immediately in writing that you dispute what he has summarized in his letter to you. If it is a sale of goods, under the Uniform Commercial Code you could be bound by the supplier's letter if you do not object to the terms within 10 days.

Q Can I write my own contracts?

You can write your own contracts and probably will in many situations. If the contracts are for large sums of money or will obligate you to do anything for any length of time, you should have your attorney review them to be sure they cover your needs.

Q Where can I get copies of contracts and agreements to use?

Professional or trade associations you belong to may have sample of industry-standard agreements. There are also numerous books containing sample contracts and agreements and explanations of the terms or suggestions of what to put in the contracts. These are often grouped by industry or subject. Among the books that have samples you may find helpful are:

Business & Legal Forms for Authors & Self-Publishers by Tad Crawford, Allworth Press, (800) 289–0963.

Graphic Artists Guild Handbook Pricing and Ethical Guidelines by Paul Basista, Graphic Artists Guild, 11 West 20th St., 8th floor, New York. NY 10011–3704, (212) 463–7730.

Legal Care for Your Software by Daniel Remer and Stephen Elias, Nolo Press, (415) 549–1976.

The Partnership Book: How to Write a Partnership Agreement by Denis Clifford and Ralph Warner, Nolo Press, (415) 549–1976.

Write Your Own Business Contracts by E. Thorpe Barrett, © 1990, 1991 by E. Thorpe Barrett; the Oasis Press/PSI Research, 300 North Valley Drive, Grants Pass, OR 97526, (503) 479–9464.

Selling through Independent Reps by Harold J. Novick, Amacom, American Management Association, 135 West 50th St., New York, NY 10020, (212) 586–8100.

Books like these are well worth reading even if you plan to have an attorney draft your contracts. The books and sample documents will familiarize you with the terms and issues involved and can give you some idea of possible conditions or special considerations your attorney will need to know about to prepare your agreements or contracts.

There is also at least one computer program that generates individualized contracts for software developers. The program, which is available for IBM PC and compatible computers, gives you several categories of contracts to choose from and lets you pick individual clauses to use in each type of contract:

Quickform Contracts, Invisible Hand Software, 3847 Whitman Road, Annandale, VA 22003, (703) 207–9353.

Q **What if I want to change something in a contract I've been asked to sign?**

Changes have to be agreed to by both parties, so call or contact the other party (or your attorney) before you make the change. If you make the change on the contract instead of printing out a new contract with the change in place, you and the other party both have to initial and date the changes.

Q **Can a letter be a contract?**

A letter, a letter of agreement, or even a memo could be a valid contract if it contains all the elements of a contract.

Q **What are the elements of a contract?**

To have an enforceable contract, the contract must be for an activity that is legal and should contain these elements:

▶ an offer to do something in return for something else by one party
▶ an acceptance of the offer and terms of the offer by another party
▶ a consideration (an obligation to do something you don't legally have to do, such as write a manual in return for a sum of money)

The terms of the contract should be carefully spelled out so there is no misunderstanding. Points covered in the terms should include:

▶ a description of the job
▶ the date by which the job should be completed
▶ the location at which the job will be performed
▶ the method and timing of payment(s)
▶ a clause stating how attorney's fees will be handled in the event of a dispute

Q **Is there any problem dealing with customers in another state?**

There's nothing wrong with dealing with customers out of state; however, it can be extremely difficult to collect payment on out-of-state accounts. If the customer decides not to pay and you decide to sue, you are likely to have to file suit and go to court in their state. Thus, if you are dealing with a one-time sale or a customer you don't know well, consider getting all or a large part of your money up-front or in progress payments.

Q **How do I decide if I should sue another company?**

Decisions about whether to bring a lawsuit against any business or individual should be made just like any other business decision: on the basis of what you stand to gain or lose by following the particular course of action. Going to court is not something to do to get even. Generally, however, the decision about whether to sue will be based on how much the lawsuit will cost you.

If the amount is small enough that the dispute could be brought to small claims court (where you don't need an attorney), you would decide to proceed or let the matter drop based on the time it would take you to prepare your case and file the papers and the time you would spend at the courthouse waiting for your case to be heard.

If the amount involved or the nature of the dispute precludes using small claims court, you have to weigh the costs of the suit against what you stand to gain if you win the case or what you will lose if you don't sue. Unfortunately, when you add up the cost of the attorney's fees and expenses, court costs, legal stenographer's fees, expert witness fees (which may exceed $20,000 alone on a relatively simple matter, according to one attorney), and other incidentals, you may find it impractical to sue anyone unless the amount of the dispute is large and you have a clear-cut case.

Q **What alternatives do I have?**

The most expedient solution, of course, would be sitting down and talking to the company or individual with whom you have the dispute and trying to work things out on your own. Before you make up your mind not to budge or give in to anything the other party says, remember that standing on your principles may be a lofty ideal, but it may not get you anywhere. The goal in settling a dispute should be to come to some kind of win-win compromise that will let both you and the other party return to the business of doing business.

If you and the other party can't work out your differences on your own, you may then want to consider some type of alternate dispute resolution such as arbitration or mediation, which let you bring your dispute before an impartial third party trained in negotiation methods. You should realize that arbitration may be binding and mediation is not.

Q **What is a nondisclosure agreement and when do I use one?**

A nondisclosure agreement (also called a confidentiality agreement) is a contract used to protect client lists, methods of doing business, proprietary processes used in a business, designs, formulations, and similar intangibles from being used by anyone without your authorization. You might use one when you are presenting a patentable idea to a manufacturer or when you are hiring employees or contractors who will have access to information you do not want made available to others or used for any purposes other than your own.

Q **Is there any way I can prevent employees from leaving and starting a business like mine?**

Depending on laws in your state you may be able to prevent former employees (or businesses you buy out) from opening up a competing operation by having them sign a covenant not to compete. However, it is likely you will only be able to do so in a limited geographic area and for a limited amount of time. If you want employees or a business you buy out to sign a noncompete agreement, you should be sure to have the agreement drafted or at least reviewed by an attorney familiar with your state's laws regarding covenants not to compete.

Q **Can I get sued if a customer doesn't like my work?**

Possibly. It will depend on what the customer doesn't like about your work, what your original agreement was, and whether the customer has time and money to pursue a lawsuit.

Q **How can I protect myself?**

To protect yourself against unwanted lawsuits you should be cautious and honest in all your business dealings. Be realistic about the capabilities of your company, and have an attorney look over important documents before you offer or accept them.

In addition, to protect yourself against financial loss, make sure you have adequate business insurance. Although you may take every precaution to avoid a lawsuit, someone may still sue you, and even if they lose the case and you don't have to pay one cent in settlements, you could literally go broke paying the costs of defending yourself. The right business insurance policies can protect against that kind of loss.

Q What are statutory damages?

Statutory damages are monetary penalties specified by law. Frequently they will be a multiple of something else, such as three times the financial loss incurred by the plaintiff.

Q What are slander and libel, and when should I be concerned about them?

Slander and libel both involve damage or injury to someone's reputation or business through disparaging remarks. Usually slander refers to verbal remarks and libel to published (written) remarks that are malicious or harmful. Attorneys often refer to the two (slander and libel) collectively as defamation. As a businessperson you might be accused of libel or slander if you imply your competition makes shoddy products, is not professional in their business dealings, or if you write or say anything that could be construed as tarnishing their reputation. You could also be sued for libel or slander if you wrongfully accuse or imply customers or employees are bad credit risks, thieves, or something similar.

Q Can't I tell people the truth if asked for credit or employment references?

By definition, truthful remarks cannot be defamatory. However, credit and employment information is protected under privacy laws in many states, and you could unintentionally violate these laws by giving out information. Furthermore, whether you actually could be found in violation of privacy or defamation laws, paying the court costs to defend yourself can be extremely expensive. To stay out of trouble, never say or imply anything about competitors, employees, or customers that you can't back up with facts. Furthermore, never make any kind of detrimental information available to the public or say or do anything that could hold the person or business up to ridicule. If ever questioned (say, about an employee who you fired), for your own protection verify only dates and names. Do not say he or she was a lousy worker or a thief. The same holds true for customers who are credit risks. Report the facts to credit bureaus, but avoid saying anything else to anyone else.

20.

Intellectual Property: How to Protect What You Create

Whether you realize it or not, your creativity may be one of your most valuable business assets. The products you invent, the artwork you design, the words you create, and the name and logo you use to represent your business all have monetary value. Under law, these products of your creativity are considered intellectual property and, like any other property you own, can be protected against theft or unauthorized borrowing if you take the proper precautions at the proper times. This chapter will help you gain a better understanding of how and when to protect your creativity.

Q **What is intellectual property?**

When you hear the word *property* you probably think of things you own, like buildings, cars, televisions, jewelry, equipment, and other kinds of real property you can see, touch, buy, and sell. There is another kind of property, however, that may be even more valuable to you as a business owner. It is intellectual property—property such as names, inventions, artwork, writing, music, computer programs, designs for products, formulas, processes, and anything else that results from creative endeavors.

Just like any other property, intellectual property has value under the law and can be bought or sold. Unlike other property, however, the value of intellectual

307

property lies in its uniqueness and often in its reproducibility. The design for a new product, for instance, may be used to produce hundreds of thousands of items worth millions of dollars. Thus, if the design is illegally copied and used to manufacture a similar product, the individual or company that created the original product could sustain a significant monetary loss.

Q How is intellectual property protected under the law?

The laws that can be used to prevent others from illegally copying and profiting from your creative efforts are called intellectual property laws. Among them are the laws covering copyrights, patents, trademarks, and trade secrets. These laws are specialized, often quite complex, and to some extent are being defined or redefined on a case-by-case basis as the law struggles to catch up with the information age and the technology that drives it.

Q How do the various intellectual property laws differ from one another?

The division lines aren't always cut-and-dried but as a general rule of thumb:

- copyright laws help protect written, drawn, photographed, and artistic works
- patents and trade secrets laws can help protect inventions, new machines, and new processes
- design patents help protect the way a product looks
- trademark and trade name regulations help protect the distinguishing identity of goods and services

Q Can a product be considered more than one type of intellectual property?

Yes, sometimes you can get protection for your intellectual property under more than one law. Gerry Elman, an intellectual property attorney and a partner in the law firm of Elman and Wilf in Media, Pennsylvania, says, for example, that some software "embodies patentable ideas and can be protected by copyright as well." This, he says, is like having belt-and-suspenders protection for your property.

Q **What is a copyright?**

Copyright gives the owner of a work the exclusive rights to:

- reproduce the copyrighted work
- prepare derivative works based on the copyrighted work
- distribute copies or phonorecords of the work to the public by sale or transfer of ownership or by rental, lease, or lending
- perform or display the copyrighted work publicly

Q **Can I copyright my idea?**

No, you can't copyright an idea. Copyright protects only the means (words, a drawing, etc.) you use to *express* the idea. It doesn't prevent others from adopting your idea and using it themselves. For instance, if you drew a picture of a uniquely shaped computer desk, you would own a copyright on the drawing, but your copyright on the drawing would not stop someone from actually building and selling thousands of desks based on your picture.

Q **Is there any way to protect ideas?**

You may be able to protect your ideas with patent or trade secret laws, which are explained later in this chapter.

Q **Can I copyright my business or product name?**

A name cannot be protected by copyright. You may be able to protect your name as a trademark, however.

Q **What can be copyrighted?**

The copyright law covers "original works of authorship that are fixed in a tangible form of expression." Among the types of works that can be covered by copyright are:

- literary works
- computer programs, which are classified as literary works under the copyright laws
- musical works, including accompanying words
- dramatic works, including accompanying music
- pantomimes and choreographic works
- pictorial, graphic, and sculptural works
- motion pictures and other audiovisual works
- sound recordings

Q How do I get a copyright?

Under copyright laws in the United States, work created on or after March 1, 1989, is *automatically* copyrighted the moment you create it in a fixed form that others can perceive.

Q What does *fixed* mean?

Fixed in a tangible medium of expression is a rather broad term designating a variety of material objects. Essentially, putting something into fixed form simply means putting what's in your head onto paper or disk or audiotape or some other format that others can read, see, or listen to. Among the things regarded as fixed formats are paper manuscripts, books, phonorecords, audiotapes, computer disks, sheet music, and films.

Q Don't I have to register the work or put some kind of notice on it?

Works published before March 1, 1989, had to bear a copyright notice or the copyright was lost. Works published on or after March 1, 1989, do not have to carry a copyright notice and don't have to be registered. Registering the copyright and putting a copyright notice on your work are both advisable, however. Putting the notice on the work alerts people to your copyright claim to the work and identifies the owner and year of the copyright. Registering the work adds these advantages:

- It establishes a public record of your ownership of the work.

- It permits infringement suits to be filed (you can't file an infringement suit until a work is registered).

- Registration made within five years of publication establishes *prima facie* evidence in court of the validity of the copyright and facts stated on the copyright certificate.

- Registration made within three months after the publication of the work or before infringement allows you to collect statutory damage and attorney's fees if you sue for infringement and win. If the copyright wasn't registered before infringement, all you can collect are actual losses related to the infringement. (Statutory damages are a penalty that can be levied in place of or above the dollar amount of any actual loss.)

Q **If I put a copyright notice on the work how should I do it?**

The copyright notice normally consists of the following three things:

- the symbol © (the letter *c* in a circle) or the word *Copyright* or the abbreviation *Copr.*
- the year of first publication
- the name of the copyright owner

For phonorecords of sound recordings, the symbol ℗ (the letter *p* in a circle) should be used instead of the circled *c*.

Q **Where do I put the notice?**

The notice should be put in a place that gives "reasonable notice" of your copyright. The first page of a manuscript, the label of a record, somewhere in the front matter (traditionally the back of the title page) of a book.

Q **If I want to register the copyright, how do I do it?**

To register a copyright you will need to send a properly completed registration form, a nonrefundable filing fee of $20, and a nonreturnable deposit of the work to the Copyright Office. All three of those things must be in the same package. The requirements for the deposit of the work vary with the type of work being registered, but it is usually one or two complete copies of works that can be easily duplicated. To get application forms, information about deposit requirements, or other information about copyright, write the Copyright Office, Library of Congress, Washington, D.C. 20559, or call the office at (202) 707–3000.

Q **I'm a free-lance programmer and technical writer. If a company pays me to write a program or manual for them, who owns the copyright on the work I produce?**

You generally own the copyright on work you create as an independent contractor (free-lancer) unless you sign an agreement assigning the copyright to your client.

This, too, is a change from the way things were done in the past. It is a result of a 1989 Supreme Court decision in a case between Baltimore sculptor James Earl Reid and the Community for Creative Non-Violence (CCNV). Prior to that case, some companies hiring contractors to do work for them assumed they owned the copyright under work-for-hire provisions of the copyright law. In the case between Reid and CCNV, the Supreme Court found that CCNV's commissioning and supervision of Reid were not enough to make him an employee and, therefore, work-for-hire rules did not apply. As a free-lancer, he owned the copyright to his work.

If you are not the only person working on the program or manual, the work would probably be considered a joint work, and you would co-own the copyright if there were no agreements specifying other arrangements.

Q **If I hire an ad agency to design ads for me, who owns the designs?**

Based on the Reid decision, the ad agency might be able to make a case for owning the copyright on anything it writes or designs for you unless you have an agreement stating otherwise. It would be a good idea, therefore, to have the agency sign an agreement assigning the rights in the work to you.

Q **If I revise a work, what year should I put in the copyright notice?**

The year of original publication. Years in which the work was revised may be included, too, but the significant date is the date of first publication.

Q   How long does copyright last?

The copyright on works created on or after January 1, 1978, is in effect for the author's life plus 50 years. If the work is a joint work, the term of copyright extends until 50 years after the death of the last surviving co-owner. Works made for hire have a term of 100 years from creation or 75 years after publication, whichever is less. The copyright duration for anonymous and pseudonymous works is the same as that for works made for hire unless the author's name is revealed in Copyright Office records.

Q   How long does it take the Copyright Office to process registrations?

It can take up to 120 days to get a certificate of registration or, if the application cannot be accepted, a letter explaining why it has been rejected. If you want to be sure the Copyright Office received your registration packet, send it registered or certified mail, return receipt requested.

Q   Do I need an attorney to get a copyright, or can I do it myself?

Registering a copyright is just a matter of filling out some forms and sending the proper fee, so you probably don't need an attorney to register your copyright. However, if you are copyrighting catalogs, advertising materials, programs or other works that were not created by you or one of your regular employees, you have to be sure you own the rights (see above).

If you are copyrighting computer software, you might want to consult an intellectual property attorney to determine if your program has patentable material and about how much of the source code might be considered a trade secret and can be blacked out when the source code is submitted to the copyright office for registration. Be sure to get Copyright Office Circular 61, *Copyright Registration for Computer Programs*, if you plan to copyright your own software.

Similarly, if the work you are copyrighting contains any kind of trade secrets or could be used in patentable items or processes, you should consult an attorney who specializes in these things.

Q **If I don't register the copyright, should I mail myself a copy of the work and save the sealed package to prove the date and authorship?**

That's a waste of time and effort. As attorney Gerry Elman explains, "It's a myth that you can date something by sticking it in an envelope and mailing it to yourself. That's because you could send an empty envelop to yourself, sealed lightly with rubber cement, keep it safe, and then when the time comes that you want to antedate something, stick your newly created letter inside and seal the envelope shut."

Instead, Elman recommends having a friend with no interest in your work or a notary sign and date your document as a witness, or better yet, simply registering the copyright.

Q **I publish a monthly newsletter. If I register the copyright, do I have to register each issue of the newsletter separately, or can I register a year's worth on one form?**

Since each issue is separately copyrightable, you have to register each one separately. A group registration is available, but it is for registering groups of works by the same author. Copyright Office Circular 62, *Registration for Serials*, explains the regulations for newsletters, bulletins, and other periodicals. Circular 104, *Group Registration of Contributions to Periodicals*, explains group registrations.

Q **I forgot to put a copyright notice on my program. Will I lose my copyright on it?**

If the program was published after March 1, 1989, no, you won't lose your copyright. It would be a good idea to add your copyright notice to future copies, though it isn't necessary.

If the program was written after January 1, 1978, and registered within 5 years of publication, the copyright may still be valid if you do your best to have a copyright notice put onto all copies that you can locate. Call the Copyright Office and ask for Circular 3 for more information.

Do I have to give the Copyright Office a copy of the source code if I register my software?

Not necessarily, but if you don't, you have to ask the Copyright Office for special relief from the strict application of the law. They will respond with a letter saying that they can't determine whether there is copyrightable authorship in the materials you sent but that they will issue a certificate under the "rule of doubt." If you do provide at least some of the code, portions containing trade secret material may be blocked out if you request another form of special relief. For additional information, get Copyright Office Circular 61.

Is there any other way I can protect my software?

You might be able to patent your software or use the trade secret law, trademark laws, or unfair competition laws to protect it. An intellectual property attorney would be the best source of information if you plan to market your software to a large commercial market.

Can I copy phone listings?

According to a March 1991 Supreme Court ruling in the case of *Feist Publications v. Rural Telephone Service Co.*, you can safely copy the white pages in the phone book. In the decision that was handed down in the case, the court said copyright is not awarded for sweat-of-the-brow work but for originality. Listings in white pages of a phone book, the court ruled, are facts with no originality in organization or expression and therefore cannot be protected by copyright.

The ruling did not automatically negate copyrights on other kinds of compilations. It would seem from the wording of the decision that compilations showing originality of organization and expression would still be protected by copyright. What is likely to be tested in future court cases is just what constitutes originality of organization and expression.

Can I reprint things I find in online databases?

Generally, no. An online database usually consists of more than a listing of mere facts; databases are usually specialized and involve some originality in selec-

315

tion, arranging, and often writing and editing. Thus, unlike the white pages in the phone book, their ability to be copyrighted would probably be upheld if challenged.

Q **I found a lot of information in an electronic library that I'd like to include in my newsletter. Am I allowed to do that since I paid to download them from the online service?**

No. The author of the text in the files you downloaded owns the copyright, and reprinting the file in your newsletter without his or her permission is an infringement of the author's rights.

Q **If I upload text or shareware to an online information service, do I give up any rights in my work to the online service?**

No, you wouldn't lose your rights in the work. You would still be the owner of your copyright. The service might claim a compilation copyright, which is simply a copyright on the particular collection of material available on the service. That doesn't take away your individual copyrights in your work, though. You are still the sole owner of your work.

Q **I have a hand scanner and want to scan some artwork I found in a book and use it in my publication. Is this OK to do?**

If the copyright has expired on the book or if the artwork included in the book is in the public domain, you should be able to scan in illustrations to use in your publication. If you are scanning from a new book of clip art or a book that is a collection of old prints, look in the front of the book to see what the company says about reuse of the material in the book.

Q **What does being in the public domain mean?**

When a work is in the public domain, it means the work is not covered by copyright protection. It can be used freely by the public without permission from the creator or his or her heirs. Among the types of work that are in the public domain are federal government publications and works for which the copyright has expired. In the past, some works wound up in the public domain inadvertently, too, because they were published without a copyright notice. Under the current law, however, copyright notice is no longer required on published works.

Q **A magazine wants to buy my craft design for reprint in the publication. The agreement with the letter they sent me reads: "I hereby agree to sell all right of copyright." Does that mean I can't resell the design to a British publication?**

Yes, it does. By signing that agreement, you give up all copyrights in the material the magazine is buying. If you want to have the design published, but don't want to sell all rights, you could try calling the publication and asking if they would be willing to change the rights clause. If you are unfamiliar with the rights that can be offered, check your library for books about selling writing. These books generally have information about the different types of publication rights.

Q **How much does a drawing have to be changed to be considered a new drawing? If I traced the outline and filled in my own details, could I sell the new design as my own?**

What you would be doing is creating a derivative work, and under the copyright law, only the copyright holder or someone the copyright holder authorizes may do that. Even if your design looked somewhat different from the original, if any of the author's expressions were copied, rather than just the idea, you would be infringing on his or her copyright.

Q **What about "fair use"? How much of a copyrighted work can I reprint without getting permission?**

The answer depends on many factors, including your intended use. The fair use rule says portions of works may be reproduced for educational, news, commentary, or research without infringement under certain circumstances. The circumstances are decided on a case-by-case basis using all four of the following criteria:

▶ the purpose and character of the use, including whether such use is of a commercial nature or is for nonprofit educational purposes

- the nature of the copyrighted work
- the amount and substantiality of the portion used in relation to the copyrighted work as a whole
- the effect of the use upon the potential market for or value of the copyright

In addition, there are a number of more specific guidelines published for reproduction of text, music, and other works by educators and librarians. These are discussed in Copyright Office Circular 21, *Reproduction of Copyrighted Works by Educators and Librarians.*

 Where do I get forms to copyright my work, and what do they cost?

You can get the forms free from the Copyright Office. (You pay a $20 registration fee when you return the completed form.) You can order them by phone by calling (202) 707–3000. Be sure to get the right forms for the type of work you are registering. The forms and what they are used for are as follows:

For Original Registration

- Form TX—for published and unpublished nondramatic literary works
- Form SE—for serials, works issued or intended to be issued in successive parts, such as periodicals, newspapers, magazines, newsletters, annuals, and journals
- Form PA—for published and unpublished works of the performing arts (musical and dramatic works, pantomimes and choreographic works, motion pictures and other audiovisual works)
- Form VA—for published and unpublished works of the visual arts (pictorial, graphic, and sculptural works)
- Form SR—for published and unpublished sound recordings

For Renewals

- Form RE—for claims to renew copyright in works copyrighted under the law in effect through December 31, 1977 (1909 Copyright Act)

For Corrections and Amplifications

▶ Form CA—for supplementary registration to correct or amplify an existing registration

For a Group of Contributions to Periodicals

▶ Form GR/CP—for registration of a group of contributions to periodicals; gets filed in addition to application form TX, PA, or VA

Q **How old do works have to be before I can assume they are in the public domain?**

Under the copyright law in existence prior to 1978 the term of copyright was 28 years, and it could be renewed for another 28 years. However, the 1978 law extended the renewal term on some works to 47 years, making the total term 75 years from the end of the year copyright was secured. Thus, anything published before 1918 would be in the public domain in 1993.

Q **If I copyright my work here in the United States is it protected in other countries, too?**

Many foreign countries abide by the same international copyright conventions that the United States does, and your work would be protected under their local laws if you comply with the provisions of the conventions. You can get a list of countries that honor U.S. copyrights from the U.S. Copyright Office. If someone in another country infringed on your copyright, you would have to sue in that country.

TRADEMARKS AND TRADE NAMES

Q **What is a trademark?**

A trademark is a word, group of words, name, device, or symbol used to identify goods you sell and distinguish them from similar goods sold by other businesses.

It can consist of words, graphics, or letters and is used to identify a product, line of products, or all the products produced by your company. A brand name like Coca-Cola or a symbol like the multicolor striped apple that identifies Apple Computer products are both trademarks. Trademarks and service marks are protected under federal law.

Q **Can I trademark a service?**

Yes. It is called a service mark.

Q **Is my business name a trademark?**

Your business name is a trade name. It is protected at the state or local level. If you opened up a lawn-care company called The GreenCarpet Lawn-Care Service, your next-door neighbor couldn't open a business with the same name or one confusingly similar, but there would be nothing to stop a company in another state, or depending on your state laws, another part of your state from opening up a company with the same name even if it was in the same business. If you registered the name as a service mark, you could protect it from being used by other lawn-care companies in the country, something you might want to do if you want to franchise your lawn-care service.

Q **If I want my business name to be my trademark, do I have to register it locally and also register it as a trademark?**

Registering your business name is a state or local process and is completely separate from registering a federal trademark. So if you want national protection for your name you would have to register the name locally and apply separately for trademark protection. If you don't need national name protection, registering the name locally may stop other local businesses from using the name. If you want statewide protection for the name but don't need national protection, you could register a trademark with your state. Your secretary of state's office should be able to direct you to the proper source of information for registering a name as a trademark in your state.

Q **Are there any restrictions on what can be used as a trademark?**

Your trademark or service mark can't be confusingly similar to others for a similar product or service, and it must do more than just describe a product or service. It has to give it a unique identity. You could not register the term *Lawn Service* as a trademark, for instance, but could probably register terms like *LawnMaker* or *Greenlawn* if those terms aren't already trademarks for similar products and services. In addition, your trademark can't be a generic term for a kind of product. Terms like *photocopier* or *tissue* can't be trademarks but *Xerox* and *Kleenex* can. In fact, you can lose your mark if it starts to be used as a generic term as in *xeroxing* a document or getting a *kleenex* to blow your nose. Major corporations wind up spending a lot of money to keep the names of popular products from becoming generic terms.

Q Should I invent a nonsense name or use something that reminds people of what the product or service does?

Your choice of trademark should be based on marketing factors as well as the ability to register the term. A truly unusual coined name will be far easier to protect as a trademark, since there will be little likelihood of there being similar names or marks in use. Xerox and Exxon are two familiar examples. A potential drawback of using a coined term, however, is that prospective customers may not immediately be able to identify the nature of your goods and might bypass your ads or sales literature.

On the other hand, a name that is too descriptive of your product or service may present problems, too. You may discover someone else is already using the clever name you chose, or that the name really won't be suitable if you expand your business in the future. Got It Message Center may be the ideal name for an answering service but would be inappropriate if you later decided to expand the business into a full-fledged order fulfillment service.

Thus, you might want to choose several possible names and test them out on friends and acquaintances and do some preliminary searches to see if they are already in use. If preliminary searches and feedback show the name sounds promising, then you can decide to search further if you want to use the name widely or just adopt it if it is not in use in your immediate geographic area.

Q How do I get a trademark?

If your mark is not confusingly similar to any others, you can acquire rights to it by using it in commerce and continuing to use it. If you can prove you were the first company to use a mark, you might be able to prevent others from using it, even if you haven't registered the mark. Like copyrights, though, it is much better to register your mark.

Q   **What are the advantages of registering a trademark?**

With federal trademark registration, you could gain nationwide protection, and if your mark was infringed, you could get federal court orders to prevent continued use of the mark. In addition, you might be able to collect money if you sued and won.

Q   **Is there anything I have to do before I start using my mark?**

Before you start using your mark, you should do a trademark search to be sure no one is already using it.

Q   **I'm only going to sell to businesses in my state. Do I have to do a national name search, or can I just do a search of local business names?**

If you are only going to be providing services locally and won't be investing a lot of money in name recognition, a local search may be sufficient. Searching the Yellow Pages listings, county and state business name listings, and ads for products or services similar to what you sell will probably be sufficient to tell you if there are companies marketing services in your area with confusingly similar names or logos. Be aware, however, that if your name should conflict with similar products sold nationally, you could be forced to stop using your name if theirs existed first. Similarly, if you later expand to other geographic regions you might run into name conflicts you didn't discover on a local search.

Q   **When should I do a search in a wider geographic area, and how would I do it?**

How extensively you should search will depend on available funds, time constraints, and the relative importance of making sure there are no conflicts. If you are going to sell products or offer services more widely and invest more money in name recognition, then a more extensive trademark search is warranted.

Your best bet for doing a national search is to hire an intellectual property attorney or a trademark search firm or information broker familiar with doing trademark searches. If you want to do the search yourself, or do a preliminary search before retaining an attorney, there are several electronic databases that will simplify the search process. The primary ones are Thomson & Thomson's Trademarkscan Federal and Trademarkscan State, which list trademarks registered at federal and state levels. Both of these databases are available on Dialog and have gateways to make them available from CompuServe and GEnie. Since not all trademarks are registered, other directories and databases should be searched as well. Dun's Electronic Business Directory, available on CompuServe, is useful since it contains names, addresses, and phone numbers of over 8.5 million businesses and professionals in the country. Yellow Pages and industry directories available in public libraries are valuable search tools, too.

The Patent and Trademark Office in Washington, D.C., has a library that is open to the public (see page 473). In addition, there are public and university libraries throughout the country that have been designated patent and trademark depository libraries. These libraries have copies of patents and federal trademark records you can search. To get information about the patent and trademark depository libraries, call the Patent and Trademark Office at (703) 308–3924.

 If I hire an intellectual property attorney or trademark search company to do the search, and they don't find anything similar, can my trademark be challenged?

Yes, your mark, even once it is registered, could be challenged as being merely descriptive for up to 5 years. Additionally, while an attorney or search firm is likely to do a more extensive and knowledgeable search than you would on your own, there is no guarantee that they will turn up all unregistered uses of your mark. Your mark, even after it is registered, could always be challenged by a prior user of the mark. If your mark starts to be used as a general term to describe a class of products, you can lose your rights to it as well. Aspirin and escalators are two examples of products that lost their trademark because they became generally accepted terms for describing a class of products rather than the product of specific company.

Q **What does it cost to register a trademark?**

The federal filing fee for registering a trademark is $200. If you have an intellectual property attorney do the search for you and prepare the applications, you can plan on paying an additional $700 to $2,500 in addition to the filing fee, depending on the extent of the searches done, the results of the searches, and the attorney you retain. Be sure you ask about fees in advance if budget is a major consideration.

Q **Must I have an attorney to register a trademark?**

No, you don't need an attorney to register your trademark. Depending on your plans for the business or product, it may be advisable, however. The extra fees buy you better searches (unless you happen to be an expert at electronic searches and other search techniques) as well as the attorney's expert judgment on whether or not the mark could be considered confusingly similar to others in use for the kind of product or service you sell. Whether retaining an attorney or registering your trademark are worthwhile at all will depend on your budget and plans for what you sell.

Q **I have a trademark I want to use, but I'm not ready to start the business. Is there a way I can keep others from using the mark?**

Yes. A 1989 amendment in the trademark law allows you to reserve a trademark you intend to use by filing a special form and paying a $200 fee.

Q **When do I use the ™ symbol and when do I use the ®?**

If you are claiming trademark rights and haven't registered the trademark or the registration hasn't yet been approved, you would use the symbol ™ to denote your claim to a trademark or SM to denote a service mark. Once registration is granted you use the symbol ® to denote the registered trademark.

Q **How do I protect my trademark?**

To protect the trademark you have to continue using it, and you have to keep it from becoming a generic term to describe a class of products. To maintain the distinction, your mark should be used as an adjective, as in Band-Aid adhesive bandages or WordSmith writing services. To further protect your mark, you should make sure it is always printed in the same way and that your trademark notice is used at least once in each printed piece containing your mark.

Q How do I actually register the trademark?

To register the trademark, you need to submit to the Patent and Trademark Office a written application, a drawing of your mark, and three samples of a label or other examples showing the mark in actual use.

You can get the application form and instructions by writing the U.S. Patent and Trademark Office, Washington, DC 20231 (mark your envelope "Trademark Information Requested") or by calling (703) 557–3158. If you have questions about trademarks or patents call (703) 308–HELP.

Q What if another company starts using my trade name or mark?

If you decide it is worth the cost of fighting the unauthorized use of your name or mark, you should contact an attorney. If you've registered your mark or name, he or she will send the company a letter demanding they stop using the name. If you haven't registered the name, the attorney can help you find out if you have common law rights to the name through first use and if it is worth the time and cost to pursue the matter.

Q Does a U.S. trademark give me any protection in foreign countries?

No. If you want trademark protection in other countries you will have to determine their laws and apply there.

Q How long does trademark protection last?

Trademark protection can last indefinitely; however, to retain trademark registration, you will have to file an affidavit between the fifth and sixth year of use saying you are still using the trademark. Additionally, at the end of the tenth year and every 10 years thereafter you have to renew your registration.

Q **Does it cost anything for the affidavit or the renewals?**

Yes. There is a $100 fee when you file the affidavit, and a $300 fee each time you renew the registration.

Q **It sound like a lot of work and money. Should I bother?**

That is a decision only you can make, and it should be based on your budget and your future plans. If you plan to stay a small local business, it probably isn't necessary to go to the time and expense of registering your name as a trademark. If you expect to grow and sell in wider geographic areas, it may be very worthwhile to apply for trademark registration.

PATENTS

Q **What kinds of things can be patented?**

Patents are granted in these broad categories:

- products, machines, processes, or compositions of matter
- major variations of existing products, processes, or compositions of matter
- new varieties of plants
- new, original designs for manufactured items (design patent)

Q **What makes an invention qualify for a patent?**

To qualify for a patent, an invention has to meet these qualifications:

- It must be new, which means it can't be patented or described in a printed publication in any country, and it must not have been used publicly or placed on sale in the United States.

- It must be useful.
- It cannot be something obvious to someone having ordinary skill in the relevant technology.

Q **How does the Patent Office interpret the terms "obvious" and "ordinary"? How can I tell if my invention is obvious?**

That's one of the sticky parts of patenting inventions. Explains intellectual property attorney Gerry Elman, "If you've got more than ordinary skill, what's possibly 'obvious' to you may not be obvious to someone with ordinary skill and may be legally patentable. If you've got a good idea, talk with a patent attorney if you think it's a money maker."

Q **Is there anything that can't be patented?**

Printed material, general business ideas, methods of doing business, scientific theories, mathematical formulas, useless devices, and obvious changes to existing devices can not be patented.

Q **How do patents differ from copyrights?**

A copyright protects the form of expression of an idea—one specific drawing, one set of words, etc. To get a copyright, your work only has to be original. A patent protects the conceptualization of an idea and has to be not only original but also *not obvious*. For instance, if Thomas Edison had copyrighted a written description of how to make a light bulb, no one would have been able to reproduce his description without infringing on his copyright. However, people could have used his description to make their own light bulbs. By patenting the light bulb, Edison prevented others from manufacturing and selling the light bulb unless they licensed the rights to do so from him.

Q **What rights does a patent give me?**

A patent protects new and original inventions or processes from being copied, produced, or sold in the United States and its territories and possessions. It gives you the right to prevent other companies from making, using, or selling your invention and the right to sue if anyone infringes patent as defined by the claims (in other words, if anyone copies or uses or sells your invention without your permission). A patent makes it possible to get a court order to stop an infringement and to sue for and be awarded money for past infringement.

Q **Does a patent give me the right to sell my invention anywhere in the United States?**

No. That's a common misconception. A patent does not give you any rights to *sell* your invention. It only gives you the right to *stop others* from selling it. The right to actually sell your product may be controlled by the FDA or some other regulatory agency or could be limited by existing patents. Suppose, for instance, you fiddle around with one of the pocket electronic organizers and devise a way to make a new plug-in card that will let the pocket organizer double as a remote control for the TV and a garage door opener. You might have a patentable invention but might not be able to sell the invention because of prior patents on the machine and/or its plug-in cards.

Q **How do I find out for sure that no one else has already patented my idea?**

You should search industry publications and catalogs and have a search of Patent Office records done to determine what patents might exist for inventions similar to yours.

Q **Where can I do such a search?**

You can search the patent records at the Patent and Trademark Office in Washington, DC (see page 473). Or, you can search records in the PTO depository libraries located throughout the United States.

Q **How long does a patent last?**

Patents on inventions are good for 17 years from the date the patent is granted, provided you pay a maintenance fee due 3½, 7½, and 11½ years later. Design patents are granted for 3½, 7, or 14 years.

Q **Can a patent be renewed?**

No. When the 17 years are up, anyone can use the invention, unless the patent is for a drug that has gone through FDA approval and has been extended by the Patent Term Restoration Act or unless the patent is extended by a special act of Congress.

Q **When do I file a patent?**

If you plan to patent an invention, do so as soon as possible. A good time is as soon as you can describe the invention in enough detail to enable someone else to make and use it. In the United States you have to apply for a patent within one year of the time you first disclose the device or start selling it. In other countries, you have to apply for the patent before it is publicly disclosed. Since disclosure includes showing your plans to others without first making them sign a confidentiality (nondisclosure) agreement, it is a good idea to get nondisclosure agreements signed by anyone you show the device to before it is patented and make marketing decisions early on.

Q **What does the Patent Office charge to patent an invention?**

The Patent and Trademark Office fee depends on the number of claims in the patent application and the size of the company filing for the patent. The minimum fee is $355 for small businesses and $710 for big businesses and covers applications with no more than three independent claims and no more than twenty total claims.

Q **Do I need an attorney to file for a patent?**

You will very likely need the services of an attorney or a patent agent. (Patent agents don't have to be attorneys to practice before the U.S. Patent Office, but they do have technical training and have passed a difficult exam.) While you are technically not prohibited from submitting an application yourself, it is usually foolish to try to do so unless you are very well versed in patent law. In fact, a form letter the Patent Office sends out to inventors whose applications are rejected reads in part:

*An examination of this application reveals that applicant is unfamiliar with patent pros-
ecuting procedure. While an inventor may prosecute the application, lack of skill in this
field usually acts as a liability in affording the maximum protection for the invention
disclosed. Applicant is advised to secure the services of a registered patent attorney or
agent to prosecute the application, since the value of a patent is largely dependent upon
skillful preparation and prosecution.*

Furthermore, an attorney can help you plan the right strategy for your purposes. Explains attorney Gerry Elman,

*The first thing to think about is—why do you want a patent? Is it because you are about
to sell a product and want to make sure nobody else can ride your coattails into the
marketplace? Or is it because you have an idea for a product and want to sell this idea
to some company that would make and sell the product, paying you a fee for each one
sold? Or do you want to be able to say you have a patent pending so that investors will
fund your business? Or, do you just want to put it on your resume and your Who's Who
listing? These different motivations would give rise to differing strategies in the expendi-
ture of time and money.*

Q **How much will it cost me to have a patent attorney file the application?**

If you do retain a patent attorney, expect to pay $2,000 to $6,000 or more. If
your invention has potential for significant profit this would be money well spent,
since the value of your patent could hinge on the way the patent claims are
written.

Q **Where do I find a patent attorney or agent?**

Look in the Yellow Pages of your phone book under "Patent" and/or under the
lawyer listings. You can also get a list of agents registered to practice before the
Patent Office from the Superintendent of Documents, Government Printing Office
(see page 472). While you may file for a patent without using an agent or attorney,
anyone else who prepares your application must have passed the Patent Office
examination and must be registered to practice before the Patent Office.

Q **What about companies that say they will patent and market your products? Are they any good?**

Some are better at marketing their services than marketing other people's products. Check around carefully before using one of these groups. Try to find other inventors and ask what their experiences have been and who they know to be truly helpful. If you can't find any inventors organizations, try calling local SCORE, SBDC, SBA (see appendix 2 for addresses and information), or university or college business school offices, and ask for references. There is also a magazine for inventors called *The Dream Merchant,* where you can get marketing information for your invention. The magazine maintains a database of inventors' groups around the country and provides referrals for subscribers. For information about *The Dream Merchant,* write the magazine at 2309 Torrance Blvd., Suite 201, Torrance, CA 90501, or call (310) 328–1925.

Q **When I file a patent can I leave out information that is a trade secret?**

No. You must disclose your invention in full so that anyone of ordinary skill in the relevant technology would be able to make and use the invention.

Q **How can I see if there is interest in my idea and protect it from being stolen by a manufacturer?**

The best way is to patent your invention before showing it to manufacturers.

Q **Can I patent a variation of a product?**

Only if the variation is not an obvious change. In addition, if your variation is patentable, the patents on the original invention—if they have not expired—might prevent you from selling your invention without the consent of the inventor of the original item.

Q **Can I patent a novel idea for using existing products?**

Only rarely. The idea would need to be an unobvious process to be patentable.

Q **Will the patent I get in the United States protect my invention from being copied and used in other countries?**

No. You will have to file patent applications in the foreign countries in which you want protection. Remember, too, that you usually must make this application before any disclosure of your invention has been made. You do not get the year's grace period that you do in the U.S.

Q **What happens if someone does infringe my patent?**

As stated previously, you have the right to sue and could be awarded money for past infringements. However, suing can be a lengthy and expensive process, pitting "little" you against the money and legal staffs of giant corporations. If you are determined and have a valid patent you might win the lawsuit in the long run, but the monetary and emotional costs can be draining. It took Robert Kearns, the inventor of the intermittent windshield wiper, 12 years to win his battle against auto companies for infringing his rights. Eventually he won a $10.2 million settlement, $8 million of which went to legal fees, and was planning to use the remainder to bring still more infringement suits. It is possible, however, to get patent owner's insurance to pay an attorney's fees for such suits.

Q **How do I protect the idea for an invention?**

If you are working on an invention and want to document your progress and the dates of your work, you could have your log signed and dated by a notary or a friend who is not involved in any way with the invention.

Q **I have already started to market the product—can I still get a patent?**

In the United States you can apply for a patent within one year of the time it is first offered for sale or disclosed publicly, so if you have been marketing the product for less than a year, you may be able to get a patent in this country. Other countries require you to apply for the patent before disclosing your invention; thus, you cannot qualify for patent protection in those countries.

Q **How can I protect a design for a new product?**

There is something called a design patent that lets you protect things such as designs on jeans, the shape of an object, and other designs used in the manufacture of goods.

Q **What is a nondisclosure agreement and when do I need to use one?**

A nondisclosure agreement prohibits others from using your confidential information or trade secrets for their own benefit or divulging that information to anyone else.

You would use one if you have employees who have access to confidential information, such as your customer list or plans for an invention, or if you have to show confidential information to others outside your company.

Q **What is a trade secret?**

A trade secret is business information you have that gives you a valuable edge over your competitors. This information may be a recipe for a cookie, an invention, the unique part of the code for a program, your customer list, plans to introduce new products, or almost anything else that is generally not known and gives you a competitive advantage.

Q **What kind of protection is there for trade secrets?**

If what you have is not generally known, and if you have taken care to maintain secrecy, you can sue the individual who disclosed your secrets. You may also take legal action to stop use of your trade secrets by others and recover damages if warranted.

Q **What do I have to do to maintain secrecy?**

Generally you have to limit access to what you consider a trade secret, be it your customer list, your recipes, or formulas. If you need to give people access to your trade secrets, you should make them first sign a nondisclosure agreement, preventing them from using or passing on what they learn. If you have employees, don't leave important papers laying out on desks or in unlocked drawers where someone working late could easily get at them. Avoid giving suppliers or bankers or anyone else you deal with access to your trade secrets, too.

Q How can trade secret laws help me?

Trade secret laws can protect your invention or your software in the development stages and can help you prevent others from profiting from your business procedures, lists, processes, or other unique parts of your operation. Some companies that have products with short lives or short budgets take their chances on trade secrets and speedy commercialization rather than go to the expense and time to apply for and get a patent. However, if another company develops on their own what you have, if you don't have a patent you have no recourse against them.

Q What is licensing and how does it work?

Licensing allows you to make money from other people's use of something you have created or you own. For instance, when you license a design you have created or software program you have authored, you give the licensee the right to use that work under specific circumstances that are spelled out in detail in a written agreement. The agreement will usually specify such things as how, when, and where the licensee may use your work, how you will be compensated for the work, and whether the licensee has exclusive or nonexclusive rights to use your work.

Q Can any attorney help me with patents and other intellectual property?

Only a patent attorney or patent agent may represent an inventor applying for a patent. An attorney in a general practice often won't have the background and experience in intellectual property law to help you protect or defend your rights to intellectual property. If the matter is something more or less routine (like registering a copyright), a general practice attorney may be able to process the paperwork. (In all probability, the attorney will "job out" the routine paperwork to a firm set up specifically to handle it.) He or she probably won't have the expertise to counsel you on how an intellectual property law (such as the copyright law or patent law) relates to your specific situation and how that situation is generally handled in contracts and in courts. Your best bet is to locate an attorney who specializes in intellectual property and is familiar with your industry.

Q How can I find an intellectual property attorney?

Intellectual property attorneys are sometimes listed as patent attorneys in your phone book. If you can't find one who knows your field, call the bar association or a trade association and ask for a recommendation. If you are in the arts (music, painting, writing, for example) you can get information and referrals by contacting the Volunteer Lawyers for the Arts. If you can't find a branch of Volunteer Lawyers for the Arts in your phone book, call the main office at 1 East 53rd Street, New York, NY 10022, (212) 319–2910, and ask for information and reference to a branch near you.

21.

Health Insurance:
Protection You Can't
Afford to Do Without

A study released by the U.S. Small Business Administration (SBA) in 1992 showed that 28 percent of U.S. workers aged 18 to 64 employed by firms with fewer than 25 employees had no health insurance coverage in 1989.* Commented Patricia Saiki, who was then administrator of the SBA, "There is no more important issue for the 20 million men and women small business owners than finding the affordable means to provide adequate health care to their employees."

Obviously, sweeping reform of the health care industry is needed to make insurance accessible to small business owners and their employees. Some states such as New York are already implementing laws towards that end. But reform is not likely to come overnight. This chapter will alert you to and may help you avoid some of the pitfalls involved with getting and keeping health insurance.

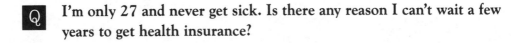 **I'm only 27 and never get sick. Is there any reason I can't wait a few years to get health insurance?**

Just because you seldom get sick doesn't mean you couldn't develop some type of long-term illness or be involved in a serious accident. A single illness or accident

* Zachary Dyckman, Ph.D, and Joanna Burnette. *Programs to Improve Health Insurance Access for Small Business: What Works and What Doesn't.* United States Small Business Administration, Office of Advocacy, 1992.

could put you in the hole for doctor and hospital bills totaling $20,000 to $30,000 in just two or three weeks if you don't have health insurance.

Q **I'm planning on quitting my job to start my own business. Can I convert my company health insurance policy to a personal one?**

If your present employer has twenty or more employees and you become ineligible for insurance under the company group plan due to a "qualifying event" (see below), you may be entitled to continue the plan for up to 18 months* under the Consolidated Omnibus Budget Reconciliation Act of 1985 (COBRA). If you become disabled, the continuation period is extended to 29 months. You will have to pay the premiums out of your own pocket, however. At the end of the continuation period you have the option of changing it to an individual conversion policy under the health care policy's regular conversion options.

Q **Does the COBRA law apply to all companies that have twenty or more employees?**

No. Some government, church, and self-insured plans are exempt from the COBRA law, so be sure to check before assuming you can continue coverage.

Q **What are qualifying events?**

The following five events are considered qualifying events under COBRA:

1. You cease to be an employee for any reason other than gross misconduct.
2. You change from full-time to part-time employment and no longer quality for the company's health care plan due to the reduction in hours you work.
3. You are the spouse of the insured and lose coverage due to divorce, legal separation, or the death of the insured.

---

* A dependent spouse who loses coverage because of the death of the insured or due to separation or divorce and children who become too old for coverage under the insured's plan or lose coverage in some other way may continue coverage for up to 36 months.

4. You are a child who ceases to be eligible for group plan benefits.
5. You become entitled to Medicare benefits.

Q **How long do I have before I have to decide whether to continue the coverage under COBRA?**

Your group plan administrator is supposed to notify you within 14 days of a qualifying event of your right to continue the coverage. You then have 60 days to elect coverage, which will be retroactive to the time you became ineligible for your employer's plan. You then have up to 45 days to pay the first premium.

Q **If the employer changes insurance plans, what happens to my coverage?**

Although you, personally, pay for the continuation coverage, it is under the employer's policy. Thus, if the employer changes to a new carrier and/or plan, your coverage changes to the same carrier and/or plan. If the employer should stop offering health insurance, your coverage would be terminated along with all the others that were under the company health plan.

Q **What will it cost me to continue my present coverage?**

The rate for the coverage is the same rate your employer is charged plus a 2 percent administrative cost. If you pay part and the employer pays part of the cost now, the amount you pay will be the combined amount (your share plus the employer's share).

Q **Can I lose this coverage in any way?**

The continuation coverage terminates at the end of the continuation period or if any of the following occurs:

▶ You don't pay the premium when it is due.
▶ You become covered as an employee under some other plan.
▶ You remarry and become included under the new spouse's group health insurance.

- You become eligible for Medicare.
- Your former employer ceases to provide group health care for all employees, terminating the plan.

Q **Can the insurance company refuse individual coverage for me or my family at the end of the continuation period?**

If you haven't let the policy lapse, they can't refuse to insure you; however, rates may be higher and coverage not as good as the group plan.

Q **Suppose my employer has fewer than twenty employees. Is there any way I can continue my health insurance if I lose my job?**

Some states have continuation laws that are similar to the federal COBRA law. Your state insurance department or an insurance broker should be able to tell you if there is some type of health insurance continuation law in your state.

Q **Is it advisable to use the conversion option in the group plan?**

The conversion option will give you continuity of insurance. It is also useful if you or your dependents have health problems that might make it difficult to get a new health care policy. If you and your dependents are healthy, however, a new, individual policy may be less expensive and better than the conversion plan.

Q **Should I join an association to get their group health insurance?**

If you will be joining an association only to get their group health plan, ask to see a copy of the policy and ask about the rates for coverage for yourself and your dependents. Not all group or association plans are created equal, and some may not give you the coverage you need.

Q **What will a good health insurance policy for myself and my family cost?**

That figure varies greatly according to where you live, how old you are, how many dependents you have, and whether you or family members have had previous health problems. In 1992, for instance, a 30-year-old woman in the southwest part of the United States was quoted prices averaging around $250 to $300 per month for health insurance coverage for herself and her two children who were under the age of 10. A 62-year-old man in the Northeast, meanwhile, was paying close to $650 per month for health insurance to cover himself and his wife. His wife had a preexisting condition that was not covered by the policy he was able to get. As a broad rule of thumb, however, in many parts of the country a family of four may have to pay $4,000 or more per year for health insurance.

Q **Isn't a group health insurance plan cheaper than individual coverage?**

Not necessarily. In fact, individual health insurance plans often cost less and offer more than small group plans. The only way you can be sure which would be best for your circumstances is to compare rates and features of a group policy to an individual policy. Make sure you read policy brochures carefully since some plans that say they are for individuals are really small group plans in disguise. One insurance company, for instance, has one plan it bills as being an "economical health insurance program for individuals" and describes another as "an opportunity for individuals to enjoy group benefits and group rates!" The two plans are identical and both are small group plans. The only differences between them are the name of each plan and the artwork in the brochures describing them.

Q **What should I look for in a health insurance policy?**

Most people choose insurance based on rates and deductibles. But rates and deductibles are less important than your ability to continue coverage, warns health insurance expert Hal Zoller. Zoller, who owns Resource Equity Group, an insurance firm in Greenville, South Carolina, specializing in health and life insurance, says it's important to "know what you are buying up front. Get information about what kind of policy you are buying . . . and under what conditions it can be canceled," Zoller says. "Make sure you are not vulnerable to losing coverage. If you have group coverage tied to employment and you go out of business or are unable to work, you will lose coverage and you won't be able to get insurance elsewhere if you have any kind of medical condition at that time."

If you are buying insurance for only yourself and your dependents or are buying it for yourself and one or two other employees, Zoller suggests you look for a policy that:

- is a true individual policy, not a small group plan being sold to individuals;
- is guaranteed renewable or conditionally renewable by state;
- does not tie eligibility to employment;
- offers comprehensive major medical coverage in or out of the hospital;
- is offered by a company that is committed to health insurance as a speciality, has an A or A+ rating by A. M. Best & Co., and at least $100 million in assets; and
- offers you some flexibility in tailoring coverage to your needs.

Q **What do *guaranteed renewable* and *conditionally renewable by state* mean?**

Guaranteed renewable means that as long as you continue to pay the premiums, the insurance company cannot cancel your insurance for any reason. Guaranteed renewable plans are getting very difficult to find. Plans that are conditionally renewable by state are the next best option on renewability. That means the insurance company must continue your policy unless they cancel every in-force policy in the state. Both of these options are available only for individual policies. If you can't get a guaranteed renewable policy, conditionally renewable by state is the best alternative.

Q **I haven't had any health problems so I don't think any insurance company would turn me down. Why do I need to be concerned with the eligibility requirements in a policy?**

Eligibility requirements govern more than just your initial eligibility to get the insurance. They also govern whether you can *keep* the insurance. For instance, if your policy pegs eligibility to employment or self-employment and you become disabled and unable to work, you would become ineligible for the insurance and could lose it at the very time you need it most. Finding new insurance at a reasonable price would be impossible because of your disability.

An insurance agent told me I might be uninsurable due to a medical condition I have. What can I do?

First, find out if the agent you are using deals only with one or two companies. If so, find an insurance broker who is experienced in handling health insurance and who is familiar with insurance offered by many companies. Since each company has its own underwriting requirements it is possible that what makes you uninsurable to one company might not make you uninsurable to another. If you do have a condition that would make you uninsurable to all companies, ask about health insurance pools and open enrollment options in your state. Health insurance pools, which accept people who have been rejected by other insurance companies, are available in twenty-three states. Open enrollment periods are another option for insurance offered in thirteen states by Blue Cross/Blue Shield. During open enrollment, everyone who applies for insurance and can pay the premium is accepted. Policies obtained through one of these options are likely to be expensive but at least should provide some coverage. Be sure to read the policies carefully, however, to see what they say about coverage for preexisting conditions.

 How can I tell whether something is a true individual policy or small group insurance being sold to individuals?

"Make sure the person selling you the insurance leaves you literature about the insurance you are considering and read it carefully," suggests Zoller. "If the coverage is described as a policy, and you are described as the policy holder, chances are it is a true individual policy. If it is referred to as a plan or program, it is probably some type of group plan."

Pay particular attention to the legal-sounding descriptions in the policy literature, too. These descriptions should explain what the document is and what parties are involved. Says Zoller, "If there are more than two parties involved (the insurance company and you), it probably is not an individual policy but some sort of a group policy with the other parties being an administrator, association, trustee, et cetera." Still another giveaway that a policy is not a true individual policy is any statement requiring continuing employment or participation in an association for eligibility.

 Is individual insurance the only kind of insurance I should consider?

Because of the renewability concerns, an individual policy would be preferable if you are self-employed and have just yourself and family or one or two other employees to cover. However, if you can't get an individual policy due to previous health problems, or can get better maternity or other benefits under a group plan, group might be preferable. Additionally, if you have more than a couple of employees, individual plans are likely to be impractical for providing coverage for all of them. In that case, you might want to consider group insurance to cover the employees and individual coverage for yourself and your dependents. No matter what your circumstances, however, differences in policies from different insurance companies and even differences in policies by state or region of the country make it imperative for you to understand exactly what kind of protection you are buying.

Q | **Do I need separate coverage for doctor bills, hospital stays, and/or surgery?**

Those coverages are usually all rolled into one comprehensive major medical policy. Policies that offer only in-hospital and surgical coverage or daily indemnity policies and policies that cover certain illnesses (such as cancer) are of questionable value. If you have a comprehensive policy, cancer and other "dread diseases" will be covered under the policy, making supplemental "dread disease" insurance superfluous.

Q | **What about policies that say they will pay back premiums minus any claims when you reach a certain age?**

Read them carefully to make sure you know exactly what you are getting. One such plan covered only in-hospital care and had a very high deductible. Since it is quite easy to pile up thousands of dollars in medical bills without ever stepping foot inside a hospital, plans like this are not good substitutes for having comprehensive major medical coverage.

Q | **What benefits should I look for in a health insurance policy?**

Make sure the policy protects you against burdensome out-of-pocket expenses for inpatient and outpatient care. Find out:

- What the deductible is on the policy (how much you have to pay per year out of your own money before the insurance company pays anything).

- What percentage of bills the insurance company pays after you reach the deductible.

- Whether the deductible is applied to each illness or injury or is figured on a calendar year basis. A calendar year basis is much better since you could be struck with two separate illnesses or injuries that are costly in one year.

- What the maximum out-of-pocket expense will be. (In other words, how much do you have to pay before the company will pick up all covered medical expenses instead of just a percentage of them?)

You also need to look at how the insurance company determines the amounts it will pay. Will they pay all usual and customary charges for your medical and hospital bills in the geographic region where you are treated, or do they pay according to a schedule of fees? If payments are according to a schedule of fees you might find that the schedule of fees allows only $2,000 for a surgical procedure you need but that all the doctors in your area charge $5,000. If that were the case, you would have to pay the additional $3,000 out of your own pocket.

Check for limitations and exclusions on coverage, too. For instance, some plans or policies limit intensive care to two or three times the regular room rate or pay only for a limited number of days. Find out what the policy says about preexisting conditions: Will it deny any claims for preexisting conditions? Will it pay claims if there is no recurrence within a set period of time? Warns Zoller, "Read the definition of a preexisting condition first, and then read when they will be covered. For example, under one policy, a preexisting condition might be a condition for which you have received treatment in the last 12 months. Under another, preexisting conditions might be defined as having *symptoms* (with no treatment). Usually preexisting conditions will be covered within 12 to 24 months, and in some states, unless excluded by a special rider, all preexisting conditions disclosed on the application are covered immediately."

Other things to look into include maternity benefits, if needed, requirements for second opinions or approvals prior to surgery or to hospital admission, and your own preferences or individual needs. Does the policy cover holistic or chiropractic care? Psychologist or psychiatrist fees? Alcohol and substance abuse? Are you likely to need these things? What about yearly checkups or routine preventive screening tests such as mammograms or bone density scans for osteoporosis?

If you choose some type of health maintenance organization or preferred provider group plan, find out what doctors, hospitals, and testing labs belong to the plan and how far away you would have to travel to use them. Find out, too, if the plan pays for care that is performed outside of the organization's member doctors and hospitals and if so, under what circumstances. You don't want to find out after you get a bill for $10,000 or $20,000 in medical bills that the insurance company won't cover them because the hospital and/or doctor wasn't part of its network.

Q **What are preferred provider and health maintenance organizations?**

Preferred provider organizations (PPOs) and health maintenance organizations (HMOs) are two forms of something known as managed care plans, which are plans designed to reduce health care costs.

HMOs are both the insurance company and the health care provider. With HMOs, insured individuals usually *must* use the HMO health care providers unless there is no suitable HMO specialist or other provider available within the HMO. If that is the case, the individual will be referred to an approved provider outside the system. The primary advantage to the insured is that actual out-of-pocket expenses can be just a couple of dollars for each doctor's visit or prescription. The disadvantage is that it may not have any coverage for health care services performed by doctors or facilities that are not part of the HMO, which can be a major problem if you should be dissatisfied with the doctors or treatment plans offered through the HMO.

Preferred provider organizations operate a little differently. Typically, health care providers who participate agree to accept payment at fees specified by the PPO and charge the patient a slightly higher copayment than the patient would pay at an HMO. (Copayment in one preferred provider plan is $10, for instance.) If the insured would rather choose his or her own health care provider, however, he or she can and will be reimbursed for out-of-pocket expenses the same as under traditional health care (fee for service) plans. The benefit of a PPO is that the premiums may be 10 to 15 percent lower than traditional indemnity health care premiums, and the out-of-pocket expenses for routine checkups and tests may be lower, too. Potential disadvantages could be lower benefits if you choose doctors who are not part of the system.

Q **Would I be better off trying to get coverage for my employees through an HMO or PPO instead of through more traditional group plans?**

Only you can make that decision based on your needs and the needs of your employees. Look at the plan details, coverages, list of preferred providers, and premiums. Then compare to more traditional plans before making your decision.

Q **An insurance broker who called here tells me he can get insurance for my employees at a much lower rate than I am paying now. Is it wise to switch companies just for rates?**

"One of the things small businesses need to watch out for is the difference between new business rates for group insurance and the in-force rates," warns Hal Zoller. It is not uncommon for companies to be notified of rate increases of as much as 50 to 100 percent when their policies renew. At the same time the insurance company may be advertising the very same plan at a very low "new business" rate. "If continuity of coverage can be maintained, the new plan appears to have a successful record and you can save more than twenty-five percent, the switch might be worthwhile if benefits are comparable to what you now have," says Zoller.

Q **Do I need to get disability insurance?**

Long-term disability insurance is often overlooked because it is expensive and because no one likes to think about the possibility of becoming disabled. Nevertheless, if you should be unable to work for a long period of time due to accident or illness, you would have long-term living expenses. Long-term disability insurance can help cover those needs.

Q **How much disability insurance do I need? Enough to replace all my salary?**

Usually people get disability insurance to cover 50 to 65 percent of their salary. Insurance companies usually will not give you coverage for your full salary since they feel a greater percentage would be a disincentive to rehabilitation.

Q **What should I look for in a disability policy?**

Look at what the policy pays, when it pays (how long the waiting period is, how long you would continue to receive benefits), and look at the policy definition of disability. Some policies will pay if you are unable to work in any occupation; others pay if you are unable to work in the trade or occupation you were pursuing when you were disabled. A policy that pays if you can't work in your own trade or occupation would be best.

Q **Isn't it difficult for homebased business owners to get disability insurance?**

If you are just starting out in your own business, it might be difficult to get adequate disability insurance, since the amount a policy will pay is based on your previous earnings.

Q **Is there any other insurance I might need?**

If you don't have life insurance, you should look into getting a simple term or low-cost universal life policy. Other insurance you may need will depend on your individual circumstances. A good insurance broker who is familiar with the needs of businesspeople and your type of business can help you identify potential risks. You may find it beneficial to deal with two insurance brokers, one for health and life insurance and one for property/casualty insurance. Once you know the risks, you will have to assess the potentials for financial loss to determine what types of insurance protection to buy.

22.

How to Protect Your Business and Personal Assets from Loss

Business insurance is something few people like to discuss and no one likes to buy. After all, who really wants to pay for something they can't see or touch and hope they never have to use?

Like it or not, however, insurance is a necessary evil. A fire or theft, an accident involving a customer or employee, or a lawsuit brought against you or your company could destroy your business and eat up your life savings if you don't have adequate insurance. This chapter alerts you to some of the risks you may face and gives you the basic facts you need to make informed decisions about what kind of business insurance you should consider buying to protect your business and personal assets from financial loss.

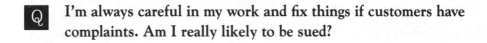 **I'm always careful in my work and fix things if customers have complaints. Am I really likely to be sued?**

No matter how knowledgeable or careful you are, you could suddenly find yourself the defendant in a lawsuit. Typical is the case of an independent consultant who recommended specific hardware and software for one of his business clients. When the software didn't work properly with the hardware configuration, the client sued and won a $100,000 judgment against the consultant. In another case a small company offering data storage and list management services as a sideline sustained a $2 million loss after it inadvertently mixed up two lists, substituting a list of credit risks for a list of prime customers.

Professional negligence is just one type of risk you may face as a business owner. Other possible exposures (risks) include product liability, personal injury (if a client or employee tripped and broke a leg in your home office, for instance), vehicular accidents involving an employee, and loss of equipment due to fire or theft.

Q I operate my business from my home. Won't my personal insurance policies protect me against losses?

Personal insurance policies offer little or no coverage for business-related losses. Homeowner's insurance usually excludes liability coverage for business pursuits and may exclude computer or other business equipment used in the home. If electronic equipment is not excluded, it is often limited to only $2,000 to $3,000, an amount far below what many home business owners have invested in their computer software and peripherals.

Q Is there any way I can get protection for my home office without getting a separate business policy?

You may be able to gain some protection by purchasing riders or endorsements for an incidental office in your home. (A rider or endorsement is an add-on to your policy.) When available these add-ons give you a limited amount of property coverage for losses to home office equipment and furnishings and a limited amount of liability coverage for personal injuries to clients or employees[*] on your premises. Sometimes these add-ons are combined into one endorsement, and sometimes they are sold separately.

Q Can I get endorsements to my home policy for professional or product liability protection?

No, product liability and professional liability (which is a form of malpractice insurance) are not available as endorsements to homeowner's insurance.

---

[*] Home office liability coverage for employees in your home office is separate from workers' compensation insurance, which you also need.

I'd like to run a day-care center from my home. Will an endorsement to my homeowner's policy cover my insurance needs for that?

Sometimes you can get an endorsement if you provide day care for only a handful of children; however, the regulations vary from state to state. Find out what the regulations are in your area, then ask an insurance agent or broker to find you an appropriate policy.

 What insurance companies offer endorsements for an office in the home?

Allstate and State Farm both offer incidental office in the home endorsements, as do most major insurance companies.

 Are the endorsements or add-on policies expensive?

The actual cost depends on what you do, how much insurance you need, and where you are located, but usually they are quite inexpensive. The additional amount you pay to add one or more business endorsements to your home policy could be as low as $10 to $20 per year.

You could pay more for an endorsement, too, and not get the best possible coverage for your needs. An insurance agent on Long Island, New York, told me about getting one home business owner an endorsement for his homeowner's policy to cover $20,000 worth of computer equipment. The endorsement added $400 a year to the cost of the businessperson's homeowner's policy. When I asked the agent to look up the cost of a businessowner's policy that would provide the same amount of coverage for the computer equipment, he found the cost was $275 ($125 less than the endorsement) for a policy that would have covered the computer equipment and given the person a million dollars in liability protection against business-related personal injury claims.

Moral: get comparison prices from several insurance brokerages and ask about all options that might be available to you. Work with the insurance agent or broker who is most willing to help you find the right insurance for your needs and budget.

 Will the extra casualty and liability insurance from an endorsement be enough?

It all depends on what kind of business you run. For instance, if you have an endorsement to your homeowner's policy, the limit of coverage (the most the insurance company will pay) for injury to clients or employees will be the same as the limit stated in your home policy. This is usually quite a bit less than the limit in a commercial policy. If you rarely have business clients come to your home office and don't have employees, however, it may be adequate for your needs.

If you don't have much data processing or other specialized business equipment and don't store equipment that belongs to other people on your property, the added endorsements may give you all the casualty insurance you need. On the other hand, if you *do* have a lot of money invested in data processing equipment, the additional fire and theft and data processing protection you can buy this way may not be adequate.

The limits and the premiums vary from company to company, too, so be sure to ask what they are. Make the agent or broker look up the figures and give you something in writing (preferably a copy of the policy and endorsements). If you don't, you may not be getting the coverage you think you are buying.

In researching this chapter, for instance, I called the local office of a nationally known insurance company three times on different days. On each call I spoke to a different agent in the office and asked the identical question: What are the limits for equipment coverage on your company's incidental office in the home rider? *Each agent gave me a different answer.* One said she thought it was $5,000; another said he thought it was $2,000; and a third said he thought it was $8,000. None of them bothered to look up the actual value. They expected me to accept the figure they "thought" was right.

Be aware, too, that endorsements usually cover only specified perils and will generally be limited by the same deductibles that are applied to your homeowner's policy.

 What happens if I don't tell the insurance company about my home office?

If you suffer a business-related loss or are sued for a business-related accident, they may refuse to pay the claim. The cost of business endorsements is usually so minimal that if you have a business in your home it would be foolish not to at least get endorsements to cover your business activities. If the insurance company you use now doesn't have such endorsements available, shop around for one that does.

Will an incidental office in the home endorsement pay to replace my computer system if I drop it and break it while moving it from one place to another?

No. The endorsement will only give you the same kind of insurance protection you have for other household goods: namely fire, theft, and other specified perils. To cover accidental breakage, spills, and so on, you need a special form policy for the computer equipment.

 What is a special form policy?

Special form policies cover you for everything except situations specifically excluded in a policy. A named perils policy protects you only for named (listed) exposures or hazards. For instance, if you had a named perils policy that states it protects against fire and theft but does not mention accidental breakage, you wouldn't collect if you accidentally broke some piece of property that was covered by the policy. However, if you have a special form policy that says the property is covered for all risks except earthquakes, you could recoup your losses from accidental breakage or damage that was not caused by an earthquake. *Special form policies* is the term now used for what used to be called "all-risk" policies. The name was changed because they do exclude some perils, and the name was therefore confusing. As with any policy, be sure to read the policy and make sure it covers the risks you want covered. If anything is unclear, ask your broker for an explanation.

A friend told me he had bought computer insurance real cheap from a company that sells it mail order. Is it really wise to buy computer insurance that way?

Like anything else you will need to comparison shop; however, you might save money buying computer coverage through mail order. A company called Safeware, which has been in business for more than 10 years, offers a good, all-risk policy at a reasonable price and has an excellent reputation for handling claims. The insurance covers most losses, including accidental breakage, spills, and power surges. A few risks are excluded (not covered). These include earthquake damage and theft of computer equipment left in an unattended car; however, endorsements can be added to cover those two and other special situations.

The rates on the Safeware policies are based on the replacement costs of your computer system. In 1992, the company was charging $129 for a replacement value policy that protected up to $14,000 in computer equipment. Policies for computer systems with lower or higher replacement values were available as well. If you have or are considering buying a businessowner's policy (BOP) you might want to compare Safeware's rates and coverages with endorsements available to your BOP.

Q **Does Safeware sell insurance where I live? I didn't see them in the phone book.**

Safeware sells insurance in most parts of the United States. To find out if their insurance is available in your area and to get current rates, you can contact the company at (800) 848–3469.

Q **I write about computer equipment and have a little repair business on the side, so I often have equipment that doesn't belong to me in my home office. Does my insurance cover loss of those items if there's a break-in or fire?**

If you do not have a commercial insurance policy, you probably would not be covered for that type of loss. You need either a businessowner's policy with coverage for property of others or separate bailees' insurance. (Bailees' insurance has nothing to do with bail for criminals. The term *bailee* means anyone who has temporary possession of someone else's property.)

Q **I'm a professional musician and use my truck to transport equipment from one engagement to another. My insurance broker says I need commercial insurance because my regular insurance might not cover my equipment if it's lost or damaged on one of these moves. Is he just trying to make extra money?**

No, he's not just trying to make an extra buck, he's giving you good advice. If something got lost or stolen in transit neither your homeowner's nor your truck insurance would be likely to cover the loss. To cover losses in transporting equipment you need inland marine insurance. Despite the term *marine* in the name, inland marine insurance has nothing to do with ships, recreational boating, or bodies of water. Instead, the name was originally associated with the concept of insuring goods after they are taken off the boat and are in transit to some other location. Today, however, inland marine insurance offers protection against a broad range of perils including the transportation of equipment.

 When do I need regular business insurance?

You will need regular (commercial) business insurance if your business office is not located in your home or if you are a homebased business with insurance risks that aren't covered by endorsements to your homeowner's policy. You may also be required by your state, regional, or local governing bodies to have some specified kind and amount of insurance to get a license. A carpenter might be required to have $500,000 worth of liability insurance, for instance. These regulations vary from one locality to another, so you will have to check with your town, city, county, and state governments to determine what rules apply. You may also have to be bonded for some types of work.

 My business office is not in my home. Will I need separate insurance policies to protect me against robberies, theft, injury to customers, and the like?

You will probably be able to get one comprehensive policy called a business-owner's policy or businessowner's packaged policy (BOP) that will cover your business for a variety of perils. Be sure to give your broker enough information so he or she can evaluate what risks you may be exposed to, search for the right policy, and let you know if other insurance is advisable.

 Under what conditions might a home business need a separate business policy?

Some examples of when you might need businessowner's coverage for a home business include:

‣ if you store other people's property in your home office
‣ if you have more computer equipment than your homeowner's fire and theft provisions will cover

▶ if you need business interruption insurance
▶ if you frequently have customers or independent contractors who come to your home

Policies and individual business needs vary, so read the policies you are considering and make sure you understand what you are buying.

Q **What does a businessowner's policy cover?**

A businessowner's policy gives you coverage for a variety of property and liability risks. These policies are available for many small offices, stores, and apartment houses and may be either named peril or special form (all-risk) policies. Businessowners' policies are usually tailored for specific businesses but are likely to offer:

▶ liability coverage against slips and falls and other physical injuries to customers
▶ accidental libel or slander* and similar nonphysical injury to individuals
▶ casualty insurance (fire and theft)
▶ business interruption insurance (replaces business income and pays for extra expenses after a fire, theft, or other insured loss so you can pay the rent, equipment leases, and other ongoing business expenses plus extra costs incurred to get the business running again)
▶ insurance for property of others while it is on your premises

Don't just assume a BOP will meet all your needs, however. Get specifics. "Each insurance contract is unique," explains Ed Coyle, a property and casualty insurance broker in Wheaton, Illinois. He warns that the variations can be confusing: "There is no generic policy. Each company tends to add their own bells and whistles to make their policy different."

Depending on circumstances, you may need extra protection against employee theft, glass breakage, machinery or boiler breakdown, or other perils. Computers and computer equipment would be covered as other property but may not be cov-

---

* The protection against accidental libel and slander available in most BOPs does not apply to publications. If you publish newspapers, magazines, books, or other written media, you will need to get separate coverage if you want protection against libel and slander. One source is the Inland Press Association, 777 Busse Highway, Park Ridge, IL 60068, (708) 696–1140.

ered against losses due to brownouts, spikes, and so on. If you want that type of protection you might get a separate computer policy.

Q Is a businessowner's policy expensive for a home office?

No. A businessowner's policy suitable for a home office will probably cost about $150 to $250 a year, an amount that is quite reasonable for the extra insurance coverage you get. The businessowner's policy would be completely separate from and in addition to your homeowner's policy.

Q How do I know I have enough of the right kind of insurance?

The most important thing you can do is find a good insurance broker who understands your business and who will help you understand what your risks are and how to protect against them. If you don't have an insurance broker and don't have friends who can recommend a good one, look in the Yellow Pages under "Insurance." When you call agents, explain what kind of business you are in and ask what they recommend. Be sure they understand the way your business operates and be sure you know exactly what the policy or policies they suggest will or won't cover.

Q What's the difference between an insurance agent and a broker?

The definitions vary somewhat from state to state, but in general an insurance broker represents the customer and finds the right policy or policies from among the offerings of many different companies. An insurance agent may represent only one insurance company (such as Allstate or State Farm) or may be an independent agent who represents many companies and functions like a broker.

Q What is errors and omissions insurance?

Errors and omissions insurance is malpractice insurance for professionals who aren't medical practitioners. Often called E & O insurance or professional liability insurance, it protects professionals from financial loss due to claims involving negligence, errors, omissions, and wrongful acts. Traditionally, coverage included all legal fees, court costs, and settlements up to the limits of the policy. John Mitchell of the Morley Agency in Southampton, New York, warns, however, that "some policies now being written have first dollar exclusions [deductibles] on legal fee coverage or reduce the maximum the policy will pay in a settlement by the cost of the legal fees." Therefore, be sure to read your policy very carefully.

If you are involved in a traditional profession, such as accounting, real estate, or personnel recruiting, you may be able to get a policy or references to companies that offer suitable policies through your professional association. If you are in a profession with few practitioners, finding a suitable policy can be quite difficult.

Q **Don't businessowners' policies include professional liability coverage?**

Professional liability is different from and usually purchased separately from other kinds of liability insurance. The exception seems to be for printers. Several companies offer E & O insurance as an add-on to their businessowner's policy for printers.

Q **What does errors and omissions insurance cost? Isn't it expensive?**

Unfortunately, we live in a society where people like to sue one another. That makes E & O insurance quite expensive for many businesses. Rates are based on a variety of things, including the type of business, dollar volume of the business, the number of customers, and experience in the field, and often start at $1,000 to $2,000 a year or more. In 1992 one company was charging computer consultants a minimum rate of $1,000 for $100,000 of E & O coverage or $1,750 for a million dollars in liability coverage. The rates increased for consultants with more than $200,000 in sales.

An E & O policy for individual personnel recruiters in 1992 cost approximately $700 to $1,000, depending on the insurance company issuing it.

The high price of professional liability insurance means many people who run small homebased businesses feel they can't afford E & O insurance. "They can't justify the cost because it's a struggle for them to pay for basic health insurance and automobile insurance," says Coyle.

Q **A friend of mine who is a consulting engineer says he doesn't need liability insurance because he put the house and everything else in his wife's name and he is careful in his work. Is that a safe way to avoid buying errors and omissions insurance?**

If you need E & O insurance there really is no completely safe way to avoid the cost. Many very small companies do choose to go without E & O insurance because of the cost; however, doing so is a gamble. You have to understand what your risk is and be willing to live with the risk and the consequences should you be sued. If your friend has put everything in his wife's name without the advice of an attorney he may not have the protection he thinks he does. State marital laws might consider his wife a partner in the business and equally liable for the business.

Q **I have errors and omissions insurance now but plan to retire soon and will be discontinuing the insurance then. Will my current insurer still cover me if someone sues me 5 years after I retire for something they claim I did before I retired?**

If you had an occurrence policy at the time referenced in a claim, the insurance company issuing the policy that was in effect when an incident occurred would be responsible for paying the claim up to limits in effect at the time the incident occurred. Thus, if the policy at the time offered a maximum of $100,000 and you were now being sued for $1 million, all the occurrence policy would cover is $100,000.

If you have a claims-made policy, the policy in force at the time a claim is made is the one that covers the claim. To insure coverage after you retire if you have a claims-made policy, you can buy tail-end coverage, which covers you for some period of time into the future for claims based on your actions while the policy was in force.

Q **I'd like to switch insurance companies. What happens after I do? Who covers professional liability claims made in the past? The present company or the old one?**

If you switch companies, you should ask about something called prior acts coverage, which will extend your present level of protection backward to years past at present levels of coverage.

Q **Can't I incorporate to protect my personal assets in case I'm sued for professional malpractice?**

Contrary to popular belief, incorporation does not automatically protect your personal assets from liability in malpractice (or other) lawsuits. Although incorporation makes the business a separate legal entity from its owners, there are numerous circumstances that can cause that status to be lost. In fact, a good attorney could probably find a way to strip away corporate status of almost any small business based on criteria such as these:

- the business failed to keep corporate financial affairs distinctly separate from personal financial matters
- the business didn't hold required shareholders' and directors' meetings or keep adequate records
- the business was undercapitalized
- the business didn't file an annual report or filed it late

Even if you were able to maintain your corporate status and/or were found not guilty of any personal negligence, you could still lose a tremendous amount of money due to the high cost of legal fees. In 1989, for instance, the average cost of legal fees to defend a corporate director in a liability suit was $1.2 million. While the costs for a liability suit against your small business might not come up to those average costs, you would still be looking at five- or six-figure bills for legal and court costs if you were sued.

Q **I went to a seminar on starting a business and heard someone mention being bonded. What is bonding and how does it protect me?**

There are two basic types of bonding that businesses sometimes need to be concerned with: surety bonds and fidelity bonds. Surety bonds don't protect you. They protect the customer by guaranteeing something will be done in a certain way. Bid bonds and performance bonds that are often required on construction projects are an example. Essentially they guarantee that the work you contract to do will be completed and that suppliers will be paid. If you default on the contract, the bonding company becomes responsible for completing the job and paying suppliers and will come after you to make good on their losses. Other types of surety bonds are those required of pawnbrokers to protect owners of property from loss and bonds required of liquor stores to assure the state will be paid if the liquor store breaks any laws.

Fidelity bonding is honesty insurance. Fidelity bonds are purchased to protect businesses from financial loss due to fraud, theft, embezzlement, or other dishonesty by their employees. If there is a loss the bonding company pays the business and goes after the employee. Banks and other concerns where employees handle money or the equivalent often bond employees.

Q **How do I get bonded?**

If a municipality or other governing agency requires you to be bonded in order to get a license to practice your business they should be able to suggest names of companies to contact. You can also get names of companies to contact by looking in the Yellow Pages under the heading "Bonds."

Q **Can I get bonded if my business is a start-up?**

Bonding works a little like credit. If you are a start-up company with little or no history of completed jobs you may have to build up gradually to the point where you can be bonded for major projects. For instance, at first, $50,000 might be the largest bond you can get, and you might be able to get it only if you put up collateral. As you gain experience and build a history of successful completion of projects, the amounts of bonding you will qualify for will increase. If you need to be bonded to do work for a municipality or government agency, ask if they have programs to help you get the bonding you need. Your local SBA or SCORE office (see appendix 2) or state or regional economic development agency may also provide help.

Q **I'm planning to hire someone to work for me part-time. Is there any kind of insurance I have to get?**

You will have to get workers' compensation insurance. You will also have to pay the employer's share of Social Security insurance and withhold the employee's share and taxes. (See chapters 23 and 24 for tax requirements.)

Q **Who and what does workers' compensation cover?**

Workers' compensation compensates employees for work-related injuries and illnesses. It also provides liability coverage to pay the employer's legal fees if the employee or employee's family file suit against the employer for an injury, illness, or death.

In most states employers are required to get workers' compensation for most types of employees. Domestic workers, farm workers, and casual laborers are sometimes excluded from those requirements. Workers' compensation compensates employees for medical bills, a percentage of lost wages, funeral expenses, and survivor's benefits as appropriate due to work-related injuries or diseases. The amounts and percentages and length of time benefits are paid are regulated by state laws.

The specific illnesses or accidents a worker may be compensated for are also regulated at the state level; however, loss of limbs, back injuries, and other typical and easily identifiable work-related injuries are generally covered. In some states, less easily identifiable conditions such as stress-related or psychological illnesses are considered compensable conditions as well.

Q **Do I have to get workers' compensation if I have just one employee?**

Some states only require businesses to provide workers' compensation when there are three or more employees. Other states require it for all employees. If your state does not require you to carry workers' compensation if you only have one employee, you should consult an insurance broker and/or attorney to determine how best to protect yourself against possible work-related injury lawsuits.

Q **What does workers' compensation cost?**

The cost of workers' compensation depends on the industry, the classification of the individual workers, the size of your payroll, and something known as experience rating. The cost of premiums can be as little as $1 or $2 per hundred dollars of payroll or as high as $25 or more per hundred in high-risk industries.

Q **Can I avoid getting workers' compensation by having employees work for me as independent contractors?**

Many companies are attempting to cut costs by calling their employees independent contractors. By using independent contractors instead of having employees, employers also eliminate their share of Social Security and some other payroll taxes, the need to pay for health insurance and other benefits, plus a lot of bookkeeping.

If the people who work for you are really employees, however, treating the employee as an independent contractor is risky at best. If the contractor is injured working for you, he and the courts may consider the relationship to be an employee/employer situation, and you would not only be liable for the costs of medical care and lost wages but also be assessed statutory damages (a penalty) for not having workers' compensation. Calling an employee an independent contractor is also risky from a tax standpoint. The IRS and state tax departments are cracking down on abuses. (For a list of guidelines the IRS uses to determine whether someone is an employee or independent contractor, see chapter 23).

Q **Is there any way I can keep workers' compensation costs down?**

The most important thing a small business owner can do to keep workers' compensation rates as low as possible is to make sure your business is classified properly. "Most business owners don't realize their workers may actually fall into several different rate categories," says Linda Jasper, president of Suffolk Sidewalks, Inc., a construction company in Miller Place, New York. "Most insurers will automatically lump your entire payroll into one classification: the highest one. But not all work your employees do will actually fall into that higher classification."

In the construction business, Jasper explains, the rate for a concrete worker who does foundations is higher than the rate for a concrete worker doing flat-work since there's more danger of injury with the foundation work. "If you are aware of these categories and keep good records showing what percentages of man-hours go into high-rate and low-rate jobs, you can save money by having some of your workers classified in low- or medium-rate categories instead of having them all lumped together into the highest rate categories."

If you pay more than $5,000 a year in workers' compensation, another way you may be able to cut costs is with experience rating. This is a system that set rates based on actual claims history of your company compared to others in the industry in the previous year. Dividend insurance plans might be another option. Dividends are paid on premiums but are not guaranteed. They are dependent on the insurance company's claims experience with all the companies it insures.

Q My office is in my home. Won't my homeowner's insurance cover me if an employee trips in my home office and gets hurt?

No, homeowner's policies and business pursuits endorsements usually don't cover injury or work-related diseases of employees of your business. Household workers (people who come in and clean your home, for instance) may possibly be covered by your policy, however.

Q I have an employee who drives his own car to do errands for me. Do I need special auto insurance for that or will his own insurance cover it?

You need to get insurance. Even if your employee were driving his car, if he were on a business errand for you and injured someone, you could be sued. The kind of insurance that offers you protection is called employee nonownership and hired car liability, which protects the owner of the business for the actions of the employees while they are driving their personal autos. Depending where you live, it may cost as little as $75 a year.

Q How much will business auto insurance cost?

The cost will vary considerably according to the following factors:

- the number of vehicles insured by the business
- the type of use and cargo of the vehicles
- the size of the vehicles
- the business location (where the vehicles are garaged)
- the area (radius) of operations

Q Where can I get business automobile insurance?

The company from which you buy your personal vehicle insurance might also sell business vehicle insurance. It would be advisable to call several brokers and get information, or better yet, call several business owners in your area and ask them which broker they use for insurance and how satisfied they are. You can find names of insurance brokers in the Yellow Pages of your phone book.

Q If I rent equipment and it is damaged while it is in my office, will my insurance cover it?

Probably not. You may be able to purchase a floater (special policy) to cover the potential risk, however.

Q I'm testing a new product for woodworkers. Do I need to get product liability insurance if I put clear instructions and warnings in the package I sell?

Yes. No matter how clear your warnings are or how the user abuses a product, you could be sued if someone suffers an injury as a result of your product.

Q Won't all my other insurance protect me?

No. Product liability is one type of insurance, like professional liability, that usually must be purchased separately.

Q It sounds like I could spend every cent I earn just buying insurance. How do I decide what kinds of insurance I really need and how much I should buy?

Keeping insurance costs under control is something that concerns businesses of all sizes. Key to the process is something known in the insurance industry as risk management. Coyle explains that risk management is a four-step process:

1. Identification of sources from which losses may arise.
2. Evaluation of the financial risk involved in each exposure based on expected frequency, severity, and impact.
3. Treatment of risk by elimination, reduction, control, or transfer to others (such as an insurance company).
4. Monitoring the results of your efforts.

Q Isn't risk management just for big businesses?

Even very small businesses can put risk management techniques into practice. Begin by making a realistic determination of all the ways you might possibly suffer financial losses. On your list should be all possible business-related losses. Include casualty and theft losses, embezzlement (if you have employees), injury to others from products or services you sell, personal injury to customers or employees due to a fall or some other accident while on your business premises, libel or slander (knocking the competition or talking about customers with bad credit ratings can get you sued), and even things such as the loss of income from your business if it should be interrupted by a fire or theft or some other insurable catastrophe.

Decide which are most likely to occur and which of those would be most devastating to your business or personal assets. Cover what you can with insurance, and at the same time try to reduce risks of the loss and the cost of any insurance coverage.

Q How can I reduce risks of something happening?

There are literally hundreds of different ways to reduce risk. Among them:

- Don't accept work you aren't qualified to perform.
- Be meticulous about labeling, dating, and backing up all client work.
- Make backups or copies of important documents, records, and data, and consider storing them off premises. A large customer list, your receivables, work in progress, and other important documents might be difficult or impossible to recreate should a fire, computer system outage, theft, or other disaster hit your place of business.
- Remove or correct any obvious hazards in the workplace. For example, get rid of anything people are likely to trip on, repair broken banisters or railings, make sure stairways and walkways are kept free of snow or ice or other slippery substances.
- Learn how to lift boxes and heavy items without putting excessive strain on your back and teach employees to do the same.
- Set and enforce safety rules, such as not opening all the file drawers in a cabinet at a time.
- Make sure electrical circuits aren't overloaded.

- Protect computer equipment at minimum with surge protectors.
- Consider shutting down small home computer systems (unplugging them) during severe electrical storms. Even a good surge protector isn't likely to withstand a lightning strike on an electric line.
- Check references before hiring employees.
- Make sure employees who will be driving for you have in-force driver's licenses.
- Make sure your employees are properly classified in your workers' compensation policy.
- Deposit receipts nightly.
- Don't let any one employee have unsupervised control of the books, cash, or any aspect of your business.
- Have regular health checkups and encourage your employees to do the same.
- Live a healthy life-style.

Q **How will reducing risks cut costs?**

Reducing risks helps you avoid or reduce losses, which in turn keeps rates down on policies that are based on your claims history. Reducing your risks also will keep out-of-pocket expenses down for uninsured losses.

Q **Where can I get more information about business insurance?**

The Insurance Information Institute is an excellent source of information about business property and liability insurance. They have a consumer information hot line you can call if you have questions about any kind of insurance except health and life insurance. The Insurance Information Institute is located at 110 Williams St., New York, NY 10038. Their telephone number is (212) 669–9200.

23.

Taxing Issues

Few things in life are quite as taxing as having to pay taxes. For starters, you know you are going to have to pay the IRS a painfully large chunk of your hard-earned income. Then, to make matters worse, you know you will have to give up a healthy chunk of your time to collect the receipts you need and read up on the latest changes in tax laws.

To add insult to injury, you are likely to stumble on the estimated preparation time in the instructions to Form 1040 and realize: (1) The estimated time figures couldn't possibly be accurate, and (2) the IRS used your tax dollars to pay someone to tell you how long it should take to prepare your tax return.

While nothing may dispel your aggravation with the system, this chapter and the next one will help you gain a better understanding of tax regulations governing self-employment and home offices. In them you will find dozens of answers to frequently asked self-employment and home office tax questions. The subjects covered run the gamut from the most basic "Do I have to report it" questions to what you should do if you inadvertently run afoul of the tax laws.

The information in this chapter applies only to questions arising from Schedule C or Schedule C-EZ self-employment income. Schedule C is the sole proprietor business return; Schedule C-EZ is a simplified Schedule C designed for use by businesses with gross receipts of $25,000 or less and business expenses of $2,000 or less. While every attempt has been made to insure the accuracy of the information, neither this chapter nor any book or source of general information can substitute for your own personal tax adviser. Tax laws change frequently and the interpretation of the laws, in some instance, can vary according to specifics of your individual situation.

INCOME AND TAXES—SORTING THEM OUT

Q I sell handcrafts at flea markets and just make a little extra spending money. Do I have to report this income to the IRS?

Yes. The income has to be reported on your tax return. You will have to pay income tax and possibly self-employment tax on your profits (net income). In addition, if your state has a sales tax, you probably should be collecting sales tax on the items you sell.

Q Do I have to report *all* income I make on my own to the IRS?

Yes. Whether you make money from full-time self-employment, from moonlighting, from a hobby, or from work as an independent contractor or free-lancer, the IRS expects you to report the income and pay taxes on it.

Q Suppose I don't get paid in cash. Do I still have to report the income?

Yes. If you barter what you sell for other people's goods and services, or for credits toward goods and services, the IRS expects you to report the value of the trade. If you run a business, the income from bartering (value of goods and services received) is also subject to self-employment tax.

Q My records show one of my clients reported less on the 1099 form they submitted to the government than they actually paid me. Can I use their figures in reporting my income on my tax return?

No. You should report the actual income you received, and ask the company to file a corrected 1099.

Similarly, if a company reports too much income on a 1099, checks off the wrong box on the 1099 (marking your earnings as lotto winnings, for instance), or makes any other mistake, you should ask them to file a corrected information return.

Q. **I did work for a company based in another country. They paid me but didn't send a 1099 to the U.S. government. Do I have to report that income?**

Yes.

Q. **How will the IRS know whether or not I report all my income?**

There are any number of ways the IRS can and does find out about unreported income. Here are a few of them:

▸ 1099 information returns filed by companies are matched against your income tax returns by computer.
▸ Jealous neighbors or associates you have a falling out with could report you.
▸ One of your customers could be audited and trigger an audit of companies with which it does business.
▸ Your return could be kicked out at random for a compliance audit.
▸ Some other circumstance could cause the IRS to audit part of your return and, due to your answers or some discrepancies, cause the IRS to dig deeper, getting bank records and/or examining the way you live to determine if you are hiding income.
▸ Your return might have attracted notice because you made a large (over $10,000) bank deposit or cash purchase.

No matter what the mechanism, if the IRS discovers you have purposely underreported income (or misrepresented facts on your return) you could be charged with fraud.

Q. **Do I have to file a business return to report my spare-time income, or can I just include the income on Form 1040?**

The answer depends on how regularly you make money at what you do and whether or not you carry out the income-producing activity in a businesslike way. If you regularly seek customers and regularly make money, you will need to report the income as business income on Schedule C or Schedule C-EZ. You will also have to pay self-employment tax if you make more than $400 profit. (See the questions on self-employment tax in this chapter.)

If you seldom make money from the activity and it is something like scuba diving or tole painting that could be considered a hobby, you may not have to file a business return.

You will need to report the income, though, and may benefit from reporting the income on Schedule C or Schedule C-EZ (see below).

Q **I wrote and sold three short novels this year. All of my self-employment income came from advances against royalties on those books. Since the payments were royalty, can I report the royalty payments as supplemental income (Schedule E), and avoid the self-employment tax?**

No. Writers, photographers, artists, and others who create books, dramatic works, artworks, music scores, and other creative works have to report royalties on Schedule C as business income.

Q **Are there any benefits from reporting part-time self-employment income as business income?**

Yes. Here are several:

▸ Almost all ordinary and necessary business expenses are fully deductible on Schedule C. If you use Schedule C-EZ you can deduct up to $2,000 in business expenses. The same expenses, if reported as a miscellaneous deduction on Form 1040, Schedule A, are subjected to the 2 percent floor on miscellaneous expenses, which means they are only deductible to the extent that they exceed 2 percent of adjusted gross income (AGI).

▸ If you are running a business and your expenses exceed your income, you can use the loss to offset other income. If you don't file a business return, deductions for expenses for hobbies or other income-producing activities will be limited to the amount of income from the activity.

▸ If you report income on Schedule C and have a room that qualifies as a home office, you may be able to take a substantial home office deduction. The IRS does not allow a home office deduction if what you do is termed a hobby.

▸ Interest on personal loans is no longer deductible. However, interest on business loans *is* deductible. Thus, if you borrow money to buy a computer for your home business you can deduct the interest on the loan on Schedule C prorated to your business use of the computer. You could not deduct the interest on a personal loan for a computer to use in conjunction with your hobby. If that same computer were used more than 50 percent for business, you could also expense or depreciate the cost. (See "Can I deduct the cost of my home computer and car phone?" on page 386 in the next chapter.)

Q Who should use Schedule C-EZ?

Schedule C-EZ is aimed at those who have few business deductions and a limited amount of income from a small business. To use this schedule to calculate your taxes you may have no more than $25,000 in gross receipts and no more than $2,000 in business expenses for the year. In addition, you cannot use the form if you take the home office deduction, show a loss for the year, have more than one business that you run as a sole proprietor, have employees, have to File Form 4562 (for depreciation and amortization expenses), or have unallowed passive activity losses from the business from a previous year. Having inventory at any time during the year also disqualifies you from using Schedule C-EZ.

Q Can I have a full-time job working for someone else and file a business return, too?

Yes. If your income-producing activity qualifies as a business, you can file a Schedule C return even if you have a part-time or full-time job working as an employee in another business.

Q **Do I have to have a separate business checkbook to file a business return?**

The IRS doesn't require you to have a separate business checking or savings account to file either a Schedule C or a Schedule C-EZ. However, having a separate business account will simplify record keeping for you and help prove your business intent to the IRS should you ever need to.

Q **Do I have to be registered as a business or have a business name to file a business tax return?**

For IRS purposes, you do not have to have a business name or be registered as a business with any government authorities. Some states and some municipalities do require anyone who operates a business to get a business certificate or license. Such laws, where they exist, have nothing to do with federal income tax laws, however.

Q **Don't I need an employer identification number to file a Schedule C?**

You don't need an employer identification number (EIN) unless you hire employees or start certain types of pension plans.

Q **How many hours a week do I have to work for myself for the IRS to consider what I do a business and not a hobby?**

The IRS doesn't set any minimum number of hours. Instead, it wants to know if you have a profit motive for pursuing the activity and if you are carrying out the activity in a businesslike way.

Q **How do I show a profit motive?**

The easiest way is by making a profit. If you make a profit pursuing the activity in 3 of the last 5 years including the current one, the IRS will assume the activity is a business. If the activity you are involved in is raising race horses, the time frame for making a profit is extended to 2 of 7 years.

Q **What happens if I don't make a profit within the specified time? Will the IRS automatically declare my business a hobby?**

Not necessarily. The three-out-of-five-year guideline (known as the hobby-loss rule) is a major factor, but not the only one the IRS will look at in determining if something is a business or a hobby. Other things they will consider are:

- Do you carry out the activity in a businesslike manner? (Keep good records. If you don't keep copies of receipts, correspondence, etc., you aren't going to look very businesslike.)
- Does the time and effort you put into the activity indicate you intend to make the activity a profitable business?
- Do you have the expertise necessary to carry on the activity as a successful business?
- Do you depend on income from the activity for your livelihood?
- Are losses due to circumstances beyond your control, or are they normal for the start-up of your kind of business?
- Have you changed your methods of operation to attempt to improve the profitability of the activity?
- Have you previously been successful making a profit in a similar business?
- Will you be able to make a profit in the future from appreciation of assets?
- Do you materially participate (take an active part) in the business?

Q **Is any activity that makes a profit considered a business?**

No. Occasional profit-making transactions (say, the sale of your childhood stamp collection) would not be considered a business. Additionally, the IRS does not consider you to be in business if what you do is manage your own stock or investment portfolio.

Q **What about independent contractors? I do a lot of work as an independent contractor for one company. Could the IRS call me an employee and deny my business deductions?**

The independent contractor issue can be complicated. Many companies try to call employees independent contractors to avoid the hidden costs of having employees. Those hidden costs can easily amount to one-third or more of the actual salary paid to the worker. They include such things as the unemployment taxes, employer's share of FICA, and workers' compensation, as well as things like medical insurance, sick pay, vacation and holiday pay, pension plans, and so on.

To prevent this kind of abuse, the IRS has tried to establish criteria to distinguish employees from independent businesspeople. Generally speaking, these criteria say that if you are a writer, attorney, speaker, consultant, or other professional or tradeperson who operates independently and offers services to the public (in other words, to multiple clients), you are not an employee. However, the IRS also says you will be considered an employee if the client company has the right to control and direct the means and methods of accomplishing the work you perform for them.

To clarify these two broad rules, the IRS has developed a list of twenty factors it considers on a case-by-case basis to determine whether an individual is an employee or independent contractor. The importance of each factor—according to the IRS—varies with the occupation and the individual circumstances under which the services are rendered. Here are the twenty factors and how the IRS views each:

1. *Instructions:* An employee is told when, where, and how to do the work; an independent contractor performs work without being told when, where, or how to do the job.
2. *Training:* Training is for employees; independent contractors would use their own methods, receiving no training from the client.
3. *Integration:* If an individual's services or job is integrated into the daily business operations (the business can't operate well without the service), the person performing the service is considered an employee.
4. *Performance:* An employee is expected to personally perform the job hired for; an independent contractor may assign others to do the work.
5. *Assistants and cost of goods:* An employee would not bear the cost of hiring and training assistants or employees and does not pay for cost

of goods out of his/her own pocket. An independent contractor would be responsible for hiring, training, supervising, and paying assistants and for paying the costs of materials as part of the job contract.

6. *Work relationship:* An employee performs work frequently at recurring intervals as part of a continuing relationship with a company; independent contractors don't maintain similar continuing relationships.

7. *Schedule:* The employee must keep hours set by the employer; the contractor chooses his/her own hours.

8. *Hours worked:* An employee is likely to work full-time for only one company; a contractor is available to work for multiple companies.

9. *Location of work:* An employee works on the employer's premises or on a route specified by the employer; the contractor is not restricted to working on the client's premises.

10. *Sequence of work:* The employee follows company instructions and routines; the independent contractor does work in whatever sequence he/she deems best.

11. *Reports:* The employee must account to the employer for daily actions and activities; the contractor does not account to the client for his/her daily activities.

12. *Method of payment:* Employees are usually paid by the hour, week, month, or year; contractors are usually paid by the job or on straight commission.

13. *Expenses:* Employees have business and travel expenses paid for them by employers; independent contractors pay their own business and travel expenses.

14. *Tools:* The employee is often (but not always) furnished with significant tools or equipment to do a job; the contractor supplies his/her own tools or equipment.

15. *Investment:* Employees have no significant investment in what they do; independent contractors put significant investment in equipment or facilities used to perform services.

16. *Profit or loss:* The employee gets paid and is not subject to losses. Independent contractors do not get salaries; they make a profit or suffer losses.

17. *Number of business customers:* The employee works with one business or one primary business at one time; contractors may perform services for multiple companies at once.
18. *Availability:* An employee is not available to others for work; a contractor is available to work for multiple companies.
19. *Ability to be fired:* An employee can be fired; a contractor has to be paid if he/she produces the results specified in the contract.
20. *Right to quit:* An employee can quit without incurring liability; a contractor is legally obligated to meet contract terms or risks financial loss.

In summary, if you look like you are an employee (work a regular schedule in the client's office and never work for anyone else), chances are the IRS would call you an employee if you or the company was ever audited.

Q **What about programmers and others who take on long-term contracts on government or other projects requiring work be done on-site? Does the IRS consider them employees or contractors?**

Many such occupations fall into a category the IRS calls "technical service specialist," which is defined as an individual who is an engineer, designer, draftsman, computer programmer, systems analyst, or in a similar line of work. These technical service specialists are considered employees if they are working under contracts arranged by a third party such as a job shop or temporary employment agency.

The IRS says, however, that the designation technical service specialist doesn't automatically doom someone to be an employee. Someone considered a technical service specialist can be an independent contractor if he or she contracts directly with the client firm and doesn't appear to be an employee based on the criteria described above.

Q **What happens if the IRS says I'm an employee?**

A company that wrongly classifies you as an independent contractor would have to pay unemployment taxes on your earnings and might also be liable for a penalty of 100 percent of the tax they didn't withhold. You would lose any home office deductions and deductions for payments to pension plans. Business deductions would have to be reported on Schedule A rather than Schedule C and would thus be subject to the 2 percent limitation on miscellaneous deductions.

Q What taxes do I have to pay when I work for myself?

You have to pay federal income tax and, if your profits from self-employment amount to more than $400 for the year, self-employment tax. You may be liable for state and local income taxes as well.

Q What is self-employment tax?

Self-employment tax is a combination of Social Security and Medicare taxes. When you are an employee in someone else's company, Social Security and Medicare contributions are withheld from each paycheck you receive. These withholdings are called FICA (Federal Insurance Contributions Act) and are matched by equal amounts your employer must contribute on your behalf.

When you are self-employed, you have to pay both the employee's share *and* the employer's share of these taxes. To compensate somewhat for this double whammy, you get a slight break on Schedule C (in the form of an adjustment to self-employed income), and you can subtract an amount equal to one-half of your self-employment tax from your income on line 25, Form 1040 (adjustments to income).

Like FICA withholdings, self-employment tax is calculated on Schedule SE separately from and in addition to any income tax you owe.

Q How much is the self-employment tax?

The self-employment tax rate is a percentage of income based on two separate rates—one for Social Security and one for Medicare. For the 1993 tax year, the Social Security rate is 12.4 percent on the first $57,600 of net self-employment income. The Medicare tax rate is 2.9 percent on the first $135,000 of self-employment income. Thus, the total self-employment tax rate works out to be 15.3 percent on the first $57,600 of net self-employment income (12.4 percent + 2.9 percent) and 2.9 percent on any income between $57,600 and $135,000.

The rules and income ranges change periodically, so be sure to check the actual rates each year you have self-employment income.

 I have a full-time job and work for myself on the weekends. My full-time employer withholds FICA from my salary. Do I have to pay self-employment tax, too?

If the wages from your full-time job are under $135,000 you will have to pay some self-employment tax on the money you make on your own. However, the maximum amounts you have to pay in for Social Security and Medicare are based on your total income.

For instance, suppose you earn $45,000 at your full-time job, and make an additional $22,000 (after the adjustment to income on Schedule C) working for yourself. The maximum income for the 15.3 percent self-employment tax rate is $57,600. The $45,000 in wages (which have had FICA withheld) is applied towards that maximum first. You pay the 15.3 percent on combined income up to the $57,600 Social Security income maximum. Thus:

$57,600   *(income base for the 15.3 percent Social Security tax rate)*
$-\$45,000$ *(wages)*

$12,600 *(amount subject to the 15.3 percent tax rate)*

In addition to this amount, however, you have to pay the 2.9 percent Medicare tax on all income over $57,600 and up to $135,000.

That means the remaining $9,400 of your self-employment income ($22,000 minus the $12,600) is taxed at the 2.9 percent rate.

The total self-employment tax you would owe on the $22,000 you made on your own would be:

$12,600 at the 15.3% rate	*$1927.80*
plus	
$9,400 at the 2.9% rate	*+ $272.60*
	$2200.40

Q **Do I have to pay self-employment tax if I'm retired?**

The same rules apply whether you are retired or not. Thus, if you make more than $400 in profit from self-employment you are liable for self-employment taxes even if you are already collecting Social Security.

Q **Do I just put aside the money and pay the income tax and self-employment tax when I file my income tax return each year?**

The answer depends on your personal tax situation. If you expect to owe more than $500 over and above any withholdings or tax credits for the year, you will probably have to pay estimated tax payments. These tax payments are usually paid in four equal installments on April 15, June 15, September 15, and January 15.

As a general rule, you will have to pay quarterly estimated taxes if you expect to owe more than $500 in income and self-employment tax *and:*

> ▶ your withholding and credits for the year will be less than 100 percent of your previous year's tax liability

or

> ▶ your withholding and credits will be less than 90 percent of the tax liability for the current tax year

At the end of 1991, our legislators, in all their infinite wisdom, saw fit to further complicate that general rule by adding several ifs, ands, and buts. At this writing, paying 100 percent of last year's tax liability in estimated payments this year may not protect you from penalties for underpayment. Under the new regulations, you are required to project your current year's income and pay at least 90 percent of the taxes in quarterly estimates if *all three* of these circumstances apply:

> ▶ you made any estimated tax payments in the prior three years
> ▶ you anticipate your adjusted gross income for the year to exceed $75,000 (or $37,500 for married taxpayers filing separate returns)

and

> ▶ you expect your adjusted gross income to be more than $40,000 higher than your adjusted gross income for the preceding year

If all three of these circumstances did not apply to your income in a particular year, you could avoid penalties by making estimated tax payments that equalled 100 percent of the taxes you paid in during the previous year.

To simplify all of the above, if you think you will owe the IRS money at the end of the year, your safest bet (and the easiest on your pocketbook at the end of the year) is to pay the money in four quarterly payments. If your income has jumped a lot and is expected to be over $75,000, plan the payments to equal at least 90 percent of the tax due at the end of the year to avoid penalties.

Q My income is never spread out evenly during the year. Some quarters I make a lot of money and some I make almost nothing. Do I have to pay the estimated tax in four *equal* payments?

No. You will need to annualize your income and then calculate what percentage of the total you made in the present quarter. Then calculate your estimated taxes based on that percentage. If you plan to use this method you will need IRS Publication 505 and Form 2210.

Q All my income is from self-employment, and it looks like it will be a lot less this year than it was last year. Will I have to pay a penalty if I pay less than one-fourth of last years taxes for each quarterly payment?

As long as you have paid in 90 percent of the tax due for each quarter you shouldn't have to pay a penalty.

Q How do I go about sending in the payments?

Use IRS Form 1040-ES. The form includes a worksheet for your records and vouchers you fill in and submit with each payment so the payments are credited to you.

Q What happens if I miss an estimated tax payment or don't pay in enough during the year?

You pay a penalty for amounts you owe on each separate installment. The penalty for 1992 taxes was 11 percent of the unpaid amount for the first installment and 10 percent of unpaid amounts for each subsequent installment. However, the IRS method for calculating the penalty is complicated. If you miss an installment, the IRS suggests you divide what you owe among remaining payments (so you don't underpay for the remainder of the year) and then use Form 2210 at the time you submit your taxes to annualize your income and calculate any penalty you may owe. Alternately, the IRS will calculate the penalty for you.

Q **Do I have to pay estimated taxes to the state, too?**

If your state has an income tax, chances are you will need to pay a separate estimated tax to the state. Your local IRS office may have state tax information and forms. If they don't, call or write your state tax department for information. The addresses and phone numbers are listed in appendix 4.

24.

What Can I Deduct?

One of the benefits of being self-employed is you can take a variety of deductions you might not otherwise qualify for. If you keep good records and are aware of what you may and may not deduct as a business owner, owning your own business can help you lower your taxes substantially. Here are a number of questions and answers to get you started considering ways your business can cut your personal taxes.

Q **What expenses for starting my business are deductible?**

Start-up expenses (expenses you incur before you are ready to take work from customers) are considered capital expenses and have to be either included in basis (the starting value of your business and its assets) or amortized (spread out over several years). To be amortizable, the expense has to be something that would be deductible if you were already in business and paid before the business started operation.

Such start-up costs include costs of studying a prospective business and the costs for actually launching it such as initial advertising expense, employee training, equipment, etc.

Q **From a tax standpoint, when does my business actually begin? Is it with the first customer?**

You can be in business if you are ready to accept customers. The actual event that triggers you being in business (as opposed to starting a business) will vary by the type of business and your own personal way of operating. Something as simple as registering a business name, having business cards made up, or even accepting money for something you have done for free up to now (teaching friends to use computers, for instance) can be the grand opening of a homebased business.

Thus, from a tax standpoint, you might want to consider putting off as many business purchases as you can until after you are actually in business. But remember: while you don't have to have acquired any customers or made a profit to be in business, if you don't make a profit in 3 out of 5 years you could trigger the hobby-loss rule as discussed in the previous chapter.

Q **Once I'm in business, what expenses can I deduct?**

Any product or service purchased for use by or in your business is deductible if it is ordinary and reasonable for the type of business you run. Schedule C filers will generally find their deductions fall into these broad categories:

- ▶ deductible business expenses
- ▶ depreciable business property
- ▶ the home office deduction
- ▶ cost of goods sold (if you are a manufacturer or sell products)

Q **What kinds of expenses are deductible business expenses?**

The specific expenses that will be deductible for your business depend on what you do and what would be ordinary and necessary for your business. Some typical examples of expenses follow.

Business Expenses

Deductible the Year in Which the Expense Is Incurred

advertising expenses	bad debts*
advertising giveaways	bank fees
airplane and cab costs on business trips	beeper service
association dues	blank computer floppy disks
auto mileage or car expense*	books related to your business

Business Expenses—*Continued*

business cards (if you are in business
 already)
business gifts*
business insurance fees
calendar
cellular phone service
college courses to improve business skills*
commissions
consultant fees
copy paper
copyright registration fee
employee salaries*
file folders
hotel/motel fees*
industry directories
ink cartridges
interest on business loans
interest on business credit cards
licenses
meals
notepads
online service usage related to your
 business*
paper daybook/scheduler
pencils
pens
postage
professional fees (attorney, CPA, etc.)
professional journals and trade magazines*
publicity expense
repairs of business property or equipment
ribbons for typewriters or printers
seminars*
stationery
telephone call expenses*
tolls and parking fees
toner for copier, fax, printer
trade show and conference fees

trade show booth fees
training tapes (audio and video)
travel*
voice mail or answering service
wages paid to employees

Home Office*

Rent, real estate taxes, mortgage interest,
and utilities are fully deductible for non-
homebased businesses; home businesses
may allocate part of these expenses to
business.

Assets to Depreciate or Expense*

answering machine
beeper
bookshelves
car*
cellular telephone
computer*
computer memory
desk
facsimile machine
fax boards
filing cabinets
hard drive
improvements to business property
in/out baskets
label printer
modem
office chairs
office drapes, blinds, decorative pictures
other computer boards
printers
scanner
shrink-wrap machine
storage cabinet
storage racks

*Items are discussed in more depth elsewhere in this chapter.

Business Expenses—*Continued*

telephone handsets	legal fees prior to opening
tools	other start-up costs
trucks	patent purchase
workbench	research to start a business

Amortizable Costs
computer software
customer list

Q **Can I deduct the sales tax on supplies I bought for my business or only the actual price of the supplies?**

You can deduct the sales tax you paid on the price of supplies used in the course of business. You can't deduct sales tax or freight on capital assets used in your business, however. The sales tax on those have to be capitalized in the cost of the asset.

Q **I translated some documents for a small company, but the company never paid me and is now out of business. Can I deduct the money the company owed me as a bad debt?**

Not if you are a cash basis taxpayer as most homebased and very small businesses are. A bad debt only qualifies as a deductible expense if there is a true creditor/borrower relationship, if there has been an actual loss of money (you lent the customer money, for instance), or if you are an accrual basis taxpayer and have already reported the debt as income.

Q **I run my business from my home and only have one phone line. Can I deduct anything for all the business phone calls I make?**

If you have only one telephone line coming into the house or apartment, you cannot deduct any part of the line charge (basic service charges) for having the phone in the house. You can deduct the cost of any long-distance or other calls you can separate out from your bill and verify as business calls. Voice messaging, call waiting, or other special services would be deductible if you can prove the business purpose.

If you have a completely separate telephone line coming into the house and use it exclusively for business, *all costs* including the line fee and basic monthly charges could be deducted. The second line is also advisable to make sure business calls are always answered professionally. Despite the growth of homebased businesses, customers don't appreciate hearing a five-year-old pick up the phone and say, "Daddy's in the pool" or hearing spurts of rock music every time your teenage daughter picks up the extension to see if you are still on the telephone.

Q   **Can I deduct the cost of my home computer and car phone?**

Computers, computer peripheral equipment, car phones, and other property that might be used for entertainment value as well as for business are called listed property and must comply with special rules. If you can provide the business purpose, you can deduct the business portion of their cost using one of two methods: the first-year expense method (Section 179 deduction) and depreciation. If your business is classified as a hobby by the IRS (see pages 372–373 in chapter 23), the Section 179 expense may not be allowable in full due to the limitations of the hobby-loss rule.

Q   **What is the Section 179 expense deduction?**

The Section 179 expense deduction lets you write off certain equipment costs in one year instead of spreading them out (depreciating them) over time. To take the deduction you must:

▸ use the equipment more than 50 percent of the time in your business and be able to prove it;

▸ prorate the cost to your business usage (if you use the equipment 60 percent of the time for business, you can expense 60 percent of the cost); and

▸ recapture (pay back) a portion of the deduction if you dispose of the property or stop using it for business before the end of its useful life. (The IRS considers computers, copiers, etc., to have a useful life of 5 years.)

Additionally, these limits apply:

▸ The total amount of equipment you may expense in one year is limited to a maximum of $10,000 or your net income, whichever is lower.

▸ The $10,000 limit is per taxpayer, not per business. Thus, if you have more than one business the maximum you can expense is $10,000.

▸ Married individuals filing separate returns are treated as one taxpayer (together their expense deduction may not total more than $10,000). Members of partnerships or S corporations must follow special rules and should consult their accountants or a good tax guide before taking the 179 expense deduction.

▸ Automobiles may be expensed only up to certain IRS stated maximums. In 1991, the maximum expense deduction you could take for an automobile placed into service for your business was $2,660.

▸ If you put more than $200,000 of equipment into service in the year, the amount you may expense is reduced by one dollar for each dollar over $200,000. Thus, no expense deduction may be taken if you put $210,000 of equipment into use.

Q **What do I have to do to prove the business use of a computer, car phone, or similar equipment?**

To prove the business use of equipment, you must keep a log of usage. For computers and other office equipment you would need a log showing when each thing was used, the amount of time it was used, and the purpose of the business use. For automobiles you would need to keep track of the date of each use, the business purpose, the mileage for each trip and the total car mileage for the year. (See Table 24.1.) If you have a computer and modem and subscribe to any of the online services, you'll find templates and/or programs for logging expenses in online electronic libraries. Some of the files you find will be free for the price of the download; others will be try-before-you-buy shareware.

Table 24.1: Mileage Expense Log

| Date | Destination/Purpose | Mileage | | | Tolls/Parking |
		Leave	Return	Total	

Q **Can I deduct any equipment expenses if I don't use the equipment more than 50 percent of the time for business?**

You could depreciate the business portion using the IRS tables for straight-line depreciation.

Q **Can I use the Section 179 deduction to offset income from my daytime job if my business shows a loss?**

Under the rules that were in effect at the time this book was written, you can use the 179 expense deduction to offset other earned income such as wages from employment, earnings from rentals, royalty income, and farm income.

Q **What's the difference between a business asset and a business expense?**

A business asset is something you buy or acquire or develop that has or is expected to have monetary value and will use in your business for more than one year. Examples of assets are land, equipment, patents, buildings, and franchise rights. For tax purposes, a business expense is money a business pays out for products or services that will be used within the current year.

Q Are they treated differently for tax purposes?

Yes. The cost of business expenses is immediately deductible from income. The cost of an asset has to be spread out and deducted over a period of years or be added to the value of the asset and not deducted at all.

Q How are amortization and depreciation different?

Amortization means spreading out the cost of an intangible asset, such as a patent or goodwill; depreciation refers to spreading out the cost of tangible business property (things you can see or touch), such as machinery, buildings, etc. Generally, expenses that have to be amortized have to be spread out over a longer time period than expenses you can depreciate.

Q How do I know whether to consider a purchase a deductible expense or to depreciate it?

Generally, equipment or anything else you buy that has a useful life of more than a year has to be depreciated. Cost of things like bank fees, legal fees, advertising costs, office supplies and postage, and other costs that are incurred repeatedly would be expenses that are deductible in the year they were incurred for cash-basis tax payers.

Q How do you know what the useful life is of something?

The IRS publishes tables showing the allowable useful life of various classifications of business assets. You'll find these lists in IRS Publication 534, *Depreciation*.

Q Is it a good idea to expense the car I just bought?

For most home businesses, it probably isn't a good idea to expense a car. (For additional help read the information on deducting car expenses in this chapter.)

Q What automobile expenses can I deduct?

You can take a depreciation deduction for the use of your car in business. This may be done in one of three ways:

▶ Calculate the business mileage driven and take a deduction based on this number. For 1992, the business mileage rate was 28 cents a mile. Thus, for every 1,000 business miles you drive you would get a $280 deduction using this method.

▶ Calculate the business mileage as a percentage of the personal mileage and prorate the value of the automobile at the time it was placed in service to the business usage. Then use the MACRS 5-year property rules to depreciate the car. (If you bought a new car for $12,000 and used it 50 percent of the time for business, you would depreciate $6,000 of the purchase price. The other $6,000 would be a personal expense and is not depreciable.)

▶ Use the Section 179 deduction to expense the business portion of the car in the first year of use. The amount you may expense was a maximum of $2,760 in 1992. Thus, for many taxpayers, expensing the car is not a wise decision.

Q **Can I deduct the cost of business travel?**

Yes. If you are making a business trip you can deduct the costs of traveling to do business or to attend trade shows, conventions, and conferences that are related to your business. You can deduct the full cost of your airfare or train fare; cab fare while away; room charges; incidentals (laundry, dry cleaning); tips; baggage fees, including insurance; and telephone, telegraph, and fax calls. Additionally, you can deduct 80 percent of the cost of your meals while you are traveling and 80 percent of business entertainment costs if you are meeting clients and taking them to the theater or a ball game. If you drive your own car rather than take an airplane or train, you can deduct your auto mileage at the business mileage rate allowable in the year you take the trip.

Q **Can I deduct the cost of a business trip to another country?**

Rules get stricter for out-of-the country travel for self-employed people and major shareholders of small corporations. But if the trip is a week or less in length or you spent less than 25 percent of your time on vacation, you should be able to deduct the cost of foreign travel as you would travel in this country; however, you should read the rules for foreign business travel carefully in advance of your trip. Those rules can be found in IRS Publication 463, *Travel, Entertainment, and Gift Expenses.*

Q   What about conventions held in other countries?

If the convention is held within North America, the general business tests for foreign travel apply. If the convention is held outside of North America, you have to show a reasonable explanation why the convention was outside North America.

Q   Is travel or conventions on cruise ships deductible?

If you use a cruise ship to reach your business destination, the deduction for travel is limited to twice the allowable per diem federal travel rate. If meals and entertainment are paid for separately, these have to be calculated first at 80 percent of cost. The cost of the journey other than meals is then added on to the meals up to the maximum allowable amount for the trip.

If you are attending a convention on a cruise ship, numerous rules apply involving the ship's ports of call, time spent on business activities, and so on. You will need to document and submit records for hours spent at on-board business meetings, schedules of activities, etc. If you meet all the rules, then you are allowed up to a $2,000 deduction per year for a convention on a cruise ship.

Warning: If you plan foreign business travel or conventions overseas or on a cruise ship, be sure you understand all the rules governing deductibility of your trip before you make the arrangements. If you don't, or if you don't save all the necessary documentation, your deductions could be denied.

Q   I took the vice president of an out-of-town company I do business with on a tourist boat trip around Manhattan. Can I deduct both our fares?

You can deduct 80 percent of your expenses if the entertainment was ordinary and necessary for your business *and* if the entertainment was directly related or associated with business *and* if the expense isn't considered lavish or extravagant. Essentially, if you discussed business with the visiting VP before, during, or after the trip, the expense would probably be allowable.

Q Could I deduct expenses for taking the VP's spouse and mine along on the excursion?

If the two of them were traveling together and it was impractical for you to entertain the client without the spouse, and your spouse goes along because the customer's spouse is there, the cost of tickets for both spouses would be considered ordinary and necessary and be deductible as entertainment expenses.

Q If I travel into the next state on business, can I deduct the cost of my lunch?

Not if you return home the same day. There's no such thing as a tax-free (or 80 percent tax-free) lunch unless you are away from your "tax home" overnight or long enough to require sleep.

Q What is my "tax home"?

Your tax home is your place of business. To be away from your tax home, you have to be away from the area or city surrounding your tax home. If you regularly work in two or more widely separate areas, your tax home is the area you select as your principle place of residence.

Q Suppose I want to combine a vacation with a business trip. Can I still deduct my trip?

If the primary purpose of the trip is business and the trip is within the United States, you can deduct all your costs to and from the location plus the hotel and other business-related costs described above for the business part of the trip. Money you spend on transportation, meals, or entertainment during the vacation part of the trip are not deductible. If, however, the primary purpose of the trip is vacation or personal, no part of your transportation costs from your tax home to your destination are deductible. The transportation costs after you arrive that relate to the business activity would be deductible.

For example, say you travel to Disneyland for a vacation for a week. While there, you drive to the next county to visit a client and, because of the distance, return to your hotel the next day. You could deduct the costs of reaching the client and the overnight hotel fee plus 80 percent of food costs as business expenses, but the rest of your expenses for the week plus your airfare to Disneyland would be nondeductible personal expenses.

However, if you were attending a week-long business convention at Disneyland and spent a day visiting relatives before returning home, you could deduct your entire plane fare plus the hotel cost and meals (at 80 percent) and other incidentals while at the hotel. The costs of traveling to your relative's town and expenses you incurred that day would not be deductible.

Q **Can I deduct the cost of college courses I take?**

You can deduct the costs of educational courses you take if you can prove they maintain or improve the skills you need to run your present business; however, you cannot deduct the cost of any education that would qualify you for a new trade or profession even if it also improves the skills you need for your current line of work. For instance, a psychiatrist was allowed to deduct costs of studying to become a psychoanalyst since that was regarded as upgrading her skills. A computer repair person with no college degree who returned to college to become a computer programmer would be considered to be taking classes to qualify for a new occupation and the deduction would be disallowed.

Q **What about seminars? Are they deductible?**

If there's a sound business reason for attending a seminar or other short-term course, you can deduct the costs. If you have to travel to get to the seminar and the majority of your trip is spent attending the seminar, you can also deduct your travel costs as a business expense. If you spend more time on personal activities than attending the seminar (say, take a four-week vacation after you attend a one-week seminar on the opposite side of the country from your business), your travel would be disallowed but the seminar cost allowed.

Q Can I deduct subscriptions to trade and business magazines on Schedule C?

Yes, if they are necessary for your business, they are fully deductible on Schedule C. List them under the miscellaneous deductions below travel and entertainment.

Q I run a computer-training business. Can I deduct the cost of using online computer information services?

You can deduct the business use of the services. If you use the services partly for business and partly for pleasure, you can only deduct the time spent online for business. You should keep a log recording the amount of business time spent online and the charges.

Q What is the home office deduction?

The home office deduction is a deduction you can take for the costs of operating the business portion of the home. If your office space qualifies and if you have a net profit from your business, the home office deduction can lead to a significant tax savings. It is separate from and in addition to deductions for everyday business expenses such as pens, paper, legal fees, etc., and must be deducted from income after all other business expenses. It allows you a deduction for a portion of your mortgage interest, real estate taxes, gas, electric, water, garbage disposal, and home repairs. And it allows you to depreciate (take a deduction spread out over a period of years) the business portion of your home. You cannot use the home office deduction to show a business loss, however.

Q What are the qualifications for the home office deduction?

To qualify, your home office:

▸ must be used exclusively and regularly for business, and
▸ must be:

- your principle place of business
- a place you meet with customers, patients, or clients in the regular course of your business, or
- a separate structure on your property used in connection with your business
  - your business may *not* be a hobby or passive activity such as managing investments

If you are an employee of a company rather than self-employed, you may be able to take a home office deduction if the use of your home is for the convenience of the employer and you are not renting your home office to your employer.

Q **Are there any exceptions to the exclusive use rule?**

Yes. The area you use for your home office does not have to be used exclusively for the business if:

- your home business is a day-care center or
- you use part of your home to store inventory you sell in your business

If you store inventory, however, the space you use must meet all five of these criteria:

- your business is selling products wholesale or retail
- the inventory is kept for use in your business
- your home is the only fixed location of your business
- you use the storage space regularly
- the space you use is separately identifiable and suitable for storage

For instance, suppose you sell novelty items at an indoor flea market. You store your inventory on shelves in your basement and use it to stock your booth as needed. You also have a Ping-Pong table in the basement that the kids use occasionally. The space used to store the inventory would be deductible even though the room is not exclusively used for your business pursuits.

Q I use part of my den to run a word processing business from my home. The family uses the other part as a family room. Can I take a home office deduction for the part of the room I use?

The answer is probably not, but it would depend on circumstances. If you work at a little desk squeezed in between the TV and the sofa, your office would not pass the exclusive test and would be disallowed. If the area you use for your business could be easily separated from the rest of the room by a panel or wall or other divider and your part of the room is furnished with office equipment, your deduction might be upheld if you were audited, but there is no guarantee.

Q What about other businesses for which paperwork is done in a home office, but services are performed (and income actually made) in other locations?

That question was the subject of a Supreme Court case that was decided in January 1993.

Nadir Soliman, a self-employed anesthesiologist, had taken a $2,500 deduction for a home office he maintained to do paperwork and administrative chores. The IRS disallowed the deduction on the grounds that the home office was not the doctor's principle place of business since the services for which he was paid were performed at several hospitals in the area.

The U.S. Supreme Court, overturning a lower court ruling, agreed with the IRS. They ruled that even though a self-employed individual may find it necessary to maintain a home office to handle administrative functions, the office may not necessarily be deductible.

The court's opinion, rendered by Justice Anthony Kennedy, outlined two criteria for determining whether or not the home office is the principal place of business:

- the relative importance of the activities performed at each location
- the amount of time spent in each location

Factors that should be considered in determining the relative importance of the home office, stated Justice Kennedy, are whether the taxpayer meets with customers or clients in the home office and whether the home office is the actual place of delivery of the products or services. "We do not regard the necessity of the functions performed at home as having much weight in determining entitlement to the deduction," he wrote.

At this writing it remains to be seen whether the ruling will apply only to self-employed individuals who have certain specified locations away from their home offices at which they regularly deliver services, or if the IRS will attempt to apply the ruling to landscapers, consultants, and others who perform services at miscellaneous and constantly changing locations away from their home offices.

 How do you determine the amount of the home office deduction?

The amount you can take as a home office deduction will depend on:

▶ the percentage of your home used for business
▶ the direct costs of operating your home office
▶ the indirect costs of operating the office
▶ your income after business expenses have been subtracted on Schedule C

You calculate the deduction on Form 8829. Start by calculating the percentage of your home used for business. To do that you divide the square footage of your home office by the total square footage of your home. The directions for Form 8829 say you can use any other "reasonable method" of calculating the percentage of your home used for business. However, when you fill out Form 8829, you are asked to record the total area of your home and the area occupied by your office.

For example: If you use a 10-by-15-foot room for your home office (150 square feet), and the total square footage of your home is 1,500 square feet, the percentage of space used for business would be 10 percent.

Then, you complete a series of calculations step by step on Form 8829 that lead you through the process of deducting allowable expenses in the order they are allowed. First comes mortgage interest, real estate taxes, casualty losses, and any carryover from previous years; then, if you still show a profit, you can deduct utilities, maintenance, and repairs; finally, if you still show a profit, you can deduct an amount for depreciation on your home office.

Q **What is the difference between indirect and direct costs?**

Indirect costs are any costs you split between your home and home office, such as the 10 percent of your first mortgage interest if your office uses 10 percent of your home space, for instance, or 10 percent of your real estate taxes.

Direct costs are those related only to the business portion of your home. For instance, if you built an addition onto your home to accommodate your office and used it for no other purpose, the interest on a second mortgage you took out to pay for the addition and the extra real estate taxes that would be assessed on the addition would both be direct costs.

Q Do I include my office phone bill in utilities or are they a Schedule C expense?

Phone bills go on Schedule C. Remember, you can't deduct any portion of the basic line charge for the first phone line coming into your home (your home phone). (For additional information, see the question on telephone deductibility on page 385.)

Q What utility expenses are deductible?

Electricity, heating, air-conditioning, water, and garbage removal, if separate from your real estate taxes.

Q Can I deduct the cost of the lawn service and the ornamental trees we planted?

Landscaping costs are not allowed as home office deductions unless your office is located in a separate building on your property. Then you may deduct whatever landscaping costs apply to the separate building.

Q Our roof was leaking and we had a new roof put on the house. Can I deduct a portion of that cost?

No. A new roof is considered a permanent improvement because it adds to the useful life of the property. Thus, the cost has to be capitalized and cannot be deducted. The business portion of the cost could be depreciated though. In addition, you would add the expense to the basis of the house.

What is basis?

Basis is the base or starting point for figuring depreciation, amortization, gain, loss, or depletion. You use it in determining the value of assets you place into service in your business. If you buy a piece of equipment you depreciate, your basis in that piece of equipment is the cost of the equipment. If you convert personal tangible property to business property (a computer you bought for home use, then later decided to use in your business), the basis is the fair market value of the property at the time you put it into business use.

 Can I use the current fair market value of my house for determining depreciation?

Probably not. Basis for figuring depreciation on your home is either the fair market value at the time you placed it in service or the adjusted basis, whichever is lower. To find the adjusted basis, you subtract the cost of the land the house is on from the total purchase price of the house. Add in the cost of any permanent improvements made to the house, and subtract any casualty losses that have occurred.

Thus, if you purchased your home for a total purchase price of $125,000 and if the land the house sits on is worth one-third of the total purchase price of the house, and you made no permanent improvements to the house since you bought it, your basis in the house is:

purchase price	land value		basis of the house
$125,000	− $41,250 ($125,000 × .33)	=	$83,750

If the home office occupies 10 percent of the house, the basis of the home office would be $8,375. It would be this amount on which depreciation is calculated.

 How do I calculate the depreciation on the home office?

Under current rules, a home office placed in service from 1991 on is depreciated over 31.5 years under something known as the straight line MACRS rates. These rates (as well as rates for other depreciation methods for other property) are published each year in the free IRS publication called *Depreciation* (Publication

534). To figure your depreciation, you get the appropriate percentage rate from a table in the publication, which tells you what the rate is for each year the property is in service. Then you multiply that rate by the portion of the home basis allocated to your office space.

Thus, in the example above where the office portion of the basis was $8,375, if you place the office in service at the beginning of 1992 and the MACRS rate is 3.042 percent, your depreciation allowance for the year would be $255 (rounded up to the next dollar).

basis of home office	$8,375
first-year MACRS rate	× $.03042
for 31.5-year property	$254.767

Q **Suppose you rent an apartment instead of owning a home. If you use a room exclusively for business can you deduct a portion of your rent?**

Yes. You would calculate the square footage used for business purposes (your office space in relation to your total apartment living space) and then include the cost of your rent in the "other expense" section under indirect expenses on Form 8829.

Q **If I deduct 10 percent of the mortgage interest and real estate tax costs on Form 8829, can I still deduct mortgage interest and real estate taxes on Schedule A?**

Yes, but only the unused portion. In other words, if you deducted 10 percent on Form 8829, you would deduct the remaining 90 percent on Schedule A.

Q **What is the advantage of deducting the business portion of the mortgage interest and real estate taxes on Form 8829 instead of Schedule A?**

The advantage is that the home office deduction lowers your net business income, which in turn lowers your self-employment tax and your adjusted gross income (AGI). Since several personal deductions and one possible penalty (see discussion on estimating taxes on pages 379–381) are tied to the AGI, the more you can legally reduce your AGI, the better off you may be from a tax standpoint.

Q. **Are there any business expenses I can't deduct, depreciate, or amortize?**

Expenses that are considered capital expenses cannot be written off. Neither can expenses for intangible property if the useful life can't be determined. In some cases the deductibility of an expense depends on how the transaction is set up. Here is a list of some items that either cannot be deducted or that can only be deducted under certain circumstances. You should consult your accountant before spending any substantial sums on these transactions to assure the transaction is set up in the best possible way for your business.

- Land. (Land can never be depreciated. Clearing, grading, and landscaping usually cannot be depreciated either; however, they could be added to your basis.) If you are using the land for mining or logging, it can be depleted, however.
- Trademarks and trade names.
- Goodwill (not depreciable).
- Franchises, designs, drawings, and patterns (depreciable only if they have a useful life that can be determined).
- Customer lists, subscriber lists, etc. (depreciable only if you can separate their value from the value of goodwill that goes with the business).

Q. **Won't taking the home office deduction increase the risk of audit?**

That is a possibility, but the number of returns audited each year for any reason is relatively small, and if you have all the documentation and receipts you need to prove your deductions there is no reason to not take all the deductions you are legally entitled to take.

Q. **What happens when I sell the house? Won't I have to pay capital gains tax on the business part of the house even if I buy a more expensive house?**

The answer depends on whether or not your office qualifies for a home office deduction *in the year the house is sold.* If it is a qualified home office, meeting the exclusive and regular tests, you have to split the sale price between the business and personal use of the house. However, if your office doesn't qualify for the deduction in the year of the sale (it fails the exclusive or regular tests, for instance), you would be able to defer the full sale price of the home as though you had never had an office there.

Recapture of depreciation applies here as well under the same rules. If the home office deduction is taken in the year of sale, you have to pay tax on the recapture of depreciation even if you purchase a home that costs enough to defer all the gain. If the office deduction isn't taken, you can defer all the recapture. Therefore, it would be wise to use the office for purposes other than business in the year of sale.

Q   How do I value property I bring into a business?

You have to determine the value of the property at the time it was placed into service. For most equipment this will be less than the purchase price if the equipment is not new.

Q   Can I deduct the cost of health insurance I pay for myself?

In recent years, self-employed persons have been allowed to deduct 25 percent of the premiums they pay for health insurance for themselves and their family if they are not covered by a spouse's or any other employer's health care plan. The rule allowing this deduction was not permanent at this writing, however. You will have to check current tax regulations before taking the deduction.

Q   My children work for me. Can I deduct their wages as a business expense?

Yes, you can deduct wages you pay your children. You must be able to prove the work your children did was work for the business and that the wages you paid them were ordinary and reasonable for the type of work performed.

Remember, too, that in hiring your children or spouse you become an employer and will have to comply with additional IRS requirements.

Q   What additional IRS requirements will I be subject to if I hire my children?

Any of your children who work for you will need a W-4 form filled out, and you will have to withhold income taxes from their salary and remit it as you would for any employee. If your business is a sole proprietorship, you do not have to withhold or pay the employer's share of Social Security or federal unemployment tax for any of your children under the age of 18 who work for you in your business. Be sure, however, to check state employment regulations, since they may be different. If your business is a partnership or corporation you will have to withhold Social Security and federal unemployment tax. In either case, you will need to be able to prove the children really did work for you if challenged by the IRS.

Q **How do I prove my children and spouse worked for me?**

Have them keep a log showing when they worked and what they did, pay them by check, and have them deposit the checks in their own bank accounts.

Q **Do I have to pay Social Security for my spouse if he or she does some work in the company?**

You have to withhold Social Security and income tax but not federal unemployment tax.

Q **Under what circumstances do I have to report money I pay to other freelancers or independent contractors?**

If the total amount you pay to anyone who is not an employee and not operating as a corporation amounts to $600 or more during the year, you have to report the total to the IRS at the end of the year on Form 1099, which is called an information return. You need to file a separate 1099 for each individual whom you have paid $600 or more during the year.

Q **What happens if I don't file a 1099?**

You will have to pay penalties both for failing to file the return with the IRS and for failing to send the copy to the recipient. The IRS penalty starts at $15 per return (up to 30 days late) and increases to $30 (return filed before August 1) and then $50 for returns filed after that or not filed. The penalty for failing to send the recipient their copy is $50. For both the IRS and the recipient statement, the penalty applies if you send the statements but not all the required information or if you report the information incorrectly.

Q **Can I deduct contributions to a pension plan?**

Yes. There are several types of pension plans available to you when you are self-employed. The amount you may contribute depends on your income and the type of plan you choose.

Q **What types of pension plans are there, and which is the best for a one-person business?**

It depends upon your goal. A defined benefit plan will let you choose the amount of money you want to receive each month when you retire and then specify how much you have to put in the account each year to meet that goal. Administering this type of plan is difficult, says CPA Jack Slick, because it requires the use of actuaries and mortality tables.

"The simpler plans such as money purchase plans, profit-sharing plans, and simplified employee pension plans (SEPs) are much easier to administer, and contributions to the plans are discretionary," says Slick. Most people opt for the simpler types of plans.

All of the plans allow you to defer taxes on the income until you reach retirement. Unfortunately, contributions to the plan on your own behalf are not deductible for self-employment tax purposes.

The SEP, often referred to as a SEP IRA, is the easiest to implement. Slick explains that it is similar to a normal IRA but has higher contribution limits. Contributions to a retirement plan can't exceed $30,000 on behalf of a self-employed individual. In addition, the simpler plans place a limit on the deduction based upon a percentage of income. For money purchase plans this limit is 25 percent of business income; for profit-sharing plans and SEP IRAs the limit is 15 percent of business income. The actual rate is lower, however, since you have to reduce your income by half of the self-employment taxes paid before calculating your contribution and calculate the contribution using a formula that lowers the rate. The formula is the contribution rate divided by one plus the contribution rate. So in the case of a money purchase plan with a 25 percent income contribution rate, the maximum actual rate that is applied equals 0.25 divided by 1.25, or 20 percent. That 20 percent rate would be figured not on the total business income, but on the business income minus 50 percent of the self-employment tax.

Money purchase plans and profit-sharing plans are generally referred to as Keogh plans. These plans must be in place and approved by the IRS by the end of your tax year in order for you to make a contribution to them for that year. SEP IRAs can be opened and money contributed to them for the tax year anytime before your return for that year is actually due. This period also includes any valid extensions you obtained on your return.

Q   If I decide to hire employees, do I have to include them in the plan, too?

If you have full-time employees they must also be covered under your retirement plan. In some cases this can substantially reduce the amount of money you were expecting to put away on your own behalf. If you are thinking about starting a retirement plan, it's worth your trouble to talk to a person that specializes in this area so that you can implement a plan that matches your needs and concerns and doesn't overly stress your business.

Q   If I have a Keogh or SEP IRA, can my spouse keep contributing to an IRA, too?

Yes, as long as your spouse is working, but, because yours would be a qualified pension plan, his or her IRA contributions would only be fully deductible if your combined income is under $40,000. Limited deductions would be allowed between $40,000 and $50,000.

Q   What if I can't pay my taxes?

If you can't pay federal or state income taxes, you should complete your return and mail it on time without payment. (If you can make a partial payment, by all means do so.) You will have to pay both a penalty and interest on the unpaid amounts, but the penalty and interest if you file and don't pay will be less than if you don't file.

Q What are the penalty and interest charges if I file a return without sending in the money due?

If you file but don't pay the tax, you will be subject to a penalty of one-half of one percent of the unpaid tax for each month or part of a month the tax is unpaid up to a maximum of 25 percent of the tax. This penalty is avoidable only if you can show failure to pay is due to a reasonable cause. (Not having the money is not a reasonable cause. Neither is not knowing you had to pay taxes. You were supposed to have known the laws and put aside enough money to cover your tax liability.)

You will also have to pay interest on the unpaid amount. The interest is based on short-term Treasury bill rates and is adjusted quarterly. It was approximately 10 percent compounded daily at the time this book was being written.

Q What is the penalty for not filing a return at all?

Failure to file a return brings steeper penalties. If you don't file a return the penalty is 5 percent of the unpaid tax for each month or part of a month the tax is unpaid, up to a maximum of 25 percent of the tax. Failure to pay penalties may also apply. If your return is more than 60 days late, the failure to file penalty will be at least $100 or the tax due, whichever is lower.

Q My business got some publicity and we have been so busy I don't know where I'll find the time to get my personal tax return done on time. I'll only owe a couple hundred dollars in taxes for last year and don't want to get hit with stiff penalties, but I don't see how I can possibly get the return done on time. Is there anything I can do?

Yes. File Form 4868, which is an application for an automatic four-month extension of the filing deadline. If you can't get to a tax office, your public library or post office is likely to have copies of this form. Filing the form only extends the deadline for filing. It does not extend the deadline for having your tax payments in to the IRS. All taxes have to be paid by the due date of your return, which is generally April 15, or you will be assessed applicable interest and penalties.

Q **How many years after I file a return can the IRS come back and challenge it?**

The IRS normally can come back and ask for more taxes within three years from the due date of the return. However, if you neglect to report an item of income that amounts to 25 percent or more of your income the IRS has up to 6 years to tap you on the shoulder. Additionally, if fraud is suspected, the IRS can come after you at any time. There is no statute of limitations on prosecuting and collecting extra taxes due in the case of fraud.

Q **What are my chances of being audited?**

It depends partly on what your income is. In 1989, an average of 0.8 percent of all returns were audited. The rate was 0.74 percent for individual nonbusiness returns with incomes between $25,000 and $49,999 and 1.09 percent for individual nonbusiness returns with incomes of $50,000 to $100,000 and 4.71 percent for incomes over $100,000.

By comparison, the audit rate for Schedule C filers appears to be higher, but the income ranges were specified differently. For Schedule C filers with incomes between $25,000 and $99,999, the audit rate was 1.86 percent in 1989; for Schedule C filers with incomes in excess of $100,000, the audit rate jumped to 3.38 percent.

Q **What should I do if I get audited?**

If you are audited, be sure you understand what information the IRS wants. Gather that information and arrange it neatly, making photocopies of any receipts or documents the IRS asks for. Mail the information or appear at a scheduled appointment as requested. (If you can't make the appointment, call well in advance and reschedule it.) If you are asked any questions during the audit, answer them directly, politely, and succinctly. Don't volunteer any information.

If the amount in question is large or if you are the nervous or talkative type, you may want to consider having your accountant go to the audit in your place.

Q **What tax records do I have to keep and how long?**

Keep tax returns forever.

Keep all papers regarding the cost of your house and mortgage and improvements to it for at least 5 years after you sell the house.

Save the supporting documents for income tax returns (expenses, income) for at least 5 years.

Q **What happens if your deductions are disallowed during an audit?**

You will have to pay interest and, depending on the reason and amounts involved, perhaps penalties. If the IRS suspects fraud, the penalties can be steep.

PULLING IT ALL TOGETHER: RESOURCES TO HELP

Q **Are the income tax guides sold in bookstores and on newsstands every year any good?**

Yes, the major tax guides available each year can be helpful if you do your own taxes. They can help clarify instructions or regulations that are unclear and will alert you to tax law changes effecting the current year's return. Although each of the books provides the same basic information, you may find one better than another for your personal needs since each organizes and presents the facts in slightly different ways. Since tax laws change almost yearly, if you use such tax guides, it is wise to buy a new one each year.

Q **Does the IRS have a help line?**

Yes. Your nearest IRS office may have a number you can call (look in your phone book), or you can call (800) 829–1040. If you think you will need help, don't wait until the last minute to call. The closer it gets to April 15, the more difficult it is to get through on the IRS help lines.

Q **What other help does the IRS offer?**

Local IRS offices generally have representatives available to help you figure out how to fill out forms or how to handle different types of deductions. This help is free, friendly, and nonthreatening (since you are asking for information, not being audited). However, don't wait until a couple of days before your taxes are due if you think you will need help. The office will be busy then, making the wait for help lengthy and the time representatives can spend with any individual somewhat limited.

The IRS publishes numerous help booklets, too. Some are instructions for specific forms; others are general guides on specific topics. Some of these have quite clear and easy-to-follow explanations. Among the IRS publications that may be of use to you are:

Name	Publication Number
Business Expenses	535
Business Use of Your Car	917
Business Use of Your Home	587
Depreciation	534
Miscellaneous Deductions	529
(covers what you can deduct for hobbies if your income producing activity doesn't qualify as a business)	
Tax Guide for Small Business	334
Taxpayers Starting a Business	583
Travel, Entertainment, and Gift Expenses	463

Before you hire employees get these:

Circular E: Employer's Tax Guide	15
Your Business Tax Kit	454-A
(which includes the following items)	
Business Reporting	1057
Form 1040 ES	
Form SS-4, Application for Employer Identification Number	
Tax Calendars	509

In addition to the help available to the general public at IRS offices, the agency also sponsors a program called the Small Business Tax Education Program (STEP), which teaches business owners and others some of the intricacies of dealing with IRS forms, record-keeping requirements, deposit of withholdings, and other business tax issues. For information, call the IRS at (800) 829–1040.

Q Where can I get copies of forms I need?

You can pick up copies of forms and publications at your local IRS office, or you can order them for free by calling (800) 829–3676.

Your public library will also have forms available. If you don't see the forms you need where other forms are located in the library, ask the reference librarian for help. Often they have reproducible copies of every form in existence in a book that remains (for safe-keeping) at the reference librarian's station. The post office may have forms as well.

Q Are the computer tax programs any good? Do they really save any time?

Yes, they are very useful. They automatically copy the data you enter or import it to the right places on each form or schedule you have to complete and automatically update all of them if a change is made in any one.

They also help prevent you from making mistakes in the way you fill out the return and in the calculations.

However, the programs are not a substitute for being aware of the tax laws and how they apply to your personal situation. But if you have some familiarity with the laws, they can be of tremendous help.

Q Can I use the forms in tax programs to send to the IRS?

Tax forms have to be approved for use by the IRS. The program you are using should indicate whether or not the forms it generates are approved for use. TurboTax (for IBM-compatible computers) and MacInTax (for Macintosh computers) are two popular commercial programs that have forms that have been approved for IRS use.

Q Can I file my own return electronically?

Although there have been some tests done on having taxpayers file their own returns electronically, taxpayers who want to file electronically to get their refunds sooner have to do it through a service authorized by the IRS. Accounting firms, companies that sell tax software, and even some of the widely advertised loan companies have this service available (usually for a fee) at income tax time.

Q Is there any other place I can get tax help?

Local community groups and libraries occasionally offer tax help. If you have a computer and modem, check the online computer information services for tax help. The Home Office/Small Business RoundTable has a very active tax help section on GEnie, and there are areas on Prodigy and America Online that also have tax help available. In addition, you can find shareware programs and spreadsheet or database templates online to help you complete your taxes and online help from publishers of major commercial tax software packages such as ChipSoft (TurboTax and MacInTax) and Parson's Technologies.

Q Now that I've read this chapter, am I aware of everything I need to know about taxes for self-employed individuals?

This chapter only touches on the basics for self-employed taxpayers. Depending on your situation, rules that haven't been discussed here such as passive loss rules, alternate minimum tax, and others may apply. Be sure to check the IRS instructions and other tax publications to determine what rules do apply to your situation, and if necessary, get help from a tax adviser or the IRS itself. When it comes to taxes, what you don't know can hurt you.

V.

Managing
It
All

25.

How to Gain Control of
Your Time

It's ironic. One of the biggest attractions of self-employment is the opportunity it offers to free up commuting time and simplify life. Yet in a 1992 survey of home office and small business owners 36 percent of the respondents cited lack of time as one of their major problems. *

Indeed, rather than looking for things to do with all their spare time, people who start their own business quickly gain new insight into the meaning of words like "cope" and "juggle," particularly if they work at home. They become adept at talking to clients on the phone while simultaneously gesturing at squabbling off- spring and mouthing *Cut it out or I'm going to wring your neck when I get off the phone!* They also become the master of the white lie, being able to devise a plau- sible business reason for putting a client or customer on hold the instant they spot bubbles oozing out of the dishwasher and realize it wasn't a good idea to substitute laundry soap for the dishwasher detergent they forgot to buy.

Fortunately, there are ways to make time management easier even if you don't have any employees to whom you can delegate work. The following pages contain dozens of ideas for managing your time more efficiently and improving your pro- ductivity.

* The results are based on the responses of more than nine hundred people who responded to a survey run on the GEnie computer information service by the Home Office/Small Business RoundTable.

Why is managing time so difficult for the self-employed?

When you are self-employed you don't have the support staff you'd have in a corporation. There's no switchboard operator, no secretary-typist, no file clerk, and no bookkeeper. Neither are there salespeople, copywriters, or a public relations department. You do it all. You wear all the hats.

To make matters worse you are likely to have to do it all in relative isolation. Without the benefit of daily contact with business associates, it is easy to lose sight of your goals and spend far too much time chasing rainbows or doing nonproductive busywork.

 Most mornings I boot my computer before I start making coffee. By the time my neighbors are leaving for work, I've already been at work for an hour or more. And I'm still working long after they return home. What am I doing wrong?

Sometimes long hours are unavoidable. I was printing out labels on a dot matrix printer at about 7:30 A.M. one day when I got a call from Tom Gabrielli, a self-employed commercial artist. Tom was doing a rush job for one of my clients and needed some information before he could send the work off to the printer. Knowing I work from home, Tom wasn't surprised that I answered the phone at that hour instead of letting my answering machine pick up the call. But when he heard the clatter of the printer in the background, he said, "Oh no, not you, too! I've been working since six A.M. What time did you start?"

As a commercial artist, Tom's work is somewhat cyclical. During the busy times of the year he is likely to start early and work late; but in summer, when his business tends to slow down a bit, he gets to travel or relax on sunny beaches while his corporate counterparts are watching the car temperature gauge inch towards hot in a rush-hour traffic jam.

If your business has busy seasons, you may find there are times when there is no good way to avoid long hours of work. But if you are regularly overworked or regularly behind schedule, chances are you need to gain control over the way you use your time.

 What can I do to control the way I use time?

There are dozens of ways to control the way you use time. Some involve doing very simple things such as keeping a list of office supplies that are running low. Referring to such a list and replenishing your stock before you run out will help you avoid frantic last-minute races around town to pick up some supply you need to finish a job. If some of the supplies you use are hard to find (colored printer ink or transparency film for an inkjet printer, for instance) ordering them ahead of time could save your neck as well as your time. A client wouldn't be very happy to hear her job won't be delivered in the morning because you ran out of some crucial supply last night.

Other time and clutter management tips may require a willingness to change lifelong habits and attitudes. If you were born to clutter, procrastinate, and start umpteen projects at once, you may need to manage your time more efficiently by focusing your activities and/or restructuring your environment for productivity.

Gaining control of your time is a three-step process:

1. Decide what you want to achieve with your time now and in the long run.
2. Pinpoint activities or interruptions that interfere with what you want to achieve.
3. Implement appropriate changes to eliminate or minimize the obstacles to attaining your goals.

Q How do I get started?

Getting in touch with yourself doesn't have to be a long, involved or unduly emotional project. It simply means thinking about the things you most want to do and what you need to do to accomplish those things. You can break the process of getting yourself more organized into these four simple steps:

- Make a written list of long- and short-range goals.
- Keep a time log to monitor the way you now use your time.
- Evaluate how the way you use time relates to the goals you want to achieve.
- Restructure your activities environment, habits, and/or work loads one by one to eliminate inefficient habits and time-wasting routines.

This all sounds like a lot of busywork. How is it going to help me get more done in less time?

Effective time management isn't a matter of completing more activities in less time. It is a matter of using your time efficiently (managing it) to achieve your goals.

For example, suppose Mary Jones offers word processing and mailing list maintenance services to small businesses near her home. She has a couple of steady customers and gets sporadic business from several shopkeepers in the area. Now that the twins have started junior high school, she has more time to work and realizes she'll probably need extra money in a few years to help pay for their college tuitions.

Which of the following should she do?

▶ look for new customers by sending a mailing to all local businesses telling them about her services
▶ create a newsletter or flier to demonstrate her skills and have it distributed with the local chamber of commerce mailing
▶ advertise resume preparation and word processing in the Yellow Pages and local weekly newspapers
▶ look for a job teaching word processing
▶ try to get typing jobs from bigger businesses or organizations
▶ start a temporary employment agency specializing in providing highly skilled word processors to industry
▶ get a "real" job during the day and type resumes at night

Almost any of these options might bring in some additional income. In fact, Mary might be tempted to try all of the above activities at once to bring in more work. The new work she brings in might make her very busy, but if it all comes from one-time customers or requires her to spend a lot of nonbillable time talking to new clients or learning new skills, she might be very busy but still not meet her income objectives.

If Mary wants to make the best possible use of her income-producing time, she will need to focus on her goals and plan around them. First, she should decide how much money she wants to earn or needs to earn, how many hours she is willing or able to work to bring in that amount of income, and what kind of work

418

she likes to do. Then she should look for the best ways to produce the amount of income she needs in the number of hours she can allot to income-producing activities.

Thus, if she needs an extra $200 a week, and local shopkeepers tend to have only small, one-time jobs—and quibble over the price of those, to boot—doing a mailing to small shopkeepers will be a waste of Mary's time and money. However, if she has some background working in a legal or medical office, she might do well to focus on soliciting business from attorneys in a 20-mile radius.

If Mary has the time, energy, and desire to expand her one-person business and can raise sufficient capital to start a temporary employment agency, the best way for her to spend her time at the moment might be researching whether the community could use another employment agency and what she would need to do to start one.

The same kind of carefully thought-out approach can help you better manage your time to meet your goals.

 I've heard a lot about goal setting. Does it work? Do I really need to write goals down?

Goals are a lot like vacations. To make them happen you have to pick a destination and map out a route to reach the destination. Writing your goals down and asking yourself what, specifically, you need to do to achieve each goal can give you the focus and direction you need to reach them.

 I want to be rich, and I also want to finish writing my customer's program by the end of the week. Which do I write down on my list of goals?

Start by listing your long-term goals, but be as specific as possible. Getting rich is not specific. Boosting personal net income to $500,000 a year by 1996 is a specific goal. Once you have a specific goal, determine the steps necessary to reach that goal and set a date for doing so. If "buy a house" is your long-term goal, write down the amount of the down payment you are willing to pay and how much money you'll need to earn to keep up with the mortgage payments, maintenance, utilities, and other bills. Consider what steps you need to take to make your business grow to achieve that level of income. Set realistic target dates and you will be

Table 25.1: Sample Goal-Setting Worksheet

Goals to Achieve

Writing out your goals and the steps to achieve them makes them more attainable. A form such as this can help organize your thoughts.

Long-term goal: Buy $250,000 home		Achieve by: 6/96
Requirements	**Actions**	**Do By (date)**
$50,000 cash down payment (save additional $30,000)		3/96
have net income of $85,000		12/95
	hire 3 employees add microcomputer repair services to increase income 30%	12/93
	bring in 2 corporate accounts to increase income 20%	12/94

well on your way to reaching your goal. See the sample goal-setting worksheet above (Table 25.1).

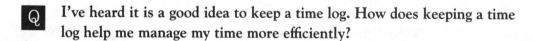

Q **I've heard it is a good idea to keep a time log. How does keeping a time log help me manage my time more efficiently?**

Keeping the log will let you quickly detect patterns in the ways you use and abuse time. For instance, your log may show you that, like your corporate brethren, you are wasting anywhere between 35 and 45 minutes a day just looking for things on your desk or in your files. Or it may show that you are spending a lot of time making or accepting phone calls that have nothing to do with reaching any of your goals. If you waste even 5 minutes on each of a dozen calls during the day, you have wasted an hour of your time—plus the cost of any calls you made.

In addition to helping you spot patterns in the way you waste time, a time log can help you identify patterns relating to the profitability of various jobs or contacts. When you look over your log, you may be surprised to see it takes you only three hours to complete a $250 job you do weekly for Smith & Sons, but you spent 5 hours on work for Rainbow City that also brought in $250. If the cost of doing each job is the same, you don't have to be a mathematical genius to figure out which produces more income for your time.

Q **Can most people find such patterns in their work week?**

Yes. In fact, the 80/20 principle or the Pareto principle (for the Italian economist who first expounded it) holds true for most businesses and individuals. In essence the principle says that 80 percent of your business will come from 20 percent of your customers or, alternatively, that 20 percent of your efforts will produce 80 percent of your income.

Your time log will help you pinpoint the customers and activities that produce the bulk of your income. To streamline your business and increase profits, focus on finding more customers like the 20 percent who now provide the bulk of your profit, and spend less time doing work for the type of customers whose work is marginally profitable.

Q **How do I keep a time log?**

It's simple. Just record all your activities for a week. Every time you start or stop an activity, get interrupted by a phone call, stop working to throw a load of clothes in the washing machine, make a brief notation about what you did. Try to write these notes at the time you start or stop an activity, not later in the day when you may forget what you did, or how long it took. You can use a format like the one on page 422, or just keep a running tally of start and stop times on a pad of legal paper or in a notebook. The important part is to keep the log.

Q **How long should I keep recording my activities?**

Keep the log for at least a week.

Table 25.2: Time Log

Here is a very simple time log to use. Every time you start, finish, or change activities, write down the time and the nature of the activity.

Keep the log for at least a week. At the end of the week, look at your patterns of activity. How many jobs did you start? How many did you finish? What kept you from finishing the jobs? If you've written down everything you did during the week, you should be able to see at a glance how you are spending your time and when and how you are being interrupted or change activities.

Activity	Start Time	Stop Time	Completed? Y	N

Q **My work varies a lot from week to week. How can I see patterns?**

While the type of work you do may vary, chances are the way you deal with your work load and interact with customers won't change much from day to day or job to job. Here are some questions to consider that may help you spot time-wasting activities or inefficient ways of dealing with your work load:

- Did you start each day with a plan of what you wanted to accomplish?
- Did you try to do too much?
- Did you usually finish one task before starting the next?
- Did you get a lot of incoming phone calls that weren't important?
- Were all the phone calls you made necessary?
- Did you spend too much time making unimportant decisions?
- Have you developed standardized letters and procedures for dealing with recurring situations?
- Are you grouping jobs for maximum efficiency?
- Are your methods or equipment up-to-date and adequate for your needs?
- Did you tend to spend time day-dreaming instead of working?
- Did you spend a lot of time looking for things?
- Did you spend more time organizing your work or your work space than doing work?
- Did you delegate business or personal chores to others, or did you let others delegate their chores to you?
- Did you put off starting big, important jobs while you got lots of little chores out of the way?
- Did you have to run to the store frequently for business or personal items you forgot to buy?
- Did you do things for other people you really didn't want to do?
- Did you spend a lot of time worrying about problems?

Q **What do I do with the log after I've made it?**

At the end of the week review your notations. Consider which things helped you to achieve long- or short-range goals and which didn't. Determine what kinds of activities or interruptions got in the way of reaching your goals. Among the things to watch for: How many jobs did you start? Did all of them have to be done? How many did you finish? What kept you from finishing the jobs? If you've written down everything you did during the week, you should be able to see at a glance how you are spending your time and when and how you are being interrupted or change activities.

Once you identify time-wasting activities, you can improve your efficiency by adapting some of the suggestions in the next chapter.

26.

Practical Ways to Save Time in Your Home Office or Small Business

Even if you were a good time manager when you worked for a corporation, you may find that managing your time in a home office or other small business is extremely difficult. One reason is that corporate time-saving strategies just aren't practical for businesses with low budgets and few if any employees. Another is simply that your work load is likely to be heavier when you work for yourself than it is when you work for other people.

In either case, managing your time is something you must learn to do if you expect to succeed. Here are dozens of time management tips you could put to work in your home office or small away-from-home business.

GETTING THE WORK OUT

Q **I start off each morning with good intentions but somehow get side-tracked. By the end of the day I find I haven't accomplished anything. What can I do?**

Make sure you start off each day with a schedule. If at all possible, make the first task on your schedule the most important thing you have to do. At the end of each day, write out your schedule for the next day, allowing yourself reasonable time limits for completing each task or portion of a task. Get everything together to start the next day's work, and leave it where you'll see it first thing in the morning if you find you have trouble getting down to work when you first enter your office.

Q **My projects tend to be long-term. It could take me a month or two to develop an inventory control system for a big customer, for instance. How can I schedule something like that?**

Keep a master project calendar. Break the task down into steps (or milestones), and then schedule each step according to when it has to be completed.

Q **How does keeping a To Do list help?**

Listing tasks on a sheet of paper offers these benefits:

- reminds you of jobs to be done
- helps keep your desk free from clutter (a list of five things to do takes up a lot less room on your desk than five stacks of papers and folders)
- makes it easier to prioritize tasks
- gives you a feeling of accomplishment when you cross off items on the list as you finish them

Q **Is a To Do list different from an appointment calendar?**

They can be the same, but often a To Do list will contain things that can be done at any time, while the appointment calendar is for meetings with other people or things that have to be done at specific times, such as calling a client between 10 and 11 A.M. on Friday. You can keep both the To Do list and the appointment schedule on the same sheet of paper, however (see the illustration on page 426).

Q **What if I can't do everything I scheduled?**

Consider whether you can cancel a task or activity, give it to someone else to do, or simply work extra hours this week and learn not to take on so much next

Table 26.1: To Do List and Appointment Schedule

Day: _____   Date: _____

Appointments

9:00
10:00
11:00
12:00
1:00
2:00
3:00
4:00
5:00
6:00

Things To Do

Item	Time to Complete	Priority

Notes:

week. If you routinely have more work to do than you have time to do it, it's time to either hire help or be more selective in the type of work you accept.

Q I make schedules but can't seem to stick to them. What could be wrong?

You may be scheduling too many things for each day or not allowing yourself time to account for occasional interruptions or delays. One solution is to schedule a block of time to do catch-up chores. This could be one hour a week or one day a week. It should be used only to finish jobs that haven't been completed or to do those non-income-producing tasks you keep putting off, like filing, bookkeeping, etc.

Another possible reason you find it difficult to get everything you've scheduled done is you may be scheduling activities that don't fit into your long-range plans.

For instance, you may be teaching a programming course one night a week, doing the bookkeeping for your uncle once a month, and selling advertising specialties as a sideline, all while you try to keep up a computer consulting business. As a result, you may be torn in so many pieces you simply can't devote the time needed to any one activity. If this is your problem, choose what is most in line with your goals and focus your attention on that activity and eliminate any that don't help you accomplish your goals.

Q I'm having trouble getting started on a big project. What should I do?

The best procedures to follow when you can't seem to get going on a project are these:

> Break the job down into small pieces and tackle one piece at a time.
> Set deadlines for yourself. Work often expands (and slows down) to fill the time allotted for it.
> Establish milestones and reward yourself with a trip to the beach or the movies, or by doing something else you enjoy each time you reach one of the milestones.
> Delegate less important jobs to others, or if you have no one to delegate the work to, consider subcontracting the work out to a helper.
> Be sure you have all the information you need to proceed with the pro-

ject. If you don't, get the needed facts and the job may start to fall into place.

DEAL WITH DISTRACTIONS

Q **I never seem to get one thing finished before I have to start another. What can I do?**

List tasks you need to perform on a To Do list. Assign priorities to work you have to do. If you have trouble finishing tasks or tracking multiple projects, put the most important thing you have to do at the top of your list, make that the first thing you do, and continue working at it until it is finished; then, tackle the next item on your list. At the end of the day, leftover tasks—if still important—get moved to the next day's To Do list.

Tip: If you use a computer system consider buying one of the calendar alert programs that beeps at you and/or puts a message on your screen to remind you of appointments, projects, etc. Some have calendars and appointment books as well as the alert feature and/or a To Do list that pops up automatically on the screen when you turn on the computer.

Other methods that may work for you are assigning the most difficult tasks you have to do to the hours of the day you tend to be most productive or when you are least likely to be interrupted.

Q **I'll be working, remember something I wanted to do, and before I know it, I'm in the middle of doing the new thing and have put aside the project I started earlier. How can I keep from interrupting myself?**

That's a common problem. To solve it, keep a notepad near you when you work and write down all the things that you remember you have to do. Then, do the tasks all at once near the end of your work day if they still seem important. You will be surprised how many of those little things you thought were important earlier in the day are no longer important near the end of the day.

Other ways to handle distracting tasks are to set aside one day a week to finish projects you've started during the week or one day a week as the only day you'll start new projects or pursue new ideas.

Q **But isn't that procrastinating? Isn't it better to do things right away?**

Procrastination is putting off things because you don't want to or don't know how to get started on them. Grouping tasks lets you concentrate on one thing at a time and accomplish each more efficiently. It can also help you spot unnecessary or marginal chores and eliminate them.

If you have employees, you may also find you can delegate some of the tasks to one of your employees.

Q **Usually an interruption is a customer or a family member who needs something done right away. How can I avoid those interruptions?**

Learn to distinguish between urgent tasks and important ones. An urgent task is one that demands to be done *now!* An important task is something that furthers your longer-term objectives. Some tasks seem pressing because someone else wants you to drop what you are doing so you can help them immediately accomplish their goals. A spouse who calls home and expects you to stop working to go out and pick up a part they need or a customer who calls and expects you to answer grammar and usage questions because you write their advertising copy (and of course does not expect to be billed for your time) are two examples of urgent tasks that don't foster your goals.

Tip: If you have one or more people you don't want to anger but who frequently make such urgent calls, letting the answering machine pick them up may avoid unwanted confrontations. If you are unavailable, the person trying to reach you might take care of the problem himself or herself. If not, be assured, the person will call back.

If you have customers who make a habit of calling you for free advice or information, consider billing for phone time or charging a retainer fee. Warn the customer a little in advance, and ask which they'd prefer: a retainer contract or to be billed for each call.

 You can't put off a baby that needs a diaper change or the parcel post guy at the door. What do you do when you are frequently interrupted by family obligations or household duties?

Don't try to play superman or superwoman. You may need to hire household help. If you can't afford household help on a regular basis, consider having someone come in once every other week to help out, and try to get more cooperation from other members of your family on a daily basis. In addition, schedule work that needs a lot of concentration for times when someone else can attend to the baby's needs or when the doorbell isn't likely to ring.

 Are those personal organizers and planning systems any good?

Sure—if you use them. Their benefit is they let you keep all your notes and records about projects, people, appointments, and expenses in one place. They can serve not only as an appointment reminder and scheduler (daybook) but also as a tickler file and record of business activities for tax purposes.

Generally, they have pages on which you can list daily or weekly appointments and To Do lists; a monthly and/or yearly planning calendar; sections for addresses and phone numbers, expenses, and notes. Some offer project planning sections, graph paper, a ruler, miniature envelopes for receipts, trip records, and other forms, and miscellaneous information guides. Since the planners are usually loose-leaf format, forms or sections may be added or removed to customize the planner to your own use.

The main problem with such systems is the human one. If you don't use the diary regularly or make legible entries in the diary or if you overschedule appointments for yourself, it won't do you any good.

 Where can I find these planning books?

Four companies that make these planners are Rolodex, Day-Runner, Day-Timers, and Franklin International Institute. The Rolodex and Day-Runner systems are sold in many office supply stores. The systems from Day-Timers and Franklin are generally not available in stores. You can get catalogs of their products by contacting the companies. The phone number for Day-Timers is (800) 556–5430. The phone number for Franklin is (800) 654–1776.

Q **How much do these planning systems cost?**

The initial cost can run anywhere from around $30 to $250 depending on the size of the binder, the type of binder (zippered or non-zippered, for instance), the quality of the covering (vinyl, simulated leather, real leather), and what types of planning tools you want to put in it (To Do list forms, expense records, daily calendar, etc.).

Q **What about the electronic organizers?**

If you buy one of the better ones they, too, can be invaluable—if you use them and if you don't lose or misplace them. They can store names, addresses, phone numbers, appointments and can be used as a calculator, clock, and memo pad. Some of the better ones can transfer information to and from a computer (with the purchase of cables and software) and have memory cards available that allow you to use the organizer as a dictionary, for financial planning, or even for a limited amount of word processing if you can type on the tiny keys.

Q **Are there similar time management systems for computer users?**

Yes. Both Day-Timers and the Franklin Institute have developed software for MS-DOS and Macintosh computer users that functions like the paper planning systems. Other companies make software (often called personal information managers or PIMs) that perform similar tasks. Computer magazines and catalogs should have ads for this type of software. Check back issues of computer magazines for reviews of the products if the prices are high.

Q **How do I know which system is best?**

Think about how you work and where you work. Do you need something small and portable? Do you travel a lot? Could you discipline yourself to make regular entries in a planner? (If not, they will all be a waste of money to you.) Do you need something that can transfer data to your computer system?

Send for catalogs and brochures and look at the planning guides in the stores. Try to determine how much space you need and how you want to organize appointments and notes. Then choose the one that seems most suited to the way you want to work.

Q **How can I motivate myself to get more done?**

If you tend to plod along without the stimulation of someone looking over your shoulder to see if work is done, give yourself deadlines and make yourself stick to them. Make it a contest with yourself, or a race with the clock (actually set an alarm clock), or program your computer to alert you at a certain time.

Q **It takes me a long time to make decisions. How can I quicken the process?**

Learn to look at the big picture. What do you want to achieve? What is the relative importance of the decision you are about to make? If it makes little real difference whether you choose A or B, choose either and move on to something else. (Flip a coin if you have to, but make the decision and move on to your next task.)

Q **What if the decision _is_ important or could cause a big loss?**

If you can't make a decision any other way, take out a sheet of paper and divide it into two columns. On the top of one column write "Pros," and at the top of the second column, write "Cons." Put the reasons for making a positive decision under the pros, the reasons for a negative decision under cons, and compare the two. Sometimes just writing it all down can help you clarify your thinking.

Q **It's one thing to know what I _ought_ to do to get organized and quite another to make myself do it. How can I motivate myself to get more organized?**

If reminding yourself of your long- and short-term goals doesn't help, try reminding yourself how much your time is worth. If you bill at $60 an hour, every minute you waste doing unproductive tasks or making unnecessary phone calls costs you a dollar.

GAIN CONTROL OVER TELEPHONE CALLS

 I don't have anyone to screen or place calls for me. How can I reduce the amount of time I spend on the phone?

Here are a few suggestions that work for even the one-person home office:

Use an answering machine or voice mail system to answer phone calls. The advent of voice mail has given telephone answering systems new respectability. Where once an answering machine message was a good indication the business you had called was very small and probably located in someone's kitchen, now it is quite common to call even major corporations and hear various versions of "I'm sorry. I'm away from my desk or helping another customer. At the tone . . ."

If you have your own answering machine, set the answering machine to let you monitor calls and cut in only if the call is important. If you don't need to monitor calls, however, don't. Monitoring them may disturb your concentration on a project, defeating one of the purposes of having the machine pick up the calls in the first place.

Make all outgoing phone calls at one time. Set aside a specific block of time (say 11:00 A.M. to 11:30 A.M.) to make phone calls, and stick to it. Instead of reaching for the phone each time you *think* you need to make a call, make notes to yourself about who you want to call and why. When the time you've set to make calls rolls around, place those calls you still think are necessary.

Grouping calls this way will help you reduce or eliminate the number of unimportant impulse calls you make. Since you have a specific time frame in which to make and complete all calls, you will be less likely to waste time chitchatting about nonbusiness matters.

 Is there any way to avoid chatting about inconsequential things during phone calls?

To keep business calls more focused, make mini-agendas for your calls. List the key points you want to discuss and check off each point as you go over it, noting any items that will be followed up at a later time. When you have gotten to the end of your agenda for the call, sum up the main points covered, and if both parties agree everything has been covered, say good-bye and hang up. You'll save your own time, the time of the person you were talking to, and cut your phone bill as well.

Q **How else can I reduce the time I spend on the telephone?**

Here are several ways:

Use electronic mail. How many times has something like this happened to you? You need to talk to your contact at a client's office for information about a project you are doing. You call but your contact is out of the office. Your contact calls you back, just after you leave for an appointment elsewhere. You return the call when you get back and the contact is in a meeting.

If you use computers and modems, this kind of phone tag could be eliminated with electronic mail. Often called *email,* electronic mail is simply a way of sending information from one computer to another without the computers having to be hooked up. Much like regular mail, when you send electronic mail it gets deposited in the recipient's electronic mailbox and waits there for the recipient to pick it up at his or her convenience any time during the day or night. Unlike regular mail, delivery to the recipient's mailbox is usually immediate.

To use electronic mail, you and your customers will need access to an electronic mail system. You don't have to have a private or custom setup. All of the commercial computer networks such as GEnie, America Online, MCI mail, and CompuServe offer electronic mail services. Generally, it is best if you and your clients use the same service for electronic mail, but some kinds of electronic mail can be sent from one service to another if necessary.

Other time-saving benefits of using electronic mail are that it can help avoid aimless small talk if you have a client who can't stop talking once on the telephone. If you need to get information to a customer in a hurry, email can also cut down on the delivery time and avoid busy or turned-off fax lines. Finally, if your customers live in other countries and you choose a service with international access, you and your customers can communicate at the hours you are each most alert.

Send a fax instead of calling. Most businesses have fax machines and leave them on constantly. If you have frequent dealings with certain businesses, ask for their fax number and ask if it is OK to send messages by fax. Besides using fax for messages, you can order parts and supplies, send for and receive literature, and even order your lunch or enter radio contests.

Tip:

> If you don't have a fax machine, but do have a computer and modem, many of the computer networks let you send a fax from your computer even though you don't have a fax machine. You won't be able to send graphics or a copy of your letterhead, but you can send text files to any fax machine in areas served by the services.

CONQUER CLUTTER

Q **I waste a lot of time looking for things. Either I put things away and don't remember where I put them, or they get buried under something on my desk. What can I do?**

If you frequently misplace things in your office, consider these solutions:

▶ *Make sure you have adequate storage space.* It's hard to keep things organized and neat if you don't have any place to keep your business files, equipment, supplies and tools, etc.

▶ *Work out orderly and convenient storage and filing systems.* Think about what you need to do your work and how you can organize your work space efficiently. It is likely that you actually use only 20 percent of the files, equipment, tools, or other items in your work area on a regular basis. Make sure those are located close to where you work so they are easy to put away or file as soon as you are done with them. Could you install shelves in your work area? Put up pegboards or racks to store frequently used tools near your working area? Look around the home improvement stores and discount department stores as well as office supply stores for ideas about storage furniture and supplies.

▶ *Do filing and straightening regularly.* Set aside 10 minutes at the end of each day to put away anything you've taken out. Make sure you always put things back in the same place, too. If you group your phone calls and have a speaker phone or a phone with a long cord, you can do your filing and straightening while you are making your phone calls.

▶ *Cross reference your files.* Could a piece of paper be filed in two places? Put the paper in one file and put a note about where to find it in the other.

▶ *Use your computer to store names, phone numbers, and reminders.* A database program or a personal information management (PIM) program can put names, numbers, and notes where you can find them quickly. If you don't have a database program or a PIM, put the names of all contacts in one word processing file and use the search feature of your word processor to find the information when needed.

Q **What's the best way to clear the clutter off my desk?**

Rediscover your wastebasket. Unless you have already trained yourself to toss out all but important documents and mail, some 50 to 75 percent of the items on your desk are outdated or refer to things you don't need to do. Set aside a half hour to an hour to clear your desk of everything you no longer need. If you have several months worth of accumulated clutter to sift through, set aside a little bit of time each day for the project, tackling one part of the area at a time, or even one corner of the desk or workbench at a time.

If you keep magazines and newsletters because you might need a name or number or the information in an article, copy down the name and number or tear out the article from the newsletter and file those things in appropriate files. Then throw out the remainder of the publication. Not only will it save room, it will make it possible to find the names, numbers, or information you were saving without having to go through stacks of old publications.

Don't leave things out so you'll remember to do them. Instead, put a description of what needs to be done and a due date on a To Do list, and put the associated paper, materials, or other paraphernalia away until it is time to do the job. If you think you will forget where you put the things you were going to leave out, include a notation on the To Do list about where you put the materials you'll need.

Q How do I decide what to keep and what to throw out?

If you are trying to organize a home office that has become so cluttered it would make a typical 10-year-old's room look neat, the best approach is to clear desks, bookcases, and work surfaces of *all* stacks of papers, magazines, newspapers, etc. Pile the stacks into cardboard boxes, keeping them separated as they were on your desk if you worry about losing things you might need.

When all is clear, start putting items back in place. Start with essential equipment and tools first (computer or typewriter, Rolodex, desk calendar, telephone, etc.). Then start sorting piles of paper you think contain the most current items. Toss out any piece of paper you don't have a specific need for.

Leave all the other piles of paper in the boxes you put them in, and move the boxes to a storage area away from your office (a basement, closet, or garage would do). Retrieve papers or items from the boxes only as you need them over the next several months. After 6 months, consider tossing all the papers and files you haven't needed into the recycling bin since it is unlikely you'll ever look at them again.

Warning: If you are so unorganized that your business certificate, tax returns, or other documents that must be saved might be buried in the piles of clutter, beg or pay a friend or spouse to sort through it all for you before tossing it out.

Q How can I deal with my "pack rat" tendencies?

Do you save mail, odds and ends of supplies, scraps of material, notes to yourself, magazines, newsletters, etc., just *in case* you need them? If you absolutely can't bring yourself to throw out those odds and ends, try this: Keep a cardboard box under your desk or elsewhere in your work area. Throw in all the things you are afraid to throw out but don't have a specific use for now.

Once a month, go through the box and throw away everything that is outdated or no longer seems important. Do not add a second box when the first is filled.

Force yourself to take the time to go through the box. If you never seem to find the time to go through the box, consider doing this: Take the top half of the materials out of the box and set them aside. *Remove the remaining items from the box and throw them out without looking at them.* If they were buried in the box for over a month because you weren't sure if you needed them you will never miss them. Put the items you set aside (the newest ones) back in the box. Repeat the procedure each month.

 What can I do with all the business cards I accumulate? I wind up moving them from one place to another on my desk for weeks and then can't find the one I want when I need a contact.

Get a Rolodex with plastic sleeves to hold business cards. Ask people to give you *two* business cards. Store one under their name in your Rolodex and the other under an industry or other classification. For instance, John James, a computer consultant, might be filed under J for James and under C for consultant. Alternately, type the name and contact information into a searchable computerized database. Print out the database and store a paper copy so you will be able to find contact names if your computer has to be repaired or can't be used due to a power outage.

 I don't have enough room to add more storage space. What can I do?

Empty file cabinets of old or outdated files. Although we live in the information age, it's not necessary to save every piece of information that comes into your office. According to a 1987 report published in *Personnel Journal,* Americans create 30 billion original documents a year and ignore 85 percent of what they keep on file. If you purge your file cabinets of material you no longer need, you will free up storage space and make it easier to stay organized. If you aren't sure what documents you should keep and what you can safely throw out, see the Records Retention Chart beginning on page 502. The chart lists typical office and business documents and suggests a length of time such items are normally stored or useful.

 My housemate is always hounding me about the mess in my office, but I find structure stifles my creativity. Is there a way to be a free spirit and be neat, too?

There are a couple of things that might work. First, try organizing your space a little. Take a few hours to put away things you seldom need or use and to arrange the rest into some kind of order. You may find that just organizing things a little actually lets you be more creative because you can concentrate on your work rather than going crazy looking for some tool or piece of information you need.

The other possible solution is to try to close off your office area from your housemate's view. If you have a separate room for it, close the door. If you don't have a separate room, look for ways to screen off your corner so the clutter isn't visible to your companion or can be hidden when you aren't working in the office. Inexpensive folding screens from discount department stores are one possibility, decorating magazines might offer other ideas.

Tip: If you use a computer system and your desk or filing cabinet is cluttered, your computer hard drive is likely to be cluttered, too. You can speed up file searches by periodically removing unneeded files from your hard disk and by running a hard disk optimization program. These programs "pick up" after you, fitting your files into orderly patterns on the hard disk so the head (something like a phonograph needle) that has to read the data doesn't have to constantly jump from one part of the disk to another to retrieve or store information.

Q What about old tax records and other files I have to save? What can I do with them?

Move inactive files you can't throw away to some other location. If you do not have to refer to them often, move them to some other storage area such as a basement, attic, garage, or rented space in a storage facility. Use suitable storage containers to protect the records from being destroyed by moisture or by mice if either are a problem. Metal or plastic garbage pails (clearly marked so they aren't thrown away) make inexpensive home storage containers.

Q Is there any good way to deal with all the mail I get?

Some of these techniques will help:

- Set aside a specific time each day to take care of your incoming mail. If practical, schedule mail chores for mid-afternoon. The change of pace late in the workday will be welcome. A mid- or late-afternoon slot for reading mail will also ensure you won't blow the whole day on unimportant tasks if you get distracted by something you spot in a piece of junk mail or magazine article.

- Open, read, and handle all of your mail in the allotted time.

- Open you mail over the wastebasket or the recyclables container, immediately discarding envelopes, ads, or catalogs you don't need. Unless you have a very specific reason for not doing so, also throw out all mail you are tempted to save "just in case" you want to refer to it later.

- If you have been sitting for most of the day, stand while you open and read the mail. The change of position will be good for you, plus you are likely to take less time opening and reading the mail if you are standing up.

- File mail you need to save *before you sit down again.* Once you sit, inertia is likely to set in, and the piece of mail you were going to file later will still be on your desk the next day.

- Ask to be taken off the mailing lists if you don't use the products in mail order catalogs you receive or if you don't read the newsletters or trade publications you get. You'll be helping to reduce landfills as well as the clutter on your desk.

Q How else can I save time?

If you think about the way you work and the jobs you do, you will probably be able to discover dozens of ways to save time. Here are some ideas to spark your own creativity:

Group jobs in batches and automate the work as much as possible. If you have a computer, learn to use it to speed multiple mailings, do your accounting, or cut down on other tedious chores. If you are cutting out fabric for craft items, cut the material for numerous items at once, rather than one at a time.

Delegate some business chores to family members. Even 5- and 6-year-old children can stuff envelopes, fill bean bag frogs, or sort things by size or color. A 7- or 8-year-old could probably file, staple, sort, and make photocopies, too. Older children or a spouse can proofread your letters, enter data in a mailing list, or do any number of other tasks if you show them how.

Learn to do two things at once. If you have to do something boring or repetitious or that doesn't require much concentration, try to do something else at the same time. Here are just a few examples:

▶ Do your filing while you talk on the telephone. A telephone with a built-in speaker will not only let you move about the room while holding a conversation but it can also keep you from getting a stiff neck if you do a lot of calling.

▶ Hook up a portable phone to your business line and fold laundry or do the gardening while making routine business calls.

▶ Take a tape recorder or a Dictaphone with you when you travel any distance in the car, and dictate letters, outline client proposals, or develop ideas for your own marketing plans.

 Tip: A remote microphone hooked up to a standard tape recorder makes it easy to control the recorder without taking your hands off the steering wheel or eyes off the road.

▶ Use a car phone to make routine customer calls while you are stuck in traffic jams.

▶ Use the tape deck in your car radio to listen to instructional tapes or books on tape. It is a great way to acquire certain types of information and training you wouldn't have time to get any other way.

- If you use a computer and don't have a print spooler for your printer, get one. A print spooler is a program that lets you queue up and print one or more documents while you continue to work on the computer. Without a spooler, printing documents may prevent you from doing any work on your computer until the printer is finished.

- If you can't perform spool printing, let your computer print out work while you do other business or personal tasks.

- Relax and work at the same time. You can fold and stuff and label envelopes, insert business cards in folders, and do other rote tasks while watching your favorite TV shows at night.

Carry reading material or small jobs with you when you have an appointment away from your office. That way, if you get stuck waiting, you can accomplish something productive during the delay.

Devise standardized letters and product literature to send in response to routine situations. If you have the kind of business that requires you to send out capabilities statements or other promotional material, assemble packages in advance so you can just add a cover letter and mail out the material quickly instead of hunting through various file folders to find press releases, brochures, resume testimonials, or magazine articles.

Devise standard formats for computerized documents. That way, every time you have to type a letter you can open a file and with one or two keystrokes insert all the margin settings, type size and font specifications, the date (if your software has a function that automatically inserts the date), etc.

Learn to use the mail merge features of computer software to add addresses to mass mailings or to call up and insert boilerplate paragraphs if you frequently need to create documents containing certain standard information.

Schedule breaks or changes in your routine to eliminate fatigue. You can get far more work accomplished when you feel up and ready to tackle it than you can when you are overtired or burned out. If your work keeps you cooped up or isolated for long periods of time, force yourself to take a break. Schedule lunch with a friend, take the baby for a walk in the park, do the shopping daily, go for a walk or a swim, etc. You'll feel refreshed, get more done, and feel better about yourself, too.

Try to limit the number of hours you work each week. Productivity slips when you work long hours on a regular basis.

Learn to say no. Don't let the whole family give you their errands to do because you are home. If you are running a business from home, establish a schedule and stick to it just like you would have to if you were going out to work.

Be forewarned: your spouse, children, relatives, and friends who have been used to you always being willing to do anything they want on a moment's notice won't appreciate your change in attitude. But unless you set priorities and stick to them you won't stay in business very long.

Learn to cut a deal. If Johnny wants you to drive him to Billy's house on the other side of town (picking up three other friends on the way), make sure (1) he first finds someone else to commit to driving the crew home, and (2) he does a specific chore (dust or vacuum a room, clean a bathroom, etc.) before you take him to the friend's house. If hubby wants you to take his car in for inspection, have him do the grocery shopping on the way home from work. If your neighbor Bill asks you to type his resume as a favor, ask if he'll drop your books off at the library. And if your wife gets upset that you are typing Bill's resume when you *still* haven't put together the bookcase she bought last month, have *her* type Bill's resume while you take care of the bookcase.

 Tip: If you have your children work for you, structure what you give them to do according to their age and abilities, and take the time to show them how to do jobs properly. In addition:

- Remember that a child is likely to take longer than you to accomplish a task, and plan accordingly.

- Break jobs up into pieces they can accomplish in reasonable amounts of time.

- Let them have their friends help with chores. Three or four 10-year-old girls can turn an occasional stint at stuffing and sealing a couple thousand envelopes into a game and get the work done in record speed. One child faced with stuffing and sealing a bunch of envelopes on her own is likely to think of all sorts of reasons she can't do it today.

▶ Consider whether you need to lower your standards for housework somewhat. If the living room looks neat and picked up, does it really matter whether or not Mark vacuumed under the sofa this afternoon?

Learn to make effective use of mail delivery services. You can order almost anything you need and have it delivered to your door these days. You can also have almost anything picked up at your door for shipment by any of a number of delivery services, including the U.S. Postal Service. Shipping supplies such as envelopes and labels are often free, too. Airborne Express, for instance, picks up parcels for free and will even bill you if you have an established business. The post office will pick up parcels for a small fee, charging one fee whether they are picking up one package or fifty at your location.

Courier services can also be a tremendous time-saver for local or regional deliveries. You can avoid having to spend hours traveling to a client's location just to drop off a package. They offer same-day delivery service to many areas, and if your package is heavy, it may cost less to use a courier service than it would to ship the same package by overnight mail.

For information about the services of the post office, call (800) 222–1811, or write U.S. Postal Service, Marketing Communications, 6 Griffin Rd. N., Windsor, CT 06006–0833. Airborne Express can be reached by writing to Airborne Express Customer Assistance Center, P.O. Box 662, Seattle, WA 98111–9926. Check the Yellow Pages in your phone book for contact information for other delivery services.

27.

Expanding Your Business

What makes the difference between businesses that fail and those that grow and prosper?

Opportunity-chasers and dream-seekers will tell you it takes luck, timing, and plenty of money to succeed in business. But people who have built small businesses usually have a different story to tell.

Although luck and money are nothing to sneer at, people who have created viable businesses know that what it *really* takes to succeed is vision, not dreams; hard work and industry knowledge, not luck; careful planning and persistence, not untold wealth.

Combine those ingredients with a little bit of business smarts and a sincere desire to satisfy customer needs, and most businesses will thrive and grow in time. But with growth can come a whole new set of problems, often involving cash flow and personal satisfaction with the business.

Q What's the best way to expand a successful business?

The first thing to do is to stop and consider what you want to achieve. Often businesses that are profitable and satisfying when they are small turn into cash-gobbling, ulcer-producing monsters when the owner tries to expand the business without considering all the implications of growth.

Therefore, before plunging ahead, take a realistic look at your own motivations and preferences. Ask yourself:

> Why do I want to expand my business?

> How big do I want the business to grow? (What sales volume do I want to achieve? How much profit will that bring me?)

> How long will it take (realistically) to reach that goal?

> Am I willing and able to devote the time and money to reach that goal?

> Am I ready to hire employees, delegate authority, and manage the business instead of work at it? Or am I willing to hire a business manager to make decisions for me?

> Will what I have to do to expand the business make it worthwhile personally as well as financially?

Your answers to those questions will help you decide how fast and how big to grow your business and if you should expand at all.

If you are sure you are ready and willing to expand your business, take the time to update your business plan. Work out all the market data and financial information, being sure to consider these points:

> Which of your products or services are most profitable to sell?

> Could you sell more of them to the same customers?

> Are there related products that might sell well to your customers?

> How could you increase the number of customers for what you sell now?

> What will it cost to produce or buy more of what you sell?

> What will it cost to market more products or to market to a wider area?

> How many employees will you have to hire, and what will it cost you not only for salaries but also for benefits and for workers' compensation, employer's contribution to FICA, etc?

> Will you need to rent office or warehouse space? Move to bigger quarters? Add on to the house?

> Will you need to borrow money or give up ownership to raise money to expand or to maintain cash flow? What will it cost to borrow the money?

Plug all your figures into your business plan, and then ask your accountant to look it over. His or her input can be valuable in helping you spot problems or opportunities you may not see.

Q **Is there any way to expand the business if I don't want to borrow a lot of money or give up ownership control?**

You can grow the business slowly out of your profits. It may take you longer, but if you aren't in a hurry and plan carefully it can work.

Q **Should I hire temporary workers to fill in during work overloads?**

If your business is not located in your home, using temporary workers is one good way to handle work overloads—one that many small and big companies alike find valuable. However, if your office is located in your home, you are likely to find it difficult or impossible to get temporary workers through an agency. Large agencies, for insurance reasons, generally make it a policy not to send temps to home-based businesses.

Q **Should I hire family or friends?**

A family business often turns out to be a satisfying team effort. While Mom may no longer be whipping up egg creams at the soda fountain as Pop sweeps the floor, the mom-and-pop shop is not dead. It's just moved home. In many cases Mom takes the orders while Pop produces the product, or Pop may do sales while Mom does customer support. Or Pop may bake cookies while Mom makes arrangements for packaging, shipping, and distribution.

And when it works it can be one of the most satisfying ways to run a business. But sometimes family or friends just don't make good employees or business partners. Sometimes they don't have the needed skills, and other times, they just don't have the desire to work as hard at the job as you would like them to. Although it can be difficult to do, before hiring or agreeing to work with family or friends, evaluate their capabilities and attitudes using the same standards you would for anyone else. And if your spouse is the one you will be hiring, be sure you can do without his or her income from another job and that you can also pay for the health insurance that he or she will be giving up by quitting.

Q **How can I keep good employees when I find them?**

Treat your employees with respect and consideration, and pay them what they could expect to earn elsewhere. If you have an employee who is of crucial importance to your operation, consider offering him or her some kind of sweat equity deal, trading ownership in the company for his or her efforts in building the company. Your accountant should be able to help you work out an equitable arrangement.

Q **I lost my biggest customer. Now what do I do?**

Pick yourself up, brush off the dirt, and see what you have to do to get back in the race and stay there. Do the best you can to determine what caused the loss of the customer, but don't dwell on the loss. What you want to know is why you lost the customer and, what, if anything, you can do to prevent a similar problem from arising in the future.

If you lost the work because the customer is having cash flow problems or went out of business, consider whether other customers you have in the same industry might also go belly-up. Be realistic. Times change. Needs change. Industries change. The small business that stays in business is the one that looks to the future as well as the present. If an industry or the local economy is changing, the time to take steps to deal with the change is before the bottom falls out, not after.

Finally, try never to let one customer be the primary source of your company's income.

Q **Should I hire someone who's retired?**

There's no reason not to hire someone who is retired if the person wants to work. Along with the gray hair will come years and years of experience and often a work ethic that can be hard to find in younger employees.

Q **How do I keep employees from stealing my customers or ideas?**

If the possibility of an employee quitting to start a competing business is real, ask your attorney about drawing up a noncompete agreement that would be effective in your state, and then make sure all employees sign it. If your customer list is crucial, try to make sure only trusted employees have access to it and, if possible, that no one employee has access to all of the list.

Q **What if I have to fire someone?**

If you have to fire someone, try to let them know what the reason is, but don't let them talk you out of firing them. They'll always resent the fact you intended to fire them and could try to sabotage your business.

Q **Is there any way to avoid the high costs associated with hiring employees?**

If the work you need done doesn't have to be performed in your office, consider using a reliable independent contractor to do the work. The fee you pay the independent contractor would be deductible on your income taxes, but if the individual works from his or her own home using personal equipment and is free to offer services to other businesses, you can probably avoid having to pay payroll taxes. If you are the only business the individual works for, you might be considered an employer by the IRS, so ask your accountant for guidance if you have any doubt about the nature of the arrangements. You will also avoid the need to buy extra equipment and office furniture.

Another option is to subcontract out jobs to other businesses as the opportunity arises. You could subcontract out an entire job to one or more people (hire one person to write a product brochure and another to do the graphic design and layout) or subcontract out just part of it (you do the writing and hire someone else to do the design). In fact, if you find several reliable independent contractors you might be able to greatly expand the services you offer and the number of clients you can handle.

Q **How can I keep costs down as I grow my business?**

If you work at home, keep the business in the house as long as it is feasible to do so. If you need more space, see if there is a place within the house to expand. An attic or garage or part of the basement might give you the space you need to breathe until the business is making enough money to allow you to move into bigger quarters.

Whether you work at home or away from home, try to determine why you need more space, too. Is it to store files, books, equipment? If so, do you really need to save everything? And if you do, must you retain it in your office? Self-storage facilities might be able to hold what you don't need regularly and allow you to avoid moving to more expensive quarters.

If you do need more space, could you sublet office or warehouse space from another business? Could you rent warehouse space and use it for an office to cut costs? If you will be buying furniture or equipment, consider whether used items might be just as good as new for your purposes.

Another option if you need more space is to add on to your home or to buy a bigger house. If you can do neither, consider whether any relatives might have storage space in their home that you could use. Pay them rent for the space, and you get a business deduction and provide them with some extra income. If the rent you pay them is less than you'd pay for storage space or a larger office, you both benefit.

Q **Where can I get help if I run into problems I don't know how to handle?**

Small businesses today have a wealth of inexpensive or free resources available to them. The appendices in this book contain just a small sampling of the many places you can turn for information and help.

These organizations include the Small Business Administration (SBA), the Service Corps of Retired Executives (SCORE), Offices of Women and Minority Business, the small business specialist at Department of Defense and other government offices, Small Business Development Centers (SBDCs), Small Business Investment Corporations (SBICs), and state, city, or county offices of economic development (see appendix 2). Business and industrial associations, college and university business schools, adult education courses, and online information services can also help your business flourish.

In addition to these resources there is the one resource that will always be close at hand: you.

In the long run it will be *your* vision, *your* ingenuity, and *your* ability to learn from others, work with others, and even help others reach their goals that will carry you and your business into a prosperous future.

Afterword

Do you have a story to share or questions you'd like addressed in future books? Although it is impossible for me to correspond personally by mail with each of you, I am interested in hearing about the problems and successes you have encountered in starting and running your business. Please send your stories as well as any comments you may have about this book to me in care of Attard Communications, P.O. Box 223, Centereach, NY 11720. I can also be reached by electronic mail:

Service	*Electronic Mail Address*
America Online	Janet AC1
GEnie	J. ATTARD

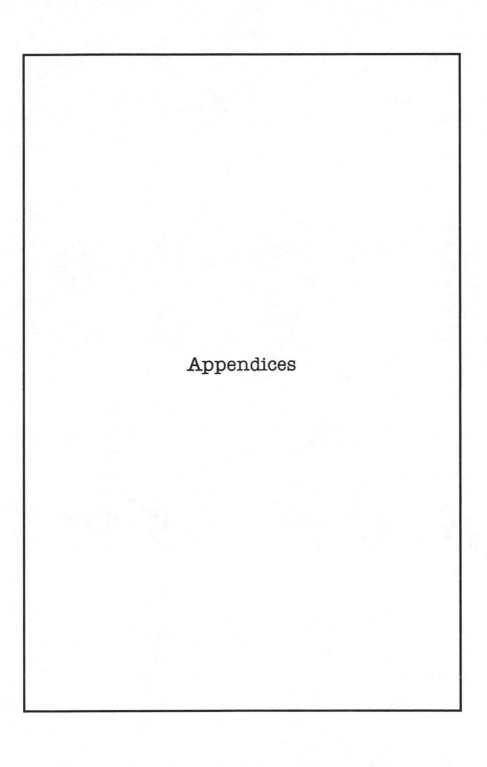

Appendices

Appendix 1

250 BUSINESS IDEAS

The ideas below are presented to get you thinking about the many different types of businesses you might start. The list includes businesses that could be homebased and businesses that would not normally be run from the home. It also includes products or services that might be incorporated as additional profit centers into existing businesses. If you don't see anything in this list that interests you, browse through the Yellow Pages of your phone book, the classified, and the "back of the book" advertising in local newspapers and trade magazines and other speciality publications.

AUTOMOTIVE

auto detailing	quick oil change and lube
body shop	repair shop
car wash	window tinting
custom painting/pinstriping	used-car dealer

BUILDING/HOME SERVICES

carpet cleaning	house and office cleaning service
chimney sweeping	inspection service
closet organizing	landscaping

lawn maintenance
moving company
tree spraying
lawn-care

upholstery/drapery cleaning
water damage cleanup
yard cleanup services

BUSINESS SERVICE

advertising agency
answering service/voice mail service
billing
bookkeeping
collection agency
computer software training
coupon mailer service
database entry and maintenance
desktop publishing/design
desktop publishing/typesetting
employment agency
executive recruiting service
fax broadcast service
freight broker service
job shop
legal transcription
mailbox service

mailing (lettershop) services
mailing list maintenance
market research consultant
medical billing
medical transcription
meeting planner service
newsletter publishing
public relations agency
resume printing
resume typesetting
resume writing
secretarial services
sign shop
temporary employment agency
translation
word processing

COMPUTER-RELATED

computer programming
computer repair

computer systems analyst
computer training

CONSULTING

audiovisual consultant
broadcast consultant
cultural diversity consultant
drug-free workplace

pollution control consultant
recycling consultant
toxic waste consultant

CREATIVE

artist
cartoonist
fashion designer
photographer

writer (see "Writing and Editorial"
    below)
songwriter/composer
bandleader

CRAFTS

custom framing
decorative wood accessories
doll making

jewelry design
pattern design
pottery design

ENVIRONMENT

asbestos inspection
hazardous waste control

hazardous waste inspection
radon testing

FOOD

bed and breakfast inn
candy distributor
catering service
convenience store
delicatessen
delivery services

gourmet café
gourmet lunches
grocery shopping service
meal delivery service
pizza parlor
specialty cookies

FOREIGN TRADE

import-export agent

INFORMATION

computer bulletin board service
information broker
private investigator

self-improvement seminars
seminar promoting

MAIL AND SHIPPING

courier service

lettershop (fold, stuff, meter, prepare mail for bulk mailings)

mail list broker

mail list rental

packaging store

MISCELLANEOUS

annual plants sales

auctioneer

clown

disc jockey

farm stand

home carpentry

home inspection

home painting

laundromat

piano tuner

special events promotions

tax preparation

TV producer

vending machine route

videocassette rental and delivery service

MOBILE SERVICES

ambulette transportation to doctors' offices

car detailing

mobile car wash

pet grooming

traveling auto repair

PERSONAL SERVICE

astrologer

airport taxi

balloon delivery service

beautician

child care

companion to sick

computer dating service

day-care for elderly

dry cleaning pickup and delivery

financial planner

gift basket business

gift shopping

hair salon

interior design

limousine service

medical claims processing

nursing service

pool cleaning/start-up

pool parlor

referral services

shopping service
singing telegram service

tailor
wedding planning

PETS

mobile pet grooming service
pet boarding
pet shop

pet sitting
pet supply mail order

PROFESSIONAL

accountant
anesthesiologist
attorney (general practice)
dentist
doctor
financial manager
franchise attorney

intellectual property attorney
investment banker
orthodontist
physical therapist
sports medicine clinic
veterinarian

PUBLISHING

booklet publisher
local small business directories

newsletter publisher
(also see "Writing and Editorial," page 461)

RENTAL

car rental
equipment rental

prom and wedding gown rental
tuxedo rental

REPAIR

appliance repair
computer repair service
electrician
heating and air conditioning repair

office machine repair
oil burner repair
plumber
TV and VCR repair

RETAIL

antiques dealer
consignment shop
fashion boutique
flea market vendor
florist

health food store
jewelry store
motorcycle and lawnmower parts
sports merchandise
T-shirt shop

SALES

advertising novelties sales
advertising specialities
business brokerage
business machines
computer VAR
computers
custom T-shirts
direct mail catalog sales
discount phone services
household goods

independent distributor
independent sales representative
insurance
makeup
pet supply mail order
print broker
real estate broker
recharged laser cartridges
shareware sales
telemarketing company

TEACHING/INSTRUCTIONS

business writing
computers for kids
crafts
creative writing
dance
drawing/painting
driving school
horseback riding
music

painting
sewing
skiing
spreadsheets
swimming/diving
tennis
tutoring
word processing

WRITING AND EDITORIAL

book reviewer
computer hardware or software
  reviewer
copy editor
copywriter
financial writer
health writer
novelist

proofreader
publicist
science writer
script writer for TV
script writer for audiovisual
  productions
technical writer

Appendix 2

BUSINESS RESOURCES

Associations, Guilds, and Societies

There are trade associations for just about every imaginable industry or specialty. Here are just a few.

American Association for Medical
  Transcription
P.O. Box 576187
Modesto, CA 95357
(800) 982–2182

American Association of Exporters &
  Importers
11 West 42nd Street, 30th fl.
New York, NY 10036
(212) 944–2230

American Bakers Association
1111 14th Street, NW, Suite 300

Washington, DC 20005
(202) 296–5800

American Business Women's Association
9100 Ward Parkway
P.O. Box 8728
Kansas City, MO 64114–0728
(816) 361–6621

American Electronics Association
5201 Great American Parkway
Santa Ana, CA 95054
(408) 987–4200

American Institute of CPAs
1211 Avenue of the Americas
New York, NY 10036
(212) 575–6200

American Society of Interior Designers
608 Massachusetts Avenue, NE
Washington, DC 20002
(202) 546–3480

American Society of Journalists and
    Authors, Inc.
1501 Broadway, Suite 302
New York, NY 10036
(212) 997–0947

American Society of Composers, Authors
    & Publishers
ASCAP Building
One Lincoln Plaza
New York, NY 10023
(212) 621–6000

American Society of Magazine
    Photographers, Inc.
419 Park Avenue South
New York, NY 10016
(212) 889–9144

American Society of Travel Agents
1101 King Street
Alexandria, VA 22314
(703) 739–2782

American Translators Association
1735 Jefferson Davis Highway, Suite 903
Arlington, VA 22202–3413
(703) 892–1500

American Trucking Association
2200 Mill Road

Alexandria, VA 22314
(703) 838–1800

Associated Master Barbers & Beauticians of
    America
1318 Starbrook Drive
Charlotte, NC 28210
(704) 552–6233

Associated Locksmiths of America
3003 Live Oak Street
Dallas, TX 75204
(214) 827–1701

Association of Independent Information
    Professionals (AIIP)
c/o Burwel Enterprises, Inc.
3724 FM 1960 West, Suite 214
Houston, TX 77068
(713) 537–9051

Association of Information Imaging
    Management
100 Wayne Avenue, Suite 1100
Silver Spring, MD 20910
(301) 587–8202
For businesses in the migrographics field.

Association of Management Consultant
    Firms
230 Park Avenue, Suite 544
New York, NY 10169
(212) 697–9693

Association of Shareware Professionals
Executive Director
545 Grover Road
Muskegon, MI 49442–9427
(616) 788–5131

Association of Venture Clubs
265 East 100 South, Suite 300
P.O. Box 3358
Salt Lake City, UT 84110–3358
(801) 364–1100

The Authors Guild, Inc.
330 West 42nd Street
New York, NY 10036–6902
(212) 563–5904

Automotive Parts & Accessories
  Association
4600 East West Highway, Suite 300
Bethesda, MD 20814
(301) 459–9110

B/PAA
Metroplex Corporate Center
100 Metroplex Drive
Edison, NJ 08817
(201) 985–4441
Business-to-business advertising and
marketing.

Computer Press Association
7000 Bianca Avenue
Van Nuys, CA 91411
(818) 996–7000

Center for Family Business
5682 Mayfield Road
Cleveland, OH 44124
(216) 442–0800

Direct Marketing Association
11 West 42nd Street
New York, NY 10036–8096
(212) 768–7277

Direct Selling Association
1776 K Street, NW, Suite 600
Washington, DC 20006
(202) 293–5760

Electronic Industries Association
2001 Pennsylvania Avenue, NW
Washington, DC 20006
(202) 457–4900

Federation of Small Business
407 S. Dearborn, Suite 500
Chicago, IL 60605
(312) 427–0206

Florists Transworld Delivery Association
29200 Northwestern Highway
Southfield, MI 48034
(313) 355–9300

Graphic Artists Guild
11 West 20th Street, 8th fl.
New York, NY 10011–3704
(212) 463–7730

IEEE
345 East 47th Street
New York, NY 10017–2349
(212) 705–7910

Independent Computer Consultants
  Association
933 Gardenview Office Parkway
St. Louis, MO 63141
(800) 438–4222 or (314) 997–4633

Independent Music Association
317 Skyline Lake Drive
P.O. Box 609
Ringwood, NJ 07456
(201) 831–1317

Information Industry Association
555 New Jersey Avenue, NW, Suite 800
Washington, DC 20001
(202) 639–8262

Inland Press Association
777 Busse Highway
Park Ridge, IL 60068
(708) 696–1140
Professional association for daily and
weekly publications.

International Advertising Association
342 Madison Avenue, Suite 2000
New York, NY 10173–0073
(212) 557–1133

International Association of Business
Communicators (IABC)
1 Hallidie Plaza, Suite 600
San Francisco, CA 94102
(800) 776–4222

International Association for Financial
Planning
2 Concourse Parkway, Suite 800
Atlanta, GA 30328
(404) 395–1605 or (800) 945-IAFP

International Car Wash Association
One East 22nd Street, Suite 400
Lombard, IL 60148
(708) 495–0100

International Communications Industries
Association
3150 Spring Street
Fairfax, VA 22031
(703) 273–7200

International Council for Small Business
3674 Lindell Boulevard
St. Louis, MO 63108
(314) 658–3850

International Franchise Association
1350 New York Avenue, NW
Washington, DC 20005
(202) 628–8000

International Reciprocal Trade Association
9513 Beach Mill Road
Great Falls, VA 22066
(703) 759–1473

Investigators Online Network, Ion
Resource Line
6303 S. Rural Road, Suite #1
Temple, AZ 85283
(602) 730–8088

Latin American Management Association
419 New Jersey Avenue, SE
Washington, DC 20003
(800) 522–6623 or (202) 546–3803

Manufacturers Agents Association
23016 Mill Creek Drive
Laguna Hills, CA 92653
(714) 859–4040

Mothers' Home Business Network
P.O. Box 423
East Meadow, NY 11554
(516) 997–7394

National Association for the Cottage
Industry
P.O. Box 14460
Chicago, IL 60614
(312) 472–8116

National Association of Convenience
 Stores
1605 King Street
Alexandria, VA 22314–2792
(703) 684–3600

National Association of Realtors
430 N. Michigan Avenue
Chicago, IL 60611
(312) 329–8200

National Association of Secretarial
 Services
3637 Fourth Street North, Suite 330
St. Petersburg, FL 33704
(813) 823–3646

National Association of Systems Integrators
P.O. Box 440
560 Dedham Street
Wrentham, MA 02093
(508) 384–5850

National Association of Tole and
 Decorative Artists
P.O. Box 808
Newton, KS 67114
(316) 283–9665

National Association of Wholesale
 Distributors
1725 K Street, NW, Suite 710
Washington, DC 20006
(202) 872–0885

National Association for the Self-employed
United Group Service Center
P.O. Box 1116
Hurst, TX 76053–1116
(800) 232–6273

National Association of Women Business
 Owners
600 S. Federal Street, Suite 400
Chicago, IL 60605
(312) 922–0465

National Association of Women in
 Construction
99 Bridge Road
Hauppauge, NY 11788
(516) 348–0505
Association for women who own
construction businesses.

National Candy Wholesalers Association
1120 Vermont Avenue, NW, Suite 1120
Washington, DC 20005
(202) 463–2124

National Cosmetology Association
3510 Olive Street
St. Louis, MO 63103
(314) 534–7980

National Decorating Products Association
1050 N. Lindbergh Boulevard
St. Louis, MO 63132
(314) 991–3470
Dedicated to promoting the independent
decorating products dealer.

National Federation of Independent
 Business, Inc.
600 Maryland Avenue, SW, Suite 700
Washington, DC 20024
(202) 554–9000

National Notary Association
8236 Remmet Avenue
P.O. Box 7184
Canoga Park, CA 91304–7184
(818) 713–4000

National Pest Control Association
8100 Oak Street
Dunn Loring, VA 22027
(703) 573–8330

National Roofing Contractors Association
10255 W. Higgins Road, Suite 600
Rosemont, IL 60018
(708) 299–9070

National Small Business Network
P.O. Box 223
Centereach, NY 11720
(516) 467–6826

National Small Business United
1155 15th Street, NW
Washington, DC 20005
(202) 293–8830

National Speakers Association
3877 N. Seventh Street, Suite 350
Phoenix, AZ 85014
(602) 265–1001

National Tour Association
546 E. Main Street
Lexington, KY, 40508
(606) 253–1036

Owner-Operator Independent Drivers
 Association
311 Mize Road
Grain Valley, MO 64029
(816) 229–5791

Professional Photographers of America
1090 Executive Way
Des Plaines, IL 60018
(708) 299–8161

Professional Picture Framers Association
4305 Sarellen Road
Richmond, VA 23231
(804) 226–0430

Self-Service Storage Association
60 Revere Drive, Suite 500
Northbrook, IL 60062
(708) 480–9627

Small Business Foundation of America
1155 15th Street, NW
Washington, DC 20005
(202) 223–1103
Focuses on exporting.

Society of American Florists
1601 Duke Street
Alexandria, VA 22314
(703) 836–8700

Software Publishers Association
1730 M Street, NW, Suite 700
Washington, DC 20036–4510
(202) 452–1600
Association for those involved in the sale of
software through traditional methods.

Specialty Advertising Association
 International
1404 Walnut Hill Lane
Irving, TX 75038
(214) 580–0404

Trade Show Bureau
1660 Lincoln Street, Suite 2080
Denver, CO 80264
(303) 860–7626
Marketing information about conducting
and exhibiting in trade and consumer
shows.

Travel Industry Association of America
1133 21st Street, NW
Washington, DC 20036
(202) 293–1433

Video Retailers Association (VRA)
2455 East Sunrise Boulevard
Ft. Lauderdale, FL 33304–1877
(305) 561–3505

Video Software Dealers Association
3 Eves Drive, Suite 307
Marlton, NJ 08053
(609) 596–8500

Magazines

ASD/AMD NEWS
2525 Ocean Park Blvd
Santa Monica, CA 90405–5201
Free to members; lists the trade shows; of interest to flea marketers.

Brabec's National Home Business Report
P.O. Box 2137
Naperville, IL 60567

Board Watch
5970 South Vivian Street
Littleton, CO 80127
(800) 933–6038
Covers electronic bulletin board systems.

Business Marketing
Crain Communications, Inc.
740 Rush Street
Chicago, IL 60611
(312) 649–5200

Catalog Age
6 River Bend Center
P.O. Box 4949
Stamford, CT 06907–0949
(203) 358–9900

CD-ROM *World*
Meckler Publishing
11 Ferry Lane West
Westport, CT 06880
(203) 226–6967
A trade magazine for information industry professionals and libraries.

CD-ROM *Professional*
Online, Inc.
462 Danbury Road
Wilton, CT 06897–2126
(203) 761–1466
A trade magazine for information brokers.

Clark Publications
2156 Cotton Patch Lane
Milton, FL 32570
For flea marketers.

Closeout News
202 W. 29th Street
Holland, MI 49423

Computers and Libraries
Meckler Publishing
11 Ferry Lane West

Westport, CT 06880
(203) 226–6967
A trade magazine for information industry
professionals.

Database
Online, Inc.
462 Danbury Road
Wilton, CT 06897–2126
(203) 761–1466
A trade magazine for information brokers.

Database Searcher
Meckler Publishing
11 Ferry Lane West
Westport, CT 06880
(203) 226–6967
A trade magazine for information industry
professionals.

Direct Marketing
224 7th Street
Garden City, NY 11530
(800) 229–6700

Direct Marketing News
19 West 21st Street
New York, NY 10010–6805
(212) 741–2095

The Dream Merchant
2309 Torrance Boulevard, Suite 201
Torrance, CA 90501
(310) 328–1925
A magazine for inventors.

Entrepreneur
2392 Morse Avenue
P.O. Box 19787

Irvine, CA 92714–9438
(800) 274–6229
Focuses on small businesses and franchises.

Environmental Lab
Leo Douglas Publications
9607 Gayton Road, Suite 201
Richmond, VA 23233
(804) 741–6704
Bimonthly; subscription $57 per year;
information for environmental laboratories.

Fair Times
P.O. Box 692
Abington, PA 19001
Flea market publication.

Home Office Computing
730 Broadway
New York, NY 10003
(212) 505–3580

Inbound/Outbound
12 West 21st Street
New York, NY 10010
(212) 691–8215
Telemarketing.

Inc.
38 Commercial Wharf
Boston, MA 02110
(617) 248–8000

Information Today
Learned Information
143 Old Marlton Pike
Medford, NJ 08055
(609) 654–4888

InfoText Magazine
34700 Coast Highway, Suite 308
Capistrano Beach, CA 92624
(714) 493–2434
A trade magazine for the information
industry. Focuses on regulatory and other
issues in pay-per-call businesses.

Library Software Review
Meckler Publishing
11 Ferry Lane West
Westport, CT 06880
(203) 226–6967
A trade magazine for libraries.

Link Up
Learned Information
143 Old Marlton Pike
Medford, NJ 08055
(609) 654–4888
Trade publication about the online
industry.

Marketer's Forum
Forum Publications
383 East Main Street
Centerport, NY 11721
(516) 754–5000
Flea market.

Midnight Engineering
111 E. Drake Road, Suite 7041
Fort Collins, CO 80525
(303) 225–1410
For "entrepreneurial" engineers.

Nation's Business
1615 H Street, NW
Washington, DC 20062
(800) 638–6582

New Business Opportunities
2392 Morse Avenue
P.O. Box 19787
Irvine, CA 92714–9438
(800) 274–6229

Office Systems
941 Danbury Road
P.O. Box 150
Georgetown, CT 06829
(203) 544–9526

Office Dealer
941 Danbury Road
P.O. Box 150
Georgetown, CT 06829
(203) 544–9526

Online
Online, Inc.
462 Danbury Road
Wilton, CT 06897–2126
(203) 761–1466
A trade magazine for information brokers.

Online Access
Chicago Fine Print, Inc.
920 N. Franklin Street, Suite 203
Chicago, IL 60610
(312) 573–1700
Quarterly magazine about online computer
services. Available on newsstands or by
subscription.

Small Business Opportunities
Harris Publications, Inc.
1115 Broadway
New York, NY 10010
(212) 807–7100

Success Magazine
P.O. Box 3038
Harlan, IA 51537
(800) 234–7324
Focuses on small business.

Teleconnect
12 West 21st Street
New York, NY 10010
(212) 691–8215
Focus on telecommunications and long-distance technology.

Telemarketing
One Technology Plaza
Norwalk, CT 068854–9977
(800) 243–6002

Water & Engineering Management
380 E. Northwest Highway
Des Plaines, IL 60016–2282
(708) 298–6622
Focuses on the water and wastewater industry.

Writer's Digest
1507 Dana Avenue
Cincinnati, OH 45207
(800) 333–0133

U.S. Government

Bureau of Economic Analysis
Washington, DC 20230
(202) 523–0777

Census Bureau
Washington, DC 20230
(202) 763–7662

Commerce Business Daily
Daily publication listing U.S. Government contracts and grants. Available by subscription from the superintendent of documents or by computer access from the Air Force Small Business RoundTable on the GEnie online service. Superintendent of documents phone: (202) 783–3238; GEnie client service phone: (800) 638–9636

Consumer Information Center
Department 91
Pueblo, CO 81009
Offers a free catalog that lists two hundred free or very low-cost informative booklets published by the U.S. government on subjects such as getting loans, getting jobs, and dieting.

Copyright Office
Library of Congress
Washington, DC 20559
Information and forms order line:
(202) 707–3000

Defense Logistics Agency
P.O. Box 1370
Federal Center

Battle Creek, MI 49017–3092
(616) 961–7014

Department of Agriculture
14th Street and Independence Avenue, SW
Cooperative State Research Service
Washington, DC 20250
(202) 720–4423

Department of Commerce
Bureau of Economic Analysis
Washington, DC 20230
(202) 523–0777

Department of Defense
U.S. Air Force Office of Small and
Disadvantaged Business Utilization
Air Force Small Business Bulletin Board
Procurement information and help doing
business with the government, offered on-
line through the GEnie service.

Department of Education
National Institute on Disability and
    Rehabilitation Research (NIDRR)
Washington, DC 20202–2572
(202) 732–1134
Grant information: (202) 732–1207

Department of Energy
1000 Independence Avenue, SW
Washington, DC 20585
(202) 586–5000

Department of Housing and Urban
    Development
Program Information Center
451 7th Street, SW
Washington, DC 20410
(202) 708–1420

Department of Labor
200 Constitution Avenue, NW
Washington, DC 20210
(202) 523–6666

Environmental Protection Agency
Small Business Ombudsman
(800) 368–5888
An advocate and source of information for
small businesses about hazardous wastes,
asbestos abatement, and environmental
regulations.

Export-Import Bank
811 Vermont Avenue, NW
Washington, DC 20571
(202) 566–8990
Help with exporting and importing.

Federal Communications Commission
1919 M Street, NW
Washington, DC 20554
(202) 632–5050 and (202) 632–6363

Federal Domestic Assistance Catalog
General Services Administration
300 7th Street, SW
Washington, DC 20407
(202) 708–5082
Lists U.S. government assistance programs
and grants.

Government Printing Office
941 N. Capitol Street, NE
Washington, DC 20401
(202) 783–3238
Offers a catalog of the many useful business
information publications issued by the
government. You can order publications by
writing the Superintendent of Documents

Office, Washington, DC 20402, (202) 783–3238.

Internal Revenue Service (IRS)
Tax Help Line
(800) 829–1040
This IRS tax help line will put you in touch with a live person (rather than a recording). If you need help with your taxes, the IRS offers taxpayer assistance and training programs as well as one-on-one help. You can also get dozens of useful publications from the IRS to help explain the tax laws.

International Trade Administration
Washington, DC 20230
(202) 377–2000
Offers help with import/export issues. Offices located throughout the country.

Library of Congress
Washington, DC 20540
(202) 707–5000

National Agricultural Statistics Service
Washington, DC 20250
Phone: (202) 447–4021

Office of Minority Business Enterprise
14th Street, between E Street and
   Constitution Avenue, NW
Washington, DC 20230
(202) 377–2000

Patent and Trademark Office
Washington, DC 20231
For forms, call: (703) 557–3158
For answers to questions, call: (703) 308-
   HELP
For information about patent and
   trademark depository libraries call (703)
   308–3924

Service Corps of Retired Executives
(SCORE)
Offers one-on-one counseling for business start-ups in hundreds of offices located throughout the United States. Help comes from volunteers who have built successful businesses themselves. Find the nearest SCORE office by calling the SBA Answer Desk at (800) 827–5722 and following the instructions to get information about local assistance. If there is an SBA office or SBDC (see pages 474–482) near you, they should be able to point you to a SCORE office as well.

Small Business Administration

Small Business Administration (SBA)
1441 L Street, NW
Washington, DC 20461
(800) 827–5722
The Small Business Administration was created by Congress in 1953 to foster the growth of small businesses in the United

States. It sponsors a variety of programs that help businesses gain management skills, get loans and bonds, and obtain government contracts. The agency also functions as an advocate for small business, representing small business concerns to Congress and federal agencies. To find out more about the SBA and help that may be available to you, look in the blue pages of your phone book under the United States government listings for the nearest Small Business Administration office. If you can't find a listing, call the SBA Answer Desk at (800) 827–5722, or call one of the regional offices below and ask where you can get help and information locally.

SBA Small Business Answer Desk
1441 L Street, NW

Washington, DC 20461
(800) 827–5722
Prerecorded information for businesses and referrals to local SBA offices.

SBA Pass
U.S. Small Business Administration
P.O. Box 9000
Melbourne, FL 32902–9919
Database of small businesses designed to help prime contractors find subcontractors.

SMALL BUSINESS ADMINISTRATION REGIONAL OFFICES

SBA Region I Office
60 Batterymarch Street, 10th fl.
Boston, MA 02110
(617) 451–2030

SBA Region II Office
26 Federal Plaza, Room 31–08
New York, NY 10278
(212) 264–7772

SBA Region III Office
Allendale Square, Suite 201
475 Allendale Road
King of Prussia, PA 19406
(215) 962–3700

SBA Region IV Office
1375 Peachtree Street, NE, 5th fl.
Atlanta, GA 30367–8102
(404) 347–2441

SBA Region V Office
230 South Dearborn Street, Room 510
Chicago, IL 60604–1593
(312) 353–0359

SBA Region VI Office
8625 King George Drive, Building C
Dallas, TX 75235–3391
(214) 767–7643

SBA Region VII Office
911 Walnut Street, 13th fl.
Kansas City, MO 64106
(816) 426–2989

SBA Region VIII Office
999 18th Street, North Tower, Suite 701
Denver, CO 80202
(303) 844–3984

SBA Region IX Office
450 Golden Gate Avenue
Box 36044
San Francisco, CA 94102
(415) 556–7489

SBA Region X Office
2615 Fourth Avenue, Room 440
Seattle, WA 98121
(206) 442–5676

Small Business Administration
Office of Innovation, Research and
  Technology
409 Third Street, SW, 8th fl.
Washington, DC 20416
(202) 205–7777

The U.S. government's Small Business Innovation Research Program (SBIR) funds selected technological research. To find out what general research projects are coming up each quarter, write to the SBIR at the above address and ask to be put on the mailing list to get presolicitation announcements.

SBIR Contacts at U.S. Agencies

U.S. Department of Education SBIR
SBIR Program Coordinator
U.S. Department of Education
555 New Jersey Avenue, NW, Room
  602F
Washington, DC 20208
(202) 219–2050

U.S. Department of Energy SBIR
SBIR Spokesperson—ER-16
c/o SBIR Program Manager
U.S. Department of Energy
Washington, DC 20585
(301) 903–5867

U.S. Department of Health and Human
  Services SBIR
SBIR Program Manager
Office of the Secretary
U.S. Department of Health and Human
  Service
Washington, DC 20201
(202) 245–7300

U.S. Department of Transportation
  SBIR
Chief, University Research, Technology

Innovation and Programs Office (DTS-
  22)
U.S. Department of Transportation
  Research and Special Programs
  Administration Volpe National
  Transportation Systems Center
Kendall Square
Cambridge, MA 02142–1093
(617) 494–2051

U.S. Environmental Protection Agency
  SBIR
SBIR Program Manager
Research Grants Staff (RD-65)
Office of Research and Development
Environmental Protection Agency
401 M Street, SW
Washington, DC 20460
(202) 260–7473

U.S. Aeronautics and Space
  Administration SBIR
Program Director, SBIR Office—Code
  CR National Aeronautics and Space
Administration Headquarters
Washington, DC 20546
(703) 271–5659

National Science Foundation SBIR
SBIR Program Manager
National Science Foundation—V-502
1800 G Street, NW
Washington, DC 20550
(202) 653–5002

Nuclear Regulatory Commission SBIR
SBIR Program Representative
Program Management, Policy
    Development, and Analysis Staff
U.S. Nuclear Regulatory Commission
Washington, DC 20555
(301) 492–3625

U.S. Department of Agriculture SBIR
Director, SBIR Program
U.S. Department of Agriculture
Aerospace Building, Room 323-J
901 D Street, SW
Washington, DC 20250–2200

U.S. Department of Commerce SBIR
Director, Office of Small and
    Disadvantaged Business Utilization
U.S. Department of Commerce
14th Street and Constitution Avenue,
    NW
HCHB, Room 6411
Washington, DC 20230

DOC SBIR Program Manager
Suitland Professional Center
SPC, Room 307
Suitland, MD 20233
(301) 763–4240

U.S. Department of Defense SBIR
SBIR Program Manager
OSD/SADBU
U.S. Department of Defense
The Pentagon-Room 2A340
Washington, DC 20301–3061
(703) 697–1481

SMALL BUSINESS DEVELOPMENT CENTERS (SBDCs)

Small Business Development Centers (SBDCs) are jointly funded by the Small Business Administration and by state governments. They provide a wealth of resources for business people, including low-cost or free seminars, counseling, help in understanding how to write business plans, etc. SBDCs are often located at colleges and universities. There are hundreds of them throughout the United States. The list below contains the contact information for each state director's office. Call or write to find your nearest SBDC.

ALABAMA

Alabama Small Business Development
  Center
University of Alabama at Birmingham
Medical Towers Building
1717 11th Avenue South, Suite 419
Birmingham, AL 35294–4410
(205) 934–7260/FAX: (205) 934–7645

ALASKA

University of Alaska
Small Business Development Center
430 West 7th Avenue, Suite 110
Anchorage, AK 99501
(907) 274–7232/FAX (907) 274–9524

ARIZONA

Arizona Small Business Development
  Center
9215 N. Black Canyon Highway
Phoenix, AZ 85021
(602) 943–9818/FAX: (602) 943–3716

ARKANSAS

Arkansas Small Business Development
  Center
University of Arkansas at Little Rock
Little Rock Technology Center Building
100 South Main, Suite 401
Little Rock, AR 72201
(501) 324–9043/FAX: (501) 324–9049

CALIFORNIA

California Small Business Development
  Center
California Department of Commerce
Office of Small Business
801 K Street, Suite 1700
Sacramento, CA 95814
(916) 324–5068/FAX: (916) 322–5084

COLORADO

Small Business Development Center
Office of Economic Development
1625 Broadway, Suite 1710
Denver, CO 80202
(303) 892–3809 or (303) 892–3840
FAX: (303) 892–3848

CONNECTICUT

Connecticut Small Business Development
  Center
University of Connecticut

School of Business Administration
368 Fairfield Road
Box U-41, Room 422
Storrs, CT 06268
(203) 486–4135/FAX: (203) 486–1576

DELAWARE

Delaware Small Business Development
  Center
University of Delaware
Purnell Hall, Suite 005
Newark, DE 19716
(302) 831–2747/FAX: (302) 831–1423

DISTRICT OF COLUMBIA

District of Columbia Small Business
  Development Center
Howard University
6th and Fairmount Street, NW, Room 128
Washington, DC 20059
(202) 806–1550/FAX: (202) 806–1777

FLORIDA

Florida Small Business Development Center
  Network
University of West Florida
11000 University Parkway
Pensacola, FL 32514
(904) 474–3016/FAX: (904) 474–2092

GEORGIA

Georgia Small Business Development
  Center
University of Georgia
Chicopee Complex

1180 East Broad Street
Athens, GA 30602
(404) 542–6785/FAX: (404) 542–6776

HAWAII

Hawaii Small Business Development Center
University of Hawaii at Hilo
523 W. Lanikaula Street
Hilo, HI 96720–4091
(808) 933–3515/FAX: (808) 933–3683

IDAHO

Idaho Small Business Development Center
Boise State University
College of Business
1910 University Drive
Boise, ID 83725
(208) 385–1640/FAX: (208) 385–3877

ILLINOIS

Illinois Small Business Development Center
  Network
Illinois Department of Commerce and
  Community Affairs
620 East Adams Street, 6th fl.
Springfield, IL 62701
(217) 524–5856/FAX: (217) 785–6328

INDIANA

Indiana Small Business Development
  Center
Economic Development Council
One North Capitol, Suite 420
Indianapolis, IN 46204
(317) 264–6871/FAX: (317) 264–3102

IOWA

Iowa Small Business Development Center
Iowa State University
College of Business Administration
Chamberlynn Building
137 Lynn Avenue
Ames, IA 50010
(515) 292–6351/FAX: (515) 292–0020

KANSAS

Kansas Small Business Development Center
Wichita State University
1845 Fairmount
Wichita, KS 67260–0148
(316) 689–3193/FAX: (316) 689–3647

KENTUCKY

Kentucky Small Business Development
  Center
University of Kentucky
Center for Business Development
College of Business and Economics
225 Business and Economics Building
Lexington, KY 40506–0034
(606) 257–7668/FAX: (606) 258–1907

LOUISIANA

Louisiana Small Business Development
  Center
Northeast Louisiana University
Adm. 2–57
Monroe, LA 71209
(318) 342–5506/FAX: (318) 342–5510

MAINE

Maine Small Business Development Center
University of Southern Maine

99 Falmouth Street
Portland, ME 04103
(207) 780–4420/FAX: (207) 780–4810

MARYLAND

Maryland Small Business Development
Center
Department of Economic and Employment
Development
217 East Redwood Street, 10th fl.
Baltimore, MD 21202
(410) 333–6995/FAX: (410) 333–6609

MASSACHUSETTS

Massachusetts Small Business Development
Center
University of Massachusetts
205 School of Management
Amherst, MA 01003
(413) 545–6301/FAX: (413) 545–1273

MICHIGAN

Michigan Small Business Development
Center
2727 Second Avenue
Detroit, MI 48201
(313) 577–4848/FAX: (313) 577–4222

MINNESOTA

Minnesota Small Business Development
Center
Department of Trade and Economic
Development
900 American Center Building
150 East Kellogg Boulevard
St. Paul, MN 55101
(612) 297–5770/FAX: (612) 296–1290

MISSISSIPPI

Mississippi Small Business Development
Center
University of Mississippi
Old Chemistry Building, Suite 216
University, MS 38677
(601) 232–5001/FAX: (601) 232–5650

MISSOURI

Missouri Small Business Development
Center
University of Missouri
University Place, Suite 300
Columbia, MO 65211
(314) 882–0344/FAX: (314) 884–4297

MONTANA

Montana Small Business Development
Center
Department of Commerce
1424 Ninth Avenue
Helena, MT 59620
(406) 444–4780/FAX: (406) 444–2808

NEBRASKA

Nebraska Small Business Development
Center
University of Nebraska at Omaha
60th and Dodge Streets
CBA, Room 407
Omaha, NE 68182
(402) 554–2521/FAX: (402) 554–3747

NEW HAMPSHIRE

New Hampshire Small Business
Development Center
University of New Hampshire

108 McConnell Hall
Durham, NH 03824
(603) 862–2200/FAX: (603) 862–4468

New Jersey Small Business Development
  Center
Rutgers Graduate School of Management
University Heights
180 University Avenue
Newark, NJ 07102
(201) 648–5950/FAX: (201) 648–1110

New Mexico Small Business Development
  Center
Santa Fe Community College
P.O. Box 4187
Santa Fe, NM 87502–4187
(505) 438–1362/FAX: (505) 438–1237

New York Small Business Development
  Center
State University of New York at Albany
State University Plaza, S523
Albany, NY 12246
(518) 443–5398 or (800) 732–7232
FAX: (518) 465–4992

North Carolina Small Business
  Development Center
University of North Carolina
4509 Creedmoor Road, Suite 201
Raleigh, NC 27612
(919) 571–4154/FAX: (919) 571–4161

North Dakota Small Business Development
  Center
University of North Dakota
118 Gamble Hall
Box 7308
Grand Forks, ND 58202
(701) 777–3700/FAX: (701) 777–5099

Ohio Small Business Development Center
Department of Development
State Office Tower
P.O. Box 1001
Columbus, OH 43266–0101
(614) 466–2480/FAX: (614) 466–0829

Oklahoma Small Business Development
  Center Network
Southeastern Oklahoma State University
Station A, Box 2584
Durant, OK 74701
(405) 924–0277 or (800) 522–6154
FAX: (405) 924–8531

Oregon Small Business Development
  Center Network
Lane Community College
99 W. 10th Avenue, Suite 216
Eugene, OR 97401
(503) 726–2250/FAX: (503) 345–6006

Pennsylvania Small Business Development
  Center

University of Pennsylvania
The Wharton School
444 Vance Hall
Philadelphia, PA 19104–6374
(215) 898–1219/FAX: (215) 573–2135

PUERTO RICO

Puerto Rico Small Business Development
 Center
University of Puerto Rico
Box 5253-College Station
UPR-Mayaguez Campus, Building B
Mayaguez, PR 00681
(809) 834–3590/FAX: (809) 834–3790

RHODE ISLAND

Rhode Island Small Business Development
 Center
Bryant College
1150 Douglas Pike
Smithfield, RI 02917
(401) 232–6111/FAX: (401) 232–6416

SOUTH CAROLINA

South Carolina Small Business
 Development Center
University of South Carolina
College of Business Administration
Columbia, SC 29208
(803) 777–5118/FAX: (803) 777–4403

SOUTH DAKOTA

South Dakota Small Business Development
 Center
University of South Dakota
414 East Clark
Vermillion, SD 57069
(605) 677–5272/FAX: (605) 677–5427

TENNESSEE

Tennessee Small Business Development
 Center
Memphis State University
South Campus (Getwell Road)
Building #1
Memphis, TN 38152
(901) 678–2500/FAX: (901) 678–4072

TEXAS

North Texas Small Business Development
 Center
Dallas County Community College
1402 Corinth Street
Dallas, TX 75215
(214) 565–5837/FAX: (214) 565–5857

UTAH

Utah Small Business Development Center
University of Utah
102 West 500 South, #315
Salt Lake City, UT 84101
(801) 581–7905/FAX: (801) 581–7814

VERMONT

Vermont Small Business Development
 Center
One Blair Park, Suite 13
Williston, VT 05495–9404
(802) 878–0181/FAX: (802) 878–0245

VIRGINIA

Virginia Small Business Development
 Center
1021 East Cary Street, 11th fl.

P.O. Box 798
Richmond, VA 23219
(804) 371–8258/FAX: (804) 371–8185

VIRGIN ISLANDS

Virgin Islands Small Business Development
  Center
University of the Virgin Islands
Grand Hotel Building, Annex B
P.O. Box 1087
St. Thomas, VI 00804
(809) 776–3206/FAX: (809) 775–3756

WASHINGTON

Washington Small Business Development
  Center
Washington State University
245 Todd Hall
Pullman, WA 99164–4727
(509) 335–1576/FAX: (509) 335–0949

WEST VIRGINIA

West Virginia Small Business Development
  Center
West Virginia Development Office
1115 Virginia Street, East
Capitol Complex
Charleston, WV 25301–2406
(304) 558–2960/FAX: (304) 558–0127

WISCONSIN

Wisconsin Small Business Development
  Center
University of Wisconsin
432 North Lake Street, Room 423
Madison, WI 53706
(608) 263–7794/FAX: (608) 262–3878

WYOMING

Wyoming Small Business Development
  Center
111 West 2nd Street, Suite 416
Casper, WY 82601
(307) 235–4825/FAX: (307) 473–7243

Office of Women's Business Ownership

The Office of Women's Business Ownership (OWBO) was created to offer potential and established women entrepreneurs a range of services and resources, which include counseling, training conferences, workshops, and technical and financial information. The following list contains the addresses of OWBO offices throughout the country.

ALABAMA

Business Development Specialist
Small Business Administration
2121 8th Avenue, Suite 200
Birmingham, AL 35203–2398
(205) 731–1338

ALASKA

Business Development Specialist
Small Business Administration
Federal Building, #67
222 West 8th Avenue
Anchorage, AK 99513–7559
(907) 271–4022

ARIZONA

District Counsel
Small Business Administration
2828 N. Center Ave., Suite 800
Phoenix, AZ 85004–1025
(602) 640–2316

ARKANSAS

Minority Small Business
Small Business Administration
320 West Capitol, Suite 601
Little Rock, AR 72201
(501) 324–5871

CALIFORNIA

ADD/Business Development
Small Business Administration
2719 N. Air Fresno Drive, 5th fl.
Fresno, CA 93727–1547
(209) 487–5189

Business Development Officer
Small Business Administration
330 N. Brand Boulevard, Suite 1200
Glendale, CA 91203–2304
(213) 894–2956

Region IX Coordinator
5900 Wilshire Boulevard, #700
Los Angeles, CA 90036
(213) 938–3933

Loan Specialist
Small Business Administration
660 J Street, Suite 215
Sacramento, CA 95814–2413
(916) 551–1431

Business Development Officer
Small Business Administration
800 Front Street, Room 4-S-29
San Diego, CA 92188–0270
(619) 557–7252, ext. 46

Regional WBO Coordinator
Small Business Administration
71 Stevenson Street, 20th fl.
San Francisco, CA 94105–2939
(415) 744–6432

Business Development Specialist
Small Business Administration
211 Main Street, 4th fl.
San Francisco, CA 94105–1988
(415) 744–6771

Business Development Specialist
Small Business Administration
901 W. Civic Center Drive, Suite 160
Santa Ana, CA 92703–2352
(714) 836–2494

COLORADO

Surety Bond Guarantee Specialist
Small Business Administration
999 18th Street, Suite 701
Denver, CO 80202
(303) 294–7067

ADD/Business Development
Small Business Administration
721 19th Street
Denver, CO 80202
(303) 844–3986

CONNECTICUT

Business Management Specialist
Small Business Administration
330 Main Street, 2nd fl.
Hartford, CT 06106
(203) 240–4642

DELAWARE

Program Assistant
Small Business Administration
One Rodney Square, Suite 412
920 North King Street
Wilmington, DE 19801
(302) 573–6295

DISTRICT OF COLUMBIA

OWBO SCORE Liaison
Small Business Administration
409 Third Street, SW, 6th fl.
Washington, DC 20416
(202) 205–6673

OWBO Director
Small Business Administration
409 Third Street, SW, 6th fl.
Washington, DC 20416
(202) 205–6673

Women's Business Representative
Small Business Administration
1111 18th Street, NW
Washington, DC 20036
(202) 634–1500, ext. 258
Main number: (202) 634–1500

FLORIDA

Business Development Specialist
Small Business Administration
1320 S. Dixie Highway, Suite 501
Coral Gables, FL 33146
(305) 536–5521

Region IV Coordinator
141 Green Heron Court
Daytona Beach, FL 32119
(612) 825–4971

Business Development Specialist
Small Business Administration
7825 Bay Meadows Way, Suite 100B
Jacksonville, FL 32256–7504
(904) 443–1912

GEORGIA

Surety Bond Guarantee Specialist
Small Business Administration
1375 Peachtree Street, NE
Atlanta, GA 30367
(404) 347–2386

Business Development Specialist
Small Business Administration
1720 Peachtree Street, NW, 6th fl.

Atlanta, GA 30309
(404) 347–2356

HAWAII

ADD/Business Development
Small Business Administration
30 Ala Moana, Room 2213
P.O. Box 50207
Honolulu, HI 96850–4981
(808) 541–2973

IDAHO

WBOR
Small Business Administration
1020 Main Street, Suite 290
Boise, ID 83702
(208) 334–1780

ILLINOIS

Business Development Program Specialist
Small Business Administration
300 South Riverside, Room 1975S
Chicago, IL 60606
(312) 353–7702

ADD/Business Development
Small Business Administration
500 West Madison Street, Suite 1250
Chicago, IL 60606
(312) 353–4578

Business Development Specialist
Small Business Administration
511 West Capitol Street, Suite 302
Springfield, IL 62704
(217) 492–4416

INDIANA

WBOR
Small Business Administration
429 North Pennsylvania Street, Suite 100
Indianapolis, IN 46204
(317) 226–7269

IOWA

Region VII Coordinator
2613 Cedar Heights
Cedar Falls, IA 50613
(319) 266–6631

Loan Specialist
Small Business Administration
373 Collins Road, NE
Cedar Rapids, IA 52402
(319) 393–8630

Business Development Specialist
Small Business Administration
210 Walnut Street, Room 749
Des Moines, IA 50309
(515) 284–4762

KANSAS

General Attorney
Small Business Administration
110 East Waterman Street
Witchita, KS 67202
(316) 269–6191

KENTUCKY

Loan Officer
Small Business Administration
Dr. Martin Luther King, Jr., Plaza,
    Room 188

Louisville, KY 40201
(502) 582–5971

Baltimore, MD 21202
(301) 962–2235

LOUISIANA

Business Development Specialist
Small Business Administration
1661 Canal Street, 2nd fl.
New Orleans, LA 70112
(504) 589–2354

MASSACHUSETTS

Commercial Marketing Representative
Small Business Administration
155 Federal Street, 9th fl.
Boston, MA 02110
(617) 451–2040

Business Development Specialist
Small Business Administration
10 Causeway Street, Room 265
Boston, MA 02222–1093
(617) 565–5636

WBOR
Small Business Administration
1550 Main Street, Room 212
Springfield, MA 01103
(413) 785–0268

MARYLAND

National Volunteer Director
907 Sextant Way
Annapolis, MD 21401
(301) 266–8746

Business Development Specialist
Small Business Administration
10 North Calvert Street, 4th fl.

MAINE

Business Development Assistant
Small Business Administration
40 Western Avenue, Room 512
Augusta, ME 04330
(207) 622–8242

MINNESOTA

Region V Coordinator
Johnson Consulting Services
P.O. Box 32372
Minneapolis, MN 55432–0372
(612) 571–3101

MICHIGAN

Business Development Specialist
Small Business Administration
477 Michigan Avenue
Detroit, MI 48226
(313) 226–6075, ext. 23

Business Development Specialist
Small Business Administration
610 C Butler Square
Minneapolis, MN 55403
(612) 370–2312

MISSOURI

WBO Coordinator
Small Business Administration
911 Walnut Street, 13th fl.
Kansas City, MO 64106
(816) 426–5311

Loan Specialist (Commercial)
Small Business Administration
1103 Grand Avenue, 5th fl.
Kansas City, MO 64106
(816) 374–6701

Public Affairs Specialist
Small Business Administration
815 Olive Street, Suite 242
St. Louis, MO 63101
(314) 539–6600

Business Development Specialist
Small Business Administration
620 South Glenstone, Suite 110
Springfield, MO 65802–3200
(417) 864–7670

MISSISSIPPI

Loan Officer
Small Business Administration
1 Hancock Plaza, Suite 1001
Gulfport, MS 39501
(601) 863–4449

ADD/MSB
Small Business Administration
101 West Capitol Street, Suite 400
Jackson, MS 39201
(601) 965–5323

MONTANA

Business Development Specialist
Small Business Administration
301 S. Park Avenue, Room 528
Helena, MT 59626–0054
(406) 449–5381

NEBRASKA

Loan Specialist
Small Business Administration
11145 Mill Valley Road
Omaha, NE 68154
(402) 221–3626

NEVADA

ADD/Business Development
Small Business Administration
301 East Stewart, Box 7527
Downtown Station
Las Vegas, NV 89125–2527
(702) 388–6611

NEW HAMPSHIRE

Business Development Assistant
Small Business Administration
55 Pleasant Street, Room 211
Concord, NH 03301
(603) 225–1400

NEW JERSEY

Business Development Specialist
Small Business Administration
Military Park Building
60 Park Place, 4th fl.
Newark, NJ 07102
(201) 645–3683

NEW MEXICO

Business Development Specialist
Small Business Administration
625 Siver SW, Room 320
Albuquerque, NM 87110
(505) 766–18879

NEW YORK

Business Development Officer
Small Business Administration
445 Broadway, Room 236-A
Albany, NY 12207
(518) 472–6300

Business Development Technician
Small Business Administration
111 W. Huron Street, Room 1311
Buffalo, NY 14202
(716) 846–4517

Assistant Branch Manager
Small Business Administration
Elmira Savings Bank Building
333 East Water Street
Elmira, NY 14901
(607) 734–8142

Business Development Specialist
Small Business Administration
35 Pinelawn Road, Room 102E
Melville, NY 11747
(516) 454–0753

WBO Coordinator
Small Business Administration
26 Federal Plaza, Room 3108
New York, NY 10278
(212) 264–1046

WBO Representative
Small Business Administration
26 Federal Plaza, Room 3100
New York, NY 10278
(212) 264–1458

Region II Coordinator
16 Cady Street
Rochester, NY 14608
(716) 328–8012

Business Development Technician
Small Business Administration
Federal Building
100 State Street
Rochester, NY 14614
(716) 263–6700

Business Development Technician
Small Business Administration
100 S. Clinton Street, Room 1071
Syracuse, NY 13260
(315) 423–5375

NORTH CAROLINA

Business Development Specialist
Small Business Administration
200 North College Street, Suite A2015
Charlotte, NC 28202–2173
(704) 371–6587

NORTH DAKOTA

Region VIII Coordinator
2450 15th Street S., #202
Fargo, ND 58103
(710) 237–4366

Business Development Specialist
Small Business Administration
657 2nd Avenue North, Room 218
P.O. Box 3088
Fargo, ND 58102
(701) 239–5131

OHIO

Business Development Specialist
Small Business Administration
550 Main Street, Room 5028
Cincinnati, OH 45202
(513) 684–2814

Business Development Specialist
Small Business Administration
85 Marconi Boulevard
Columbus, OH 43215
(614) 469–6860, ext. 274

Business Development Specialist
Small Business Administration
1240 E. 9th Street, Room 317
Cleveland, OH 44199
(216) 522–8236

OKLAHOMA

Support Services Supervisor
Small Business Administration
200 N.W. 5th Street, Suite 670
Federal Building
Oklahoma City, OK 73102
(405) 231–4884

OREGON

Loan Officer
Small Business Administration
222 S.W. Columbia Avenue, Room 500
Portland, OR 97201–6605
(503) 326–5202

Region X Coordinator
7931 North East Halsey, Suite 200
Portland, OR 97213
(503) 257–0803

PENNSYLVANIA

ARA/Business Development Specialist
Small Business Administration
475 Allendale Square Road, Suite 201
King of Prussia, PA 19406
(215) 962–3729

District Counsel
Small Business Administration
960 Penn Avenue, 5th fl.
Pittsburgh, PA 15222
(412) 644–2785

PUERTO RICO

Business Development Specialist
Small Business Administration
Carlos Chardon Avenue
Hato Rey, PR 00918
(809) 766–5001

RHODE ISLAND

Region I Coordinator
73 East Hill Drive
Cranston, RI 02920
(401) 944–4008

Business Management Specialist
Small Business Administration
380 Westminister Mall
Providence, RI 02903
(401) 528–4598

SOUTH CAROLINA

Business Development Specialist
Small Business Administration
1835 Assembly Street, Room 358
Columbia, SC 29202
(803) 253–3360

SOUTH DAKOTA

Business Development Specialist
Small Business Administration
101 S. Main Avenue, Suite 101
Sioux Falls, SD 57102
(605) 330–4231

TENNESSEE

Business Development Specialist
Small Business Administration
50 Vantage Way, Suite 201
Nashville, TN 37228
(615) 736–7176

TEXAS

Business Development Specialist
Small Business Administration
400 Mann Street, Suite 403
Corpus Christi, TX 78401
(512) 888–3333

Business Development Specialist
Small Business Administration
8625 King George Drive, Building C
Dallas, TX 75235–3391
(214) 767–7687

Business Development Specialist
Small Business Administration
1100 Commerce Street, Room 3C36
Dallas, TX 75242
(214) 767–0386

Loan Officer
Small Business Administration
10737 Gateway West, Suite 320
El Paso, TX 79902
(915) 540–5564

Business Development Specialist
Small Business Administration
222 E. Van Buren Street, Suite 500
Harlingen, TX 78550
(512) 427–8533

Business Development Specialist
Small Business Administration

2525 Murworth, Suite 112
Houston, TX 77054
(713) 660–4426

Business Development Specialist
Small Business Administration
1611 10th Street, Suite 200
Lubbock, TX 79401
(806) 743–7462

Contact Representative
Small Business Administration
7400 Blanco Road, Suite 200
North Star Executive Center
San Antonio, TX 78216
(512) 229–4535

Region VI Coordinator
7610 Basque
Waco, TX 76610
(817) 750–3600

VERMONT

Loan Specialist
Small Business Administration
87 State Street, Room 204
P.O. Box 605
Montpelier, VT 05602
(802) 828–4422

WASHINGTON

Business Development Project Officer
Small Business Administration
2615 4th Street, Room 440
Seattle, WA 98121
(206) 553–2460

WBOR Representative
Small Business Administration

915 2nd Avenue, Room 1792
Seattle, WA 98174
(206) 553–4436

Loan Officer
Small Business Administration
West 601 First Avenue
10th Floor East
Spokane, WA 99204
(509) 353–2815

UTAH

Paralegal Specialist
Small Business Administration
Federal Building
125 South State Street
Salt Lake City, UT 84138–1195
(801) 524–3203

VIRGINIA

Business Development Technician
Small Business Administration
400 North 8th Street, Room 3015
P.O. Box 10126
Richmond, VA 23240
(804) 771–2765

VIRGIN ISLANDS

Loan Specialist F&I
Small Business Administration
United Shopping Plaza, Room 7
4 C/D State Sion Farm
Christiansted, St. Croix
Virgin Islands 00801
(809) 778–5380

Business Industry Specialist
Small Business Administration
Federal Office Building, Room 283
Veterans Drive
St. Thomas, Virgin Islands 00801
(809) 774–8530

WEST VIRGINIA

Loan Officer
Small Business Administration
168 West Main Street
P.O. Box 1608
Clarksburg, WV 26302
(304) 623–5631

WISCONSIN

Business Development Specialist
Small Business Administration
212 E. Washington Ave., Rm. 213
Madison, WI 53703
(608) 264–5516

Business Development
Small Business Administration
310 West Wisconsin Avenue
Milwaukee, WI 53202
(414) 291–3941

WYOMING

Business Development Specialist
Small Business Administration
100 East B Street, Room 4001
P.O. Box 2839
Casper, WY 82602
(307) 261–5761

Minority Business Development Centers

The Minority Business Development Agency has established 103 Minority Business Development Centers (MBDCs) and Indian Business Development Centers (IBDCs) in thirty-six states. These centers, listed below by region, provide counseling and managerial and technical assistance to minority entrepreneurs in an effort to increase their business opportunities in U.S. and international markets.

ATLANTA REGION

Alabama	Georgia	Mississippi	South Carolina
Florida	Kentucky	North Carolina	Tennessee

MBDA Regional Director
1371 Peachtree St., NE, Suite 505
Atlanta, GA 30309
(404) 347–4091

Business Development Specialist
MBDA Miami District Office
Federal Office Building, Room 928
51 S.W. First Avenue
P.O. Box 25
Miami, FL 33130
(305) 536–5054

Atlanta MBDC
75 Piedmont Avenue, NE, Suite 256
Atlanta, GA 30303
(404) 586–0973

Augusta MBDC
1208 Laney Walker Boulevard
Augusta, GA 30901–2796
(404) 722–0994

Birmingham MBDC
2100 16th Avenue South, Suite 203
Birmingham, AL 35205
(205) 930–9254

Charleston MBDC
701 E. Bay Street, Suite 1539
Charleston, SC 29403
(803) 724–3477

Charlotte MBDC
700 East Stonewall Street, Suite 360
Charlotte, NC 28202
(704) 334–7522

Cherokee IBDC
Alquoni Road, Box 1200
Cherokee, NC 28719
(704) 497–9335

Cherokee IBDC
165 French Broad Avenue
Asheville, NC 28801
(704) 252–2516

Columbia MBDC
2700 Middleburg Drive
Columbia, SC 29204
(803) 256–0528

Columbus MBDC
1214 First Avenue, Suite 430

Columbus, GA 31902–1696
(404) 324–4253

Fayetteville MBDC
114½ Anderson Street
Fayetteville, NC 28302
(919) 483–7513

Greenville/Spartanburg MBDC
300 University Ridge, Suite 200
Greenville, SC 29601
(803) 271–8753

Jackson MBDC
1350 Livingston Lane, Suite A
Jackson, MS 39213
(601) 362–2260

Jacksonville MBDC
333 N. Laura Street, Suite 465
Jacksonville, FL 32202–3508
(904) 353–3826

Louisville MBDC
835 W. Jefferson Street, Suite 103
Louisville, KY 40202
(502) 589–7401

Memphis MBDC
5 North Third Street, Suite 2000
Memphis, TN 38103
(901) 527–2298

Miami/Ft. Lauderdale MBDC
1200 N.W. 78th Avenue, Suite 301
Miami, FL 33126
(305) 591–7355

Mobile MBDC
801 Executive Park Drive, Suite 104
Mobile, AL 36606
(205) 471–5165

Montgomery MBDC
770 S. McDonough Street, Suite 207
Montgomery, AL 36104
(205) 834–7598

Nashville MBDC
404 J. Robertson Parkway, Suite 1920
Nashville, TN 37219
(615) 255–0432

Orlando MBDC
132 E. Colonial Drive, Suite 211
Orlando, FL 32801
(407) 422–6234

Raleigh/Durham MBDC
817 New Bern Avenue, Suite 8
Raleigh, NC 27601
(919) 833–6122

Savannah MBDC
31 W. Congress Street, Suite 201
Savannah, GA 31401
(912) 236–6708

Tampa/St. Petersburg MBDC
5020 W. Cypress, Suite 217
Tampa, FL 33607
(813) 228–7555

West Palm Beach MBDC
2001 Broadway, Suite 301
Riveria Beach, FL 33404
(407) 393–2530

CHICAGO REGION

Illinois	Iowa	Minnesota	Ohio
Indiana	Kansas	Missouri	Wisconsin
	Michigan	Nebraska	

MBDA Regional Director
55 E. Monroe Street, Suite 1440
Chicago, IL 60603
(312) 353–0182

Chicago 1 MDBC
35 E. Wacker Drive, Suite 790
Chicago, IL 60601
(312) 977–9190

Chicago 2 MBDC
600 Prudential Plaza
Chicago, IL 60601
(312) 565–4710

Cincinnati MBDC
113 W. Fourth Street, Suite 600
Cincinnati, OH 45202
(513) 381–4770

Cleveland MBDC
601 Lakeside, Suite 335
Cleveland, OH 44114
(216) 664–4150

Columbus MBDC
37 North High Street
Columbus, OH 43215
(614) 225–6959

Detroit MBDC
65 Cadillac Square, Suite 3701
Detroit, MI 48226–2822
(313) 961–2100

Gary MBDC
567 Broadway
Gary, IN 46402
(219) 883–5802

Indianapolis MBDC
617 Indiana Avenue, Suite 319
Indianapolis, IN 46202
(317) 685–0055

Kansas City MBDC
1000 Walnut Street, Suite 1000
Kansas City, MO 64106
(816) 221–6504

Milwaukee MBDC
3929 N. Humboldt Boulevard
Milwaukee, WI 53212
(414) 332–6268

Minneapolis MBDC
2021 E. Hennepin Avenue, Suite 370
Minneapolis, MN 55413
(612) 387–0361

Minnesota IBDC
3045 Farr Avenue
Cass Lake, MN 56633
(218) 335–8583

St. Louis MBDC
500 Washington Avenue, Suite 1200
St. Louis, MO 63101
(314) 621–6232

DALLAS REGION

Arkansas	Montana	Oklahoma	Utah
Colorado	New Mexico	South Dakota	Wyoming
Louisiana	North Dakota	Texas	

MBDA Regional Director
1100 Commerce Street, Room 7B23
Dallas, TX 75242
(214) 767–8001

Albuquerque MBDC
718 Central SW
Albuquerque, NM 87102
(505) 843–7114

Austin MBDC
301 Congress Avenue, Suite 1020
Austin, TX 78701
(512) 476–9700

Baton Rouge MBDC
2036 Woodale Boulevard, Suite D
Baton Rouge, LA 70806
(504) 924–0186

Beaumont MBDC
550 Fannin, Suite 106A
Beaumont, TX 77701
(409) 835–1377

Corpus Christi MBDC
3649 Leopard, Suite 514
Corpus Christi, TX 78404
(512) 887–7961

Dallas/Ft. Worth MBDC
1445 Ross Avenue, Suite 800
Dallas, TX 75202
(214) 855–7373

Denver MBDC
4450 Morrison Road
Denver, CO 80219
(303) 937–1005

Houston MBDC
1200 Smith Street, Suite 2800
Houston, TX 77002
(713) 650–3831

Laredo MBDC
777 Calledelnorte No. 2
Laredo, TX 78401
(512) 725–5177

Little Rock MBDC
One Riverfront Place, Suite 415
North Little Rock, AK 72114
(501) 372–7312

Lubbock/Midland-Odessa MBDC
1220 Broadway, Suite 509
Lubbock, TX 79401
(512) 762–6232

McAllen MBDC
1701 W. Business Highway 83, Suite 1108
McAllen, TX 78501
(512) 687–5224

New Mexico IBDC
2401 Twelfth Street, NW
Albuquerque, NM 87197–6507
(505) 889–9092

New Orleans MBDC
1683 North Clayborne
New Orleans, LA 70116
(504) 947–1491

North Dakota IBDC
3315 University Drive
Bismarck, ND 58501–7596
(701) 255–3225

Oklahoma City MBDC
1500 N.E. 4th Street, Suite 101
Oklahoma City, OK 73117
(405) 235–0430

Oklahoma IBDC
5727 Garnett, Suite H
Tulsa, OK 74146
(918) 250–5950

Salt Lake City MBDC
350 East 500 South, Suite 100
Salt Lake City, UT 84111
(801) 328–8181

San Antonio MBDC
UTSA, Hemisphere Tower
San Antonio, TX 78285
(512) 224–1945

Shreveport MBDC
202 North Thomas Drive, Suite 16
Shreveport, LA 71108
(318) 226–4931

Tulsa MBDC
240 East Apache Street
Tulsa, OK 74106
(918) 592–1995

NEW YORK REGION

Connecticut | Massachusetts | New York | Vermont
Maine | New Hampshire | Puerto Rico | Virgin Islands
| New Jersey | Rhode Island |

MBDA Regional Director
26 Federal Plaza, Room 3720
New York, NY 10278
(212) 264–3262

District Officer
MBDA Boston District Office
10 Causeway Street, Room 418
Boston, MA 02222–1041
(617) 565–6850

Boston MBDC
985 Commonwealth Avenue
Boston, MA 02215
(617) 353–7060

Bronx MBDC
Call (212) 779–4360 for current
information.

Brooklyn MBDC
16 Court Street, Room 1903
Brooklyn, NY 11201
(718) 522–5880

Buffalo MBDC
523 Delaware Avenue
Buffalo, NY 14202
(716) 885–0336

Connecticut MBDC
410 Asylum Street, Suite 243
Hartford, CT 06103
(203) 246–5371

Manhattan MBDC
51 Madison Avenue, Suite 2212
New York, NY 10010
(212) 779–4360

Mayaguez MBDC
70 West Mendez Bigo
Mayaguez, PR 00708
(809) 833–7783

Nassau/Suffolk MBDC
150 Broad Hollow Road, Suite 304
Melville, NY 11747
(516) 549–5454

New Brunswick MBDC
134 New Street, Room 102
New Brunswick, NJ 08901
(201) 247–2000

Newark MBDC
60 Park Place, Suite 1404
Newark, NJ 07102
(201) 623–7712

Ponce MBDC
19 Salud Street
Ponce, PR 00731
(809) 840–8100

Queens MBDC
110–29 Horace Harding Expressway
Corona, NY 11368
(718) 699–2400

Rochester MBDC
111 East Avenue, Suite 218
Rochester, NY 14604
(716) 232–6120

San Juan MBDC
207 O'Neill Street
San Juan, PR 00936
(809) 753–8484

Virgin Islands MBDC
81-AB Princess Gade
St. Thomas, VI 00804
(809) 774–7215

Williamsburg MBDC
12 Heywood Street
Brooklyn, NY 11211
(718) 522–5880

SAN FRANCISCO REGION

Alaska	Arizona	Hawaii	Oregon
American Somoa	California	Nevada	Washington

MBDA Regional Director
221 Main Street, Room 1280
San Francisco, CA 94105
(415) 974–9597

District Officer
MBDA Los Angeles District Office
977 North Broadway, Suite 201
Los Angeles, CA 90012
(213) 894–7157

Alaska MBDC
1557 C Street, Plaza, Suite 200
Anchorage, AK 99501
(907) 274–5400

Anaheim MBDC
6 Hudson Center Drive, Suite 1050
Santa Ana, CA 92707
(714) 542–2700

Arizona IBDC
2111 East Baseline Road, Suite F-8
Tempe, AZ 85283
(602) 831–7524

Bakersfield MBDC
218 South H Street, Suite 103
Bakersfield, CA 93304
(805) 837–0291

California IBDC
9650 Flair Drive, Suite 303
El Monte, CA 91731
(818) 442–3701

Fresno MBDC
2010 N. Fine, Suite 103
Fresno, CA 93727
(209) 252–9551

Honolulu MBDC
1001 Bishop Street, Suite 2900
Honolulu, HI 96813
(808) 536–0066

Las Vegas MBDC
716 South Sixth Street
Las Vegas, NV 89101
(702) 384–3293

Los Angeles MBDC
3807 Wilshire Boulevard, Suite 700
Los Angeles, CA 90010
(213) 380–9541

Oxnard MBDC
451 W. Fifth Street
Oxnard, CA 93030
(805) 483–1123

Phoenix MBDC
1661 East Camelback, Suite 210
Phoenix, AZ 85016
(602) 277–7707

Portland MBDC
8959 S.W. Barbur Boulevard, Suite 102
Portland, OR 97219
(503) 245–9253

Riverside MBDC
1060 Cooley Drive, Suite F
Colton, CA 92324
(714) 824–9695

Sacramento MBDC
530 Bercut Drive, Suite C&D
Sacramento, CA 95814
(916) 443–0700

Salinas MBDC
123 Capital Street, Suite B
Salinas, CA 93901
(408) 754–1061

San Francisco MBDC
One California Street, Suite 2100
San Francisco, CA 94111
(415) 989–2920

San Jose MBDC
150 Almaden Boulevard
San Jose, CA 95150
(408) 275–9000

Santa Barbara MBDC
4141 State Street, Suite B-4
Santa Barbara, CA 93110
(805) 964–1136

Seattle MBDC
155 N.E. 100th Avenue, Suite 401
Seattle, WA 98125
(206) 525–5617

Stockton MBDC
5361 N. Pershing Avenue, Suite F
Stockton, CA 95207
(209) 477–2098

WASHINGTON, DC, REGION

Delaware	Maryland	Virginia	West Virginia
	Pennsylvania	Washington, DC	

MBDA Regional Director
14th & Constitution Avenue, NW, Room
  H-6711
Washington, DC 20230
(202) 377–8275

Business Development Specialist
MBDA Philadelphia District Office
Federal Office Building
600 Arch Street, Room 10128
Philadelphia, PA 19106
(215) 597–9236

MBDA Pittsburgh District Office
614–16 Federal Office Building
1000 Liberty Avenue
Pittsburgh, PA 15222
(412) 644–6659

Baltimore MBDC
2901 Druid Park Drive, Suite 201
Baltimore, MD 21215
(301) 383–2214

Newport News MBDC
6060 Jefferson Avenue, Suite 6016
Newport News, VA 23605
(804) 245–8743

Norfolk MBDC
355 Crawford Parkway, Suite 608
Portsmouth, VA 23701
(804) 399–0888

Philadelphia MBDC
801 Arch Street
Philadelphia, PA 19107
(215) 629–9841

Pittsburgh MBDC
Nine Parkway Center, Suite 250
Pittsburgh, PA 15220
(412) 921–1155

Washington MBDC
1133 15th Street, NW, Suite 1120
Washington, DC 20005
(202) 785–2886

Books for Further Reading

COMPUTERS

Banks, Michael A. *The Modem Reference.* Englewood Cliffs, NJ: Brady/Simon and Schuster, 1991.

Glossbrenner, Alfred. *Glossbrenner's Guide to Shareware for Small Businesses.* New York: Windcrest/McGraw-Hill, 1992.

Pournelle, Jerry, and Mike Banks. *Pournelle's Guide to PC Communications.* Redmond, WA: Microsoft Press, 1991.

Shenot, Robert. *The Shareware Book.* 1992. (How to make money writing and selling shareware. Available by downloading from online services; or in printed format, by contacting Robert Schenot, Compass/New England, Broad Street, P.O. Box 117, Portsmouth, NH 03802–0117; 603–431–8030.)

DIRECTORIES AND GUIDES

Kissling, Mark, ed. *Writer's Market.* Cincinnati: Writer's Digest Books, 1992. (Listing of places writers can sell their work.)

Martindale Hubbell Law Directory. Martindale-Hubbell, a division of Reed Publishing. Published annually.

Pratt's Guide to Venture Capital Sources. Edited by Venture Economics staff. Phoenix: Oryx Press. Published annually.

Standard Rate and Data Service (SRDS), a series of media directories.

DO-IT-YOURSELF LAW BOOKS

Barrett, E. Thorpe. *Write Your Own Business Contracts.* Grants Pass, OR: The Oasis Press, 1991.

Clifford, Denis, and Ralph Warner. *The Partnership Book: How to Write a Partnership Agreement.* Berkeley: Nolo Press, 1991.

Crawford, Tad. *Business & Legal Forms for Authors & Self-Publishers.* New York: Allworth Press, 1990.

Kramer, Felix, and Maggie Lovaas. *Desktop Publishing Success.* Homewood, IL: Business One Irwin, 1991.

Levinson, Jay Conrad. *Guerrilla Marketing.* Boston: Houghton Mifflin, 1984.

Levinson, Jay Conrad. *Guerrilla Marketing Attack.* Boston: Houghton Mifflin, 1989.

McQuown, Judith H. *Inc. Yourself; How to Profit by Setting Up Your Own Corporation.* New York: HarperCollins, 1992.

Remer, Daniel, and Stephen Elias. *Legal Care for Your Software.* Berkeley: Nolo Press, 1987.

Salone, M. J., and Stephen Elias. *How to Copyright Software.* Berkeley: Nolo Press, 1989.

MISCELLANEOUS BUSINESS BOOKS

Arden, Lynie. *The Work-at-Home Source Book.* Boulder, CO: Live Oak, 1992.

Basista, Paul. *Graphic Artists Guild Handbook, Pricing and Ethical Guidelines.* New York: Graphic Artists Guild, Inc., 1991.

Bolles, Richard Nelson. *What Color Is Your Parachute.* Berkeley: Ten Speed Press, 1992.

DuLude Claudia. *How To Start Your Own 900 Service.* Denver: IdealDial (You can order by writing to: IdealDial, 910 15th Street, Suite 900, Denver, CO 80202, 800–582–3425.)

Mastin, Robert. *900 Know-How: How to Succeed with Your Own 900 Number Business.* Newport, RI: Aegis Publishing Group, 1992. (Write: 796 Aquidneck Avenue, Newport, RI 02840, or call 401–849–4200.)

Mooney, Sean. *Insuring Your Business.* New York: Insurance Information Institute Press, 1992.

Novick, Harold J. *Selling Through Independent Reps.* New York: AMACOM, 1988.

Rugge, Sue, and Alfred Glossbrenner. *The Information Brokers Handbook.* New York: Windcrest/McGraw Hill, 1992.

TAX GUIDES

Bernstein, Peter W., ed. *The Ernst & Young Tax Guide.* New York: John Wiley & Sons. Published annually.

Esanu, Warren H., Barry Dickman, Elias M. Zuckerman, and Michael N. Pollet. *Consumer Reports Books Guide to Income Tax Preparation.* New York: Consumer Reports Books. Published annually.

H & R Block Income Tax Guide. New York: Collier Books. Published annually.

J. K. Lasser Institute. *J. K. Lasser's Your Income Tax.* Englewood Cliffs, NJ: Prentice Hall. Published annually.

Appendix 3

SUGGESTED RETENTION SCHEDULE FOR BUSINESS RECORDS*

The retention schedule below was compiled by Fellowes Manufacturing Company and is based on a combination of record storage experts' recommendations and a survey of actual business practices. The list is reprinted here courtesy of the Fellowes Manufacturing Company.

The schedule is presented here as a general guideline only. It may have to be adapted to meet legal requirements of your state and/or of any federal agency regulations** with which your business must comply. Be sure to check with appropriate state and federal authorities or with your CPA for any specifics for your business. In addition, there may be a very good reason to keep records longer than legally required for historical reference purposes.

 Key:

The letter *P* means Permanently, *O* stands for Optional; otherwise figures represent the suggested number of years for retaining the records.

---

*Fellowes Manufacturing Company, © 1986. Reprinted with permission of Fellowes Manufacturing Company.
**For retention requirements established by federal laws and regulations, see the current "Guide to Record Retention Requirements" published annually in the Federal Register, which can be obtained at nominal cost from the Superintendent of Documents, U.S. Government Printing Office, Washington, DC 20402.

Accounting and Fiscal Records

Accounts, charged off	7	Correspondence, credit and collection	7
Accounts payable ledger	P	Cost account records	7
Accounts receivable	10	Customer ledger	P
Accounts receivable ledger	10	Donations	7
Balance Sheets	5	Drafts paid	8
Bank deposit record	6	Earnings register	3
Bank reconcilement papers	8	Entertainment, gifts and gratuities	3
Bank statements	8	Estimates, projections	7
Bills collectible	7	Expense reports, departmental	5
Bills of sale of registered bonds	3	Expense reports, employees	5
Bill stubs	7	Financial statements, certified	P
Bonds cancelled	3	Financial statements, periodic	P
Bonds registered	P	Fixed capital records	P
Bonds, sales or transfer	15	General cash book	25
Budget work sheets	3	General journal	10
Building permits	20	General journal supporting papers	P
Capital stock bills of sales	P	General ledger	P
Capital stock certificates	P	Notes, cancelled	10
Capital stock ledger	P	Note ledgers	P
Capital stock transfer records	P	Payroll register	7
Cash books	25	Petty cash records	3
Cash receipts and disbursement records	10	Plant ledger	P
Cash sales slips	3	Profit and loss statements	P
Charge slips	10	Property asset summary	10
Check records	7	Royalty ledger	P
Check register	10	Salesperson commission reports	3
Checks, dividend	10	Stock ledger	P
Checks, expense	10	Tabulating cards and magnetic tape	1
Checks, paid and cancelled	9	Traveling auditor reports	15
Checks, payroll	7	Trial balance, accounts receivable	3
Checks, voucher	6	Trial balance sheets	P
Checks, warrants	P	Uncollectible accounts	7
Correspondence, accounting	5	Work papers, rough	2

Administrative

Audit reports, internal	10	Classified documents; control, inventories, reports	5
Audit reports, public and government	P		
Audit work papers, internal	6	Correspondence, accounting	5

Correspondence, advertising	3	Forms control	5
Correspondence, credit and collection	7	Inventory cards	3
		Inventory, plant records	P
Correspondence, engineering and technical	10	Organized charts	P
		Requisitions	3
Correspondence, general	3	Research reports	20
Correspondence, personal	6	System and procedure records	P
Correspondence, sales and service	3	Telegram and cable copies	3
Correspondence, tax	20	Telephone records	P
Correspondence, traffic	6		

Advertising

Activity reports, media schedules	5	Estimates	2
Contracts	10	House organs	P
Contracts, advertising	7	Market data and surveys	5
Correspondence	5	Samples, displays, labels, etc.	P
Drawings and artwork	P	Tear sheets	3

Corporate

Annual reports	P	Incorporation records and certificates	P
Authority to issue securities	P	Licenses, federal, state, local	P
Authorization and appropriations for expenditures	3	Permits to do business	P
Bonds, surety	10	Records of mergers, consolidations, acquisitions, dissolutions, and reorganizations	P
Capital stock certificates	P		
Capital stock ledger	P		
Capital stock transfer records	P	Reports to Securities and Exchange Commission	P
Charters, constitution, bylaws, and amendments	P	Stock applications for issuance	P
Contracts, employee	P	Stock certificates, cancelled	10
Contracts, government	P	Stock, stock transfer and stockholders records	P
Contracts, labor union	P		
Contract, vendor	10	Stockholder minute books, resolutions	P
Dividend checks	10		
Easements	P	Stockholder proxies	10
Election ballots	20	Stockholder reports	P
Election records, corporate	10	Voter proxies	15
General cashbooks, treasurers', auditors'	25		

Executive

Correspondence	2	Research reports	20
Policy statements, directives	P	Speeches, publications	10
Projects, ideas, notes	P		

Insurance

Accident reports	11	Expired policy, hospital	6
Appraisals	P	Expired policy, inspection certificates	7
Claims, automobile	10	Expired policy, liability	7
Claims, group life and hospital	4	Expired policy, life	7
Claims, loss or damage in transit	7	Expired policy, marine	7
Claims, plant	P	Expired policy, property	8
Claims, workers' compensation	10	Expired policy, surety	10
Expired policy, accident	7	Expired policy, workers' compensation	10
Expired policy, fidelity	7		
Expired policy, fire	6		
Expired policy, group	6		

Legal

Affidavits	10	Copyrights	P
Charters	P	Patents and related data	P
Claims and litigation of torts and breach of contract	P	Trademarks	P

Manufacturing

Authorities for sale of scrap	3	Job records	10
Bills of material	5	Journals	10
Blueprints	30	Ledgers	P
Correspondence, engineering and technical	10	Operating reports	10
Correspondence, production	2	Order register	6
Credit memoranda	5	Production reports	6
Credit ratings and classifications	2	Quality control reports	5
Drafting records	8	Receipts, delivery	3
Drawings and tracings, original	P	Reliability records	P
Inspection records	5	Specifications, customer	P
Inventory records	16	Store issue records	3
Invoice copies	5	Time and motion studies	P
Invoices, received	7	Tool control	5
		Work orders	5

Personnel

Accident reports, injury claims, settlements	11	Payroll records, after termination	P
Applications, changes, terminations	3	Pension plan	P
Attendance records	6	Pension plan, applications	P
Clock records	4	Pension plan, claims	P
Correspondence	6	Pension plan, correspondence	P
Daily time reports	5	Rating cards	5
Disability and sick benefits records	8	Salary and rate changes	10
Earnings records	P	Salespeople auto records	2
Employee service records	P	Salespeople performance records	P
Employee contracts	7	Salespeople expense accounts	4
Fidelity bonds	3	Time cards	5
File, individual employee, after separation	3	Time tickets	5
		Time tickets, receipted	5
Garnishments	7	Training manuals	P
Health and Safety bulletins	4	Union (collective bargaining) agreements after termination	6
Injury frequency charts	10		
Insurance records: group, employee	6	Withholding exemption certificates after termination	8
Medical folders, employee	5		
Pay checks	P	Workers' compensation reports	10

Plant and Property

Appraisals	P	Plans and specifications	P
Damage reports	7	Plant account cards, equipment records, historical folders	P
Deeds, titles	P		
Depreciation schedules	3	Purchase, lease records	1
Inventory records	6	Sales	7
Leases	6	Space allocation records	2
Maintenance and repair, buildings	10	Taxes	P
Maintenance and repair, machinery	5	Water rights	P

Purchasing

Acknowledgments	3	Purchase requisitions	1
Bids, awards	3	Quotations	3
Contracts	5	Receiving reports	6
Correspondence	5	Receiving slips	4
Exception notices	6	Vendors' contracts	P
Purchase orders	3		

Sales and Marketing

Claims (loss or damage)	5	Invoices, received	7
Complaints	5	Mailing and prospect lists	2
Contract progress reports	3	Market research studies and analysis	P
Contracts, customers	6	Market surveys	5
Contracts, representatives, agents, distributors, etc.	3	Orders acknowledgment	4
		Orders filled	8
Correspondence	3	Price lists	P
Discount rates	5	Shipping notices and reports	4
Guarantees, warranties	6	Tax-exempt sales	5
Invoices, copies	6		

Taxation

Agent's reports	P	Excise reports	5
Annuity or deferred payment plan	P	Inventory reports	16
Correspondence	20	Real estate	15
Depreciation schedules	3	Sales and use	P
Dividend register	P	Social security	P
Employee withholding certificates (after termination)	8	Tax bills and statements	P
		Tax returns and working papers	P
Exemption status	P		

Traffic

Aircraft operating and maintenance	10	Receiving documents	5
Bills of lading	3	Routing records	1
Delivery of reports	3	Shipping instructions	6
Employee travel	1	Shipping tickets	6
Export declarations	4	Title papers	P
Freight bills	5	Tonnage summaries	P
Freight claims	5	Tracer reports	P
Leases	6	Vehicle operation and maintenance	4
Manifests	1		

Appendix 4

STATE TAX DEPARTMENT ADDRESSES AND PHONE NUMBERS

You will need to comply with state as well as federal tax laws. The list below contains the addresses, phone numbers, and official names of the tax departments in all of the states. New York City and Washington, DC, tax department numbers are included as well.

ALABAMA

Department of Revenue
Income Tax Forms
P.O. Box 327410
Montgomery, AL 36132–7410
(205) 242–1000

ALASKA

Department of Revenue
State Office Building
P.O. Box 110420
Juneau, AK 99811
(907) 465–2320

ARIZONA

Department of Revenue
Attention: Forms
1600 West Monroe Street
Phoenix, AZ 85007
(602) 542–4260

ARKANSAS

Department of Finance and Administration
Revenue Division
P.O. Box 3628
Little Rock, AR 72203
(501) 682–7255

508

CALIFORNIA

Franchise Tax Board
Tax Forms Request
P.O. Box 942840
Sacramento, CA 94240–0070

COLORADO

Department of Revenue
1375 Sherman Street
Denver, CO 80261
(303) 534–1208

CONNECTICUT

Department of Revenue Services
State Tax Department
92 Farmington Avenue
Hartford, CT 06105
(203) 566–8520

DELAWARE

Department of Finance
Division of Revenue, Delaware State
  Building
820 N. French Street
Wilmington, DE 19801
(302) 577–3300

FLORIDA

Department of Revenue
Supply Department
Carlton Building
Tallahassee, FL 32310
(904) 488–6272

GEORGIA

Income Tax Unit
Department of Revenue

Trinity-Washington Building
Atlanta, GA 30334
(404) 656–4293, 4071

HAWAII

First Taxation District
830 Punch Bowl Street
P.O. Box 259
Honolulu, HI 96809
(808) 548–3270

IDAHO

State Tax Commission
P.O. Box 36
Boise, ID 83722
(208) 334–3660

ILLINOIS

Illinois Department of Revenue
P.O. Box 19010
Springfield, IL 62794–9010
(217) 782–3336

INDIANA

Indiana Department of Revenue
100 N. Senate Avenue
Indianapolis, IN 46204
(317) 232–2189

IOWA

Iowa Department of Revenue and Finance
Taxpayer Services Section
Hoover State Office Building
Des Moines, IA 50319
(515) 281–3114

KANSAS

Department of Revenue
Division of Taxation
Taxpayer Assistant Bureau
P.O. Box 12001
Topeka, KS 66612–2001
(913) 296–0222

KENTUCKY

Revenue Cabinet
Property and Mail Service
Frankfort, KY 40620
(502) 564–3658

LOUISIANA

Department of Revenue
P.O. Box 201
Baton Rouge, LA 70821
(504) 925–7532

MAINE

Bureau of Taxation
Income Tax Division
State Office Building
Augusta, ME 04333
(207) 289–3695

MARYLAND

Comptroller of the Treasury
Income Tax Division
State Income Tax Building
Annapolis, MD 21411
(301) 974–3117

MASSACHUSETTS

Massachusetts Department of Revenue
Taxpayer Assistance Bureau

100 Cambridge Street
Boston, MA 02204
(617) 727–4545

MICHIGAN

Michigan Department of the Treasury
Revenue Administrative Services
430 West Allegan
Treasury Building
Lansing, MI 48933
(517) 373–3200

MINNESOTA

Minnesota Department of Revenue
Mail Station 4450
St. Paul, MN 55146
(612) 296–3781

MISSISSIPPI

Mississippi State Tax Commission
P.O. Box 960
Jackson, MS 39205
(601) 359–1141

MISSOURI

Tax Administration Bureau
P.O. Box 2200 "A"
Jefferson City, MO 65105
(314) 751–3505

MONTANA

Montana Department of Revenue
Income Tax Division
P.O. Box 5805
Helena, MT 59604
(406) 444–2981

NEBRASKA

Nebraska Department of Revenue
Box 94818
Lincoln, NE 68509–4818
(402) 471–2971

NEVADA

Department of Taxation
Capitol Complex
1340 South Curry Street
Carson City, NV 89710
(702) 885–4892

NEW HAMPSHIRE

Department of Revenue Administration
State of New Hampshire
61 South Spring Street
Concord, NH 03302
(603) 271–2191

NEW JERSEY

Division of Taxation
50 Barrack Street—CN240
Trenton, NJ 08646
(609) 292–5185

NEW MEXICO

Taxation and Revenue Department
Revenue Division
P.O. Box 630
Sante Fe, NM 87504
(505) 827–0700

NEW YORK CITY

NYC Department of Finance
Bureau of Tax Collection

P.O. Box 3900
Church Street Station
New York, NY 10008
(718) 935–6739, 6000

NEW YORK STATE

Department of Taxation and Finance
Taxpayer Service Bureau
W. Averell Harriman Campus
Albany, NY 12227
(518) 457–2772

NORTH CAROLINA

NC Department of Revenue
P.O. Box 25000
Raleigh, NC 27640
(919) 733–3991

NORTH DAKOTA

Office of State Tax Commissioner
State Capitol
600 East Boulevard Avenue
Bismark, ND 58505–0599
(701) 224–3450

OHIO

Department of Taxation
Income Tax Division
P.O. Box 2476
Columbus, OH 43266
(614) 433–7750

OKLAHOMA

Oklahoma Tax Commission
Income Tax Division
2501 Lincoln Boulevard

Oklahoma City, OK 73194
(405) 521–3108

OREGON

Oregon Department of Revenue
955 Center Street, NE
Salem, OR 97310
(503) 378–4988

PENNSYLVANIA

Commonwealth of Pennsylvania
Department of Revenue
Strawberry Square
Harrisburg, PA 17128
(717) 787–8201

RHODE ISLAND

Rhode Island Division of Taxation
1 Capitol Hill
Providence, RI 02908
(401) 277–3934

SOUTH CAROLINA

South Carolina Tax Commission
Individual Income Tax Division
P.O. Box 125
Columbia, SC 29214
(803) 737–5000

SOUTH DAKOTA

Department of Revenue
700 Governors Drive
Pierre, SD 57501–2276
(605) 773–3311

TENNESSEE

Department of Revenue
Andrew Jackson State Office Building
Room 807
500 Deaderick Street
Nashville, TN 37242
(615) 741–3133

TEXAS

Comptroller of Public Accountants
State of Texas
111 East 17th Street
Austin, TX 78711
(512) 463–4600

UTAH

Utah State Tax Commission
160 E. 300 S. Heber Wells Building
Salt Lake City, UT 84134
(801) 530–6306

VERMONT

Vermont Department of Taxes
Pavilion Office Building
Montpelier, VT 05602
(802) 828–2515

VIRGINIA

Department of Taxation
Taxpayers Assistance
P.O. Box 1115
Richmond, VA 23208–1115
(804) 367–8031

WASHINGTON

Department of Revenue
General Administration Building
Olympia, WA 98504
(206) 753–5540

WASHINGTON, DC

Government of District of Columbia
Department of Finance and Revenue
Room 2053
300 Indiana Avenue, NW
Washington, DC 20001
(202) 727–6104, 6105

WEST VIRGINIA

State Tax Department
Taxpayer Service Division

P.O. Box 3784
Charleston, WV 25337–3784
(304) 348–3333

WISCONSIN

Wisconsin Department of Revenue
P.O. Box 8903
Madison, WI 53708
(608) 266–1961

WYOMING

The State of Wyoming
Secretary of State
Capitol Building
Cheyenne, WY 82002
(307) 777–7378

Glossary

2/10 net 30

If this phrase or one like it appears on an invoice, it means that the purchaser of the goods may take a 2 percent discount if they pay the bill within 10 days. If they choose not to pay in 10 days, the full amount of the bill is due in 30 days.

Accounts payable

These are your bills—the money you owe suppliers and vendors.

Accounts receivable

Money (bills or account) that is owed to you for goods or services purchased by customers but not paid for at the time of sale.

Adjusted gross income (AGI)

On income taxes, your total income minus any adjustments to income. Taxable income is your adjusted gross income minus your deductions.

Agent (insurance)

An insurance agent is a salesperson who represents one or more insurance companies. An exclusive agent represents only one company; an independent agent is an independent contractor who is a sales representative for more than one insurance company. See also *broker*.

All-risk insurance policy

This term used to describe a type of insurance policy that protects you against all possible causes of loss except any specifically excluded and listed in the policy. Most companies now call these policies "special form" policies instead of "all-risk."

Amortization

A method of spreading out certain kinds of business costs over a period of years. Similar to depreciation, but usually the recovery period is longer.

AOD

Acknowledgment of delivery.

Arbitration

A way of resolving legal disputes without a formal trial. The disagreeing parties agree to have a third party or panel of experts hear both sides of the dispute and make an award or decision on how the dispute should be settled.

ASCII

American Standard Code for Information Interchange. This is a computer standard for creating text that can be read on any computer.

Asset

A business asset is something you buy or acquire or develop, has or is expected to have monetary value, and will use in your business for more than one year. Examples of assets are land, equipment, patents, buildings, and franchise rights.

Assumptions (financial— in business plan)

As used by financial types, assumptions are predictions about future circumstances and future business activities. If you are predicting what your sales will be next year, for instance, you have to make some predictions (informed guesses) about how many customers you will have and how many sales you will make to those customers.

Backup

A copy of computer data that can be stored independently from the hard disk or floppy disk on which the data was originally stored. You need to backup your data so you can recreate the information if something happens to the data you originally created.

Balance sheet

A summary of your assets (what you own), your liabilities (what you owe), and what you are worth (the difference between the assets and liabilities).

Basis

The beginning figure for calculating depreciation, amortization, gain, loss, or depletion.

Baud

A term used to describe how fast modems and faxes transfer data.

Body copy

Body copy refers to the text of press releases, printed articles, or advertising.

Boilerplate

Standard information or forms, such as standardized contracts or personalized sales letters in which only a small amount of information (such as a name or address) changes from one document to another.

BOP

See *Businessowner's policy.*

Break-even analysis

An analysis of how many sales you have to make at a given price in order that your sales cover your expenses.

Broker (insurance)

An insurance broker is a marketing specialist who represents the buyer of insurance and selects proper coverage from among the offerings of many companies. See also *agent.*

Bulletin board system (BBS)

An electronic communications center where messages can be posted for other people to read using their computers.

Business interruption insurance

As the name implies, business interruption insurance offers coverage against losses due to a temporary interruption of business due to fire or other insured risks. It covers lost net profits and continuing expenses such as rent.

Businessowner's policy

This is a special type of insurance policy for small businesses that combines many separate insurance coverages, such as fire, theft, and personal liability, into one policy. Often abbreviated BOP.

Card deck

Card deck advertisements are ads that are printed on index-sized cards and mailed to subscribers of certain magazines or people who are known to buy a certain type of product or service through the mail.

Cash flow	Literally, the flow of cash (money) through your business from outlays for supplies, products, raw materials, sales, and operating expenses to income from sales or other sources. A cash-flow analysis compares the income your daily operations generate to your expenses.
CEO	Chief executive officer. The chief executive officer of a company is usually the person who controls it.
CFO	Chief financial officer. This person is responsible for managing all the financial aspects of a company.
Chargeback	A chargeback is a credit card transaction that is literally "charged back," or billed to the business that made the original sale. Chargebacks occur when credit card holders dispute charges on their bill either because they never made the purchase or because they are dissatisfied with their purchase and the merchant refuses to correct the problem. The merchant is liable for chargebacks even if the merchandise was shipped.
Clip art	Artwork you license to use in your publications. You actually may cut or clip the art out of a book that is distributed to you, hence the name *clip art*. Clip art (artwork you have the right to reproduce) is available in various computer formats as well as high-quality printouts.
Close, closed, or closely held corporation	A private corporation as opposed to one that is publicly traded. Often its shareholders are close friends or family members. Special rules sometimes apply to closed corporations.
COBRA	See *Consolidated Omnibus Budget Reconciliation Act of 1985*.
Compliance audit	A compliance audit is an audit conducted under the Taxpayer Compliance Measurement Program (TCMP) to help the IRS determine who is most likely to cheat on which types of deductions. The audit looks in depth at all of your finances.

Confidentiality agreement Also called a nondisclosure agreement. This is an agreement you may be asked to sign if you will have access to trade secrets of projects under development. It legally prevents you from disclosing trade secrets or other information to other parties.

Consideration (law) Consideration is what you receive in return for doing something you don't have to do—usually money. If you agreed to write a technical manual for $5,000, the fee would be the consideration.

Consolidated Omnibus Budget Reconciliation Act of 1985 This law provides a way for people to continue health care coverage after they leave their jobs, divorce their spouse, or lose eligibility for health insurance through some other means. The law applies to companies with twenty or more employees.

Contingency fee A fee that is paid when the outcome of something such as a lawsuit is successful.

Continuous form Forms or computer paper that comes in one continuous strip. It is usually perforated so it can be separated easily into page-sized sections. The edges on continuous forms have holes in them to allow them to be pulled through a printer by a mechanism that has sprocket or pins to grab and move the paper.

Copy See *Body copy*.

Corporation A separate entity chartered by the state to do business.

Covenant not to compete Sometimes called a noncompete agreement. It is a contract employees or others sign stating they will not compete with the employer for a set period of time. There are a variety of state laws that govern such agreements, so if you plan to use one be sure to have an attorney look it over and make sure it is enforceable in your state.

Damages Money awarded as the outcome of a lawsuit.

Data file Any information or document you create with a computer program (letter, ad, drawing, etc.).

DBA "Doing business as." A term used to designate the certificate one gets after registering a business name with appropriate local or state officials.

Debt financing Debt financing simply means financing your business with loans. You borrow a specified amount and are expected to pay it back in a specified period of time at a specified interest rate.

Debt-to-worth ratio Amount owed creditors divided by the value of the business.

Depreciate A tax deduction that allows you to recover what you paid for property by deducting its cost over a period of years.

Download To transfer information from a remote computer to your own and save it on disk.

Dunning letters Letters demanding payment for bills.

Equity financing Equity means ownership. Equity financing means trading ownership for money. How much ownership must be given up varies with the deal.

Estimated taxes Estimated taxes are money you must pay in advance toward your expected year-end tax liability. You only have to pay estimated taxes if the income and social security tax (FICA) withheld from any wages you earn will not cover all the tax you will owe at the end of the year. Generally, if you expect to owe more than $500 in income and self-employment tax than you will have contributed through salary withholdings, you will have to pay estimated taxes. The tax gets paid in four installments during the tax year.

Factor or factoring Factoring is the sale of accounts receivable to a third party. It is a way of speeding up collection of receivables; in which you sell your receivables (what's owed you) to a third party for a percentage of what the actual amount owed is worth.

Once receivables are sold, the factor accepts all the risk for collection. Billing functions remain either with you or get transferred to the factor, depending on the individual arrangements.

FICA

The Federal Insurance Contributions Act, which made into law the withholding of Social Security contributions from employees' paychecks.

Financials

The financial projections and financial historical data used in a business plan.

Fiscal year

Any 12 consecutive months used for accounting for business activity. The fiscal year may or may not start and end at the same time as the calendar year.

Floor

In the preparation of income taxes, a floor is a base amount that expenses must exceed to be deductible. The floor is calculated as a percentage of adjusted gross income.

Floppy disk

Floppy disks store small amounts of computer data and are removable from the computer. Originally, floppy disks were thin and flexible, hence the name *floppy*.

Freeware

Software that is distributed for free use but for which the author retains the copyright.

Gross income

The total of all income with no expenses or deductions subtracted.

Guaranteed renewable

An insurance term meaning an insurance company cannot cancel or refuse to renew your policy as long as you continue to pay the premiums, and it continues to sell the kind of insurance you've purchased.

Hard disk

A hard disk is a type of mass storage device for computer data. It is used to store computer programs and data files.

Hardware

Pieces of a computer system you can actually touch, like the keyboard, printer processing unit, monitor (screen), hard drive, etc.

Health maintenance organization (HMO)	A managed health insurance plan where the insurer is also the health care provider. Usually HMOs cover only the fees of doctors or other providers who are part of the plan. If you go to a doctor or hospital outside the HMO, the insurance won't cover your costs.
HMO	See *Health maintenance organization*.
Income statement	Also called a profit and loss statement or operating statement. It summarizes the profitability of a business, showing what's left over (or lost) when you subtract cost of goods sold and operating expenses from the total sales.
Independent contractor	A self-employed individual who performs a specific job for a business either under a formal contract or by verbal agreement with the company. Generally, independent contractors offer their services to more than one business. In fact, people who work only for one company sometimes have trouble proving their independent contractor status to the IRS.
Inland marine insurance	A type of insurance that was originally designed to cover goods *after* they were taken off ships and were in transit inland. Now it is used to cover a wide range of perils including some for which nothing else is appropriate, such as electronic data processing equipment and media. Other things often covered by inland marine policies or floaters are goods in transit, jewelry, fine art, personal effects, as well as bridges, highways, and other things having to do with transportation or communications.
ISO	Independent Sales Organization. A distributor who buys products or services and resells them at a profit. ISOs operate in a variety of fields. Companies that offer merchant card processing services to vendors are one type of ISO.
Jaggies	Refers to the jagged edges that are produced when some computer printers print alphabetical characters or drawings with rounded edges.

Keogh plan	One type of tax-deferred retirement plan for the self-employed.
Letter of agreement	A letter of agreement sums up points you and another party agreed on. It can serve as a contract.
Liabilities	In accounting, all debts your business owes. This includes money you owe vendors (accounts payable), money you owe in income taxes, money you owe on long-term loans, etc.
Mediation	A way of attempting to settle disputes without a lawsuit. A third party (called a mediator) brings disagreeing parties together and encourages them to settle the dispute themselves.
Megabyte (MB)	A unit used to measure disk space and computer memory.
Merchant status	Authorization for a business to accept credit cards in payment for goods and services. A business with merchant status will have the charges processed through their "merchant account" with a bank or other credit card processor.
Modem	A device that converts computer data into a format that can be sent over telephone lines and converts incoming telephone signals into computer data on the receiving end.
Net income	Total income minus expenses; in other words, your profit.
NOL	Net operating loss (when sales minus expenses produces a loss).
Noncompete agreement	See *Covenant not to compete*.
Nonexclusive right(s)	A right to sell a product that may be granted to more than one person or organization at a time.
NSF	Nonsufficient funds (said of a checking account that doesn't have enough money in it to cover a check).

Online service

Any of a number of large, commercial computer services that offer information, news, searchable databases, discussion forums, and in many cases, software you can download, store, and use on your own computer system. To access an online service you need a computer, a modem, a telephone line, and a subscription to the online service.

Overhead

Any expenses a business has that can't be directly tracked to a product or service. Examples of overhead costs are expenses you pay for heat, light, telephone, insurance, supplies, and indirect labor. Overhead costs should be allocated and included in the price of every product or service you sell.

Partnership

A legal form of business where two or more individuals share work and/or financial responsibility for running a business.

Phonorecords

A term the Copyright Office uses to denote musical records you play on a phonograph.

Port

A data passageway on a computer. In other words, a place to plug printers, scanners, and other devices into the computer system.

PPO

See *Preferred provider organization*.

Preferred provider organization (PPO)

A health care plan where you have the option of using any of the providers in a network of preferred doctors, laboratories, hospitals, and other providers or using doctors and other providers outside the system. Generally, there is a small copayment per visit ($2 to $10) for using the plan's providers; if you use providers outside the plan's network, you pay and send in the bills to the company to collect your share.

Prime contractor

The business that is responsible for successful completion of a government contract. Prime contractors usually subcontract (give work out to other companies) various parts of contracts.

Print spooler	Software that lets you print out work on a computer printer while you continue to work at the computer.
Pro forma	Projected or expected financial data.
Prorated	Proportioned or allocated. In figuring your taxes, you pro-rate an expense to the percent business usage of the item. For instance, if you bought a $2,400 computer for your home office and used it 60 percent of the time for business, the amount you could depreciate or expense would be 60 percent of $2400, or $1440.
Public domain	Works (artwork, writing, software, etc.) that do not have copyright protection.
RAM	Random access memory. The temporary memory a computer uses to process work. Every time you shut down the computer, and often when you change tasks, the contents of the RAM are lost.
S corporation	Formerly called subchapter S corporation. This is a special type of corporation that affects the way profits and losses are handled for taxation. Many small businesses are S corporations.
Sales projection	An estimate of the number and dollar amount of sales over a specific period of time and sometimes in a specific region.
Scanner	A computer device that converts images on paper into a format that a computer can read. Different scanners have different capabilities. Some can convert only pictures; others with the appropriate software can convert words into a format the computer can edit.
SCSI	Small computer system interface (pronounced "scuzzy"). A computer passageway (port) through which data can pass at very high speeds. A SCSI port is simply a place to attach a disk drive or some other device to a microcomputer.
Self-employment tax	Social Security tax and Medicaid tax individuals pay when they are self-employed.

SEP	See *Simplified employee plan.*
Shareware	Software that you can try before you buy. This can be downloaded from online services or local electronic bulletin boards or can be purchased in disks sold by mail order and sometimes on racks at novelty stores and bookstores. You can buy the disk for a few dollars, try the software, and, if you like it, buy it from the author of the program.
SIC	Standard industrial code. is a code the U.S. government uses to classify businesses by industry.
Simplified Employee Plan (SEP)	A type of IRA retirement plan where the employer makes the contribution, not the employee.
Software	Programming (instructions) that tells the computer what to do with what you type at the keyboard.
Sole proprietorship	A business owned by only one person. The business may have employees, but the actual ownership is in one name.
Source code	Source code is a computer code that can be read like English.
Spool	See *Print spooler.*
Statute	A statute is a law created by a governing body.
Statutory damages	An amount of money specified by law. Often statutory damages are penalties; for instance, three times the amount set by a jury or three times the value of a property.
Telecommuter	An employee who works at home and uses a telephone and computer to communicate with the employer.
Telemarketing	Using a telephone to market or sell goods and services or to get appointments to meet with customers.
Trade secrets	Information such as customer lists or formulas that gives a business a competitive edge in the marketplace, provided

the information is kept secret. Unauthorized use of your trade secrets can be against the law.

Turnkey business

A turnkey business is a business that is complete and ready to go. It is usually a business concept that comes with plans to follow, equipment, and perhaps some training videos or manuals. Like with a car, someone just has to get behind the figurative wheel of the business, turn on the key, and drive it.

Upload

To send information from your computer "up" to some other computer. In other words, to transfer information from your computer and store it on the remote computer system.

Useful life

The amount of time an asset is expected to last and be useable.

Weekly shopper

Weekly shoppers are publications that consist of almost all advertising and have little or no editorial content. They may be mailed or tossed on driveways or stoops and contain ads for plumbers, garage sales, hair salons, tire dealers, etc.

Widget

A term used by business writers to mean any type of gadget or product a business might sell.

Working capital

Your current assets minus your current liabilities.

Index

Italicized page numbers refer to tables.

Overhead costs for small offices, 126
Ownership, 173–86
  corporations, 173, 179–86
  partnerships, 173, 175–79
  sole proprietorships, 173–75

Packaged (turnkey) businesses, 62–68
Packaging, 84
Paper, 33, 86–87, 189, 190
Paperwork, managing clutter in, 435–44
Partnerships, 173, 175–79
  advantages and disadvantages of, 175–77
  agreements between, 177–79
  corporations vs., 179
  limited, 179, 183
  spouse and, 177
  Uniform Partnership Act (UPA), 177
Past due notices, 271–75
Patents, 326–33
  attorneys for, 329, 330
  categories of, 326
  copyrights vs., 327
  cost of, 329
  for designs, 332–33
  duration of, 328–29
  filing, 329–30
  marketing products based on, 331
  in other countries, 332
  protecting, 332–33
  protecting ideas, 331, 332
  qualifications for, 326–27
  renewal of, 329
  restrictions on, 327
  rights granted by, 327–28
  sales and, 328
  searches for, 328
  trade secrets and, 331
Payment, customer, 263–75
  check clearance and, 81
  collecting late, 264, 268–75
  contracts for, 271
  credit cards as, 81
  discount for early, 267
  lawsuits for collecting, 270, 275

length of time to collect, 263–64
online business credit report for, 268
past due notices, 271–75
regulations on collecting, 272
reinvoicing for, 264
speeding collection of, 264–68
Pension plans, 404–5
Performance bonds, 359
Permits, 30–32
Personal guarantee for debts, 151
Personal insurance, business-related coverage of, 349–53, 363. *See also* Health insurance
Personal organizers, 430, 431–32
Personal service corporations, 183–84
Pfeiffer, Tim, 280, 282, 286
Phillips, Holly, 26
Photocopiers, 194–95, 197
Photography/photographs
  in brochures, 260
  going rates for, 143
  with press releases, 234
Planning. *See* Business plans
Planning systems, personal, 430–32
Postcards, past due notices on, 274
Preferred provider organizations (PPO), 345–46
Press kit, 234–36
Press release, 229–34
  advance time for, 233
  contact after sending, 232–33
  effectiveness of, 232
  format for, 230–31
  frequency of, 233–34
  photographs with, 234
  writing, 229–30
Pricing, 122–45
  accurate sales and cost estimates for, 127–29
  charging by hour or by job, 129–31
  charging family and friends, 133
  commission earnings and, 127
  contingency fees, 131
  differential, 134